Reunderstanding
Indian Philosophy

Reunderstanding Indian Philosophy

— Some Glimpses —

S.S. Barlingay

DK PRINTWORLD
Publishers of Indian Traditions

Cataloging in Publication Data — DK
[Courtesy: D.K. Agencies (P) Ltd. <docinfo@dkagencies.com>]

Barlingay, S.S. (Surendra Sheodas), 1919-1997.
Reunderstanding Indian Philosophy.
Includes bibliographical references (p.).
Includes index.
ISBN 13: 9788124601075

1. Philosophy, Indic, 2. Philosophy, Hindu.
3. Philosophy, Buddhist. 4. Jaina philosophy.
I. Title.

ISBN 13: 978-81-246-0107-5

First published in India in 1998
Second impression in 2014

Printed and Published by:
D.K. Printworld (P) Ltd.
Regd. Office: "*Vedaśrī*", F-395, Sudarshan Park
(Metro Station: Ramesh Nagar)
New Delhi – 110 015
Phones: (011) 2545 3975; 2546 6019; *Fax*: (011) 2546 5926
e-mail: indology@dkprintworld.com
Web: www.dkprintworld.com

To the memories of

K. J. Shah & E. R. Srikrishna Sarma

and to my friends

Awadhoot Hardikar, S.R. Talghatti,
Shankarrao Kharat, Da. Go. Deshpande,
Vinayak Shirke, Sultan Ali Shaida, K. P. Jog and
Ouseparampil

Foreword

While the book was at a preparatory stage, our beloved father, Prof. S.S. Barlingay passed away. Publication of one of his last works remained our sole consideration. When Shri Susheel K. Mittal of D.K. Printworld wished to continue with the publication, our gratitude knew no bounds. We are extremely grateful to Shri Mittal for taking personal interest in the publication of this work.

We are equally grateful to Dr. S.E. Bhelkey, Reader, Department of Philopophy, Pune University, without whose help, this monumental task would have become impossible.

Since the publication of this work was completed after the demise of Prof. Barlingay, some lapses might have remained inspite of all our efforts. We tender our apology for the same.

Pune
17-3-1998

Dr. Kranti Pande
Mona Barlingay

Contents

The Threshold

To me philosophy is philosophising. It is neither Indian nor non-Indian. It is not determined by geographical boundaries. The expression, Indian philosophy, is an instance of transferred epithet. It is philosophy, propounded by Indian philosophers. It could be that some of the philosophical problems tackled by them are pseudo problems. But it is also possible that for some reason or the other, their problems might have been misunderstood by scholars on account of the different cultural background, in spite of their mature philosophical under-standing. Perhaps these scholars might be interpreting the problems on the basis of the trends current during their times. All this has happened in regard to philosophy of Indian origin. For when 'Indian' philosophy went in the hands of such scholars, they looked at the Indian thinkers and their thought with patronizing spirit. In fact, Indians now try to understand and interpret the philosophy that developed on this soil without being subjugated by any undue influence from outside. This is, of course, not to suggest that there should not be any exchange or communication of the philosophical thought.

Philosophical thought developed in post renaissance Europe in two different ways at least. One was called Rationalism and the other, Empiricism. We are told that Descartes was the father of rationalism whereas the other kind of thought was credited to Bacon, Hobbes, Locke, Hume, etc. But this does not mean that Malebranche, Spinoza or Leibniz merely wrote some footnotes to or gave just the explanations of the thesis propounded by Descartes. Similarly when Hume talked of 'relations of ideas' it should not be taken to mean that he had changed his faith and had become an adherent of rationalistic faith. The case of philosophy developed in India is similar. While interpreting *Vedānta Sūtra*s philosophers of

Advaitic, Viśiṣṭādvaitic or Dvaitic schools hold divergent views. But even those who belong to one tradition and have basic agreement on the fundamental thesis, differ with one another when they go to details. Thus Rāmānuja and Madhva differ basically from Śaṅkara[1] and criticize him even in *abusive terms*. But those who give basically the same interpretation of the fundamental thought like Vācaspati or Sureśvara do express their difference on details. Thus, those who come under one canopy of basic thought, are not prohibited from expressing their differences. All such things happen in a developing thought. This has happened in Buddhist thought also.

In nineteenth century Hegel and his followers dominated the European philosophical scene and they began to consider philosophy as a system. This affected 'Indian' philosophical horizons also. During my college days our philosophy teacher told us that Indian philosophy comprised of six orthodox and six un-orthodox systems, and we understood that to be 'systematic' was a great virtue and achievement of Indian philosophy. I did not realise that it was only the influence of Hegel percolated through his European and British followers like Bradley, Bosanquet, Taylor, etc., which was speaking through the mouth of my teacher. But later when I was free from the magical effect of the 'rope trick' and asked myself whether it was an achievement to treat philosophy as if it was a system or an organism I had to answer the question in negative. I thought it was to confine philosophy to certain fixed limits and not allow it to expand, develop or breathe fresh and free air. Philosophy was not a science and I wondered whether even a science could be regarded as a complete (and a closed) system? Could that which was subjected to continuous discoveries and growth, and that in the growth of which 'human reason' played a major role, be regarded as a complete system on any ground? What we called a system might itself be a (rational) human construct. Hegel did not talk of human reason. He talked of perfect 'idealised' Reason with capital 'R'. His 'system' was concerned with 'ideal'. It was of the nature of idea; and by Hegelian dialectics

1. In this threshold I have used, Śaṅkara, Ādi Śaṅkara, and Śaṅkarācārya as synonyms. Śaṅkarācārya, Bhāratī Kṛṣṇatīrtha, is the only exception. He was Śaṅkarācārya of Purī Pīṭha in the fifth and sixth decades of twentieth century.

the ideal and the real were regarded as identical. Such an ideal-real system, of course, would be beyond the reach of human reason and certainly it could not be conceived in plural number. I, therefore, did not cherish the idea of systematic philosophy, whether it took its birth in India or outside.

The cultivation of such a sceptical attitude was, of course, due to the initial influence of my father. My father was a brilliant student of Mathematics, Philosophy and Sanskrit. The great Ganganath Jha used to address him affectionately as Paṇḍitjī. He had learnt Vedānta, Pūrva Mīmāṁsā, Nyāya, Vyākaraṇa, Mathematics and Astronomy and trained some great scholars like Dr. K.L. Daftari. Finally, he did not pursue any of these studies and became a lawyer. Bhāratī Kr̥ṣṇatīrtha, Śaṅkarācārya of Purī Pīṭha had bestowed on him the honour of Mahāmahopādhyāya. It was he who introduced me, not only to Sanskrit drama and poetry but also to *Aṣṭādhyāyī* of Pāṇini, Paspaśā Āhnika of Patañjali's *Mahābhāṣya* and Brahma Kāṇḍa of Bhartr̥hari's *Vākyapadīya*. He used to tell me that one should always go to the root of the problem, that one should view the problem as one viewed the *amalaka*, placed in one's palm' (*karatalāmalakavat*). Only then with one instance one could grasp the nature of all instances coming under that category, *ekena mr̥tpiṇḍena sarvam mr̥ṇmayam iti vijñātam syāt*. This 'sceptical' attitude of mine was further cultivated by my elder brother, Dr. W.S. Barlingay and my teachers, Dr. Rasvihari Das and Prof. Gilbert Ryle. The result was that I looked at "the so-called" Indian Philosophical 'systems' rather in a sceptical manner. Nevertheless I must say that my outlook was positive. Whether it was the philosophy of Gauḍapāda or Ādi Śaṅkara, or Kaṇāda or Īśvara Kr̥ṣṇa or Bharata, Abhinavagupta, Cārvāka or Gaṅgeśa, the author of *Cintāmaṇi*, I looked at their works, with a critical eye, with an eye of the third person. I was more attracted by the vision or intuition they gave than by the systematic outer cover, with which philosophers of the East and West looked at them. Perhaps on account of such an attitude of mine my present essays also have a tone of secpticism.

Although I did not accept philosophy as a system in the Hegelian sense of the term the problems which arose in my mind in regard to 'Indian' philosophy, were important. I was attracted by different concepts like those of *Puruṣatantra*, *Puruṣavyāpāratantra*, and *Vastutantra*[2] discussed by Ādi Śaṅkara in the beginning of *Śārīraka Bhāṣya*, and also by the fine distinctions which are at the back of these concepts. Similarly, I was attracted by the distinction again made by Śaṅkara between *Bhūta* and *Bhavya*.[3] I also was struck by the question he asked about knowledge, "Is knowledge a mental process", *api jñanam nama mānasī kriyā*. I thought he was asking a pertinent and an important question which was later asked by twentieth-century philosophers like Wittgenstein and Ryle. I was also troubled by the traditional interpretations of technical terms like *nirākāra*, *nirguṇa* and *ajāta*.[4] I never agreed with the traditional interpretation of these concepts and believed that the philosophers of Advaita had something different and significant to say in this regard. If by *nirākāra* was meant having no *ākāra*, shape or form or structure what did it convey? Did it stand for what had no spatial existence? How then are we to understand the nature of space? Can we say or not that the space is *nirākāra*? Similar doubts arose in my mind about *ātman* also and I tried to read the aphorism *Anusmr̥teḥ*[5] in a new light. I asked myself about the relation between *smr̥ti* or memory and *ātman* which further

---

2. *Puruṣa-tantra* means that which is determined by the subject. It is subjective. *Vastutantra* is that which is determined by the object or the thing. It is objective. If we are talking of ontology it would be ontological of the nature of thing which existed in its own right. For me it would be cosmo-centred.

   Puruṣa-vyāpāra-tantra would be determined by the *vyāpāra* of the subject. It would stand for all those whose nature is determined by the activity of man. I feel, it represents what we now call anthropocentric.

3. *Bhūta* is that which exists, *bhavya* means that which ought to be brought into being. It means *bhavitum yogyam*.

4. *Ajāta* means that which is not born. But it may stand for two different things: (a) that which is not capable of being born anytime and, therefore, which does not exist nor will exist anytime; (b) it may mean it is not born anytime for it is always existing.

5. *Anusmr̥teḥ* — An aphorism in *Bādarāyaṇa Sūtras*, used for proving the existence of *ātman*. It tells us about two range of *ātman*'s existence. We are as if, holding the *ātman* in one pinch, which extends from the →

gave rise to the question about the role of time in this context as also in the general context of philosophy. Similarly, while reading *Māṇḍūkyakārikā* I found that Gauḍapāda talked of *viśva* as the 'knower' in *jāgarita* state. Was he not talking about the external world? What was the meaning of *taijasa* as the knower of the *svapna* state of *prājña* as the knower of the state of deep-sleep?

Coming to Sāṁkhya philosophy, there were some questions that struck me. What should be the possible meaning of, 'there is Prakṛti' or 'there is Puruṣa'; 'how should '*cit chāyā*' be interpreted? When the Sāṁkhya philosophers talked of *satkāryavāda*, were they really talking of causation? Similarly, when we go to Yoga philosophy how should we interpret the aphorism of Patañjali, '*śabdārtha-pratyayānām itaretarādhyāsāt saṅkaraḥ*'. What was the mutual relation between *śabda* (the symbol), *artha* (the bearer of the symbol) and *pratyaya* the cognition arising in our mind on account of the presence of the symbol? How were we to understand the aphorism of Patañjali (*Mahābhāṣya*), '*śabdaḥ sphoṭaḥ, dhvanistu śabdaguṇaḥ*'.

I had a similar difficulty about Buddhism and their doctrine of *pratītya-samutpāda*, and also about Buddha's *mudrā*s, '*sarvam anityam*', '*sarvam sanghātam*', '*sarvam anāmam*' and '*sarvam santānam*'. I thought that these four *mudrā*s of the Buddhist told us something very fundamental, that they acquainted us with the fact that everything in this world was flux. Nevertheless when this world of flux was presented to us in macroscopic form we understood it as if it was static and having temporal duration. In such a *sanghāta* perhaps there was no place for soul or *ātman*. However, this *sanghāta* was characterised by *santānatva*, i.e., countinuity, a flow of what W.E. Johnson called the continuant (aspect of time). The Buddhist philosophy had a social background and it further helped to discuss the human problem at the social level. To my mind, Marx was also discussing the human problem at the social

→ present time to the last point in time in our earlier life that we remember, perhaps the *mudrās*, the Buddhists talk of, have also the same thing to convey. Whether we call it *ātman* or *anātman* we are pointing to the concept of continuity and flow of our existence which has both, the occupant and the continent.

level where he followed the method of dialectic. I was thinking for a long time that there is a great similarity between the dialectic developed in Buddhism and by Marx which I discussed in my paper 'Dialectics: Buddhist and Marxist.'

Such and several other thoughts flocked in my mind when I studied 'Indian' philosophy under Paṇḍits and finally came to the conclusion that a complete re-understanding of 'Indian' philosophy was necessary if renaissance in 'Indian' philosophy was to be brought about.

In 1835, Lord Macaulay introduced a new education policy in India. It opened a new vista for the youths of India. A new career was now open to those who were educated in a new way as they could now become officers in the British bureaucratic set-up. Thus, a large number of students were drawn to the new type of education. This was, of course, not to say that Indian Education System did not require any reforms. But nobody did realise the objective of Macaulay's policy and its far-reaching effects. This was the beginning of colonization, although this experiment did not succeed in the same measure as it succeeded in respect of the Maories of New Zealand, aborigines of Australia, the original Africans of African continent and (Red) Indians of America. But it separated us (Indians) from our umbilical chord, from our moorings. It alienated the educated from the Indian culture. Those who learnt English were isolated from their past history, from their attainments. The philosophy of Indian origin naturally had a setback. Those who opted for English education could not study Indian philosophy at all. Our philosophers like President Radhakrishnan could not study Indian philosophy and Sanskrit in their university days and S.N. Dasgupta and Hiriyanna had to discover philosophy through their researches of Sanskrit (philosophical) texts. Of course, European orientalists and Sanskrit Paṇḍits like Late Ganganath Jha did some important work during this period by translating

6. There was no text of Indian tradition presented. They were verbal translations. Translations are required to present the text. But translation is not presentation. Presentation of the text presents the thought, the issue.

Sanskrit philosophical texts. But in such works, although the scholarship was present, the philosophical rigour and the vision required for philosophisation were conspicuously absent.[6] It is to the credit of European orientalists, who took their inspiration from Sir William Jones, that a good deal of Indian 'wisdom' is preserved. But it must be said that due to their lack of acquaintance with the culture of India some of their findings led to absurdities. For example, in one of the Upaniṣads, *prakṛti* is described as Ajā (unborn), *ājāmekām lohitaśukla-kṛṣṇām, bahvīḥ prajā sṛjamānām namāmaḥ*. How would it look if it was translated as, "we bow to the she goat of red, white and black colour and which gives birth to lot of young ones". But something of this kind has happened in some of the writings of the orientalists. I am afraid — some sociologist-metaphysicians might even draw a conclusion that Indians conceived god (or soul) in the form of goat.

I joined college in 1935, a hundred years after Lord Macaulay's reforms were introduced. By this time Indian philosophy was introduced in Indian universities. It was introduced in the third decade of twentieth century after the books of Professor Dasgupta and Professor Radhakrishnan were published by British publishers. I could study Īśvarakṛṣṇa's *Sāṁkhya Kārikā* and Indian philosophy in general for my B.A. and M.A. degrees. But my elder brother who graduated in 1924 could not offer Indian Philosophy for his B.A. Now a lot of 'Indian' philosophy is introduced in Indian universities, but this is the 'Indian' philosophy first exported to Europe and the Western world through the writings of European scholars and then imported back to India. In this communication quite a large part of valuable philosophical material is lost, and a big gap is created. 'Indian' philosophy is virtually reduced to some kind of oriental textual study. It is not brought in line with European philosophy and a gulf continues between them. K.C. Bhattacharya, Suryanarayana Shastri, Satkari Mukherji, Kuppuswami Shastri, B.K. Malik, Hiriyanna and several others tried to bridge this gulf. In the present generation also the efforts of J.N. Mohanty, Shivajeevan Bhattacharya, Pradyota Mukhopadhyaya, K.J. Shah, Debi Prasad Chattopadhyaya cannot be side-tracked in this context. The works of Staal and E.R. Shrikrishna Sarma also cannot be ignored. I also, in my small way, tried to do something in this regard. While discussing with Prof. Gilbert Ryle at Oxford University, the contribuion of modern analytical philosophy, it came to my mind that long ago the grammarians of India, Naiyāyikas and Mīmāṁsakas have discussed the problems of language and have propounded their theories of language. I developed this theme in my lectures which I delivered in Oslo and Manchester Universities, England. Later I wrote a paper on the contribution of Indian gramarians entitled 'The Theory of Meaning in Indian Grammar System.' A bridge is being built now over the modern philosophical structures and the ancient Indian structures. But the distance still remains. Macaulay's reforms brought about something which Indians had perhaps never thought of. The growth of Indian thought is stunted. It is still not a living discipline. The result is that everything ends in false and incorrect historising. I also feel that many a time while interpreting the concepts the orientalists did not take the cultural context into account and did not bring in the old Indian and the new thought under one canopy. This was also the case with Paṇḍits. I thought there should be a dialogue between the Paṇḍits and the modern philosophers. I, therefore, held a few seminars and arranged for some dialogues under the title, 'Sequence Seminars' in the University of Pune. This was later followed by ICPR under the scheme 'Saṁvāda'. But what is necessary is a renaissance in the domain of philosophy of Indian origin.

Daya Krishna has taken a very important step in this direction. He, for example, raises the problem about Āraṇyakas and Upaniṣads and raises a doubt about the authenticity and credibility of the Upaniṣadic texts which have come down to us traditionally. While accepting that what Daya Krishna and other Indian philosophers are doing is important, I must say that the problem does not end there. Reading the Āraṇyakas and correcting the text of Upaniṣads would not solve the problem. Daya Krishna does not suggest it either. Philosophy of Indian origin has to be looked at in a still wider perspective. Even the Upaniṣadic and other texts, as they have come down to us, are to be reunderstood. I would illustrate my point by taking the instance of the word *mithyā*. *Mithyā* is translated as illusory. But the word *mithyā* was used by Vedāntins as that which has birth, death and existence in between. It is, therefore, not equivalent to illusory. May be that some people have used it in the sense of illusory. But all have not used the word *mithyā* like that, and due credit has to be given to the intention of the writers. The relationship between the illusory and real is logical. It is a relationship similar to one of *virodha* and not of *bādhā*. The case with *mithyā* is different. It tells us that what appears now as real appears to be otherwise after a *time gap*. So *mithyā* cannot be equated with 'illusory'. There are several such words whose logical structures will have to be examined before they are used for expressing our philosophical thought.

My understanding of Cārvāka is also different and untraditional. I regard him as a robust common sense philosopher. I do not think that he was a materialist or a hedonist. I also do not think that he did not accept inference as a *pramāṇa* although he did not accept *anumāna* as a *pramāṇa*. *Anumāna* and inference are not identical. Unfortunately I could not include any of my papers on Cārvāka in the present volume. But the papers included in this volume are relevant to Indian philosophical thought.

My basic approach to 'Indian' philosophy is determined by my paper, 'Reunderstanding Indian Philosophy'. It was first presented to the Andhra University Seminar at Waltair and later, in a revised form with some additions and deletions in *Discovery of India* series in Nehru Centre, Bombay. Subsequently, it fell in the hands of Professor D.P. Chattopadhyaya who came to know about this paper and expressed his desire to publish it in JICPR.

'The Grammar of Indian Moral Concepts' germinated in my mind while I was giving an open course on Indian Ethics. Before I finalised the paper I discussed the same with Professor E.R. Srikrishna Sarma.

The paper on 'Pratītya Samutpāda, Sāmānya Lakṣaṇa and Apoha' was the Buddha Jayanti Lecture given by me before Indian Philosophical Congress at Hyderabad in 1975. Here I suggest that by Pratītya-samutpāda Buddha did not want to propound a thesis of causal process.

The paper, 'Duḥkha, Tṛṣṇā, and Vaira', which is basic to Theravāda, is in fact very crucial to Buddhist way of thinking. I have tried to explicate here the relationship between different concepts coming under *dvādaśa nidāna*. I hold the view that *nidāna* means diagnosis and not cause. This paper was published in *Jagannath Upadhyaya Commemoration Volume.*

The paper, 'Jīva and Ajīva' was presented to the World Sanskrit Conference, held in Weimar (Germany) and was published in their proceedings. This thought is developed further in my paper on the philosophy of Kunda Kunda. It is not published anywhere but a large part of it was originally written in Marāṭhī as a preface to Professor Tagare's book, *Pravacanasāra of Sri Kundakunda.*

According to tradition Gauḍapāda was the teacher of Govinda who was the teacher of Ādi Śaṅkara. He (unless there were two Gauḍapādas) seems to have written a commentary on the *Sāṁkhya Kārikā* of Īśvarakṛṣṇa. From Jacobi onwards, people have presented an extreme idealistic picture of Gauḍapāda. I do not think it is necessary to go so far. My view is that he regards *sat* as absolutely objective. But when this *sat* is operative in the human world it assumes an anthropocentric form. It now becomes a new presentation of the objective world. The traditional thought is that Gauḍapāda was a mystic and denied the external world. I am not sure of it. But his methodological approach, to my mind, is very important. He gives the logical classification of knowledge situation into four types, the *jāgarita, svapna, suṣupti* (deep sleep) and the *turya* or the fourth. The last according to him is not a knowledge situation at all; for, knowledge requires, a subject-object or a knower-known relationship, and this is absent in the fourth. Perhaps Gauḍapāda was greatly influenced by Buddhist thought.

The Buddhist thought is at least preserved till this date in Tibet, China, Sri Lanka and South Eastern and Far Eastern countries. But what happened to non-Buddhist thought is not known. With the Turkish, Afghan, Moghul and central Asian invasions a lot of destruction took place all over India and many of our prized books are lost. Some of them are now traceable, but certainly not all. Bhartṛhari's commentary on *Mahābhāṣya* was lost although it is now traced at a few places. So was the case with Bharata's *Nāṭyaśāstra*, and *Abhinava Bhāratī*. Bhaṭṭanāyaka's *Hṛdaya Darpaṇa* is still not found. But almost the whole of Sāṁkhya and early Vaiśeṣika literature is lost. The Vedāntic literature between Bādarāyaṇa and Ādi Śaṅkara is still not found, with the result that many people pronounce that due to the influence of Buddhist philosophy, the Vedāntic literature was completely wiped out. It is very difficult to make any remark on such a state of affairs.

Perhaps a new cultural movement started in the fourth century AD. I am not sure whether it could be called Brāhmaṇical revival, although people call it so. But it must be remembered that during this time many cultural strides took place. There was a revival of learning in Kashmir, in Malava and in the south. Bhoja wrote (or got someone to write) *Samarāṅgaṇa Sūtradhāra*, a monumental work on architecture. He also wrote on poetics and several other subjects. *Saṅgīta Ratnākara*, an important monograph on music, was written in Devagiri by Śāraṅgadhara. Round about this time or a little earlier, Bhāskarācārya, the last known mathematician of ancient and mediaeval India, wrote his three important works *Līlāvatī*, *Bīja-gaṇita* and *Siddhānta Śiromaṇi*. Philosophy of different brands also flourished during this time. The great Dharmakīrti also flourished during this time only and finally became a Buddhist.

My paper, 'A Background Picture of Jainism and Buddhism', was lingering in my mind for a long time. I have a feeling that any society in its enthusiasm for activity not only develops the action side but also develops the ritual side. Rituals are originally intended actions but gradually they get stereotyped and become mechanical, quasi-mechanical or ideo-motor and then they act almost like the natural instincts. They also attain a certain status and have a place in the sacred action for pleasing the God(s) or fate and pantheon. These rituals attain an important status in society and are prized both by priests and scholars. Of course, simultaneously some development of thought does continue. Thus, thought and action move almost on parallel lines. Sometime later these parallel lines bend and intersect each other and through this dialectics a kind of syncretism takes place. They become two sides of the same coin. For understanding such a development (of practice) I take the Pūrva Mīmāṁsā concept as a paradigm. By Pūrva Mīmāṁsā I do not mean what is given by Jaimini and his followers. The code prevalent in any tribe or society and which gives sanction to social practice is for me the Pūrva Mīmāṁsā of that tribe or society. Such practices in some form are followed even when different tribes tend to unite. I may further assert that even after the emergence of genuine thought, a tendency to vulgarise that thought and practices continue to affect and tone the people. We, for example, think today that Advaita Vedānta dominates and rules the society but the fact is that the Vedāntic theory continues to rule the minds of the people only after getting polluted and vulgarised by ritualistic practices. Perhaps Ādi Śaṅkara never believed in ritualism and *karma-kāṇḍa*; he perhaps never believed in caste system or Cāturvarṇya; or God as the creator of the universe. He did not believe in Individual soul or rebirth. All these things come into practice on account of ignorance and vanish when knowledge dawns on man. He certainly did not believe in distributing *aṅgārā* (or religious ash) to his devotees. But all this is taking place now and I regard this as a relic of *yajña* system or Pūrva Mīmāṁsā system. In my paper, "A Background Picture of Jainism and Buddhism", I have tried to bring out such a development in historical process.

I consider my paper on Paryāpti relation important because it explicates the concept of number. *Paryāpti* relation is a relation introduced by Naiyāyikas. Mathematicians distinguish between cardinal and ordinal number series. The cardinal series is concerned with 1, 2, 3, 4 . . . . . *n*, and the ordinal series is concerned with the order such as first, second, third, etc. We have a tendency to think that cardinal series is basic but when we talk, for example, of 'number' five, do we really talk of *one number*? In fact, we talk of five numbers and a relation, 'from 1 to 5'. Number *five* means, 'from 1 to 5', i.e., from first to fifth inclusive of both places. This presupposes the ordinal number series. In the absence of ordinal series there would not be a series of cardinals 1, 2, 3, 4, ... *n*. There would only be a series represented each time by number one, 1, 1, 1, 1, not represented by a continuous line but a series of 'discrete *ones*'. I think this is a very important truth about numbers given to us by Nyāya philosophers.

In my paper 'Buddhism and Change' I have tried to point out that although Buddhist philosophy grew as a philosophy *of flux*, in course of time it accepted '*Anityatā*, *śūnyatā* and *nirvāṇa* as *principles* (which are not in time). This was an impediment to the doctrine of *anitya*. The conceptualisation of *anityatā* took away the mobility from the behaviour which was *anitya*. It was bereft of a spatio-temporal element. This was a transition from change to changelessness and brought it very near to Advaita Vedānta. This is how Ādi Śaṅkara was criticised as veiled Buddha, *pracchanna* Bauddha. Buddha's theory got a jolt in accepting some permanent principles. Buddhists did not accept *jāti* or abstraction. But the termination *tva* in the language finally resulted in some kind of abstraction and conceptualisation.

In my paper on 'Significance of Tarka' I have taken *tarka* as a near synonym of implication. My former student and friend Professor Vijay Bhardwaj does not agree with me. He thinks that *tarka* stands for counterfactual. He is in good company. Later Nyāya philosophers did hold such a view. But, not counterfactual, but implication is basic to logic and this is indicated by *tarka*. In *Nyāya Sūtras, tarka* is described as *avijñātatve arthe kāraṇotpattitaḥ tattvajñānārtham uhaḥ tarkaḥ*. Maṇikaṇṭha Miśra who was contemporary of Raghunāth Śiromaṇi and who was himself a Nyāya philosopher understands *tarka*, the way I understand it.

To me, if India has to make any progress there must be renaissance particularly in philosophy. Svāmī Vivekānanda, to my mind, is an epitome of such philosophical renaissance. He was preceded by Raja Rammohun Roy who established Brahmo Samāja. Brahmo really means *Brahman*. He wanted to transform the ritualistic Hindu 'Religion' into philosophy. But the word 'Brahmo' does not give the idea that Raja Rammohun Roy did not want to say anything different from Upaniṣads. To me Vivekānanda does not say anything basically different from what Raja Rammohun Roy and philosophers of Brahmo Samāj say. Vivekānanda has in mind *Brahman* of Vedānta only. This is what I have tried to explain in my paper 'Practical Vedānta of Svāmī Vivekānanda'. This lecture was delivered by me in Miami University (USA) in 1992.

In this collection is also included my paper on 'Māyāvāda'. It is my first published paper. It was written in 1942 and published in 1946 in *Nagpur University Journal*. In this paper I have examined the traditional view that the world is illusory. Perhaps such a view was held by later Advaitins. I am trying to point out how difficult it is to hold such a view.

All this is reunderstanding Indian philosophy. I am aware that this is not sufficient. This is just a glimpse, a *darśana*. I must reiterate that there are Indian and non-Indian writers on philosophy but philosophy is neither Indian nor non-Indian. I do not classify my papers as papers on Indian philosophy except for practical convenience.

I am grateful to the editors of *IPQ* and *JICPR* and all those friends who published my papers in the festschrifts and also permitted me to publish them in this book.

I thank Shri Susheel Mittal and D.K. Printworld (P) Ltd. for bringing out this composition. I also thank the manager and the workers of D.K. Printworld (P) Ltd. and the press who are trying hard to bring out the book in a beautiful form.

PUNE
17-12-1997

S.S. Barlingay

1

Reunderstanding Indian Philosophy

In what sense can philosophy be Indian? The question may suggest that the so-called Indian philosophy is fundamentally different from other brands of philosophy, for example, from Western philosophy. I have no doubt that some people seriously think so; but if what they seriously think is also seriously taken note of, then it will mean that, just as some kinds of plants grow in tropical regions and not elsewhere, similarly some kinds of philosophy grow in particular regions. This may further mean that there are types of philosophy such that one is totally different from the other; that each type makes an organic whole; that, even if in a type we may be able to distinguish the parts, the parts together form a whole; and that the commonness of parts between one type and another type cannot be treated together on the basis of one commonness. This may also mean that each type is like a seed; that it grows not only in a particular atmosphere but also in a particular ethnological pattern. Indians being of Aryan race, the Indian type belongs to Aryan pattern and, in a similar way the Greek, the Barbarian, the Roman, the Anglo-Saxon and the Mongolian patterns can be distinguished. Carried further, it signifies that, if there is *cāturvarṇya vyavasthā*, then there will be one particular type of philosophy and way of life, integral and prescribable to each *varṇa*, which is sometimes very seriously thought of by those who talk of *svadharma*. It also implies that philosophy by its nature must be pluralistic, i.e., there would and ought to be varieties of philosophy from the point of view of the need and aptitude of the units in human society.

It is also possible to think that, when we talk of Indian or Western philosophy, we may not think of the logical patterns of philosophy but may think of cultural patterns; that what we call philosophy may be regarded as merely the manifestation or abstraction of the cultural patterns, although this may not mean that philosophies would be watertight compartments, that is, there would not be any communication between philosophy of one pattern and that of another pattern. Of course, it is possible to think that there could be varieties of philosophy even in one cultural pattern and similarities of philosophy in different cultural patterns, because no two men might be alike in the same cultural pattern, while two men of different cultures could be alike in thinking and may have common sympathy and understanding. It is possible, e.g., to think that British philosophy is empiricist, whereas the continental philosophy is otherwise; that by and large the British philosophers would not believe in innate ideas like the continental philosophers who may accept them. But even amongst the continental philosophers there may be critical thinkers like Kant, who may accept something of the empiricist tradition and may build a structure of critical philosophy on the same.

Sometimes by using the term Indian Philosophy I may also mean the philosophy expounded by Indian philosophers. 'Indian' in such a case would not be an adjective of philosophy but would be a case of transferred epithet in as much as it would qualify the writers and not their thought. I have a feeling that, when we talk of Indian philosophy, we have largely such usage in our mind, though other usages need not be completely ignored. I have also a feeling that, when one talks of Indian philosophy, one uses it in the sense of some assorted accumulation of various individual, cultural thought also. When, for example, one talks of 'British philosophy in mid-century', one does not necessarily talk of one particular pattern, though it is possible that the thought may move in one direction on account of the culture, region, and time. I feel that, although I have tried to clarify several possible usages about Indian philosophy, it is much better to keep the matter open and should not postulate that Indian philosophy means this and not that, because the term Indian philosophy is vague and its use is ambiguous and open.

However, when I am talking of Indian philosophy, I shall not talk of the more modern thinkers like Aurobindo and Gandhi, and shall also not concern myself with the interpreters of the old systems like Vivekānanda and K.C. Bhattacharyya or Radhakrishnan, Mahadevan and Murthy. I shall rather try to open and understand the issues once again.

Generally, when we talk of classical Indian philosophies, we talk of them as systems. What is systematic about them? Do they have some common axioms? Does each 'system' have any separate and additional axioms or postulates? Let me try to understand the basic common assumptions and separate independent assumptions of each such system.

First, any attempt at philosophizing is man's attempt at understanding reality or the world. This makes it epistemic. Understanding the world may also mean understanding one's own self and understanding other individuals. It may also refer to the norms for understanding and norms for the behaviour. Most probably time would not interfere with this concept of philosophy, although time may bring about a greater development or depth-dimension to this concepts of philosophy. Essentially, man's concept of philosophy would arise by way of introspection or retrospection on his experience which he has gradually acquired through experiencing, and human history would tell us that this human experience develops from crude experience to a less crude experience. Basically, the crudity or rawness of human experience must remain as it is, although this experience could be chiselled and polished in the course of development. I, therefore, feel thāt all the Indian philosophical systems must be understood against the anthropological background, and their basic nature must be epistemological.

Let me clarify what I want to say. A man in Vedic time as now could talk of the world or reality. But neither is the Vedic concept of reality a perfect concept for the man today, nor was it so for the man of Vedic age. Horizons of our world have gradually widened; still the enhanced world remains finite only, and the residue of the reality hidden from us is far greater and far deeper than the one that was experienced or understood either by the Vedic man or is experienced or understood by the modern man. Nevertheless, the relationship between man and the world and man's ability to understand the world remains the same. Thus, I would say that all the so-called systems of Indian thought made three assumptions:

(1) There is world which exists in its own right;

(2) There is a knower who is a part of the world but who is treated as separate from the world; and

(3) The knower can know the world.

These presuppositions are bound to be at the back of any philosophical investigation, and, therefore, there should not be any surprise if they were at the back of the so-called system of Indian philosophy. But each system had to make a few other presuppositions on account of the difference in the subject-matter. For example, at least in the early Pūrva Mīmāṁsā, the theoretical questions, such as what the world is and what a knower is do not seem to assume a prominent role; for Pūrva Mīmāṁsā had almost dogmatically (and practically) assumed varieties of things and men, and its problem was to organize a theory of action. The things were for enjoyment, and men were for enjoying. (This was also the presupposition of Sāṁkhya.*) Mīmāṁsā had accepted the superiority or inferiority, that is, hierarchy, of men, and had also accepted the limitation of human power which was supplemented by the supernatural power. It had imagined that the supernatural power helped or deferred human action, and had also believed in the dichotomy of body and soul; for, it could distinguish between a dead body and a living body, and had imagined that a body was dead when the living element in it had left it and gone elsewhere. If the living element went elsewhere, it followed that (*i*) it could go and (*ii*) that it must be living and so always be living, that is, it must be immortal. They had also imagined that different material things could be classified under different classes; and if the different particulars could be classed under one class, then there must be the deity of that class controlling the particulars. This concept seems to be at the back of Platonism also, with the difference that Platonism gives us passive 'inactive' concepts. If you imagine the deities of the concepts, you also get a 'solution' of how the concepts could be used by man; for it is the deities which help man voluntarily or through

---

**saṁghāta parārthatvāt* and *pursuṣosti bhoktṛbhāvāt*.

invocation to act in a particular way. All such things find a place in Greek or Hindu mythology, and are very usefully worked out in the epic like the *Mahābhārata*. But in the theory of Mīmāṁsā many of these things are just assumed and, therefore, the problems which arise in Pūrva Mīmāṁsā are primarily non-theoretical. There we are concerned with the relations amongst men and women or man and different men, since these relations are based on *varṇa*, *jāti*, and *āśrama*. They are also based on the notion of hierarchy, and thus certain axiological norms are either presupposed, suggested, or justified. Pūrva Mīmāṁsā is also concerned with the praise of super-human power, and it dogmatically assumes soul, immortality of soul, and rebirth. These concepts are necessarily required for Pūrva Mīmāṁsā for explaining actions and prescriptions of actions. For all these activities analysis of concepts and language also became necessary and made room for prayer, *praśaṁsā*, *arthavāda* and interpretation. Basically, therefore, a system like Pūrva Mīmaṁsa is not a system of knowing what there is. It is primarily concerned with how men ought to behave, though only in a traditional society, and it is only secondarily that metaphysical problems like those of the existence of soul, rebirth, *karma*, etc., and a very important philosophical problem like that of analysis emerge. In such an activity, there, indeed, will be a development of thought. But such a development of thought will be for defending the tradition, not for prescribing a change. Pūrva Mīmāṁsā thus, becomes a defender of orthodoxy.

The trouble with Pūrva Mīmāṁsā was that its assumptions were taken as the thesis of the system; and people forgot the distinction between the thesis of a philosophical system and beliefs of a system. Of course, there can be infinite number of theses in a philosophical system, and the uncritical beliefs of a belief system of certain class can also become the propositions in a dominating philosophical system. The reason for this is that almost every society has a certain belief system as also a pattern of rituals. This pattern of rituals is solemnized within that society; and, if the society begins to dominate over a more enlarged society on account of establishing a supremacy over other societies, then the code of conduct and the system of rituals of the dominating society becomes a system of norms, not only for the dominating society but also for the enlarged society. When this happens, the beliefs in the belief system also become the intuitive truths and become propositions of the philosophical systems. This intuitive transformation requires an authority which is supplied either by the sacred books or by the uncodified accepted pattern of norms. Naturally, one forgets that the sacred books are written by men in the society. They come down to us now by way of tradition where the authorship becomes mystified and is attributed to God, or the codified or uncodified norms assume the status of *mantras*. All this has taken place in Pūrva Mīmāṁsā, although it should be realised that a similar process has taken place in other philosophical systems also. It may further be noted that such a process is bound to take place even in a system which may be regarded as unorthodox.

Like the assumptions of Pūrva Mīmāṁsā, Sāṁkhya, Vaiśeṣika and Uttara Mīmāṁsā must also have their assumptions, although, I am afraid, that some of the assumptions of Pūrva Mīmāṁsā might have been either the common assumptions of other systems or might have been integrated with other systems at some other stage. For example, let us take the question of disembodied soul. This assumption seems to have been either integral to different systems or was incorporated into those systems. Similarly, the propositions about *karma* also seem to have been incorporated into other systems, and these incorporations made the other systems Vedic. The assumption of *karma* theory, for example, seems extremely unnatural to the Buddhist way of thinking. But the cultural grafting of two philosophical system made it possible. Similarly, the assumption that there is soul seems to be inconsistent with the Uttara Mīmāṁsā system. But to any serious student of Advaita Vedānta today this assumption seems to be so basic that it has become an intuitive proposition for the Advaitic system. In fact, such adoptions and integrations of the thesis of one system into the thesis of another system seem to be either the basic function or basic mischief of any historical method.

What are the basic assumptions of Vedānta, Sāṁkhya and Vaiśeṣika systems of thought ? Unlike Pūrva Mīmāṁsā school, the basic thought of these schools appears to be theoretical. It makes an inquiry into: What is real? What is universe? What is reality?

Advaita begins with *brahmajijñāsā*, Vaiśeṣikas enumerate the *padārthas,* and the Sāṁkhyas give a classification (or maybe a division) of the world into *prakṛti* and *puruṣa*. The questions which these systems ask are: what is truth? what is death? what is *jīva*? With such inquiry the concepts of *mokṣa, apavarga* or *kaivalya* appear to be *prima facie* inconsistent, although these three concepts are almost organically connected with these systems. The inquiry about *mokṣa* does not seem to be connected with what is true or what is real. As inquiry about *mokṣa* is basically anthropocentric, practical inquiry relates to why there should be a *rendezvous* of the two inquiries, the theoretical, i.e., basically scientific and cosmocentric, and the practical which has a significance for man only. Nevertheless, historically this has happened. In fact, in the case of Sāṁkhya as in the case of Buddhism, the inquiry starts with a practical question: how to get rid of misery? This rendezvous makes an assumption that the knowledge of what facts are will also lead to the ultimate emancipation of man. This seems to be a common assumption of all these systems over and above the theoretical assumptions. It is surprising that such an integration of practical and theoretical questions did not take place, at least in the early development of Pūrva Mīmāṁsā. The Pūrva Mīmāṁsā assumption of *svarga* has; in fact, nothing to do with the inquiry into what is true or real. It seems to be a simple and clear acceptance, whether it is an assumption of soul or *yajña*, *karma*, *punarjanma* or *svarga*. The step from theory to practice, as in the case of Advaita, Vaiśeṣika, and Sāṁkhya, seems to be very interesting, and this makes me think that there must be a code of rituals, maybe a crude code, for the adherents of these systems and so also for the followers of Cārvāka. It will be interesting to see how there was a transition from the practical to the theoretical and again to the practical questions.

Coming to the theoretical question, the first and intuitive assumption of all the above systems is that there is 'world'. This may be variously named as *Brahman*, *saṁghāta*, *sat*, etc. To say that there is world is to set an outer boundary to what we know. To say that there is world is not to say whether it is one or many. To say that it is one or many will be a further assumption or specification, and will depend on our comprehension and our power of discrimination. It will have to do with the theory of knowledge, and it will not be a basic assumption. Thus, if these further assumptions are made, it means that we have already taken into account the theory of knowledge. Thus, to me all the three systems do not just talk of 'what is real', they are also concerned with 'what we know' of the real.

The term world or its equivalent *Brahman* (and not *jagat*) does not stand for any demarcated specific whole within which you can demarcate parts. It is merely then general apprehension that there is something (indeterminate) which exists in its own right. But to say that there is world is different from saying that there is some determinate thing as the object of our apprehension. When I say that there is some determinate thing, I have, in fact, something in my mind which is more than what I say, for example, I definitely project that determinate thing against the background of the world. I also understand that there is 'I', the knower, who is outside of and different from that determinate thing. This 'I' is also projected or understood against the background of the world, and so when I say that there is something determinate my saying has also taken note of my perceiving, seeing, hearing, touching, smelling, or even tasting. But none of this happens when I am saying that there is world. The world is not projected against the background of another world, nor am I outside of this world. Since I am included in this world, I may not be conscious of my separate existence; nor would I use perception as a means of knowing this world, for perception requires discrimination, demarcation. When I say there is world, the world is indeed there. But the knowledge arises in some mysterious manner, and this is not perceptual knowledge. Whether it is to be called *śabda* or intuition or something else is a different matter. But it is necessary to recognize that the way things are distributively known is different from the way the world as a whole is known. It is necessary to understand this distinction before we begin to understand properly the *padārtha*s of the Vaiśeṣikas, on the one hand, and the *Brahman* of the Vedānta, *prakṛti* (and *puruṣa*) of the Sāṁkhya and *śūnya* of the Buddhist on the other hand. When the *Brahman* is 'known', it is not the same thing as the knowing of the Vaiśeṣika *dravya*s. This also brings us to another important point in knowing. Knowing different *dravya*s and knowing different *padārthas* are also not of the same kind. In any theory of knowledge, this sensitivity of 'different knowings' must be properly felt and realized, otherwise we are likely to be led into some kind of rigid format which will really be anything but knowing. I have a feeling that in the hands of the Paṇḍits and also the Western Orientalists the feeling of the sensitivity is either lost or reduced.

I shall take an instance from the Sāṁkhya system. It has for thesis three propositions (amongst others): (*i*) there is *prakṛti*; (*ii*) there is *puruṣa*; and (*iii*) there are many *puruṣa*s. What is the relation of these propositions to one another? To say that the propositions (*i*) and (*ii*) are true: is it equivalent to saying that there is dualism? Is it equivalent to saying that *prakṛti* and *puruṣa* have the same status? To say that there is *prakṛti* and there is *puruṣa*: is it inconsistent with the proposition that there is *prakṛti only*? To say that there is *puruṣa* and to say that there are many *puruṣa*s: is this an inconsistent position? To say that there is *prakṛti*: is this proposition of the same kind as (*a*) there is world; (*b*) there is a table; (*c*) there is *padārtha*; (*d*) there is honesty or dishonesty, etc.?

I think most of the modern thinkers on Sāṁkhya have not handled the problems which Sāṁkhya has raised with due sensitivity. I shall try to point out how these propositions may be held consistently together, and thereby point out that Sāṁkhya theory may after all mean something very different from what we have been told by our medieval traditional or modern traditional Paṇḍits.

That there is *prakṛti* may either look like a proposition that there is matter, or it may look like a proposition that there is a law or rule. It may also look like a proposition that there is (one) concrete thing or one existent reality. It is necessary to understand that, although these propositions look alike, they mean different things. When we say that there is one concrete world, we are talking about the concrete world as a whole. When we say that there is matter, or everything is matter, we are not talking of the concrete world as a whole; we are talking of some common element. Thus, for example, after looking at different stones or different metals we may say: all that is stone or metal. Or we may abstract some common element in the varieties in the fashion of Nyāya and talk of some commonness. For example, we may talk of mass in all the things or spatial character of all the things. While talking of *prakṛti*, if we are talking of concrete reality, we would talk of living and non-living reality. In that case, we would talk of two different real objects or even concrete objects or class of objects; but even then only one kind of reality would be taken into account. But if we are talking of some common element, then it will not be possible for us to count it in additive terms. Again, if the world of experience is, for example, abstracted into living and non-living or conscious and unconscious, and, if we are thinking of *prakṛti* as only unconscious, then we shall not be able to talk of unconscious elements in additive language. In the same way, *puruṣa* can be talked of either as a concrete thing or some kind of abstract notion. Perhaps either the philosophers of Sāṁkhya have not used or handled these different things delicately or the critics of Sāṁkhya have purposely misused the concepts in the style of *chala* or *vitaṇḍa*. Let us see how a consistent philosophy or philosophies under Sāṁkhya can be constructed or reconstructed using these different notions which are supposed to be basic to Sāṁkhya.

I shall present four models of such constructions.

Model 1: *Prakṛti* is conceived as a sum total of concrete reality except the human beings or self-conscious living beings (which may include the vertebrate animals). In this case, we may talk of *prakṛti* in the same way as we talk of earth or planets and may include concrete objects like metals, stones, trees, and animals except men (and higher vertebrates). In such a case, we can talk of *prakṛti* as one and *puruṣa* as many.

Model 2: We can think of *prakṛti* and *puruṣa* as conceptual division of the total reality where the *fundamentum divisionis* will be either consciousness or unconsciousness. In such a case, the body of the *puruṣa,* for example, will have to be classified under *prakṛti*, and liveliness of entities like men, animals, and trees will have to be classified under the concept of *puruṣa*.

Model 3: The concept of *puruṣa* will be the same as in *Model 2.* Nevertheless, *prakṛti* will not be regarded as abstract but as concrete reality which will consist of all things in the world including the bodies of living beings. This will mean that *prakṛti* is one and *puruṣa* also is one (under this hypothesis it is possible to think of many *puruṣa*s also). And, although we can distinguish *puruṣa* from *prakṛti*, it will be consistent to say that there is no *dvaita*, for *puruṣa* will have no structural existence. It will not exist in its own right, it will exist as dependent on *prakṛti*. It will really be a certain manifestation of *prakṛti*.

Model 4: It is possible to think that *prakṛti* is one in the sense that it is concrete, and it is also possible to think that there is disembodied consciousness as a logical abstraction; nevertheless, it should be possible to think that as a special variety what we call *prakṛti* is inseparably connected with consciousness such that each particular that is formed becomes unique and, therefore, many. They become living conscious persons.

Many more models can be presented, but I desist myself from the temptation of enumerating all of them. I am satisfied with just pointing out that in the course of history these different models could be simultaneously held in different compartments of mind, and that in the understanding of Sāṁkhya vision explanations under different models were partly collected and grouped together. For example, if we say that *prakṛti* and *puruṣa* were abstract notions, then it could be an analysis of reality but could not be the genetic basis of reality. Similarly, if we think that twenty-five *tattva*s about which the Sāṁkhya talks were the logical principles (*tattva*-principle), then it would be absurd to think that the concrete reality came out of purely logical principles. In both the cases, logical analysis is mistaken for genesis (*sarga*). Sometimes, giving an account of *prakṛti*'s creation, mistakes would creep in if proper interpretation is not given of sentences such as *buddhi* arises out of *prakṛti, ahaṁkāra* out of *buddhi* and *tanmātra* out of *ahaṁkāra*. Now, if one is referring to the process of knowledge, then such passages would be meaningful. But, if it is regarded as a real process of creation or physical division, then references to *buddhi* and *ahaṁkara* as intermediate steps between *prakṛti* and *tanmātra* are not required. One could think of *prakṛti* itself as giving rise to *tanmātra*s and also to *mahābhūta*s. But, if *prakṛti* is interpreted as an abstract principle, then this is not possible. Abstract principle cannot give rise to any concrete reality, whether it is conscious or unconscious. And, if the world manifestation is both conscious and unconscious and if it arises from one thing, then one would have to think of the primordial object or reality having both the aspects, conscious and otherwise; and could certainly think of *mahat* as such an object, and *sarga* of Sāṁkhya could start from *mahat*. The logical division of *mahat* into *prakṛti* and *puruṣa* would, in that case, be of logical and not of physical significance. The consistency of Sāṁkhya system or Sāṁkhya vision will have to be validated against the touchstone of how we conceive of *prakṛti* and *puruṣa*. Again, let us take the problem of *kaivalya*. When we talk of *puruṣa*'s *kaivalya* or *artha,* (I have a feeling that *puruṣārtha* is primarily a concept of Sāṁkhya system and *artha* is the primary *puruṣārtha*), we will have to talk of *puruṣa* as a concrete living object. He will be an embodied *puruṣa*. He will have to be a person. Only then we would be able to talk of 'his' emancipation. *Puruṣa* as an abstraction does not really require emancipation. It is always segregated. All concepts are only *kevala*. But, in such a case, *prakṛti* as an abstraction will also be *kevala*. Such an abstract *puruṣa* will not be subjected to birth, death, etc. (*janana, maraṇa, karaṇa*). The concept of rebirth (and *karma* also) would not be even relevant if *puruṣa* is taken merely as an abstraction.

To be brief, Sāṁkhya vision which has come down to us consists of several layers, and we will, skilfully have to separate these layers in the fashion of a good archaeologist or a geologist. For Sāṁkhya vision is a criss-crossing of several visions, and what we now perceive in Sāṁkhya text is a foggy picture of the depth where we are not able to differentiate between the nearer and the distant parts of the depth.

Just as ethical problems arise only for a man in society, i.e., only when he recognises the existence of other men, similarly ethical problems arise only for a person who has body, not for consciousness, pure and simple. In fact, all our actions, desires, wishes, pains, and pleasures are for a person with body. If this is not recognized, we would be committing a fallacy which may at times be subtle and at times gross. For example, if the husband is to be of any use for the fulfilment of one's (i.e., *ātman*'s) desire (*ātmanastu kāmāya patiḥ priyo bhavati*), then that *ātman* should be with the body. It is not a disembodied soul which has urges, for the urges are manifested in and through the body. The bodiless *ātman* does not have sex, although the terms *jīva* and *ātman* are of masculine gender and *ruh* and soul of feminine. When we talk of any action, the first presupposition is that it must be an action of an embodied soul. It appears to me that many a time this particular fact is not paid heed to, and interpretation of passages in the classical philosophy is given in such a way that a muddle or confusion is created. If ethical problems as also the problems concerning action are to be considered in Sāṁkhya, then the first thing that is to be recognized is that in this context *puruṣa* means an embodied self-conscious being. It is only in this way that we can understand plurality of *puruṣa* in Sāṁkhya. It is only of the embodied *puruṣa* that we can talk in terms of *janana, maraṇa* and *karaṇa*. They occur at different times and at different places. Sāṁkhya here accepts the concept of time. *Ayugapat pravṛtti* or non-simultaneous or successive occurrence is a temporal concept, and it is accepted in Sāṁkhya. Similarly, there is the concept of individuality or *ahaṁkāra*. This *ahaṁkāra* is of two types. This is also mentioned in the Sāṁkhya system. This *ahaṁkāra* gives (*a*) personality to the consciousness and (*b*) differentness to things or *saṁghāta*. This individuality (*ahaṁkāra*) requires that each consciousness should be bordered out. This cannot be done unless it is 'imprisoned' by body. Although I am using the terms consciousness, 'imprison', and 'body', I am using them only figuratively; otherwise, there is every chance of our thinking that there is disembodied consciousness which also exists in its own right. When consciousness is determined by space, time, and matter, it becomes a person; it gives identity to the self; and it is this self-identity which is important for action, as well as social and moral life. It is necessary to know that the problem of *ahaṁkāra* is the same as the problem of self-identity or personal identity, and this can be determined in the case of an individual — a conscious individual — in two ways. From his own side it is determined by his awareness of 'I' or I-consciousness, i.e., the consciousness has its spread-out and control only in the area of his body which is determined by space and time. As an embodied person, it has common features with other embodied things, which have no consciousness and which are not controlled by the object itself. When others look at this embodied soul, they find his separate individuality as distinguished by (*ayugapat pravṛtti*) non-simultaneity and positions at different places. Things have both *ayugapat pravṛtti* and *parārthatva:* for an embodied consciousness there is *ayugapat pravṛtti*, for other people there is *parārthatva*, and for the person himself there is *svārthatva*. This makes one individual different from another individual and one thing different from another thing. Sāṁkhya has brought this out by bringing in the concept of *ahaṁkāra*. Without *ahaṁkāra* and the concept of discrimination, our knowledge that we are different from one another and also that things are different from one another will not arise.

One thing more. Sāṁkhya starts with man who is an individual. It is not the *puruṣa* of a conceptual nature. The conceptual *puruṣa* cannot be many. Such *puruṣa*s are manifestations of *prakṛti* only. Conceptual *puruṣa* cannot be an existent. *Puruṣa* made out of *prakṛti* on account of *cidichāyā* alone can be many. In fact, we have to think of many *puruṣa*s if we are talking of the individuals in the world. It is they who have both *janana* and *maraṇa* — birth and death — and they also have consciousness. It is such *puruṣa*s who will also have pain and pleasure; and if at all there is any ethics, it is for such *puruṣa*s.

What is the *puruṣārtha* of these *puruṣa*s? What do they want? Sāṁkhya answers that, once these *puruṣa*s are recognized, the world is divided into *saṁghāta* and *puruṣa*. *Saṁghāta* is *prakṛti* where consciousness (of macro level) is not noticed. It can be regarded as material, although it may take a variety of forms. It has no ethics, it is to be enjoyed by others —saṁghāta *parārthatvāt*. *Puruṣa,* on the other hand, is an enjoyer. He is an enjoyer of *saṁghāta*, and, if it is accepted that *puruṣa* is also a *saṁghāta* on account of his having a body, he not only enjoys an ordinary *saṁghāta* but also enjoys 'other' *puruṣa*s' which account for the social communication as well as sex activity. For women also in this language would be *puruṣa*s. Man includes woman.

A belief system may also play a part. It is possible that the beliefs in soul and its immortality, and rebirth, *karma*, may enter here, and we may think of *sarga* now, not in a logical way but in a Mīmāṁsā way, i.e., as a matter of beliefs. The beliefs persist. And, if the implications of the beliefs are to be refuted, they will have to be refuted by a deeper understanding of reality. Knowledge alone gives us this deeper understanding of the reality. It would tell us that the only *puruṣārtha* is to know the limitations of the empirical *puruṣārthas*, to know that *puruṣa* as such is only a concept and not an existent. *Puruṣa* in us is only the 'shadow' of this concept of consciousness. As soon as this is done, the dance-drama will come to an end. And, just as the dancer returns to the green-room after performing the dance-drama, so also we would realize that the *sarga* is only due to ignorance. Not that it does not continue, but (in a different way) now the whole thing becomes meaningless. This is the *kaivalya*, the loneness, recognition of the purposelessness of the pseudo union of the *prakṛti* and *puruṣa*. As soon as this is realized, one would know that there is neither rebirth nor *karma* nor *svarga*, for the *puruṣa* as an epiphenomenon would not exist. And this would also be the recognition of the fact that what we call misery is only a necessary accompaniment of the empirical world.

The Advaita system of Vedānta has been the most accepted philosophy in India for the last several hundred years. It is supposed to be the interpretation of Upaniṣads, and so it is accepted as a very orthodox philosophical thought. However, to my mind it appears that, in order to understand the basic tenets of Advaita, it is equally necessary to understand the background, at least the logical background, which has given rise to the Advaita way of thinking. This background is supplied by the Pūrva Mīmāṁsā, Sāṁkhya, and Buddhism. The main tenets of Pūrva Mīmāṁsā, are the following:

(1) The Vedas must be accepted as infallible.

(2) The Vedic sentences basically give us prescriptions and injunctions, i.e., what we must do and what we must not do. These prescriptions and injunctions, at least for the members of the higher class, are centred around the rituals connected with sacrifice.

(3) Man must always act, for action is prescribed in the Vedas.

(4) A man who is living is divisible into two parts, the body and the soul. Our soul, being the agent of action, has freedom and responsibility to act.

(5) The soul exists in its own right. (Contrary to this it is also believed that soul requires body to act.)

(6) The action exists in its own right and modifies or gears the soul to action. The circle of action is not complete during one's life period. So the soul and action exist beyond death. Therefore, in order to fulfil the actions or suffer the consequences of action, the soul takes rebirth.

(7) It also has to pay for the actions in the other world, either in the heaven or in hell.

(8) Each action or the object of the action has a deity, and a man must please the deity through sacrifice.

It also takes for granted inequality in society, thanks to *karma*, and provides a justification for *cāturvarṇya* and also for *jāti vyavasthā*. It would naturally believe in many souls which would remain as souls. And so philosophy would either be the philosophy of society of men or it will be the philosophy of society of souls.

In a way, Advaita like Sāṁkhya and Buddhism tried to raise a banner of revolt against this system. The Pūrva Mīmāṁsā school thinks that there are several souls. Advaita points out that each soul gets its identity only so long as it is limited by a certain body. It illustrates this from the example of *ākāśa*. We can talk of a particular space in a particular pot, but spaces are not many. It is only one space limited by different pots. Similarly, different *jīva*s cease to be *jīva*s as soon as they are considered in the context of the whole reality. Advaita Vedānta suggests that when we are talking of consciousness or *caitanya* we cannot talk of *jīva*s. It is not possible to talk of *this caitanya* and *that caitanya*. As soon as we begin to talk of *caitanya*, the individuality which characterizes *jīva*s is lost; in fact, there is a subtle inconsistency involved in talking of *jīva*s. We get, the plurality of *jīva*s on account of what Sāṁkhya calls *ahaṁkāra*. This *ahaṁkāra* determines the identity of *jīva* from within, but, if a third man is to know the *jīva*s, there must be specificness of the *jīva*s knowable to the third man. To me it appears that this cannot be done unless the third man knows or imagines spatio-temporality regarding the *jīva*, and this is not possible in regard to a 'disembodied *jīva*'. It is difficult to imagine a disembodied *jīva*, and so when we so imagine we somehow imagine it with some kind of 'ethereal body' which is really inconsistent with our own assumptions. What we do is that we isolate the consciousness from the usual body and then reinforce it with another body. A better hypothesis, therefore, is to think that when the body is destroyed the individuality itself is destroyed. This may happen either at the time of death or when the *liṅga-deha* or subtle body is destroyed. But when the body is destroyed, will the consciousness persist? Here, Advaita will resort to another kind of argument. It is based on *satkāryavāda*. If consciousness is experienced as effect, then it must also exist as cause. It cannot come into existence as an accident. It must be there right from the beginning. And so, even after the individuality is lost it must be potentially present. In fact, it must constitute the cosmos. Furthermore, what we call individuality may itself be a play of consciousness. When we talk of individual consciousness, consciousness is taken as something that is subjective. When the individuality is lost and consciousness is conceived to be still persisting the question arises as to whether such consciousness can really exist outside the bounds of spatio-temporality. To me it appears that Advaita is not clear on this point, that is, it may allow spatio-temporality and even matter occupying space and time in its thesis. The matter will be charged with consciousness. In fact, like the quantum physics the reality can appear as matter from one point of view and consciousness from another. It is not the body that is denied to consciousness; it is only some gross body, that gives self-consciousness which is denied. It is not that it does not come into existence but that which comes into existence perishes. The self-consciousness comes into existence but 'perishes' into the ocean of consciousness, and liquidates itself into that. The self-consciousness in a body gives subjectivity. It is this realization that the subjectivity eliminates itself into the cosmos (i.e., the consciousness that is objective), which provides the thesis that I am *Brahman* (*ayam ātmā brahma* or *prajñānam brahma*). This realisation is equivalent to saying: I am not, the *Brahman* is. There is no identity between 'I' and *Brahman*. 'I' simply do not exist when there is a realisation that there is only *Brahman*. Śaṅkarārcārya in *Ṣaṭpadī* has very clearly stated that *taraṅga* is *samudra* but *samudra* is not *taraṅga*. This means that a self-conscious being cannot be without body; that it is the self-conscious being who can have aspirations which can be mundane or supramundane. It is with these aspirations that the concepts of *karma*, *dharma* and *svarga* are connected. It is with these that the concepts of birth and death are connected. If this self-conscious body is denied or if it is realized that the self-conscious body comes into being and is destroyed in the course of time, all problems which Pūrva Mīmāṁsā raises would vanish. This, I think, is the main thesis of Uttara Mīmāṁsā. Sāṁkhya aids this thesis, for it is in Sāṁkhya that *puruṣa* or consciousness is taken out of what they call union of *prakṛti* and *puruṣa*. When *puruṣa* is taken away from *prakṛti*, it is no more *jīva*; and such *puruṣa* cannot have any aspirations of either doing anything or achieving anything. Both *karma* and *karma-phala* are denied to him, for they are of no significance to him. The concepts of *svarga* and *naraka*, as also birth and rebirth, become redundant. Nevertheless, all these concepts find their shelters in Uttara Mīmāṁsā doctrines and also in the Sāṁkhya and Buddhist doctrines. This makes the whole thing complicated, and no clear view is arrived at. It should be remembered that the naive uncritical belief of a common man is that there is a disembodied soul, although it is accepted that such a disembodied soul has also a microscopic body. This belief is perpetuated and presupposed in the Pūrva Mīmāṁsā thinking. Sāṁkhya points out that we can legitimately accept disembodied consciousness as a concept existing in its own right, because consciousness or sentience is a fact of experience. But only such disembodied sentience would be inactive. This is indirect admission that, when we distinguish body from consciousness or matter from consciousness, we have started or initiated the process of abstraction. But to say this, is not to say that consciousness or sentience is unreal. Whatever is experienced in the form of effect must be potentially present as cause or in the form of cause also. There is a difference between sentience or *puruṣa* of Sāṁkhya and *jīva* of a tiny or micro-living being. A *jīva* cannot exist unless it is a complex of matter and sentience, for it is this complexity which gives it self-consciousness or self-identity. It is this argument which is carried forward by Advaita. Instead of using the word, *jīva*, it prefers using the word *ātman*. *Jīva* is an empirical existence. It is not segregated from body. Perhaps, when one talks of *jīva*, the emphasis is on sentience. But it should not mean that the sentience exists in its own right. The operation of each *jīva* is strictly within certain bounds and is comparable with space limited by a certain pot. The model is of *chatācvacchinna ākāśa.* This limitation gives it its identity. But the sentience like space is not unreal. It is to be presupposed as real, and would constitute the very nature of reality or *Brahman*. Sentience is not *mithyā*. The ontological status of sentience is not denied in the context of *Brahman*. But its manifestation in the form of individual is different from the general status of sentience. It is not regarded as a function of the body; nevertheless, it is regarded as inseparable from the body so long as the body exists. But, when body perishes the separate existence of the individual sentience also perishes, although the sentience as such does not perish. This position does not allow the persistence and influence of *karma* over either the sentience or the individual, beyond a certain point. The sentience, when it is manifested as a complex, takes the form of awareness, and so paves the way for epistemology. Cārvāka would differ here on one point. He is likely to say that sentience does not persist beyond death, for it is the function of the body, function of the four *mahābhūta*s when they came together in a unique and particular way. But both Cārvāka and the Advaitin should agree that in a living body the function of the sentience should be epistemic, and also that it should act and behave as agent and controller of the body. Everything that the body does would appear now as being directed by the agent; and, in a way, though within limits, the function of the *jīva* and the function of this agent would be similar. This agent would be called *ātman* or *ahaṁ*, and he should be responsible, along with the several other *ātman*s, for the construction of *jagat* and *prapañca,* the 'human' universe. This agent would never have a cognition that it dies, although, as a matter of fact it does perish; and so, if one is not careful enough, the trap for identifying the *ātman* with *jīva* would always exist. To me it appears that this has happened again and again, and so *ātman* is many a time confused with *jīva*. But the concept of *ātman* is not the same as that of *jīva*. What *ātman* indicates is merely the *sākṣitva;* it is merely the linguistic expression of that *sākṣin* which means mere presence of sentience.

Man, who is the embodied sentience, asserts his freedom over the universe and makes further constructions over it. These constructs or constructions begin with naming, and continue with more and more elaborate and complicated forms. The variety, however, is characterized by the same sentience. And, if sentience is accepted as the general feature of this universe, then the real stuff of all this universe will be sentience. But in its appearance it will look otherwise. This difference will be partly due to sentience taking a form other than that of sentience or due to man's giving it different forms. Now, it is possible that the nature may be matter characterised by sentience or the nature may be sentience itself, though it is very queer to understand it in this sense. It is easy to understand or misunderstand matter characterised by sentience as sentience itself. But one thing is certain: if Vedāntic position is accepted, then the sentience cannot be eliminated; and it also will have to be admitted that man will give it different forms. This will be *loka-vyavahāra*. This will be the combination or copulation of *satya* and *anṛta*, and will be the extended reality, the social reality, which in its own right will be nothing but the sentience or the primordial stuff with which we have started. In a sense, we can say that the primordial stuff is real and all constructs over it are unreal, because, although there is potentially in the original stuff to take these forms, the forms are only constructs of man. They are real forms but can be regarded as appearances, and thus it becomes possible to think that the whole world that is constructed is *māyā* or illusion. Whether originally intended or not such a position has been taken up by Advaita in one of its interpretations. Constructions may be imaginary or real; distinction between the two has to be made and yet they will be nothing but constructions. What is important to note is that, whereas it is possible to think of *jagat* or constructed world as *mithyā* or illusory, it is never possible to think of *ātman* in the same way. It is always real, for it is non-different from the primordial stuff. In the constructs themselves, there are several belief systems playing their parts. The belief system of birth-and-death cycles and *karma* is one kind of belief systems. The belief system with which we live and communicate and transact with others or try to educate others is another, and the belief system connected with dreams and the supernaturals is still another. That in our life several belief systems arise does not mean that they have the same status. Some belief systems are to be disposed off instantaneously, and some off them are required for our communication with others. If we discard belief system, which lays emphasis on heavens, *karma*, and rebirth, it does not mean that we will have to simultaneously discard all belief systems.

Although all epistemological investigations begin with and presuppose consciousness or sentience as an element in experience, an element of experienced world cannot be denied. What can be denied is that consciousness *qua* consciousness is a separable unit in the complex, that is, the experienced world. How consciousness as such can exist unless it has some form, comparable either to the form of matter or energy, is the problem. What we experience is sentient matter and not sentience. But, once sentience is separated from the other part of the experienced world, it is easier and possible to think that the other part does not exist; what exists is the sentience alone. The argument for holding such a view is that, if matter can exist in its own right, why cannot sentience exist in a similar way? In fact, it is this argument which has been forwarded or is supposed to be forwarded by all idealists, including even the epistemological idealists who take for granted the knower as independent of the body. This is also the argument attributed to Advaita. The question, however, is whether such sentience *qua* sentience can exist without space and time, i.e., without spatio-temporal properties. Even those who talk of sentience *qua* sentience have to supply some kind of microscopic spatio-temporal body for such sentience. But, once one starts with the argument that sentience can exist without a body, one can also regard the world as a nebula of sentience; and one can further hold that at some stage spatio-temporal and material properties emerge from sentience and limit the sentience. It is this limitation which may give rise to a manifest self-consciousness which is only potentially present in the sentience, i.e., although existing, it is only in a hidden form. Once one makes this assumption, one is thinking of sentience as a whole. One cannot think of sentience in a pluralistic manner; one must think of it as a common substance just as a materialist conceives of matter as a whole, as a common substance. This concept of sentience is justified by man's concept of the whole. Let us imagine that the world consists of several inseparable elements, one of which is sentience. As soon as one thinks of a whole which cannot be separated into several independent parts, one has no other alternative but to imagine the world in terms of being sentient, i.e., sentience is characterised as the whole. Once we assume that the world is unity, it is natural to think that the world is sentient and that it appears to be manifold on account of spatio-temporal limitations, i.e., *samvṛtatva* or *paricchinnatva,* which also is one of the manifestations of sentience itself. But, instead of having unitary or holistic concept of the world, if one thinks of the world as a name for the manifold, then it is possible to think of a variety which may consist of both sentient and non-sentient elements, and the sentient element would not be segregated from its spatio-temporal body.

However, once one accepts sentience as an element in the world or once the world is accepted as a manifestation of sentience, the way for epistemology, not only of knowledge but also of beliefs, has been paved. It then becomes possible for one either to construct or imagine some belief systems, particularly when one goes further and further away from reality. One thus constructs a theory about *karma* and thinks that one must always be active such that one *karma* must lead to some other *karma*; and also that *karma* requires an agent too, for its performance. Therefore, the agent of *karma* must also be immortal; that it must exist beyond the point of death so that the rebirth must be possible; and that there must be heavens and hades. All these are make-belief systems. If one is self-conscious, one can know through knowledge that they are make-belief systems. And once it is so known, all the systems of make-beliefs will simply evaporate. But, so long as one is ignorant of their make-belief character they will go on haunting one as real. Our social beliefs perpetuated by Pūrva Mīmāṁsā are of this make-belief nature. These naive beliefs are shattered only when one knows that as a knower one is capable of creating them. That which is created by our make-beliefs can be destroyed by knowledge. If something is a part of physical reality, it cannot be so destroyed by knowledge. I think the main propositions of Advaita theory tell us that propositions of Pūrva Mīmāṁsā are the creations of a make-belief system. Of course, while asserting this, the Advaitin also creates certain other make-beliefs, viz. that the world is a unitary whole; that the world is an illusion, i.e., everything is a make-belief. And somehow *karma, jīva*, etc., though believed to be make-beliefs, still persist as real beliefs in some other chambers of our mind and peep into Uttara Mīmāṁsā system. On account of such further beliefs, I think, some of the basic and important propositions of Advaita Vedānta are lost to us, and we again fall in the trap of Pūrva Mīmāṁsā which starts controlling our mind.

2

Concepts in the Philosophy of Indian Origin

I

CONCEPTS in Sāṁkhya are explained on the basis of metaphysical dualism usually associated with Sāṁkhya system. In this paper I propose to find out whether such an interpretation is necessary or whether there is plausibility of some other explanation.

It is usually asserted that according to Sāṁkhya there are two realities *prakṛti* and *puruṣa* and we are also told that *prakṛti* is non-vital, but it acts, *puruṣa* is vital in nature but is incapable of any action. Such kind of explanation has given rise to criticisms and controversies at the hands of exponents of other systems. Śaṅkarācārya, for example, could say that the division between *prakṛti* and *puruṣa* will reduce both *prakṛti* and *puruṣa* to abstractions, and abstractions could not be called realities. To my mind it appears that most of the problems in philosophy arise because we regard epistemological or linguistic phenomenon as a copy of something, that something is. When something exists then we say that it is. But the word 'is' is also used along with abstractions and words in language. When I say this is my experience I am certainly saying that my experience 'is'. But this 'isness' is not the same as the 'is-ness' of things. But if the difference in these two different uses of 'is' is not taken into account then a linguistic or epistemological dualism may easily become metaphysical or physical dualism. To my mind it appears that some such magic has come into play and has led to misunderstanding about Sāṁkhya. Shall we not distinguish between something which is without consciousness and the consciousness? If we, e.g., take a living body it is theoretically possible to distinguish between consciousness and the body, and both of them can be characterised by 'is-ness'. Even when the body dies the characteristic of 'is-ness' cannot be neglected and this leads us to treat a living body, a dead body and some other material body or a thing, on par. We certainly have to characterise the consciousness with 'is-ness'. Of course, it is not customary to say 'is-ness' is, but is-ness also is, i.e., characterised by is-ness and such use of is-ness is likely to lead to infinite regress. But while we are prepared to characterise consciousness with is-ness we do not realise that characterising consciousness with is-ness and characterising is-ness with is-ness are similar. This non-realisation leads us to think that consciousness exists in the same manner as a thing exists. Such linguistic use leads us to posit some kind of metaphysical entity. It is not possible for us to avoid the use of 'is' in language or in communicating our thoughts. And so at the linguistic level we are bound to use consciousness and the object which is characterised by consciousness as two different entities and regard one as external to the other.

However, accepting that the bifurcation of consciousness and *prakṛti* is of this kind, we will have to say that *puruṣa* or consciousness in metaphysics will not have to be treated as separate from *prakṛti*, though in expression they would appear to be different and separate. To illustrate this point consider the following examples:

(1) This is my book	(2) This is my land
(3) This is my wife	(4) This is my hand
(5) This is my head	(6) This is my son
(7) This is my idea	

When I say, 'This is my book' the book is not a part and parcel of me. It can be stolen away from me, it can be torn and destroyed, without in any way affecting me, except emotionally sometimes. But the book can also be kept with me if I am fond of the book. I, e.g., may keep it in my pocket. When I say "This is my land or landed property' the logic in the first case does not work here. Land is certainly separate from me, but it is so external to me that it cannot be kept with me. I can at the most keep with me certain deeds of the land but I cannot keep the land in my pocket and I can only be inseparable from land if my cremation takes place on it. When I say 'This is my wife' and also sometimes say that there is a union of two souls the thinking system of my wife and that of mine, cannot be fused in one. The bodies also cannot be inseparable although the product of the union in the form of a child may inherit the qualities of both. Any one of the two, myself and my wife, may exist independently even after the death of one of the two. This is not the case when I say 'this is my hand'. My hand is inseparable from me as a part of the system. But if it is *amputated*, I can certainly take it into my other hand and show to people that it was my hand. But when I go from 'this is my hand' to 'this is my head', it is much more inseparable. I can of course, be beheaded. But if I am beheaded, I shall not be able to take my head into my hands and show to people and express that this was my head. It will have to be left to others to say whose head it was. If there is a soul it will be very much inseparable from me although in certain mythologies they would be regarded as separable after death.

These different uses have to be taken into account if we have to understand that propositions about metaphysical realities are to be distinguished from realities which are just linguistic.

On the basis of this distinction I have made above, let me see now, how we can understand the relation between *prakṛti* and *puruṣa*; *puruṣa* is said to be conscient as opposed to *prakṛti*. If we distinguish consciousness from the other part, this is bound to happen. We do so express it in language. If *puruṣa* is a name given to the totality of functions which is called consciousness, it will be really correct to say that *prakṛti* is non-conscient. If we use the word 'is' both in regards to the *prakṛti* and *puruṣa* it would not be out of place. But the function as such cannot act. Action is not the function of consciousness alone, it does require intelligent direction which may be called will or sometimes even intention. But the basis of this action is the movement and this is certainly not a part of intelligence, consciousness or will. So to my mind it is very legitimate to regard that in a sense it is only the *prakṛti* which is a doer and *puruṣa* has nothing to do with action, and so he is non-doer.

Another point in Sāṁkhya which is equally important in this

respect is about the characteristic of *prakṛti*, like *sattva*, *rajas*, and *tamas*; Sāṁkhya calls them *guṇa*. But they are not qualities in the sense *dravatva*, *snehatva*, etc., are *guṇa*; *rūpa* regards *rūpa*, *rasa*, *gandha*, etc., as qualities but evidently these words are variously used (and for Sāṁkhya they may actually stand for some realities). Sometimes the *guṇa*s of Sāṁkhya are regarded as constituents and such constituents are understood as inseparable parts. *Sattva*, *rajas*, *tamas* are regarded as constituents of a rope (*guṇa* means rope). And the three elements in the rope make one whole called *prakṛti*. Thus, some people begin to interpret the Sāṁkhya *guṇa*s as physical parts of *prakṛti*. This, however, does not seem to be correct. To my mind the *guṇa*s of Sāṁkhya are charasteristics only, but are still not like the *guṇa*s of Vaiśeṣika. I have pointed out above how characteristics tend to become external or internal and when we talk of qualities as in Vaiśeṣika at least some of them are external. To my mind it appears that *sattva*, *rajas*, *tamas* are inseparable characteristics of *prakṛti* and not parts of *prakṛti*, but they are also not functions of *prakṛti*. So just as in ordinary language we can say that there is consciousness, similarly we cannot say that there is *sattva* or there is *rajas* or there is *tamas*. In our language mechanism such a sentence will not be complete. Whereas we do regard a proposition of the form 'there is a consciousness' complete in itself, we do not regard a proposition of the form there is *sattva* or there is *rajas* or 'there is *tamas*' as complete in itself. (Of course, our language does permit another and independent use of such propositions, but in such a use, 'there is *tamas*' means there is darkness, and there is *sattva* means there is existence and 'there is *rajas*' means there is movement.)

So it means that one has to distinguish between a thing and its function, a thing and its parts, a thing and its separable qualities, a thing and its inseparable characteristics, and a thing and the concept of a thing. A confusion of any one of these is likely to ruin the philosophic base of a certain thought.

II

Philosophy seems to be one of the primary activities of human beings. Plato suggested Philosophy begins with wonder. This element of wonder acts in three different ways. It develops man's scientific investigation. It develops the culture and finally it develops itself into philosophy including speculative philosophy. In a way philosophy is both the scientific and the cultural activity. Man has always asked two kinds of questions:

(1) What is the cause, origin and genesis of the universe?

(2) What is the explanation of the universe?

The two questions are different, though from time to time one quesetion is always confused with the other. In the development of Indian thought too, the question pertaining to the two areas are thoroughly confused. The result is wrong formulation of philosophical questions and wrong answers. Many times two opposite groups of thinkers have purposely misrepresented the opponent's point of view. Thus, Hindu, Buddhist and Jain writers generally misunderstand other's point of view — by twisting their thesis in *pūrva pakṣa* and then criticising them. Among the Hindu writers also, we find people not caring to understand the point of view of the philosophers of other schools. Such misrepresentation however, does not necessarily lead to poverty of thought. On the other hand it is my contention that several possible interpretations do make and have made the thought richer. The two questions I refer to above are what is the cause of the universe and what is the explanation of the universe? The first enquiry is the temporal enquiry, i.e., from what thing or things the present world has come into being. It is the question of the kind, who is the father or the mother of something. The second enquiry is the classification of categorisation of the experience.

Suppose, for example, someone says that there are seven *padārathas* or nine *dravyas* — as the 'Vaiśeṣikas' assert, or if someone says — that according to 'Nyāya' there are *padārathas* like *pramāṇa-prameya* etc., then we are only trying to give an analysis of knowledge. In fact, it is, this analysis which philosophy aims at. But sometimes such an analysis is confused with causal explanation and two kinds of questions are easily confused. Sometimes the word that we use are also reponsible for such a confusion. We, for example, sometimes say that *prakṛti* is the cause of the world and the Sanskrit word that is used, namely, *kāraṇa* with the temporal notion 'cause'. But it appears to me that the word *kāraṇa* is used both in the temporal sense as well as in 'How'-sense and also used in the sense of purpose. Most of the writers of different systems have perhaps used the word in all these three senses and their philosophical thought is concerned with all the three kinds of enquiries, but this is exactly the reason why, when the tradition in Indian thought is broken, their philosophy seems un-understandable. Take, for example, such a sentence in Upaniṣad as *sadaiva saumya idamagre āsīt.* In this sentence, *agre-āsīt* are definitely temporal words and this has led to the belief that the world has come out of Brahmana as in Rāmānuja. But, for example, when we say that the world is atomic in nature or the world is ultimately energy, we do not necessarily mean that there was energy first and then came the world out of it. Explanation of the Universe is not necessarily its genetic enquiry. From this point of view it is to be seen whether the Sāṁkhya and Vedānta doctrines were, in fact, concerned with some kind of causal enquiry about the world.

As stated earlier, the development of thought in India can be traced to the transition from the 'Sāṁkhya' point of view to 'Advaita'. 'Sāṁkhya' system is not only important as a system of philosophy but is also important as it influenced several of the scientific disciplines in India like the science of medicine, the science of mathematics and the science of poetics. In a way, what Abhinavagupta did both in his philosophy as well as in his poetics was a kind of compromise between Advaitic and Sāṁkhya concepts and development of the thought arising from the compromise. In a way Rāmānuja's philosophy also showed an influence of 'Sāṁkya' concepts in his philosophical thinking.

It appears to me that people understood the 'Sāṁkhya' concept in two different ways: (1) by causal explanation, (2) by way of scientific explanation of experience. According to 'Sāṁkhya', there are 25 categories (In the hands of Kāśmīr Śaivism they became 39 or 40). These categories are: (1) *prakṛti*, (2) 7 *prakṛti-vikṛti*, (3) 16 *vikāras*, (4) *puruṣa* (they are many). The model is taken from a human family and in a way the approach is genetic. *Prakṛti* is the primary thing or an object like the mother in the house. It gives birth to 7 children which in turn give birth to 16 children. This creation could not take place without the help of *puruṣa*s as we find in actual life. The *puruṣa*s are also many because one consciousness is different from other consciousness. Thus, in this creation process *prakṛti* gives rise to *ahaṁkāra*. And in *ahaṁkāra*, there is creation in two different ways — the subjective and the objective. On the subjective side there are five sense-organs, five motor organs and *manas*. On the objective side, there are *pañcatanmātra*, *śabda*, *sparśa*, *rūpa*, *rasa*, *gandha*, which in turn give rise to *pṛthvī*, *āpa*, *teja*, *vāyu*, *ākāśa*. This creation becomes possible because everything is caused, because every cause leads to an effect.

This is what is called *satkāryavāda*. *Puruṣa* is in fact not a part of the creation and is not connected with creation in any sense of the term. It only acts as a catalytic agent. It is called *kūṭastha*. Such a position was necessary because the problem before the 'Sāṁkhya' was how to get rid of (pain and) misery which was according to them of three kinds. If *puruṣa* was connected with creation he could never have got rid of pain and misery. Therefore, the *puruṣa* must be detached from the pain. Thus the 'Sāṁkhya' theory is that pains or miseries do not belong to *puruṣa*. Here there is a confusion between the *puruṣa* and the individual. For pains or miseries nevertheless belong to the individual and if *puruṣa* is not a part of creation, there could not be many *puruṣa*s nor could the *puruṣa*s exist in the individual and experience pain. Wherefrom the 'Sāṁkhya' take this model is not known. Almost all philosophy in India starts with the problem of pain. Buddhism begins like that and so does Vedānta. How to get happiness is also a problem before Pūrva Mīmāṁsā. It may be, 'Sāṁkhya' has taken this model from the other systems of philosophy or might have discovered it themselves. The idea is, unless the *puruṣa* is separated from creation, the concept of (feeling) a way out of misery cannot be shown. So 'Sāṁkhya' said that pain and misery do not belong to *puruṣa* at all. Pain and misery do not belong to *prakṛti* also because it is not conscious, and pain and misery do not exist without consciousness. The concept of pain and misery do not arise without object. I cannot simply have pain or misery without its having a connection with something else. So for the experience of pain and misery there must be identification of the object with the subject, in 'Sāṁkhya' terminology, of *puruṣa* with *prakṛti*. The 'Sāṁkhya' solution of the problem is that this identification is false because *prakṛti* and *puruṣa* are of opposite nature. The false identification gives rise to pain and misery. Thus, if you have the knowledge that the knower, i.e., *puruṣa* is not at all connected with the object of experience, the problems of misery and pain do not arise at all.

Sometimes the 'Sāṁkhya' theory has been called as the theory of Evolution. I think it is a fundamental mistake to suppose that 'Sāṁkhya' philosophy like several other philosophies gave us a coherent and consistent system and that all the problems were related consistently with all other problems in the system. I find that in 'Sāṁkhya' psychological, logical, epistemological and ontological points of view get mixed up. Thus, for example, the kind of evolution that the traditional 'Sāṁkhya' has suggested is merely a psychological picture of how a child grows from in indeterminate person to a more and more determinate one.

But to regard the 'Sāṁkhya' problem as the problem of psychology or genesis is according to me a naïve approach to understand 'Sāṁkhya'. Just as 'Sāṁkhya' asked the question of misery and pain and thus wanted to separate individual from the experience, similarly 'Sāṁkhya' also asked a question about the nature of experience. Unless you accept the fact that 'Sāṁkhya' was connected with analysis of experience, it will be beyond anybody's understanding to find out how, from *mahat* or *buddhi* the objective world like *mahābhūta*, came into existence. The 'Sāṁkhyas' according to me were primarily concerned with experience. They were not concerned with what came out of what, which is a temporal question and so causal, but they were concerned with knowing the elements of experience. Thus, the 'Sāṁkhya' categories according to me, do not give us a tree of genesis but give us the categories under which our experience can be classified. Thus, the world can be classified under five heads *pr̥thvī*, *teja*, *ākāśa*, *vāyu*, *jala* and these again point to the elements like *śabda*, *sparśa*, *rūpa*, *rasa*, *gandha*. Similarly, our apparatus of knowing and behaviour can be analysed into five sense-organs and five motor organs. But in addition we have also to propound the concept like *manaḥ*, which is not an equivalent of mind. Similar is the case with both the concept of *tanmātra* and *pañca-jñānendriya*. I am different from another, my one thought is different from another thought:

ahaṁkāra points out this notion. But *ahaṁkāra* also points to a (higher), class where things are distinct but tend to become one. Thus, one chair may be different from another but still they are chairs. In this way, finally, in 'Sāṁkhya' analysis, there are two concepts — that of *puruṣa* and *prakṛti* which cannot be merged into one and still in one sense, that is ontological sense, they could be one and only function they would be different. The law of *satkārya* is not in fact in the law of causation but a law of identity and analysis. *Kārya* is not different from *kāraṇa*. *Kārya* is identical with the *kāraṇa* It is already in *kāraṇa*. This notion of *satkārya* is not a causal notion. *Kārya* and *kāraṇa* are identical. It gives you an equation. Just as four is equal to two plus two. Neither four nor two are governed by causal notions. This particular notion of *satkārya* has perhaps influenced the mathematics and that is why Bhāskarācārya in his *Bija-gaṇita* perhaps talks the 'Sāṁkhya language and talks of *vyakta* and *avyakta* which refer to *prakṛti* and *vikṛti*.

When we talk of philosophy as a cultural activity we have certainly to know the truth, but by this either we have tried to seek more information or tried to know the form of information or tried to express information by abstracting it. Corresponding to these three attitudes there are empirical or inductive sciences, deduction or mathematics and philosophy proper. I believe the philosophers in the different systems in India did ask the question of all the three kinds though sometimes emphasis is on the one and sometimes emphasis is on the other. I believe that whereas *satkāryavāda* points to the questiton connected with identity and mathematical equation, the 'Nyāya' theory of Causation, for example, asked a question which is connected with induction and empirical science. Take for example, the question what is reality? It may be answered in any of the three ways as suggested above. And Indian philosophers when they say *ahaṁ brahmāsmi* । *sarvaṁ khalu idaṁ brahma* । *īśāvāsyamidaṁ sarvaṁ* । *sarvaṁ śūnyam* । they asked the question which could be understood in all the three ways. 'Sāṁkhya' system, the early Upaniṣads, 'Nyāya-Vaiśeṣika' *sūtra*s made a beginning in this way and posed more and more technical questions in the times to come. This gave rise to epistemological problems like the one of the nature of knowledge.

3

Some Thoughts on the Beginnings of Religion, Philosophy and Culture in the Indian Context

BOTH philosophy and religion spring from the same source, whether it is wonder, misery, compassion or submission to higher forces. First, what is a philosophic problem? In what way is it different from a religious problem? Is it different from the problem which faces an ordinary person? The answer is complicated, for all such enquiries take their birth in a certain curiosity. All three, a philosopher, a religious person and an ordinary person, want to know the nature of reality. All of them, therefore, formulate a question which is symbolised by the words 'why', 'what', and 'how'. The difference in the explanations of a philosopher and a religious person is due to difference in attitude and methodology; the difference between that of a philosopher and an ordinary person seems to be due to the depth of curiosity. A phiolospher is not satisfied with a superficial answer and wants to go to the depth of it. Perhaps he never gets satisfaction, but at least he gets the 'feel' of the depth of the problem. A religious person tries to answer these questions by adhering to a faith and creating a system of beliefs which need have no direct bearing on reason. The questions an ordinary person, a philosopher and a religious person attempt to answer are concerned with the world, the other beings (including god and animals) and the enquirer himself or herself.

In the second phase, the inquiry becomes more technical and concerns the enquirer himself, the communication between himself and others, and with happiness, sorrow or wonder, i.e., human attitudes. It thus tends to become truly philosophical. But when the enquirer brings in 'himself', i.e., begins to talk of his own self or 'I', the misery and happiness also reach a different dimension. To know that there is misery is different from becoming aware of others' misery. To be happy is to be quite different from being aware of the happiness.

In this last phase the first person singular pronoun assumes a singular role and every inquiry becomes qualitatively different on account of the presence of 'I'. This 'I' is different from the person, although, unless we assume personhood, we cannot really assume I. The enquiry, therefore, becomes anthropocentric and finally becomes 'I'-centric. Hence, the inquiry has three aspects: (*i*) when it is world-centred or object-centred, (*ii*) when it is person-centred, and (*iii*) when it is I-centred. The I-centred inquiry has again two aspects. When one is completely self-centred it loses its validity, loses its objectivity as well as its moral content. The I-centred inquiry has also to be indifferent to 'I', i.e., it must look to any I, a common I, with the same interest or disinterest. But this I-centred inquiry is different from anthropo-centred or person-centred inquiry; for, the person-centred inquiry is a third person inquiry; here we treat a person as a third person. I may illustrate it in the following way: I see a certain person, *X*, in misery, I describe it as '*X* is in misery'. But when this third person inquiry becomes a first person inquiry it does not merely become a paraphrase of '*X* is in misery'. *X's misery* becomes *my misery* and when it becomes my misery my misery transforms itself into compassion (*karuṇā*). The experience of compassion, however, is not just a selfish experience, it is also an objective experience. When a poet has a certain experience it is elevated to second-order experience which leads to poetic creation.

Philosophical explanation is like creation. In discovering the depths of human nature, the human being, so to say, 'creates' a new universe, creates a kind of poetry. This creation, however, is not entirely restricted to philosophers, it also exists in the case of an ordinary person and the scientist. Only that, there is a difference of a degree in 'pealing the skin', of the universe and seeing the universe in a new perspective. Religious explanation also is like a creation; but this creation arises through beliefs and imagination.

In the philosophy of Indian origin these attitudes are also reflected upon. The 'why', 'what' and 'how' assume a major role in different philosophical systems. The curiosity is evidently present whether one is discussing *dharma,* or *Brahman*, or one is concerned with *duḥkha* (dissatisfaction), knowledge or ignorance; whether one is reflecting on the nature of consciousness or different aspects of consciousness. Personhood and I, therefore, assume a central role in philosophies of Indian origin, whether it is Buddhist, Jain or the traditional Hindu. Like all philosophies, therefore, Indian philosophy is also basically anthropo-centric and I-centric.

Philosophy has also to be looked at in its dynamic and anthropological form. It has gradually developed and has become more complex. Philosophy of the industrial man will not be the same as that of the cave man; likewise, philosophy of the nomad will not be the same as that of one who has started cultivating agriculture. For philosophy is essentially a cultural discipline and as culture grows or at least assumes different forms, philosophy also assumes different structures and begins to perform different roles.

Every experience is like the experience of perceiving an iceberg. The part of iceberg which is hidden from our sight is several times bigger than the part which is visible. Our experience leads us to its explanation and so we get concerned with something which is not visible to us. There is a tendency to complete the whole, and any explanation takes the form of a whole which create out of parts experienced by us. This part-needed for completing the whole is a construction and it may take several forms. It may take a mythical form as in the case of an eclipse when one says that Rāhu or Ketu swallows the moon or the sun. It may take a historical or scientific form. Even a fiction is such a construction. All these forms of construction or explanation are in fact stages of philosophising. With the anthropological development there is a variation in such explanations. Indian philosophy is not an exception. The ordinary people, as also the seers, observed and acted on phenomena that gave rise to beliefs, pseudo-scientific, scientific and supra-scientific and also offered explanation regarding the phenomena observed or acted upon. The philosophies of Pūrva Mīmāṁsā, Vaiśeṣika, Sāṁkhya, Vedānta and even Yoga are such explanations of the phenomena which have been experienced by people from time to time.

A few points must be clarified before we proceed further: (1) All Indian philosophy or at least the phenomena concerned with Indian philosophy might not have been written or experienced on Indian soil. (2) All Indian philosophy need not have been the explanation of phenomena observed by the custodians of the so-called Aryan tribes only. I have no desire to point out that the orthodox systems are the philosophisation of the Aryans or 'alien' conquerors, and that the philosophies of Buddha and others have been due to some Śaka tribes. What I mean to say is that some part of Pūrva Mīmāṁsā philosophy might have been due to the experience and action of a particular tribe, and that for such an experience it was not necessary that it should be bound to a particular region. Similarly, I want to point out that from the very early times there must have been hundreds of tribes present on Indian soil and each tribe must have constructed a world around itself — a world of experience, action and belief. That is to say people belonging to these tribes must have created a whole world-view out of their partial experience. From these several worlds of tribes, to create one world was the problem of history; and through the interaction of the world of beliefs to give one or some unified explanations of experience, and to weave a theory or theories around that experience was the problem of philosophy. If here could be a coordination in explanation, a unified theory or theories could be created. It must also be remembered that in the social process of absorption when a bigger society was being created some sections of different tribes were thrown out of the society or became peripheral to it, and either the belief systems did not become uniform or several heterogeneous belief systems continued to co-exist simultaneously. While the process of absorption and unification, i.e., making one society out of several tribes was in process, India was attacked from outside, particularly by the Islamic and the Christian civilisations. This created further complication in the unification. While the process of unification from the several heterogeneous elements was going on, another process of either disintegeration or creating heterogenity from the already formed unity was also visualised. Thus, whereas in Indian belief systems there was already a plurality which was proceeding towards unity, the unity was also being destroyed and ended towards a rather disjointed plurality on account of the attacks from other civilisations. Indian philosophies will have to be understood in all these aspects.

It is stated above that in India there are hundreds of tribes and these tribes are continuously in the process of assimilation and dissimilation. Some of these tribes might have come up from outside and pushed the earlier existing tribes either to mountains and valleys or southwards, i.e., must have displaced them from their original settlements. Traces of these movements can be found if we examine the names of towns and villages. When a settlement is shifted from one place to another the settlers are likely to give the same name to the new settlement. It is also possible that some of the tribes already present on Indian soil might have developed their own civilisation which might have been superior to that of the invaders, and the invaders could have adopted the civilisation of the original settlers; or the original settlers might have carried their civilisation to the new settlements. It is also possible that in the course of transition people might have become nomadic and might have gradually become less developed. It is, for example, said of the Baṅjārā tribes that they were originally the business-people carrying trade from one place to another but in the course of time, and on account of the situation, they were reduced to the present position. This is also said of Daṇḍakāraṇya and king Kalmāṣapāda. All the possibilities suggested above, and even more, must have shaped the civilisation and way of life of the settlers of India. Which tribe was more civilised is not our problem. In fact, what is important to know is that the less developed civilisation also influences the more developed civilisation, almost in the same way as the developed civilisation influences the less developed one (although it must be said that what counts as 'civilisation' ultimately goes in the name of the more developed civilisation).

Amongst the developed tribes there was a custom of sacrifice. Sacrifice means killing a creature or an animal and offering it as an oblation to a deity. This oblation was usually put into fire (*agni*), which itself was regarded as a deity. This fire was also regarded as a symbol of marital relations and became central to *gṛhasthāśrama* (householder station). Kindling of fire was a great step in human progress and human institutions and philosophies developed around this altar of fire. This practice being of the dominant tribe, it was also accepted by the society at large. Amongst the other tribes, also, there was a similar custom of offering oblation to some deity, and traces of such customs are not only visible amongst the present tribes-people but are also found in ancient literature like the *Rāmāyaṇa, Mahābhārata,* Purāṇas, Brāhmaṇas, and so on. However, around the oblation of the less dominant tribes no philosophic and religious system of thought gathered, or at least was not verbalised as was the case with the Gṛhyasūtras, Smṛtis,and Pūrva Mīmāṃsā, which developed out of dominant tribe.

So those who performed sacrifice, i.e., baked their animal food and created literature around it and symbolised this act with the process of family formation, became the dominant civilising thread. But in this trend also there were two stages: a stage when the tribe was nomadic and a stage when it had settled and developed an agricultural civilisation. When the tribe was nomadic the tribe must have certainly hunted animals. Later when they discovered fire they must have started cooking these animals for their food. Much later they must have reared the animals: camels, horses, bulls, cows, dogs, donkeys and even elephants. (The elephant head of Gaṇapati, is significant; it illustrates that human beings were coming in contact with elephant also.) Still later, the tribe must have formed itself into an army and used some of these animals for long marches and invasions and, as a token of victory, sacrificed some of the animals which they plundered or acquired from their enemies. They must have developed a custom of sacrificing their own horses as symbol of their victory and affluence. All this gave rise to a pattern of civilisation, creating the institution of sacrifice or *yajña*. This must have developed in a pre-agricultural stage but continued to exist in the agricultural and post-agricultural stage with new interpretations foiseted on it.

It is not our desire however to point out that the civilisation woven around the concept of sacrifice was the first. Our desire is only to point out that such a thing grew out of action and became a paradigm case for philosophy of action. Independently of it also, people must have thought of the problems of why, what and how, thus giving rise to other kinds of philosophical thinking. But it is true that a very dominant civilisation, along with its philosophy, grew around the sacrificial fire. This is the case with the philosophy of Pūrva Mīmāṁsā.

Pūrva Mīmāṃsā, I assert, is basically concerned with rituals, centred round the sacrificial fire. These rituals are of great variety and it is not possible to discuss all of them here. But each ritual had a presiding deity, there were other deities which were also to be pleased by oblations. In addition to fire being a deity, it was also the medium of offering oblation to deities. In fact, the ritual seems to be the ritual of cooking food. In this process grew a religious symbolism; the process of cooking food also became a symbolism for marital life and gradually slipped into speculations regarding life after death. It has been pointed out that each ritual had a presiding deity. In one such ritual called *agnikāmeṣṭi* or *putrakāmeṣṭi* there is no oblation made to Indra. Indra was, therefore, angry with king Bhangaswan who had performed this sacrifice. The story in the *Mahābhārata* tells us that Indra with his magic power turned king Bhangaswan into a woman. The phrase 'magic power' is very important. For kindling a fire itself was some kind of an unnatural phenomenon for the human being and had become a symbol for magic power. The introduction of heavens and life after death and rebirth are also the effects of the magic power. For, magic means make-belief and make-belief in the first instance makes one believe. This believing is due to imagination and the whole ritual becomes a 'paradigm' for a belief system. The deities were connected with these belief systems and human qualities good and bad, like envy and hatred, compassion and generority, were all woven into these belief systems, and finally the different belief systems were coordinated into one. Where the belief systems were not coordinated they splintered into different sects of different religions.

In the history of Indian civilisation, and in Hindu, Jain and Buddhist religions we find both the process of syncretism and the process of disintegration leading to different belief systems. In fact, when the Islamic civilisation invaded India and when Hindus were being converted to Islam the other process of making Islam a sect of Hinduism had also started. Had European civilisation not invaded India there was every possibility of some kind of Digambara sect being formed within Hindu religion, and some kind of Hindu sect becoming part of Islamic religion. Instances of Kabīr, Dārā Śikoh and Rasa Khān cannot, of course, be ignored.

Kindling of fire itself became a very important ritual and it was prescribed that husband-wife should kindle fire by taking *agnihotra* and should not allow the fire to be extinguished. The fire had become a symbol for continuity of the family and clan. But these rituals finally resulted in a very mature mythology and a pantheon.

Kindling fire and performing sacrifice were the acts of doing, prescribing and performing, and so the philosophy which arose out of it was in fact the philosophy of performance. Had it been restricted to kindling fire and things of this nature, perhaps science would have grown. But fire was subdued to the position of symbol and, naturally, offering oblation to fire turned into worship. Agninārāyaṇa was transformed into Satyanārāyaṇa. Mythology also played a large part in the transformation. But in addition to the mythology of the tribe playing a part, the mythology and rituals of other tribes also played their part. A kind of a syncretic ritualistic mythological belief system came into being. Nevertheless, it must be pointed out that in several parts of India, today, the official mythology or the rituals do not exist. But whatever be the social practices they are parts of similar ritualistic systems that continue to survive in one form or other.

Was the sacrifice to be made merely for cooking food? On account of the magic associated with the rituals people imagined that sacrifice would give something in the future. First, it was performed for begetting sons and daughters. Even Draupadī was born out of such sacrificial fire. It was also supposed to give wordly prowess, such as, the recognition of a ruler as a Cakravartī. After performing *aśvamedha*, (horse sacrifice), a king became Cakravartī. But finally, people imagined that the fruits of this sacrifice had also to do with life after death. 'One who desires for heaven should sacrifice' — *svargakāmo yajeta*. It is said this lead to separation of body and soul, for the body should never enjoy the heaven. But the soul without a body also could not experience enjoyment. So some kind of heavenly body was offered to the 'soul' after death. All this led to the formation of the notions of 'sin' and *puṇya* (merit) on the one side of the basic ontology, and on the other side a rich mythology. The methodology and ontology finally gave birth to moral, social and legal laws and also to philosophy. In the case of Buddhism and Jainism, altough their mythologies and rituals grew, it was not found necessary to establish separate social and legal orders (though there was seeds in their ritualism and philosophy to develop such orders). This is how the Pūrva Mīmāṁsā system became a nucleus for the Hindu religion and became the ever-growing and ever-lasting philosophy of the Hindus. But it must be remembered that the basic principles of Hindu religion and the basic concepts of Pūrva Mīmāṁsā were not separated. They rather formed a whole and led to the growth of Hindu religion and Indian culture. Nevertheless, both Hindu religion and Indian culture also drew from other philosophies, such as Sāṁkhya, Vedānta, Buddhism and Jainism, and that helped enrich the religious thought and culture of India.

4

The Significance of Pratītya-Samutpāda, Sāmānya-lakṣaṇa and Apoha in Buddhism

ACCORDING to Buddhism everything is changing and impermanent. *sarvam anityam.* I shall later on examine what made Buddha think so. But in Buddhist literature like *Dhammapada*, *Mahāparinirvāṇa-sūtra* and in Buddhaghoṣa there are references to impermanence. In the first parable of *Dhammapada* (Chinese Version) Lord Buddha seems to have said, 'Whatever exists is without endurance'.... 'The life of man is but as the earthen vessels made in a potter's mills.' And in yet another parable attributed to Buddha he says, "As the waters of river ever hasten in and flow away, and once gone, never return, such is the life of man. That which is gone knows not any return." The same notion is again repeated in Buddhaghoṣa: " Just as a chariot wheel in rolling rolls merely at one point of the tyre are in resting rests only at one point, even so the life of living being endures only for the brief period of our thought and as soon as the thought has ceased, the being too, is said to have ceased. Thus, the being of a past moment has lived but does not live nor will it live; the being of a future moment will live but has not lived nor does it live; the being of the present moment does live but has not lived and will not live." (Warren's Buddhism in translation p.150 as quoted by Yamakami Sogen: *Systems of Buddhistic Thought*, p. 11). This main philosophy of Buddhism continues in later Buddhism. Nāgārjuna, Diṅnāga, Dharmakīrti and Ratnakīrti amongst others reiterate impermanence of everything in this world: *yat sat tat kṣaṇikam*. According to Buddhism this impermanence, however, is of two kinds: (*i*) impermanance of the life period, and (ii) momentary impermanence. The first is what is experienced (ref. 1st parable), the second is what is presupposed by the first (the parable of the river). Impermanence of life period gives us immediate experience of duration and gives a scope for permanent bodies; the momentary impermanence gives us the experience of flow. The first kind of impermanence refers to phenomenal existence and allows for causation, etc., the second will not allow it. It belongs to *svalakṣaṇa*. These two kinds of change with which Buddhism is concerned can be classified as macro and micro change. As an instance of the first we may talk of birth, life and death or of beginning, continuity and end of a thing or entity. The first change is change in time. The *change of time* would come under the second kind. When one says that everything is momentary one is talking of change without any permanence. When one is talking of *macro change* one is presupposing at least some relatively permanent things and entities. But, finally, this macro change presupposes change of the micro type. Change of events for *example* presupposes a moment series; but for moment series a series of events need not necessarily be presupposed. Although these two concepts of change are related to each other, the change of events, for example, requires the concept of *causation*, the change of a series of moments — discrete moments on the other hand transcend the concept of causation. Buddhism tries to explain both these kinds of change and so it has also to explain the nature of causation as well as refute it. This may appear paradoxical. But, in fact, there is no contradiction involved in explaining and also rejecting the law of causation. When we are explaining experience from *anthropo-centric point of view*, we need tools like causation, class, and inference. All these are, concerned with *vikalpa*. They are human constructs. But when one tries to understand the nature of reality without subjecting it to human understanding and human categories one may rather have to point out the limitations of all such concepts like causation, class and inference. I feel that Lord Buddha and following him his adherents like Diñnāga, Dharmakīrti and Nāgārjuna are trying to point out such limitations of the human concept. But the limitations of the concepts may easily be confused with something else on account of *the way* these concepts are used. I think some of the misunderstandings about Buddhist philosophy are due to this kind of confusion. In what follows I shall try to explain a few of these concepts like *pratītya-samutpāda* and *apoha* and relate them and show how these concepts point to the limitations of the tools of human thought like causality and class. I may add that this study of mine is primarily based on *Pramāṇa-Vārtika* and *Nyāyabindu* by Dharmakīrti and *Apohasiddhi* by Ratnakīrti.

My first contention is that *pratītya-samutpāda* does not give us any law of causation as is thought to be the case by Mrs. Rhys Davids or following her most of the recent writers on Buddhism. Prof. Hiriyanna, for example, while talking of *pratītya-samutpāda* regards it as the law of causation, although he qualifies it as the law of contingent causation. He writes: 'It was the knowledge of these factors, with the law of contingent causation implicit in it, that flashed across Siddhārtha's mind at last and made him the Buddha' (*Outlines of Indian Philosophy*, p. 144). *Pratītya-samutpāda* is a key concept for the understanding of Buddhism and to interpret it as some kind of the law of causation is to give up the main thesis of Buddhism that everything is impermanent. I think it is not necessary to understands *pratītya-samutpāda* as the law of causation in any sense of the term. Let me try to understand the problem before Buddhism.

Like the philosophers of Sāṁkhya, Lord Buddha was also touched by suffering in this world and wanted to find a way out of it. He was not interested in any theoretical discussion of the problem; but was concerned with the removal of suffering. His doctrine of four noble truths is the proposed solution against this suffering. The concept of suffering occurs if we regard self as the unity of apperception. As Hiriyanna put it, "with the negation of self selfish impulses necessarily disappear" (*Ibid.*, p. 147) and misery being one of the selfish impulses, it can be immediately eradicated as soon as we know that there is no self. As the belief in self-identity arises out of ignorance, when this ignorance is removed naturally the suffering ends. The main problem of Buddhism is, therefore, to remove one continuous unity of self whether it is in *ātmavāda* or the theory of persistent self, or the identity of a thing in the multitude or *saṁghāta* of Sensa or identity or one *sāmānya* or Universal amongst particulars. Buddha and following him all Buddhists came to the conclusion that identity is due to illusion and everything is in fact discrete and impermanent (*niranvaya*). As a matter of fact what exists is nothing but discrete like moments and any kind of continuity that takes place is due to our own tendency to organise the discrete moments into one unity.

[*vartamāna-vyakti-saṁbandhitā hi jāter-stitā*
— *Apohasiddhi*, Ratnakīrti Nibandhāvali (Tibetan Sanskrit Works Series, Vol. III)

sa eva teṣāṁ sāmānya-samānādhāra-gocaraiḥ ।
jñāna-abhidhānair-mityārtho vyavahāraḥ pratanyate ॥
— *Pramāṇa-vārtika, svārthānumāna pariccheda*, p.81

anyat sāmānya-lakṣaṇam ।
— *Nyāyābindu, prathama pariccheda*]

We do have a tendency to unify the discrete moments into a kind of continuity of *santāna*. As we have seen earlier impermanence is of two kinds — the impermanence at the micro level and the impermanence at the macro level. At the macro level we formulate concepts like causation, inference and class. But whether it is of macro level or a micro level there is only contingency. Looked at from cosmic point of view there is no ontic reality *corresponding* to any of these unifications. They are all *vikalpa*s. From the cosmic point of view everything is moment and moment only. Lord Buddha could formulate such a thesis only by denying causation altogether and not by affirming it. His thesis is to assent discrete moments and their necessary series and deny the unity amongst them; for he wanted to get rid of suffering which is conmcomitant with the unity. In fact, what dawned on him and what is usually interpreted as the formulation of Buddhist Law of Causation — *pratītya-samutpāda* — is in fact anything but the Law of Causation though today it goes in the name of the Law of Causation known as the Law of Dependent Origination. The counterpart of this Law at the macro level in respect of Theory of Meaning is the concept of *apoha* by which unity in respect of particulars is denied. Buddha does not seem to have formulated this second concept, though it logically arises out of the fundamental concept of *pratītya-samutpāda*. It is, therefore, natural that logicians in Buddhist tradition formulated this concept while dealing with the macro experience. In this paper I propose to indicate the relation between these two important notions — the notion of *pratītya-samutpāda* and the notion of *apoha*. The notion of *apoha* will incidentally take us to the discussion of the Theory of Classes — *vyāpti* and the notions of *tādātmya* and *tad-utpatti* and *svabhāva* and the notion of *svatva*, although the discussion of all these concepts cannot be attempted in the scope of this paper.

The concept of *pratītya-samutpāda* is translated by Mrs. Rhys Davids in her book on 'Buddhism' as that being present this *becomes*. I think Mrs. Rhys Davids translated this under the influence of some theory of causation. As Hiriyanna states it in his book (*Ibid*., p. 143) "the Sanskrit expression means literally, 'arising in correlation with'" (*Ibid.*). There is no element of causal necessity involved in the theory of *pratītya-samutpāda*. Ordinarily when we say that something *A* is the cause of something *B* we somehow think that *A* has the power to or ability to create *B*; *A* we can give birth to *B*, i.e., given *A*, *B* will necessarily follow. In other words we mean that if there is an event then that event must have come into existence on account of a certain cause. Hume made a distinction between sequence and consequence and said that we can never know *A* as the cause of *B*. We only know that *A* is followed by *B*. The relation of consequence, therefore, is denied by Hume. In matters of fact we can never establish a necessity between preceding and proceeding events. We are always governed by some contingency. Kant attempted to answer Hume by saying that though it is difficult as Hune pointed out to prove the universality and necessity of causation, we can nevertheless show that in matters of fact the element of necessity can be traced. In his second analogy (*Critique of Pure Reason*) Kant makes a distinction between subjective sequence and objective sequence. If we look at a house we may decide to look at it in a way we like. The first view can be of the top, then of the middle, then of the bottom or we can go from right to left or from left to right and so on. It means that there is no objective order in our perception. The order of such preception can be reversed, and is arbitrary. But if we perceive a boat going down the stream, it is not possible for us to imagine at our will that the boat is sometimes going up the stream and sometimes down the stream.

It is not that we perceive the boat; the boat rather shows itself and in such a case the order of each succeeding perception is not determined by us but is determined by the objective situation. That is when there is an objective succession there is some kind of *necessity* involved. Objective sequence is very different from subjective sequence. I think Kant is right in distinguishing between objective sequence and subjectivce sequence and in further stating that there is an element of necessity involved in objective sequence. Hume's argument against causation was based on the fact that there is no necessity involved in matters of fact. Kant, therefore, by analogy, says that since we have shown instance of a necessity in matters of fact we need not then say on Hume's ground that there is no causation. I am here not interested in going into the merits of Kant's argument. I only want to point out that when we talk of causation we talk of two different series and of necessity governing both these series. The first such series is the series of moments and the second series in the series of events. When we talk of sequence we talk of a necessary series of moments. It is possible to conceive that a series of moments has of necessity a particular order and all the same the series of events contingent. The Law of Causation cannot be proved unless the necessity element is accepted both in the moment series and in the event series. *Pratītya-samutpāda*, according to me, accepts the first part of these two elements, viz. the necessity of the moment series. The series of objective sequence too is governed by necessity although it is quite different from the necessity governing sequence. The necessity of moment series gives us only the ground for causation. If necessity in this series is denied then the question of causation would not arise. But even if necessity in this series confirmed, it does not, however, mean that the law of causation would hold good. The relation between the moment series and the event series something like the relation that we find in the antecedent and consequent of a case of material implication. Buddha accepted the necessary order in sequences only so far as the discrete moments were concerned. What he really meant was that there was something like the law of objective sequence, that time was not reversible. If this law was misunderstood for the law of causation, it will create all the muddle in Buddha's thesis. In fact, Buddha's idea to deny the self and thereby to deny the misery or suffering cannot be achieved unless the two prongs of the law, one of the moments and the other of events, are separated. Buddha did not deny the *santāna*, i.e., a flow. There is always an order in a flow; it is always in one direction: it is not reversible and this is signified by his *pratītya-samutpāda*, i.e., there is *utpāda*, *samutpāda* — an order and it follows one particular direction. That is if there is a second moment, it cannot come into existence unless there was the first moment. If it is 2 O'clock now, 2 O' clock could not come into existence unless there was I-59 and unless 1-59 died out. We could, however, not say that 1-59 is the cause of 2, even though 2 necessarily follows 1-59.

Once you regard that unity or identity is the *human construct*, all our concepts like that of *things*, Minds or Souls, or universals fall to ground. Things are substituted by *saṁghāta*. *Ātman* is simply negated and universals are discarded. For they occur on account of the arrest of flow, *santāna*, on account of imposing some kind of unity in succeeding multitudes of states. It is something like let loosing the grip that holds the library cards in a card cabinet. So whereas we may go on using these concepts in ordinary language these concepts will really have the status of words in philosophical explanations and nothing else.

tulye-bhede yathā jātiḥ pratyāsatyā prasarpati ।
kvacinnānyatra saivāstu śabda-jñāna-nibandhanam ॥
— *Pramāṇa-vārtika,* III. 197

That is what the Buddhists mean when they say that 'class' or universal, inference, etc., belong to *vikalpa*. That is, the concepts do not have any ontological existence, that they belong to the sphere of language.

But perhaps the Non-Buddhists (and may be even some of the Buddhists) have not grasped the distinction between *svalakṣaṇa* and *sāmānya-lakṣaṇa*, the distinction which the Buddhist philosophers aim at. Many a time things are treated alike (e.g., in *Kusumāñjali*). In ordinary language, i.e., cause-effect language, for example, we speak of a seed as cause and sprout as the effect. As a part of explanation in Buddhist style it will now be claimed that a seed is to be replaced by seed-continuum and the sprout by the sprout-continuum. The seed at times T_1, T_2, T_3, etc., is not the same seed. One seed is replaced by another seed though the perceiver is never conscious of the change. And when the seed changes into a sprout there is another kind of change. So in order to distinguish a seed at time T_1, as the cause of seed at time T_2, from the seed as the cause of sprout the concept of *kurvadrūpa* is supplied by some of the Buddhist writers. The fact is that the cause-effect series in which seed and sprout are elements is a different kind of cause-effect series from the 'Seed-Seed' cause-effect series. In fact, the 'Seed-Seed' cause-effect series becomes a cause-effect series only on account of our putting that which is a cause into the cause-effect mould. In fact, in the world to which cause-effect language belongs we do not speak of 'one' seed replacing another seed. What I mean to say is that the cause-effect language belongs to the sphere of *sāmānya-lakṣaṇa*, i.e., to the onto-epistemic sphere where we treat the entities perceived as having some kind of duration or permanence and not to the ontic sphere. In the world of moments qua moment the cause-effect language is ineffective. But once we start with the theory of momentariness (*kṣaṇabhaṅgavāda*) and also allow the cause-effect language to co-exist then we are led to the conclusion that seed at time T_2, is the cause of seed at time T_1, and so on. In fact, even the word 'seed' is inappropriate to the language of *kṣaṇabhaṅgavāda*. What really undergoes a change is not the seed (but some ontological nucleus); seed is a name given to it by man and, hence, belongs to the sphere of *sāmānya-lakṣaṇa* or *vikalpa*.

In fact, the Buddhists have very clearly stated that logic itself belongs to the sphere of *vikalpa*. That is, no theory of logic can proceed without attributing some kind of 'onto-epsitemic' permanence to logical concepts. To attribute onto-epistemic permanence is to regard them as *universals*. The only thing that is necessary to safeguard against is to see that they are given any ontological status. So if the Buddhists talk of *kāraṇa-kārya*, *vyāpti*, *tādātmya*, *svabhāva* and *tad-utpatti*, they are not committing any contradiction if the ontological and onto-epistemic spheres are clearly demarcated. Once you make a division between *svalakṣaṇa* and *sāmānya-lakṣṇa* or *vikalpa* and assign all these concepts to the region of *Vikalpa* the question whether the Buddhists' use of the conceps of class, etc., is justified does not arise. Like the logicians and philosophers belonging to other schools the Buddhists are also justified in the use of such terms in their logical and philosophic techniques. Only the philosophic logic of Buddhism will differ from the philosophic logic of other schools.

Let me make my point clear both in respect of logical techniques and philosophical logic. Buddhist logicians like Dharmakīrti, Dharmottara, Ratnakīrti have, for example, used in their logical technique the word *vyāpti wherever* there is *śiṁśapā* there is *vṛkṣa*. (One may formulate it as wherever there is *śiṁśapātva* there is *vṛkṣatva* although the Nyāya philosophers would point out that such a formulation would violate the canons of Nyāya logic; *śimśapātva* and *vṛkṣatva* cannot have the common substratum, the substratum of *śiṁśapātva* being *śiṁśapā vṛkṣatva* being *vṛkṣa*). But what is pertinent is the explanation of the word *wherever*. Unless 'whatever' is conceived as *group* of 'every' *śiṁśapā* or a physical or logical space containing all *śiṁśapā*s the use of the word 'wherever' will not be significant. On the first alternative 'wherever' will signify a class of all *śiṁśapā*s although one could perhaps say that the *commonness* which holds all *śiṁśapā*s is just arbitray. But even if it is arbitrary it is motivated by the *concept* of oneness or commonness. On the second alternative even if one *śiṁśapā* is different from the other *śiṁśapā* in order to significantly use the language 'wherever there is *śiṁśapā*' one will have to imagine something 'common' signified by all *śiṁśapā*s. The Nyāya philosophers would regard this commonness as somthing real or objective, the Buddhist philosophers would merely confine it to the region of language. All *śiṁśapā*s may in actuality mean a collection of group of the individual *śiṁśapā*s. For although it is true that we use a language which for the sake of economy makes use of words standing for more things than one, the commonness may not have any reality other than linguistic. In fact, it is this feature of Buddhism which makes people think that it is nominalistic. Let us understand the concept of *śiṁśapātva*. It is indeed true that we construct our language regarding it on the basis there is something common between several *śiṁśapāṣ*. But as a matter of fact there may be nothing common between them except the word *śiṁśapā* and that may be due to our own construction or limitations of language or even practical necessity. In fact, Buddhism in its theory of *apoha* points to this limitation. We are likely to think that whenever we use any word with affix *tva* we are talking of a concept or rather a class-concept. Buddhist philosophers, as I understand them, do not accept this view. For this it will be necessary to examine their concept of *svatva* and *tādātmya*.

The Nyāya-Vaiśeṣika philosophers define *jāti* as *samāna-prasavātmikā*. That is *jāti* is characterised by a certain unity amongst different particulars. But suppose there is only one particular. Then this particular at least according to old Nyāya will not have any *jāti*. Nevertheless the particular will have *characterization.* Suppose there is only one blue object in the world, and there is nothing else which is blue. Then that object will be characterised by *blueness*; but that *blueness* will not be a *jāti*. Perhaps the old Naiyāyikas will call it an *upādhi*. It could even be regarded as *viśeṣa* or *avacchedaka*. But whether you call it *upādhi* or *viśeṣa* it does not belong to *svalakṣaṇa*; it only belongs to *sāmānya-lakṣaṇa*. It follows from this that all that which belongs to the sphere of *sāmānya-lakṣaṇa* need not necessarily be of the nature of *sāmānya* or *jāti*. Buddhist philosophers would call this *svatva*. Each particular is characterized by *svatva*. But unless you perceive a further *unity* amongst several particulars you do not characterise it by *jātitva* or classness. Whenever you talk of *tādātmya* or even *vyāpti*, the possibility of this further unity is presupposed by your conceptual framework. For example, let us take the case of 'What is *śiṁśapā* is also a tree'. It is of course true that even if there is only one *śiṁśapā* and only one tree in the world the proposition 'What is *śiṁśapā* is tree' or 'wherever there is *śiṁśapā* there is tree', would be true. But when we assent such a proposition, we do visualise the possibility that there is another *śiṁśapā* and another tree. But when we talk of another *śiṁśapā* and another tree it may be that the *śiṁśapātva* or the first *śiṁśapā* and the *śiṁśapātva* of the second *śiṁśapā* may not be identical. Such an identiy is not necessary. What is necessary is that whatever be the variation in *śiṁśapātva* it should be accompanied by *vr̥kṣatva* even if $vr̥kṣatva_1$ and $vr̥kṣatva_2$ may differ. What is really important here is the going together of *vr̥kṣatva* and *śiṁśapā*. *Vr̥kṣatva* should be the essence of *śiṁśapā*-complex. Stcherbatsky translates the relation of *tādātmya* as identity. It can be seen without difficulty that in our ordinary language *śiṁśapā* is a sub-class of tree or the scope of what we call tree is bigger than the scope of what we call *śiṁśapā*. That is, if we make a collection of *śiṁśapās* and a collection of trees then collection of trees will be bigger that the collection of *śiṁśapās*. Stcherbatsky's translation of the word *tādātmya* does not allow this. *Tādātmya* should stand for both co-extensiveness and class-inclusion. Although I am using here the words class-subclass and scope, what is really relevant here is the absence of the *vinā-bhāva* between *śiṁśapā* and tree. Treeness must be included in or integral to what we call *śiṁśapā*.

Tradition says that the Buddhists and the Nyāya philosophers hold opposite point of view about the concept of class, Buddhists denying and the Nyāya philosophers defending the concept of class. In the *Nyāya-sūtras* class has been defined as *samāna — prasavātmikā jātiḥ* — that which generates the element of commonness is *jāti*. The word *samāna* may create a difficulty. For it may mean either similarity or identity. But we need not enter into this controversy here. From the context it becomes fairly clear that the *concept* of identity is involved here. As has been pointed out earlier the concept of class or universal, like the concept of soul arises on account of the 'imposition' of the notion of identity in differnt particulars. It is like the *rod* that holds the different library cards in the card cabinet. (If this rod is taken away what remains is merely the collection or *saṁghāta* of cards). "The Commentary of Vātsyāyana on the aphorism, *samāna — prasavātmikā jātiḥ*, is siginificant on this point. It is not the notion of common cognition that is *jāti*. *Jāti* is that (substratum) where the notion of common cognition is produced. The word *that* or in Sanskrit *yā*, as in *yā samānām buddhim prasūte*, is very important in this connection." Jāti requires the notion of one substratum as also the notion of one commonness which determines the oneness of this substratum. Tradition thinks that the Nyāya philosophers being extreme type of realists thought that the substratum as well as the concept of commonness or universal were actual realities. Buddhists on the other hand deny such commonness. Whether the extreme type of realism was at back of the mind of the Nyāya philosophers is doubtful: that the Buddhists denied that we have experience of class is also far from true. They only seem to have stated that the concept of class belongs to *sāmānya-lakṣaṇa*. However, on the basis of one denying and the other defending the concept of class, a controversy did continue amongst the adherents of the Buddhists and the Nyāya philosophers. Thus, the Buddhists seem to have said in regard to *jāti*:

> *na yāti na ca tatrāsīt na cotpannam na cāṁśavat* ।
> *jahāti pūrvam nādhāram ahovyasana-santatiḥ* ॥

Similarly the Nyāya-Vaiśeṣika philosophers like Praśastapāda have bitterly criticised the notion of *apoha* which Buddhists use in giving the philosophic explanation of *jāti*.

In fact, the concept of *jāti* (or for that matter even that of all *vyakti* or *ākṛti*) is concerned with the theory of meaning. Psychologically or even epistemologically that there is a concept formation of *jāti* is not doubted. But whether the concept of *jāti* is sufficient to explain itself or whether its philosophical explanation is to be given in some other terms is the problem and the Buddhists offer their explanation in terms of *apoha*. They seem to have held that the meaning of a thing is determined or deteminable by negating it; and then by negating that negation. This is termed as *atadvyāvṛtti*, i.e., if a thing is *tad* then *atad* will be that which is different from *tad* and the *vyāvṛtti* of *atad* will be the original. The prefix *a* and the word *vyāvṛtti* are supposed to stand for the concept of difference and, hence, *atadvyāvṛtti* or *apoha* has to be regarded as the difference of difference. The concept of difference is explained in Indian logic by the *anyonyābhāva*. *Atadvyāvṛtti* has therfore come to mean the law of double difference. If the original is A, then something different from it is $(\sim A)$. And that which is different from $(\sim A)$ would be $[\sim(\sim A)]$. It will be formalized as, $A \neq (\sim A)$; $[\sim(\sim A)] \neq (\sim A)$. It is thought that, $[\sim(\sim A)] \equiv A$. The Buddhists, use of the word *apoha* or *anyāpoha* is interpreted by non-Buddhist in the sense that the Buddhists used the word *apoha* in the sense of double negation. And some Buddhist logicians might have used this concept in this sense. But, if the word *a* or *vyāvṛtti* stands for a difference then one is hardly able to conceive that, that which is different from the one that is different from the original is the original. Such a proposition cannot be an instance of the law of double negation. If the original is *A* then that which is different from *A* can be *B* or C or *D*, etc. Now, that which is different from *B* need not necessarily be *A*. It could be *C* or *D*. Thus — Nyāya-Vaiśeṣika logicians Praśastapāda, Udayana, etc. refuted Buddhist notion of *apoha* and tried to ridicule Buddhists. The critics of *apoha*, however, are not representing the Buddhist stand properly. If it is agreed that there are discrete particulars and if it is also agreed that in the explanation of these discrete particulars the concept of *jāti* through *sāmānya-lakṣaṇa* invariably comes then it follows that when we have knowledge of each particular we not only have the knowledge of the particular alone but also have the knowledge of some other particulars, just as when we read a book we not only have the knowledge of the letters but also of the knowledge of the blanks and the margins. It also follows that we have knowledge of each particular by eliminating the indistinct and marginal knowledge of other particulars. This in nutshell is the Buddhist theory of *apoha*. *Apoha* literally means total *exclusion* (*vyāvr̥tti*). It is not the same thing as *different*, although if something *A* is different from say *B*, it is true that *A* is excluded from *B* and *B* is excluded from *A*. Similarly when something *A* is excluded from *B* it follows that *A* is different from *B* and *B* is different from *A*. Nevertheless the notion of difference or *bheda* is to be distinguished from exclusion or *apoha*. Suppose in a universe there are at least five particulars (though there may be even more). Let me indicate these particulars by the capital roman letter *A*, *B*, *C*, *D*, *E*. Then the picture of the universe will be something as follows—

A,B,C,D,E. . . .

Now how is the knowledge of *A* for example, determined? The Buddhists reply that whenever you have knowledge of *A*, you also have the progressively indistinct knowledge of *B,C,D,E*, etc. You always have the configurational knowledge. It is by eliminating the relatively indistinct knowledge out of the total gestalt that you are able to have the determinate knowledge of *A*. Suppose you divide the universe into [A] and [B,C,D,E. . .] then [B,C,D,E] exclude *A* and *A* excludes [B,C,D,E. . .] Even, though [B,C,D,E. . .] may represent an open and perhaps infinite set [A] and [B,C, D,E. . .] may be regarded as complementary to each other. So the 'meaning' of *A* can be determined by excluding the complementary of *A*. This is the Buddhist theory of *apoha* or *anyāpoha* as it is sometimes called. As Ratnakīrti points out it is only the positive meaning which is intended. But this positive meaning is determined by excluding its complementary set.

> *na asmābhiḥ apoha-śabdena vidhireva kevalo abhipretaḥ* ı *na api anya-vyāvṛtti-mātram* ı *kintu anyāpoha-viśiṣṭo vidhiḥ śabdānām arthaḥ* ı — Ratnakīrti, *Apohasiddhi.*

The Buddhist concept of *apoha* cannot be explained in terms of *difference* or *bheda* and perhaps it cannot be explained even in terms of *atyantābhāva*, a concept which philosophers of Navya-Nyāya later on introduced. Or perhaps the word *bheda* or *anyonyābhāva* as used by Dharmakīrti as a technical term was different from its use in its ordinary language. But this was overlooked by the philosophers of Nyāya and Vaiśeṣka schools. For example, in the universe where there are *A*,*B*,*C*,*D*,*E*. . . as particulars not only is a set of *B*,*C*,*D*,*E*. . . different from *A*, but every particulars such as *B* or *C* or *D* or *E* is also different from *A*. But this notion of difference is far removed from that of *exclusion*. *A* is different from *B*. But something different from *B* does not indicate *A* for it may even mean *C* or *D* or *E* or. . . . For the notion that is suggested by '*A* is different from *B*' does not suggest total exclusion as *A* and *B* together *do* not exhaust the whole universe. If elephant is different from horse, horse cannot mean something other than the elephant, for this may as well apply to man, rat or anything else. Understood merely in the sense of difference as we understand in ordinary language Buddhist theory of *apoha* becomes vulnerable. But this in short is the criticism of Nyāya-Vaiśeṣika philosophers against Buddhism. Again in criticising the theory of *apoha* on the above ground the critics of Buddhism are not fair to it. It means that the Buddhist philosophers were so foolish as not to understand that 'the different from the different' need not necessarily give us the original and that the meaning of the original cannot be given in terms of the different from the different.

It will also be necessary to see whether the Buddhists really meant by *apoha* the formal law of double negation though my former explanation may easily mislead us that way. It may be granted that while talking of the theory of meaning particularly of the Buddhist type a formal law of double negation can be suggested. But it may also be noted that for the Buddhists the meaning was not formal; first the Buddhist regarded the reality *as consisting of* particulars and then these particulars were subjected to *sāmānya-lakṣaṇa*. That is the particulars as the object of knowledge were always phenomenal and empirical. The meaning of such concepts could not be understood in syntactical or formal way. Ratnakīrti emphasised this point when he says that *apoha* in fact points to the *vidhi* or the positive meaning and not merely to the negation of negation or *anyāpoha*. (*tadevaṁ vidhiḥ eva śabdārthaḥ* —*Ibid.*, p. 60) Meaning of 'empirical positive' concepts necessarily takes us to the semantic notion of meaning, as such notions are contingent and open and the meaning of such notion cannot be determined merely by the canons of logic like the law of contradiction.

The empirical concepts, so to say, have an open texture. You cannot define them. Although the empirical concepts are concepts, you do not know where the area of one concept ends that of the other concept begins. These concepts are, to use Wittgenstein's vocabulary, like a city. Just as a growth or decrease in the rows of houses does not make any difference to the city, similarly, some kind of elasticity of meaning does not make any difference to empirical concepts. In fact, eslasticity is the essence of empirical concepts. Empirical concepts are like a mould, a scheme, where we purposely ignore the difference and create some kind of common properties. What is common between one table and another or between a table and chair, when we call them pieces of furniture? They are just particulars. Perhaps only some form of spatio-temporal structure may be common to them. But is that sufficient for us to put them under one category? Perhaps it would be like roping together. *Śvā*, *yuvā* and *maghavā* under one aphorism. But although the above case in Pāṇini's grammar is sometimes pointed out as a piece of joke, the concepts that we use in ordinary language and which are concerned with experience are usually such that they allow for the jumping of one concept into another; they allow an open texture. Take, for example, the case of 'hard'. Although we have been using the words hard and soft in our ordinary language and are not worried about the definitions of words, it will be difficult to say exactly what we mean when we say something is hard. How 'hard', should a thing be in order that it should be called hard? The very fact that the comparative degrees are allowed (hard and harder) shows that if there are two things *A* and *B* such that *B* is harder than *A*, then shall we not be able to say that *A* is hard? Shall we have to say that *A* is soft? Again one may be able to say that *A* is softer than *B* but in comparison to a third thing say *D* which is not as hard as *A*, *A* may not be soft. Concepts like hard and soft are open texture concepts. And, in fact, I should generalise that all empirical concepts are open texture concepts.

When one goes further than these empirical concepts and constructs abstract concepts like hardness and softness one would find it difficult to define these abstract concepts except in relation with particular facts and if we are interested in abstractions alone then we are likely to fall in a some pitfall or will have to say that these concepts are indefinable.

The problem of meaning with which Buddhists were concerned was the problem of emprical concepts. They were concerned with the problem, how to determine the meaning of concepts that are open and elastic. The *apoha* theory of meaning is a suggested solutions to this problem. When I say something is a cow, am I concerned with cowness, that is concerned with class cow or am I concerned with this cow which is a particular, or am I concerned with the form cow? The Mīmāṁsakas answer that we are concerned with the class cow. The Nyāya philosophers say that we are concerned with all the three elements. The Buddhists say that we are concerned with particulars. They say we are concerned with the particular, because calling it a cow is just a process of naming or describing and is only subsidiary to something with which we are acquainted. Classness or form comes later in experience in the sense that it is our construction. You may not know that it is a cow, but you may know that it is *this*. Let us call this particular as *x*. Then do I know that there is class of 'this' or *x*? Do these *x*s have determinate structure such that we can put them into classes *A*,*B* and *C*, supplied to us readymade by nature, or are they our own constructs ? How am I to understands the class of Narasiṁha?

Udayana says that it is a case of Sāṅkarya or overlapping and that it goes against the very concept of class. The Buddhists say that all empirical concepts are like the concept Narasiṁha. They are instances of Sāṅkarya. And, therefore, there are not classes in the world but only individuals. In the region of empirical concepts you do not get logic-tight classes. The particulars gradually slide from one concept to another. These individuals are thought to be related to one another with similarities, and dissimilarities. When you come across a partricular individual the fact is that you have come across that particular. It is also a fact that you have knowledge of that particular. And the meaning is some sort of picture of this knowledge. The Buddhists say as pointed out earlier that the perception is of the nature of *sāmānya-lakṣaṇa* or *vikalpa*. In this *sāmānya-lakṣana* you find something distinct and definite at one end and gradually becoming indistinct and indefinite at the other end. Buddhist through their tool of *apoha* draw a wedge between the distinct and indistinct and by denying the indistinct finally determine the scope of the particular under investigation. Suppose we want to determine the meaning of tiger, then not only a particular which is called tiger is present before our mental eye but a good number of animals which together would form a complementary set to tiger would also be indistinctly present and by eliminating this complementary set we would arrive at the meaning of tiger. When we talk of particulars the problem that arises is what kind of knowledge do we have of particulars? Buddhists answer this by propounding the theory of *apoha*. The theory of *apoha* then is merely the logical continuation or development of the Buddhist theories of *pratītya-samutpāda* and impermanence which is so necessary for them for negating suffering.

5

Some Aspects of Gauḍapāda's Philosophy

TRADITION regards Gauḍapāda as the teacher of Govinda whom Śaṅkara refers to as his own teacher. The works which are attributed to Gauḍapāda and which are extinct to this day are (*i*) The commentary on the *Sāṁkhya Kārikā*, (*ii*) The Commentary on the *Uttara Gītā*, (*iii*) the *Subhagodaya Stuti*, (*iv*) the *Vidyāratna Sūtra*, and (*v*) his work which is usually known as the *Māṇḍūkya Kārikā*. There may be a few other books written by him as for example, his commentary on the *Nṛsiṁha Pūrvatāpinī Upaniṣad* (which I have not read). But at least they are not easily available. Some works of his, so it is claimed, belong to Tantra. And *Uttara Gītā* is a commentary on the text which even at the first glance appears to have Advaita bias, and the originality of Gauḍapāda, even if it is visible there, is only that of a commentator. This to my mind is not the case with his *Māṇḍūkya-kārikā*. Although scholars have held the view that the *kārikās* are some kind of a commentary on the *Māṇḍūkya Upaniṣad*, it appears to me that the genius and originality of Gauḍapāda is at work in the *Māṇḍūkya-kārikā* and what he presents is in fact the first independent treatise on Advaita philosophy.

Although he uses some of the terms used by the *Māṇḍūkya Upaniṣad*, it is simply by way of a 'take off'; he analyses these concepts, allocates them to the particular philosophical area and constructs out of these a philosophic theory of his own. It may appear that his philosophy is that of Upaniṣads. But this does not seem to be the whole truth. Upaniṣadic remarks are more or less cryptic and mostly non-epistemological. Gauḍapāda's theory on the other hand is primarily epistemological and that is perhaps the reason why Gauḍapāda is regarded as the founder of the Advaita school where the philosopohical investigation takes an epistemological turn. It is sometime alleged that Gauḍapāda is influenced by the Buddhist thought. Perhaps this is so not only with regard to philosophical results but also with regard to the epistemological method that Gauḍapāda employs. Nevertheless, there is some uniqueness in Gauḍapāda's system.

It is claimed by most people that Gauḍapāda's system is idealistic and that he not only regards the world as illusory but also thinks that it has never existed. In fact, it is this view attributed to Gauḍapāda which makes him a co-traveller with the Buddhists who are supposed to have propounded the *śūnya* (nothing) status of the world. Let us, therefore, see what Gauḍapāda actually says on all these matters.

First, whether there is world which exists in its own right is to be distinguished from whether there is an external world as the common sense conceives, viz., the world of space and time. If we deny the first alternative then we are denying the objectivity of the world. It is possible to deny the second and still accept the first, without at least being a subjective idealist. Again, to hold the first position does not necessarily make us either an objective idealist or a realist or a phenomenalist. When the philosophers use the word *sat,* they mean by it that Reality whatever be its nature exists in its own right, and so to my mind they exclude the philosophical position of subjective Idealism. It seems to me that Gauḍapāda accepts the first proposition that there is Reality which exists in its own right. Whether he accepts this position intuitively or following the Upaniṣads is irrelevant for the present pupose. However, this raises a further problem about the nature of the 'external' world. Gauḍapāda's philosophical enquiry seems to be connected with this problem. His problem takes the following two forms, and I think it is here that what may be generally called his epistemological approach manifests itself: (*i*) whether the external world can be known to have spatio-temporal properties, and (*ii*) whether there can be a good criterion for holding that there is an external world. It is clear that both these questions are epistemological in nature.

From the writings of Gauḍapāda all that can be said is that according to him we are not able to propose a good criterion for proving that there is an external world, or that the external world has such and such properties. For if we start by distinguishing between illusory and veridical experience, then according to Gauḍapāda, that by which we distinguish between the illusory and the veridical seems to be common to both these types of experience. So the very logical foundation of our distinction is uprooted.

Let us see how Gauḍapāda presents his argument. He begins by distinguishing three kinds of possible knowledge situations: (1) the *jāgarta* or where there is an established contact between the knower and the 'outside' world, (2) *svapna* or where the knower and the outside world are present but where there is inadequate contact with the outside world or where the contact is established between the knower and his memory states, and (3) *suṣupti* or where the knower and the outside world exist but where they are only juxtaposed, the knower being existent as a continuant, but in a state of sleep as an occurrent. Thus, in *suṣupti* the kind of contact that is necessary for 'knowledge' is denied. These three stages in some sense require a 'knower'. Gauḍapāda borrowing (and modifying) the terms from the *Māṇḍūkya Upaniṣad* specifically names the kind of the knower that is present in these three knowing situations. He calls these 'knowers' as *viśva*, *taijasa* and *prājña*. The corresponding Upaniṣadic terms are *vaiśvānara*, *taijasa* and *prājña*. One who is supposed to know the outside world is called *viśva*, one who knows only the 'internal' world is called *taijasa*, and one who is in juxtaposition with the object without there being 'knowledge' is called *prājña* (*pra* + *ajña*) or one who is very ignorant. (*Prājña* is sometimes regarded as one who knows absolutely. But at any rate this is not the primary meaning of the term and not the meaning here). It is necessary to note that this is naming of the knower with reference to his different states. This is the analysis of the knower that is a continuant. It goes without saying that if the continuant-knower does not exist anymore in a knowledge situation, the situation itself will become a non-epistemic situation — merely a juxtaposition of things. Such a situation will nevertheless be a case (in the world). If such disintegration is only temporary or just occasional, the total situation would be a part of a bigger knowledge situation, and the knower in the situation will have to be regarded as not totally absent, but still present in the fashion of the super-ego of Freud. Since the stream of consciousness or the knower-continuant is not completely absent or is not absent for ever, the situation can be understood on the analogy of somnambulism where the knowerness of the knower is lost and still the knower is 'aware' of the 'knower-and-the-object-of-knowledge' situation. Such a situation is only a logically limiting case of knowledge situation and is regarded by Gauḍapāda as the fourth or *turīya*. He does not seem to have anything mystical in his mind when he talks of this fourth stage.

The epistemological model that Gauḍapāda uses ordinarily requires three terms, *jñātṛ, jñeya,* and *jñāna*. But Gauḍapāda understands the limitations of these terms and so replaces it by *bhoktṛ-bhojya-model*. The history of philosophy will tell us that the word *jñāna* is much misused. A sentence 'There is knowledge' is treated almost in the same manner as we treat the sentence, 'There is *a chair*'. We begin to think that when we say that there *is* knowledge, knowledge *literally exists* in the way any physical thing exists. Knowledge is given the status of a thing or at least something that is the case. Even a theory like Plato's theory of Ideas, is a product of regarding knowledge as some kind of a thing. Somehow or other this potentiality of being misregarded as a thing is absent in the word *bhoga*. Nobody (barring the theoreticians of *karma* theory) has regarded *bhoga* as existing in its own right. Whether Gauḍapāda was aware of all the demerits which arise in the use of the word *jñāna* or knowledge is not known. But it can certainly be guessed from the internal evidence of the *kārikā* (1.3-9) that in his opinion *bhoktṛ-bhojya* model was more suitable to his philosophy. For although he talks of three kinds of *bhoga* and three kinds of *tṛpti* it does not appear that even by some distant imagination he is giving any ontic status to *bhoga* or *tṛpti*. On the other hand, in the fifth *kārikā* of the first *adhyāya* it is clearly suggested that although we distinguish three kinds of *bhoktṛ* and *bhojya,* they are really only one. It is only in the process of knowing that we distinguish between *bhoktṛ* and *bhojya*. As reality everything is only *sat*. The differentiations or *bhāva*s are created only by *prāṇa* (literally life or breath). It is needless to say that for Gauḍapāda the *prāṇa*, the knower and the *bhoktr̥s* are identical here. Thus, the creation (*janayati,* 1.6) Gauḍapāda talks of is not the ontic creation or that which is concerned with *sat* or *bhojya*. It is, indeed, true that the use of the word *prāṇa* by Gauḍapāda in 1.6 is not very happy. It may easily lead or mislead people to think that *prāṇa* is the soul and that is the soul which creates the world. The words, *prabhava* and *janayati,* are similarly very unhappy, although convenient. The word *prabhava* may either suggest the condition of knowing (*jnāpakatva*) or the condition of creating (*janakatva*). If the first is mistaken for the second, an impression may be created that *prāṇa* or the soul is the creator of everything. A greater difficulty arises with regard to the word *janayati*. The primary sense of the word is 'to create'. So it is likely to be thought that it is only the real ontological process of creation that is in the mind of Gauḍapāda. But if the context of the *kārikā* is taken into consideration, it is clear that the word *bhāva* refers to different forms of reality and that the distinction or the division of reality into different forms is done only at the level of knowing and so *janayati* merely conveys the sense of the cause or the necessary condition of differentiation in the sense that if *prāṇa* was absent the further distinctions would not be operative.

Nevertheless, it may be admitted that the real process of creation may not be entirely out of the mind of Gauḍapāda. Otherwise it would be difficult to explain the second part of the last line of the *kārikā* 1.6, *ceto'nsūn, puruṣaḥ pr̥thak*. Here, to my mind, Gauḍapāda is suggesting that the continuity of life, or to use his words, the rays of life are created by *puruṣa* or Consciousness. Does it mean that for Gauḍapāda the vital creation is the real creation and that the mechanical creation is either the creation of man or merely the cognition and recognition of forms? If this is the meaning, it would be much better to take the first two lines of the *kārikā* 1.6 with the *kārikā* 1.5. In the case the *kārikā* 1.6 would be the key *kārikā* to Gauḍapāda's philosophy, for it would refer to both the processes in Gauḍapāda's mind, the ontological and the epistemic. This also would be in keeping with the verses that follow in which Gauḍapāda is giving the views of other thinkers. It should be natural that Gauḍapāda gives his own view before referring to others' views. This, however, would mean (1) that Gauḍapāda here talks of two different processes (a) *bhāva-prakriyā* and (b) *sat-prakriyā* (2) that he further regards that the *bhāva-prakriyā* is connected with *bhoktṛ* or *bhuñjāna* and that the *sat-prakriyā* is connected with *prāṇa*. But this would be reading more than what is stated in the *kārikā*.

It is, however, plain that Gauḍapāda is not primarily concerned with the problem of the genesis or the *vistāra* of the world that exists in its own right. He is interested in pointing out that the problem of misery ends as soon as we recognise that the division of the world into *bhoktṛ* and *bhojya*, is only artificial and arbitrary; and as a matter of fact there is merely that which *is*. This state is indicated by him in the tenth *kārikā,* under the name *turīya*. It is the logical pre-supposition from which the knowing situation takes a take off. And it would also be the limiting case of knowledge situation, i.e., where the knowledge situation would be undistinguished from reality situation. Gauḍapāda says this in *kārikā*s 1.10, 11 and 12. In 1.10 he says that this *turīya* or the Fourth (state) is all-pervading, shining; it removes all miseries and here all differentiations are eliminated. He repeats the same idea again in 1.12 when he says that *truīya* is *sat*.

Gauḍapāda now explains the four (including *turīya*) knowledge situations. He does so first by distinguishing *kāraṇa* and *kārya*. His use in respect of these terms is rather peculiar. But if we keep in view the fact that Gauḍapāda is here referring to the knowledge situation his use of the word *kāraṇa* or cause and his use of the word *kārya* or effect would be clear. The *bhāva*s, *bheda*s or the manifestations or the objects of knowledge are for Gauḍapāda the *kārya* or the effect and the *sat* as the known is the *kāraṇa* or the ground for these manifestations. He says the knowers, *viśva* and *taijasa*, are always *related* as cause to the effect. For it is they who are the perceivers of the differences. The *prājña,* because he is not in contact with the world of manifestation or experience, has only the *lone status* of a knower in the sense that he is a knower but does not know anything. But *turīya* being the limiting case the distinction of knower and known disappears here. 'Even though in respect of *prājña* and *turīya* there is no perception of differentiations, the *pājña* is *bījanidrāyuta,* i.e., even though he does not know or perceive anything on account of the fact that he is in sleep, he has the ability to know or to perceive. But even this is absent in *truīya* (1.13). For *turīya* in the strict sense is not a knower. It will be interesting to know that Gauḍapāda gives different names to the knower and the knowledge situation in respect of the first three. *Viśva*, the knower is different from *jāgṛta,* the knowledge situation. *Taijasa* the knower is different from *svapna*, the knowledge situation, and the *prājña* is similarly distinguished from *suṣupti.* But Gauḍapāda does not so distinguish between the knower and the knowledge situation in respect of *truīya*. Both of them are *turīya* for the distinction of the knower and the known has (at least temporarily) broken down. In the strict sense of the term 'there is no duality' of the knower and the known. *Advaitaṁ paramārthataḥ* (1.7). Following the *Māṇḍūkya Upaniṣad,* Gauḍapāda then symbolizes the three varieties of knower, the *viśva*, *taijasa* and *prājña*, by the the letter *A*,*U*, *Ṁ*, and says that one who knows that, in spite of the distinction amongst the three, they have something common, that they are really one, is a great *muni.* This last stage of *turīya* is represented by the symbol *auṁkāra*, which has the 'commonness' of all the three namely *A*,*U* and *Ṁ* (1.22). He is also stating that just as the knowers which appear to be different are one, similarly the reality is what it is although it appears to be distinguished. The dispute about the status of reality arises only when we try to express the ultimate reality in language *upadeśā ayaṃ vādaḥ* (1.18). Gauḍapāda is here suggesting that the linguistic expression itself is regarded as creation. But the duality which is created on account of the linguistic form is a fake (1.17). The reality does not have different orders. *Jñāte dvaitaṁ na vidyate* (1.18). It is of course not clear whether in this '*one order*' Gauḍapāda is rejecting the thesis of pluralism and propounding the thesis of monism. In fact, there are at least two reasons to believe that he does not reject the possiblity of pluralism in the first order reality. He has used the word *satām* in 1.6. There was really no need to use plural number if he had in his mind only the unity and not the plurality of the first order world. Secondly, although he distinguished between *jīva* and *ātman* and states that the *jīva*s are distinguished from *ātman* just in the same way as the space in a pot is distinguished from the great space [but in fact they are not different (3.3.)], still he does not seem to have stated anywhere that the *bhojya* and the *bhoktṛ* are only one and identical. He only states that the manyness of the *bhoktṛ* is to be given up and that only one *ātman* is to be posited. But that nothing but *ātman* exists does not seem to be stated by Gauḍapāda anywhere as far as my knowledge goes. He only states that in reality which is *nirvikalpa* it is not possible to distinguish between the knower and the known. To say that we are able to distinguish or not able to distinguish is one thing; to say that there is no distinction is another. So it is possible that, whereas Gauḍapāda distinguishes the first order world (as *sat* and *ātman*) from the other-order world which is merely a *vikalpa* or *prapañca* and states that the *prapañca* or *vikalpa* is not a real creation (though he uses the words *kāraṇa* and *kārya* to denote the relation that exists between the first and the other orders), he does not deny the possiblity that in the first order there is creation or development or dynamism. In fact, if we distinguish between analysis and genesis, it is possible to think from the analytical point of view that everything (in the region of *bhoktṛ*) is *ātman* and still it would be possible to maintain that no *jīva* comes into existence unless it is produced by *jīva*. *Ātman* would be merely a collective or class name for *jīvas*. It is only on such a basis that the *satkāryavāda* in Advaita Vedānta can be explained. It is thus possible to maintain that Gauḍapāda distinguishes two kinds of processes, one the physical and the other the linguistic. He calls this other process *prapañca* and regards it as false in the sense that it cannot exist in its own right and has to be regarded as *non-different* from the first order process. But from this we need not conclude that according to Gauḍapāda there is no movement or development in the first order and that it is only static. It also does not follow, that because we talk of one order, there must be only one unitary thing there and that there could not be things of different kinds. In fact, if the first order world has more things than one, to regard that there is only one thing there would also be tantamount to *adhyāsa*. Perhaps what can be legitimately stated is that we would not be able to express that there are many thing or kinds in the first order. For as soon as we say this we have already entered the sphere of *prapañca*.

This brings us to the second part of Gauḍapāda's thesis. The key terms here are *svapna*, *vaitathya*, *saṁvṛtatva* and *bhāva*. He is asserting the *vaitathya* of all *bhāvas*. Since he has already distinguished between *sat* and *bhāva* and has regarded *bhāva*s as *vikalpa*s or *bheda*s, that is the knowledge or language products (*upadeśād ayaṁ vādaḥ* (1.18)), it should have been possible for him to regard '*bhāva*s are *vitatha*' as an analytic proposition. But he perhaps wants to strengthen his thesis by analysing experience.

Let us take *vitatha* to mean false although there seems to be a difference between other-than-the-real and the unreal or false. A construction over real may be other-than-the-real and evidently it is stated by Gauḍapāda that *bhāva*s are so constructed. *Evaṁ kalpayate prabhuḥ* (2.13, also see 2.11-12). Again *svapna* is used very technically and in fact means the object in the knowing situation when the knower is *taijasa*. Thus, any imagination or illusion, etc., will also come under *svapna*[1]. That which is suggested by the English word 'dream' will thus be the narrower sense of the word *svapna*. But here again even if we take the word in its narrower sense it should suffice to explain Gauḍapāda's argument. Next comes the word *saṁvr̥ta*. The slightly modified form of the word has been much used in the Buddhist literature. It includes in this sense whatever is included in the speech behaviour. 'Whatever is expressed in our speech behaviour along with the speech behaviour itself constitutes the realm of *saṁvr̥ti*. . . .'[2] Literally *saṁvr̥ta* means covered. In later Advaita thought the word *paricchinnatva* seems to be substituted for *saṁvr̥tatva*. So it means (1) closed inside (the mind), (2) wrapped in a concept-form, (3) limited by anything such as (*a*) language and (*b*) space and time. If I close my eyes and see an elephant, the elephant having the spatio-temporal characteristics cannot be 'inside' me. Such concepts have no bearing on existence, and so such an experience can be regarded as *vitatha*. But what about the proposition when I say, 'An idea occurred to me.' Is that idea also *vitatha*? According to Gauḍapāda such an experience is also *vitatha*. *Cittakālā hi ye antāḥ . . . . viśeṣo nānya-hetukāḥ*(2.14). It is of course possible to think that the problem of truth and falsity arises in relation to whether or not a certain thing exists. From this

1. The narrower and the wider senses of the word *svapna* are however not explained by Gauḍapāda.
2. B.K. Matilal, 'Epistemology, Logic and Grammar', *Indian Philosophical Analysis*, p. 152, (Mouton, Hague, Paris, 1971).

point of view, whether the elephant is *vitatha* would be relevant, and whether the idea is *vitatha* would not be relevant. For nobody (except the Platonist) regards ideas as existing. But if by *vitatha* is understood *unreal*, then insofar as ideas do not exist they are unreal, and so *vitatha*. Gauḍapāda uses the word *vitatha* in this second sense.

Let us now see, how Gauḍapāda uses the word *vitatha* in respect of *svapna* and *jāgaṛta* states. The problem here is not that *svapna* experience is not different from experience in *jāgaṛta*. The problem is: what are the criteria by which we can distinguish the *svapna* experience from the *jāgaṛta* experience? Here Gauḍapāda begins by analysing the common sense belief. 'The great minds have said that all *bhāvas* in *svapna* are false. (This is so) because they are *internal* and because they are *saṁvṛta*. (2.1). Here perhaps *antaḥ* and *saṁvṛta* mean the same thing; *saṁvṛta* suggests wrapped by mind, mental. Whatever we see in dream is not something actual; it is merely the mental image of something that may be externally perceived. How do I know that what I experience in dreams is not something real? Although our experience in dream is that whatever we experience is 'outside' the body, it is clear that the place of our experience in dream is the body itself. Our concepts of space and time do not cohere with our experience of (space and time in) dream. If we experience a chariot in a dream it can be proved by argument (*nyāya*) that the chariot did not exist there (2.2.3.). On account of this 'internality' when we are awake we know that the experience of *svapna* was false. But in both the cases *saṁvṛtattva* is common (2.4-5). How do you decide the *saṁvṛtattva* of a dream-chariot? Perhaps the only way it can be done is by correlating it to our ordinary spatio-temporal relations. Supposing the chariot is perceived at time T_2 (in dream) and is not perceived at time T_1 nor at time T_3. We say that the chariot that we have seen was a dream-chariot. The principle, then, on which we decide the illusoriness or falsity of a thing can be narrated thus: That which does not exist in the earlier nor in the later point of time does not have ontological existence even in the present. According to Gauḍapāda the temporal correlation seems to be the major, if not the entire, condition of *saṁvṛtatva*. The dream objects do not fit in one kind of correlation; but what we call the real objects also behave in a similar way.

Merely existing in finite time does not make an object real. At any rate this is not a sufficient criterion for deciding whether something is real or otherwise. For, this criterion is shared in common by the accepted illusory things and the real things of our ordinary belief. Gauḍapāda is not very explicit on the point, but most probably he means that those objects which are not time-governed alone are real. Perhaps space and time are themselves *vikalpa,* although Gauḍapāda seems to be silent on the point. But one important point comes out of this: in order that a thing may be real, it should not be born; that which is born is destroyed; that which has birth and death is *vitatha.* So only that thing which is not born is real. Such reality is *Brahman* or *ātman.* Such reality cannot be characterised by classness. For classness itself is the *vikalpa*, *bheda* or *bhāva*. *Ajātitā* is, therefore, the characteristic of reality. *Jātitā* is the characteristic of unreality. Hence, the *ajātivāda* of Gauḍapāda. Gauḍapāda does not mean that the world is never born as claimed by the propounders of *ajātivāda*, many a time. The world as it is, is never born in the sense that it is always there whereas the *jātitā* exists only in the human world, in the sense that *jātitā* is 'created' in the process of knowing and expressing. The determinate or the classified world that we see then is not the ontological world, but the 'needle work' that man's intellect has done over the ontological world. *Saṁvṛtatva* then means 'categorization'. To say that it is a table is to categorize the reality as table. This happens in all determinate knowledge. And whatever we experience, whether illusory or real, is always a *determinable. Saṁvṛtatva* thus seems to be connected with the very nature of *knowing*. Similarly, when we have to express or communicate, we cannot do so except by the use of linguistic or knowledge categories. Thus, if *saṁvṛtatva* means a reference to categories then, it would be common to both the experiences, the one in *svapna* and the other in *jāgarta*. *Saṁvṛtatva*, then gives us the limits of our knowledge and language, and the reality as it exists in its own right would be beyond this. To determine reality in terms of *saṁvṛtatva*, to distinguish something unreal from the real on the basis *saṁvṛtatva*, does not hold water. Gaudapāda explains this further when he refers to *saprayojanatā* or purpose in dream. When we see something in dream, it may be that later on we may say that it was without a purpose. But when we are experiencing the dream, we do not experience the futility of the purpose. Thus, it is not possible for us to discover a criterion by which we can distinguish between the dream experience and the 'real' experience. Similarly, when we express our experience in language, there is no (internal) criterion by which we can say that a particular proposition or sentence refers to something that is real and that the other refers to something that is unreal. The form of both these is exactly the same.

How do you then distinguish between false and real experience? The hypothesis that is suggested to Gauḍapāda here is that *ātman* on account of its own power or *māyā* manifests itself in the form of *bhāvas*. Gauḍapāda wants to suggest that finally the distinction that we make between *bhoktṛ* and *bhojya,* when we build up the epistemological model, is to be given up. For in the final analysis reality is indeterminable, *nirvikalpa* (2.35). This is of course not to say that although the world is seen like the magic city (*gandharva-nagara*), there is no reality at all. There is indeed the reality but in that reality there is no *nirodha* nor *utpatti*, no one is really bound, nor is any one trying to be free nor is any one free (2.32). For, all these are human categories. All the criteria that are given are about the determinate world, but they are not sufficient criteria. There is reality, but epistemological tools are not sharp enough to separate the real from the unreal.

Gauḍapāda was indeed a great thinker. But his greatness, somehow or other, was overlooked by the recent writers on Vedānta. Perhaps Professor T.M.P. Mahadevan was one of the first to introduce Gauḍapāda to the English reading world. The philosophers of India will always be grateful to Mahadevan for opening this great heritage of Indian Philosophy to the public.

6

A Background Picture of Jainism and Buddhism

It may be accepted that Pūrva Mīmāṁsā, Advaita, Jaina, and Buddhist philosophies dominated Indian horizons for ages. Some people thought, though it is not accepted now, that Buddhist philosophy was rather alien to the soil. The Buddha was regarded as belonging to the Śaka clan which came from outside. The case with Jaina Philosophy is different. It is held by the Jainas that their culture—the Śramaṇic culture was earlier than the Brāhmaṇical tradition. It may also be pointed out that according to some even the Upaniṣadic philosophy is not Vedic in the strict sense that it is in fact grafted over the philosophies which naturally emerged from the Vedas. Of course, this is a controversial matter and I do not want to enter into it. But it may be mentioned that in defending the Vedic origin of the Upaniṣads and Uttara Mīmāṁsā philosophy people refer to R̥gvedic *Puruṣasūkta* and *Nāsadīyasūkta*. In fact, these two *sūkta*s can be regarded as forerunners of Sāṁkhya and Vedāntic thought and though the Sāṁkhya philosophy is regarded as a kind of Dvaita philosophy one could find out some deeper similarity between the thought of the two *sūkta*s and Advaita. Perhaps there is some common nexus between Sāṁkhya thought and Advaita thought. But no one has claimed that the Jaina Śramaṇic culture was an offspring of Vedic culture. As stated earlier, the Jainas hold that Śramaṇic culture was earlier in origin than the Vedic culture. The sculpture of the bull in the excavations of Mohenjo-Daro is, on one interpretation, taken as a symbol of the first Jaina *tīrthaṅkara*, Ādināth R̥ṣabhadeva. It is also propounded that there is a mention of this Ṛṣabhadeva in the *Ṛgveda*. Of course, the name of Ṛṣabha appears in the *Ṛgveda* and also *Bhāgavata* and it could be that Ṛṣabhadeva of *Ṛgveda* and *Bhāgavata* and Ṛṣabhaveda of the Jainas are one and the same. There is also a legend that the very name of our country derives its origin from the name of emperor Bharata who was one of the sons of Ṛṣabhadeva. This story is also found in *Śrīmad Bhāgavaṭa*. In the *Mahābhārata* also, there is a story of one Jaḍabharata. Perhaps this has a reference to the story of emperor Bharata of the Jaina legend. One thing is certain that the name Bhāratavarṣa is not due to Bharata, the son of Duṣyanta and Śakuntalā. It is, therefore, plausible that the name Bhāratavarṣa might have a reference to emperor Bharata of Jaina tradition. From this it is possible to conclude that the Śramaṇic civilisation was contemporary or even earlier than the Vedic Brāhmaṇical civilisation. One need not even dispute that this civilisation had independent origin and independent existence. However, the similarities that are found in Jaina and Brāhmaṇical philosophies could have been either independent or due to interactions between two different thoughts. It may be pointed out that there are several such similarities between the so-called Brāhmaṇical and the Buddhist thoughts also. And, so far as similarities amongst the Brāhmaṇical, the Buddhist and the Jaina thoughts are concerned, it could be that the Vedic tradition had borrowed some thoughts from the Jaina and Buddhist traditions.

Although chronologically and historically one cannot say with certainty which civilisation is earlier, from the point of view of anthropological and social development, one could perhaps say that Yajña civilisation was a distinct step in the direction of progress. It depicts the growth or development. This is not clear from the Jaina legends, even of Mahāpurāṇa. The very first *ṛcā* of the *Ṛgveda* is *agnimīḷe purohitam*. It tells us about the discovery of fire. Of course, it is not impossible that the Jainas had also discovered fire earlier and independently. But in that case the original *karma-kāṇḍa* philosophy of Jainas, which relates its origin to some such discovery as that of fire, has not come down to us. However, today the philosophy which dominates India is certainly the philosophy of Pūrva Mīmāṁsā and is to outcome of *karma-kāṇḍa*. The *karma-kāṇḍa* in some form, is predominant even in the philosophies of

Buddhists and the Jainas. In fact, I could even say that in every kind of thought when it is being practised some kind of *karma-kāṇḍa* or rituals are bound to arise. A theory arising out of such rituals, I name as the philosophy of Pūrva Mīmāṁsā and it can be of a Brāhmaṇical, Buddhist, Jaina or any other origin and for the sake of convenience I start with the Pūrva Mīmāṁsā of Vedic origin. And in this sense perhaps Lokāyata, Buddhist, Jaina and Advaita or Uttara Mīmāṁsā philosophies in their theoretical form could be regarded as reactions to the ritual originated Pūrva Mīmāṁsā philosophy. It is true that today neither the philosopy of Pūrva Mīmāṁsā is accepted without qualification nor are the practices prescribed by it are adhered to in its original form. They have been substantially modified by the Buddhist, the Jaina and the Advaita views. But although the Yajña civilisation has disappeared to a large extent, yet our beliefs which are, so to say, commonly shared by traditional philosophies of India have their origin in the philosophy of Pūrva Mīmāṁsā or at least *karma-kāṇḍa* of some kind. I, therefore, think that the elements connected with behaviour and rituals must be prior to the thought elements in the Brāhmanical philosophy as also in the Jain and Buddhist philosophies.

In Pūrva Mīmāṁsā of Vedic origin, *jīva* and *śarira*, i.e., *bhūta*s (matter) are regarded as two independent existents. If one looks to the differences between the living man and the dead, one could early see why the independent *jīva* and *śarīra* were introduced. One could think of a living man dying and death would mean disintegration of the compound of body and soul. But once this disintegration is accomplished one could not further think that the body (matter) and the soul also further die. One could, therefore, think of immediately of soul and conversation of matter. The next step in this direction would be the introduction of the concepts of rebirth and the immortality of soul. This would also bring in the concepts of heaven and hell and a kind of *karma* theory. All this happened in Pūrva Mīmāṁsā thought.

It appears to me that for the philosophers of Jainism the philosophical problems must have arisen alomst in the same order as it came for Pūrva Mīmāṁsā philosophers. Both had realised that a living being cannot remain without *karma* or action even for a single moment: *na hi kaścit kṣaṇam-api jātu tiṣṭhatya-karma-kṛt*.

For, any living being is a temporal gestalt and such a gestalt could not remain without movement (action). Even his position of rest had to he regarded as an extension of his dynamic state. Thus, the concept of *karma* become fundamental concept in both the philosophies. Of course, this concept developed in two philosophies in different ways. In Pūrva Mīmāṁsā philosophy it became invariable concomitant of the basic substance, the *jīva,* and, therefore, it developed into some kind of ritualist theory and was brought into the framework of cause and effect. First, the Pūrva Mīmāṁsakas made a division of a living being into *jīva* and *śarīra* and then regarded this *śarīra* as something material or non-living. The paradigm before them was that of a dead body. Like Descartes they also must have thought that the body had extension, i.e., it had spatial properties. Such spatial properties could not be linked with *jīva qua jīva*. The *jīva* on the contrary was ever-living. But they also realised the difficulty in conceiving *jīva* without a body. How could it act without a body? So they attached to it what is termed as *liṅga-deha* or minute body. They could not get out of the jigsaw-puzzle of the *deha-jīva* complex. So soon as the *jīva* had the *sūkṣma-deha*, *jīva* could go anywhere and had the capacity to enjoy or suffer the effects of his action. This *jīva* with *liṅga-deha* could go to heavens or hades, enter the mother's womb, get reborn and also redie. Śaṅkarācārya has described such a position in one of his *stotras*: *punar-api jananaṁ punar-api maraṇaṁ punar-api jananī-jaṭhare śayanam.* This *jīva* has no rest any time except in some 'mundane' sense. This position reduces the concept of *karma*, as substance stretched in time series, from Time, t_1 to t_n . . . and *jīva* becomes some kind of metaphysical presupposition only. Only *karma* — a complex of *karma*, becomes significant. Therefore, it is very natural to think of this *karma* as if it was a substance having its several atomic states. In fact, in Jainism this has happened. It recognises the *aṇu*s or atoms of *karma*. But in Pūrva Mīmāṁsā too the position is not very different. Although the *jīva* still retains the primary position, his stauts is determined by his *karma*. There is so to say a symbiosis of the *karma* with the *jīva*. The *karma* is now characterised as *sañcita, prārabdha* and *kriyamāṇa.* The phenomenon of *karma* is not anything less than a law of physics, the *jīva* cannot get itself separated from *karma* and it is neither *karma* alone nor the *jīva* alone. It is the quantum of *jīva-karma* complex.

The Jaina thinkers have not made a compromise in understanding the nature of *jīva* and *deha*. For the Jainas the *jīva* and *deha* can be distinguished but not separated. They asert that *jīva* has extension. Though this extension may vary in different situations. Ordinarily the extension of *jīva* and the extension of the body is the same. This concept clearly indicates that at some level of thinking at least the Jaina philosophers did not abstract the body and soul (*jīva*) from each other. Of course, without some kind of abstraction they would not be able to explain the concept of death and so perhaps some kind of miniature body had to be associated with *jīva* in all its states. It is very important to point out here that Jainas talk of six *dravyas*: *jīva*, *ajīva* (i.e., *pudgala*), *dharma*, *adharma*, *ākāśa* and *kāla*. Of these *dravyas* the first five are *astikāyas*, that is having existence, of which it can be said that they exist. One may compare the concept of *astikāya* with that of schematism of Kant. If we think of *jīva* but do not think of its body, then *jīva* would be merely an abstraction and would be reduced to the status of concepts. Body might increase or decrease but it could not be separated physically. To avoid such a position, they brought in the concept of *astikāya*. Thus, an *astikāya jīva* would be the *jīva* that existed and it would naturally require a body. A *jīva* which is not *astikāya* would naturally by the concept of *jīva*, an abstraction of *jīva* I have a feeling that when the Jainas thought of *astikāya dravyas* they thought of deciphering them in the way of Pāṇini deciphered the *pratyāhāras* in *Māheśvara Sūtras*. The *Māheśvara Sūtras* are following *aiuṅ, eoṅ*, etc., the last being *hal*. Now the first letter along with the last consonant makes a *pratyāhāra* and such *pratyāhāra* is inclusive of all letters from the first to the last—*ādirantyena sahetā*. In giving the list of *dravyas* perhaps Jaina philosophers have used a similar technique. The *dravyas* are listed as follows: *jīva*, *ajīva*, *dharma*, *adharma*, *ākāśa* and *kāla*. Thus, if you talk of *jīva* it would include along with *jīva-ajīva*, i.e., *pudgala*, *dharma*, the cause of *gati*, i.e., the potential movement, *adharma*, the cause of static position, i.e., the potentiality to be without movement. *Ākāśa,* i.e., space and *kāla*, i.e., time. A *jīva* is a complex a gestalt of all the six. But if we talk of *ajīva*, i.e., *pudgala* it would be a gestalt of only the five (*dravyas*) from *pudgala* to *kāla,* i. e., would not have the *jīva* in it. If we think of *dharma* it would have *dharma*, *adharma*, *ākāśa* and *kāla*, but would not have *jīva* and *pudgala*. In the same way *adharma* would have the characteristics possessed by *adharma*, *ākāśa* and *kāla*. If you think of *ākāśa* we would have *ākāśa* and *kāla* but would not have the first four. And in the case of *kāla*, it will be *kāla qua kāla* and would not have either *jīva* or *pudgala*, or *dharma* or *adharma* or *ākāśa*. In the absence of these, *kāla* would have no actual existence and still it could not be brushed aside. It would not be *astikāya* but would still be. For Jainas 'existence' or *astikāyatva* is concerned with space or *pradeśa* and pure *kāla* cannot have *pradeśa*. In fact, pure space also would be a concept and unless it is coordinated with *kāla* it too would not have actual existence; but space is always so coordinated and it always has time-dimension. And since everything else is conceived under two coordinates *ākāśa* and *kāla*, everything else would be regarded as *astikāya* or having actual existence. To use Kant's language the categories would now take the form of schemata. Thus, the *dravyas* of the Jainas also would have to be treated at two levels, (*i*) the actual existents and (*ii*) as characteristics (of categories). *Kāla* and *ākāśa* together would supply a seafold for such existents. Pure *kāla* alone would be without schemata. Nevertheless it would not be a concept, it would be something real.

In Jaina theory of *karma* is of the nature of *pudgala*. This is attached to *jīva* right from the beginning, i.e., from beginning of time. This is understandable because unlike Pūrva Mīmāṁsā Jainism does not believe in *jīva* without spatial properties and so *jīva* for the Jaina philosophers would be a complex of *jīva* and *pudgala*, i.e., these two would be distinguishable but not separable. But in their enthusiasm or perhaps under the pressure of the thought which was of Pūrva Mīmāṁsā type the Jaina philosophers thought that *jīva* and *karma* were not complex but were only compound, i.e., at some stage (i.e., at the time of *jīva's* emancipation) they could be separated. The process of separation is connected to the process of *mokṣa* and the actualisation of separation is marked with the 'attainment' of *mokṣa*. This *mukta-jīva* naturally would have to be without space dimension and so would have to stay outside space, in dimensionless space. They had to invent *alokākāśa*, which was other than what we ordinarily think of, that is, *lokākāśa*. Perhaps the *jīvas* at the time of emancipation, would have to travel all the way where the horizon of *lokākāśa* would end. The *jīvas*, they say, go to *alokākāśa* and rest when they are emancipated or become *mukta*. Of course, here too they could not think of the situation which could be freed from spatial language. The emancipated *jīvas* would also require a resting place which was provided by *siddhaśilā*. *Śilā* or a stone is ordinarily conceived as having spatial dimension. *Śiddhaśilās* would not have spatial dimensions although *siddhaśilā* is conceived and expressed in the language of space. The attainment of emancipation thus lands us in the following position: (1) The concept of *karma* which was regarded as some kind of law of natrure is thus finally broken. (2) And acceptance of bodiless *jīva* would be going back to a position of Pūrva Mīmāṁsā. Once the *jīva* becomes bodiless it would not have to go through the ordial of rebirth. One can certainly think of immortal soul not taking rebirth. In a limited sense this concept is worked out by the Christians and Muslims. Like Jainas and the Mīmāṁsakas they also believe that at the time of death the *jīva* and body get separated and the body rests in the tomb and the *jīva* rests somewhere till doomsday when the process of regenerating the world is taken on by the creator god. The process of liquidating the body is explained by the Jaina thinkers by bringing in the concepts of *bandha*, *āsrava*, *saṁvara*, *nirjarā*. The process is very similar to *karma siddhānta* process of *sañcita*, *prārabdha* and *kriyamāṇa*. They illustrate it by very peculiar example. Ordinarily a gourd floats over water. But if we tie a thread around it and then put layer of the mud over the same, then on account of the weight of the mud the gourd sinks in the water. So is the case with *jīva* the *karma* at this stage is taken as external to *jīva* and it, so to say, flows into the *jīva*, makes it heavy and forces it follow the laws of *pudgala* or *karma* and makes it take rebirth. This process, however, which is started by *āsrava* or the flow of *karma* has to be stopped. This is done by *saṁvara*, nay, the *jīva* should be got rid of this too, and it is done by *nirjarā*. It is extricating the matter from *jīva*. When this is finally done the *jīva* is got rid of the bondage or *bandha* and becomes *mukta*. Roles of *pāpa* and *puṇya* are not very clear in this process. In Pūrva Mīmāṁsā, *pāpa* and *puṇya* act as levers for further action and force the *jīva* to take rebirth. This role to *pāpa* and *puṇya* is consistent with the philosophy of Pūrva Mīmāṁsā;

there is no place for *mukti* in it. One is governed by something like the Newton's law of inertia; once you are moving you are always moving. Once you are caught in the whirlwind of *karma*, you are always in it. This is not the case with *saṁvara* and *nirjarā* in Jaina philosophy, where Jainas introduced the concepts of *pāpa* and *puṇya*. *Puṇya* perhaps initiates stopping of the process and leads the *jīva* to *mukti* and *pāpa* should enhance the process and lead it to rebirth. But roles of *pāpa* and *punya* are not quite clear in the Jaina works.

To me it appears that the introduction of the concept of *mukti* in Jaina philosophy was not consistent with their original concept of *jīva* (*saṁsārī jīva*) which was inseparable from some kind of body. This has led to further inconsistencies in their thought, e.g., one such inconsistency was that the *jīva* had a gender and that females could not get *mukti*. Perhaps this was the then prevalent idea in the society, whether it was Vedic, Buddhist or the Digambara Jaina. This one inconsistency further led to another inconsistency, viz., before women got emancipated they had to be reborn as men. Jaina *Mahāpurāṇa* is a collection of mythological stories primarily about the first Jaina *tīrthaṅkara* Ṛṣabhadeva. There was a belief that husband and wife are simultaneously born in the same womb of the mother and then they live as husband and wife. But since the woman does not get emancipated Ṛṣabhadeva's consort had to be reborn as man and had to act as minister of Ṛṣabhadeva (in the previous rebirth) before she could be emancipated. It is generally believed that of the twenty-four *tīrthaṅkara*s one was a woman, Malli by name. But since this was against the social thinking of Jainas of the Digambara sect the followers of the sect did not accept it and said that the *tīrthaṅkara* was not Malli but was Mallinātha. Such kind of thinking must have come certainly only when the concept of *mokṣa* was introduced in the Jaina thought. Here Pūrva Mīmāṁsā thought, though crude, seems to be more consistent, for their *jīva* was always bodiless, and was of the nature of consistent gypsy and nomad, which never settled at any place.

I believe that ancient Indian philosophers had asked two different questions: (1) What is reality? and (2) what is man's end or objective of life? The first was in regard to the inquiry about the cosmo-centric world, and the second was about the man the anthropocentric world. Although in the philosophy that has come down to us these two questions are mixed up. I do not think that there is any straightforward relation between them. According to the traditional Paṇḍits all our philosophical inquiry leads to the ultimate question of *mokṣa* or liberation. In fact, a scholar like Dr G.V. Tagare who with equal eminence can speak about Jaina. Buddhist or 'Brāhmaṇical' thought thinks that all such thought is basically concerned with practice leading to *mokṣa* or liberation. Like Dr Tagare in fact all traditional Paṇḍits think that every theory has the objective of *mokṣa*. I am really doubtful about it. Of course, *mokṣa* is basically and directly related to man as related to the world. But now suppose that a man who has a desire to know the reality succeeds in his desire and knows the reality. Why should such realisation lead to his liberation? To know that the nature of reality is such and such should not be necessary and sufficient condition to enable him to liberate himself. Perhaps he might be able to understand that life is without ideal, without purpose (*viphala*). But to know, for example, that fire is purposess need not lead him to the traditional concept of *mokṣa*. As a matter of fact, the concept of fruitfulness or purpose is basically related to *abhyudaya*, *śreyas* and perhaps even *preyas*, and the concept of *mokṣa* might point out to the limitation of *abhyudaya* concept. But this does not follow from our understanding the nature of *Brahman*, reality or 'world'. The concept of *mokṣa* only points out to what a man should do? What a man should strive for and what the limitations of man are in respect of his striving. In our world there are phenomena represented by the object of the verb desire or will and unless this is accepted what we ought to do does not become meaningful. In fact, in the very word *jijñāsā* the concept of will or desire is latently present. Suppose we say that everything is *pudgala* or analyse the world into categories such as substance, quality, *sāmānya*, *viśeṣa*, etc., or suppose we classify the world into *jīva-ajīva*, *dharma* or *adharma*, how would this kind of knowing lead towards *mokṣa* ? In a way it is true that to know this and to know that this is true knowing is to know our nature. It is also true that to know the nature of ourselves or *jīva* should be our object or end. But this kind of end does not seem to be the same as the end indicated by *mokṣa*, at least in the traditional sense of the term.

What I feel is that man's practice and thought process tread on independent path for sometime but after sometime they get mixed up with the result that we create a false causal process and begin to think that thought is the case of practice or *vice cersa.* Of course, there is an important reason for such mix up. It is only from selecting certain atoms of thought from practice that man creates his theories, his doctrines and philosophy. I believe that basically Jainism was an inquiry regarding the nature of truth, regarding man or the world regarding the analysis of *jīva* and *ajīva*. Of course, this enquiry must have its base in their way of life. The doctrine of *mokṣa* need not have been imposed or superimposed on this analysis of *jīva* or *ajīva,* etc. It need not have been thought that as soon as a man has the understanding of the nature of the world he attains the happiness or bliss. I do understand that the heaven of the Pūrva Mīmāṁsakas falls into the catagory of desirable and the *naraka* falls into the catagory of undesirable. And every bit of heavenly enjoyment leads to the destruction of *puṇya* and you find yourself on this earth. The concept of heavens is, therefore, the kith and kin of the concept of *preyas* and perhaps the concept of *śreyas* might also be regarded as some kind of superior *preyas.*

But when we think of *mokṣa* we go beyond the concept of *śreyas*. It is the concept of *niḥśreyas,* it is not the concept of worldly prosperity. I do not understand as to why one should superimpose the concept of worldly prosperity on *niḥśreyas.* But such things become possible because we forget to distinguish between *niḥśreyas* and *śreyas.* Perhaps the concept of *śreyas* has its origin in *kāma* (may be *dharma* and *artha* also), the concept of *niḥśreyas* on the other hand is concerned with the withering away of such *kāma.* Unfortunately a common man does not distinguish between *kāma* and *mokṣa* and starts explaining *mokṣa* in terms of *kāma* only. We, therefore, begin to feel than even *mokṣa* is some kind of desirable like paradise — a desirable at some higher level.

Perhaps this kind of understanding of *mokṣa* has cropped up or interpolated everywhere Indian thought. Why should one learn Mathematics? The annswer given is, for the attainment of *mokṣa.* Why should one do *dharma*? Again the answer is the same. Why should one marry? Of course, we are told, for attaining *mokṣa*? Why should one read *Kāmasūtra*? The answer is the same. Why should one learn grammar? The answer is again the same. Such thought, however, is the contraction of the concept of *mokṣa*. It certainly is its caricature. On account of such contraction the difference between *śreyas* and *niḥśreyas* is ignored and we start thinking that whatever we do is for the sake of *mokṣa*. I believe that in Jaina thought also this has happened, and the discussion about *mokṣa* or *jīva*s striving for *mokṣa* became important.

I do agree that Jaina contribution in the area of Syādavāda, Nayavāda, Saptabhaṅgī is very important. I also believe that Jaina analysis of *jīva* cannot be ignored. Jaina concept of *pañcāstikāya* is certainly very valuable and I do not wish to underrate their use of *tattva*s like *āsrava*, *saṁvara* and *nirjarā* in separating *jīva* from *ajīva* of *kāma* and getting *jīva* freed from bondage or *bandha* and, thus, leading it to *mokṣa*. But I believe that at least in the beginning the Jainas, like the members of any other society, were interested in the concrete *jīva*. This could have been their practical interest. Further they could have been concerned with the behaviour of this *jīva* and the interrelation of this *jīva* with other *jīva*s. I think this should explain the practical over-tones in their philosophy in respect of Ācārāṅga. This should also explain the concept of *mahāvrata*s and *aṇvrata*s and their emphasis on *ahiṁsā*, *satya*, *asteya*, *brahmacarya* and *aparigraha*. In fact, today if a Jaina citizen or *śrāvaka* is known by anything it is by these concepts and the behaviour which follows from these norms in the form of *mahāvrata*s and *aṇuvrata*s. But I need not write anything on it in the present essay. What I wish to point out is that simultaneously with the code of conduct which they developed they were confronted with the metaphysics of *jīva* and *ajīva* and were not just satisfied with the idea that a *jīva* should not be a prey to violence or that it should not get attached to worldly prosperity. Thier deliberations over the concept of *jīva*, although it may have been a product of their practical concern, developed into metaphysics, logic and epistemology. But in doing this, they somehow embarked on the mission of separating *jīva* from *karma-pudgala*s and thought that they had explored the emancipated *jīva*.

The problem before the Buddha seems to be somewhat different. He was not concerned with the soul of body of man or any living being nor was he concerned with invention of fire and the culture that basically developed from performance, of sacrifice. Like the Jaina *tīrthaṅkaras* the Buddha was also a product of Indian civilisation and culturally at least he had accepted the concept of rebirth (*punarjanma*), etc., at least this is what appears from the *Jātaka* stories. But he was basically concerned with *human misery* and the problem before him was how to get rid of this misery or *duḥkha*. His problem is pointed out in what is called the four noble truths: (1) there is misery, (2) there is emergence of misery, (which is perceived), (3) there is diagnosis of misery, and (4) there is remedy for the misery. In *Buddhacarita* there is a story of how Gautama the Buddha was kept away by his father from the worldly experience as it was predicted that he would become a recluse. When he grew up and when his father thought that he was sufficiently mature to understand the worldly matters, he was taken to the royal court. But on the way he experienced four varieties of human misery. He came across a corpse, an old man, a pauper and a beggar and to find out solution to these miseries he left home and went to Sāranāth and Gayā and finally attained Buddhahood. Dr. Ambedkar tells us, and perhaps rightly, that the story is only a myth, concocted by Buddha's followers like Aśvaghoṣa and others. This might be so. Nevertheless, the story gives us a vivid description of human miseries and their varieties. The first three varieties are natural miseries which perhaps require a metaphysical solution and the fourth is a social misery.

What flashed across the Buddha's mind at the time of enlightenment is known and expressed is language as *pratītya-samutpāda*. The whole of Buddha's life was spent in spreading the message of *pratītya-samutpāda* with all its implications. These implications are expressed in the form of *Dvādaśanidāna* and *Aṣṭāṅgamārga*. *Pratitya-samutpāda* was taken to be the formulation of the law of contingent causation. I think that this was a wrong interpretation and I shall try to understand it at some later point in this essay. But when the Buddha realised the truth that everything was misery and that it could be remedied, the problem before him was only practical and it remained practical in the early Buddhism or Theravāda. But just as the nature of *jīva* confronted the Jaina philosophers and led them to metaphysics, similarly, Buddha's problem led his followers to its theory. It brought forth a few propositions like *sarvam anityam, sarvam saṁghātam, sarvam anātmam* and *sarvam śūnyam.* It also led to theorization of *pratītya-samutpāda* and Buddhism got wrapped in the logical problems of *jāti* and *apoha.*

We do not have any direct writings of the Buddha and have to depend on oral tradition. But the Buddha seems to have said to one of his disciples that it is very difficult to grasp the meaning and implications of *pratītya-samutpāda* (in Pāli *paṭiccasamuppāo*). Although it is said that at the time of the Buddha's enlightenment he had realised, *pratītya-samutpāda*, as a key to the riddle of the universe, the development of the concept was taken into consideration in later Buddhist thought. Candrakīrti in his *Mādhyamikavṛtti* says that *pratītya-samutpāda* was variously interpreted. All the definitions given by Candrakīrti, however, have one thing in common, namely, the momentary character of events, *sarvam kṣaṇikam* or *sarvam anityam. Ityaḥ* means momentary or fleeting existence and *prati* means occurring again and again. *Pratītya-samutpāda* thus meant, coming into existence of momentary existents. Perhaps this is the minimum that is implied in the concept of *pratītya-samutpāda.* Thus, in the early development of Buddhist thought it stood for momentariness and discreteness of existents which are continously changing. Later Buddhist thought changed this concept and in the hands of Rhys Davids it became the law of 'dependent-organisation'. I shall come to the examination of this definition later, but I want to point out here that in the beginning, Lord Buddha and his followers must have thought of it as the concept of continuous change and applied the same to the concept of misery and the removal of misery. Basically, however, the problem before Buddhism, whether earlier or later, was the same. In *Dhamma Cakhappayattana sutta* Buddha says, "O Bhikkhus, misery is the prime truth, birth is misery, ailment is misery, death is misery, a relationship with the disliked is misery and the *viyoga* of the liked is also misery." Buddha does not ask the question as to *why* does misery arise in this world? He, then, in the fashion of a physician, wants to diagnose several aspects and dimensions of misery and calls them *dvādaśa-nidāna* or twelve symptoms of diagnosis. *Avidyā* is one of these twelve. *Avidyā* means ignorance. When someone says something arises out of my ignorance it does not mean that ignorance is in a straightforward sense the cause of that something, it is not a proposition of the same kind as "it arises out of circumstances" or "I am born of mother". *Avidyā* like *prajñā* is an epistemic category and consciousness is presupposed by it. As a matter of fact the development of human world is either due to *avidyā* (i.e., in some sense a belief system) or is due to *prajñā*, i.e., knowledge system through *saṁyama* and *saṁkalpa*.

In the system of 'beliefs' one finds that misery or *duḥkha* is due to *vedanā* developing into *tṛṣṇā* or blind appetites. *Avidyā* and *saṁskāra* help the continuation or growth of *tṛṣṇā*. So long as *prajñā* and *saṁyama* do not interfere there is no possibulity of *duḥkha-nirāsa*. That by which *duḥkha* is controlled is called *mārga* and consists of eight constituents: *samyak pṛṣṭi*, *saṁkalpa*, *vāk*, *karmānīta*, *ājīva*, *vyāyāma*, *smṛti* and *samādhi*. It means that misery can be controlled if the proper discipline is followed. The Buddha tells us that misery is concerned with *anityatā* and the base of this misery is *tṛṣṇā*. It is the development of *sparśa* and *vedanā* through *avidyā*, *sparśa*, *vedanā* and *tṛṣṇā* are constituent conditions of misery. *Avidyā* and *saṁskāra* are its epistemic conditions. If these epistemic conditions are changed, then our attitude towards *tṛṣṇā* can change. *Prajñā* supplies such a focus and as pointed out above this new focus is the focus of discipline or *mārga* or *magga*. The Buddha's philosophy was thus practical and was concerned with the problem of disciplined behaviour. The problem is moral or social in whatever way you understand it. The early Buddhism did not want to enter into the theoretical problem. He was showing way of life, *viśuddhimagga*.

But very soon the problem was topsy-turvied and in the hands of later Buddhist philosophers Buddhism developed into serious Buddhist philosophy. Of course, here also the philosophy starts with the concept of suffering. Suffering is due to our regarding the self as the unity of apperception. Hiriyanna rightly put it, "with the negation of self, selfish impulses necessarily disappear" (*Outlines of Indian Philosophy*, p. 147). Misery is one of the selfish impulses and it can be eradicated as soon as we know that there is no self, there is no *ātmā*. It led to the theory of *anātman*, denying any unity in any experience or process. The belief in self-identity arises out of ignorance—*ajñāna* and is removed through *prajñā*—knowledge. When the *prajñā* dawned on us the suffering would naturally be removed. This theory of *anātma* or denial of persistent self was also extended to the things and instead of unity of a thing we now had *saṁghāta* (perhaps of *sensa*). Similarly, the concept of *sāmānya* was also denied as it is something common to all particulars. Both the concepts of *dravya* and *sāmānya* or *jāti* were regarded as merely the extension of the concept of *ātman*. These concepts arise on account of our tendency to unify the discrete moments into one flow or unity. Thus, here also *pratītya-samutpāda* could not be rightly interpreted as a theory of causation. In fact, it was the causal theory that was denied by the Buddhists. But in the hands of later Buddhist philosophers, Buddhism did not remain merely a way of life it became a very serious theoretical philosophy.

Buddhism and Jainism like Pūrva Mīmāṁsā started with some practical propblems. It started in a way with presuppositions which were also the Pūrvamīmāṁsā presupposition. Pūrva Mīmāṁsā accepted *jīva* as a bodiless substance. Jainism in the beginning accepted it as a substance with body but in their aspiration to get emancipated threw away the body as if it was the snake-slough and reached the point where *jīva* was regarded as bodiless. Buddhism on the other hand started with the practical consideration of *duḥkha* and ultimately denied the concept of *ātman* or self. If *ātmān* is denied *duḥkha* also gets denied automatically.

In practice, however, Pūrva Mīmāṁsā started with the elaborate rituals connected with sacrifice. Perhaps those who did not discover the fire also had some rituals and all these rituals and customs got mixed up and could not be eliminated. Perhaps in no society rituals can be eliminated. In the present society also we practise lot of rituals. Dr Ambedkar wanted to eliminate rituals from his neo-Buddhism. But his followers brought them in by a back door. In practice, whether you are a Jaina or a Buddhist or a Vedāntin you have fallen a prey to the Mīmāṁsā doctrine of rituals. The truth of *ācāraprabhavo dharmaḥ* remains in tact. Whether it was Pūrva Mīmāṁsā, Buddhism, Jainism or Vedānta, rituals dominated their philosophy.

I have tried to give the backgroud picture of Jaina and Buddhist philosophies. In the caurse of time both these philosophies grew in various directions like banyan trees. But in the beginning they were like the saplings of 'rituals' and their problems, were rather similar to those of Pūrva Mīmāṁsa (of Brāhmaṇical variety). I am conscious that in investigating and exploring these roots I am not critical and might even be wrong. I am also aware that for investigating problems of philosophy generally, a critical approach should be adopted. But I feel that when sometimes one has to depend on interpretation of uncertain histories, and when one is concerned with the problem of discovering something, I feel, one has no alternative except being speculative. This is my justification for my speculative aberrations.

7

The Theory of Meaning in Indian Grammar System*

PHILOSOPHICAL questions of real importance were, indeed, asked in ancient India and the answers suggested by the philosophers then are still worthy of our consideration. It is necessary to remove a prejudice that is current in the West, for which theosophists, *yogīs* and religion preachers are mostly responsible, that all Indian philosophy is mystical, theological, religious and idealistic. It is, indeed, true that a philosophy of this nature did exist and dominate India. It is certainly the case that it completely overshadowed analytical philosophy, misrepresented its technical terms, and imposed its own interpretations. Again, loss of the important works on systems like Sāṁkhya and Vaiśeṣika, and incorporation of some tenets of these systems by the adherents of Vedānta, helped in creating a belief that everything that was supposed to be philosophic in India was Vedāntic or idealistic. The philosophic literature that is circulated in the West has perpetuated this belief. Thus, every notion, whether it was in politics or philosophy, mathematics or art, was identified with the so-called Absolute or *Brahman*, which in turn was thought to be of the nature of bliss, hapiness, or joy.

Ryle describes the preocccupation with the theory of meaning as the occupational disease of twentieth-century Anglo-Saxon philosophy. If so, it was also the disease of the ancient Indian philosophy, whether orthodox or otherwise. The orthodox philosophy stressed the importance of the theory of meaning for the preservation

* Modified from the lectures given in Oslo and Manchester Universities.

of the Vedas. Yāska, the eighth-century BC commentator on the Vedas, mentions one Kautsa who regarded passages in the Vedas as meaningless, because he had not bothered to know the syntax and grammar necessary to understand the archaic language of the Vedas. Yāska thus laid down the necessity of the study of language structure, which has been systematized in what is now known as the *Nirukta* literature. Soon, however, 'grammar', of which the theory of meaning was a part, began to be studied for its own sake, not simply as auxiliary to the study of the Vedas. This gave rise to the schools of Mīmāṁsā (analysis and interpretation), grammar (or language analysis), and logic.

It was only at a much later stage that philosophers recognized(!) that analytical thinking was a disease and thus found out a remedy for it. But this remedy was worse than the disease, promoting quibbles and verbal controversies. Philosophy became just a part of the Hindu dogma and the edifice of knowledge was shaken. Historically, the constant invasions from the West Asia quickened the process; the centres of learning were reduced to ashes, and the books and the libraries were destroyed. Thus, the ancient learning almost came to an end, and the new philosophy that emerged was mystical in character. The first well-known grammarian is Pāṇini, who wrote *Aṣṭādhyāyī* and who is now accepted as the father of philosophy of language and linguistics. It was he who first made use of symbols in Indian thinking and gave us what may be called an axiomatic deductive system. His grandson (?) Vyāḍi seems to have propounded a well argued theory of meaning. But his work is lost. The works that are now available are the *Vārtikas* of Kātyāyana and the *Mahābhāṣya* of Patañjali. Another linguistic philosopher, Bhartṛhari, is supposed to have written a commentary on the *Mahābhāṣya*. But that too is lost.* However, a part of his work known as *Vākpadīya*, i.e., an essay concerning the sentence and the words, has survived. But, in fact, it is mainly to two works, the *Mahābhāṣya* and the *Vākyapadīya*, that reference is made in this paper.

---

* I am told it is found now and is being published by Bhandarkar Oriental Research Institute.

Rightly or wrongly, an early Indian thinker thought that, since the world was known to us through five sense-organs, it could be classified under five classes. He distinguished between the knowing process and the object of knowledge. In the absence of any other name of termed the objects of knowledge as *śabda*, *sparśa*, *rūpa*, *rasa* and *gandha* and defined them as follows:

Śabda	=	Df	The object of hearing,
Sparśa	=	Df	The object of touching,
Rūpa	=	Df	The object of seeing,
Rasa	=	Df	The object of tasting,
Gandha	=	Df	The object of smelling,

A lot of discussion has centred round these words and it was argued whether or not these objects were eternal. Most of the discussion is based on certain confusions. Although it is irrelevant what is more important for our purpose is that these words were re-employed, as technical terms, for explaining certain important notions like language and art. *Śabda,* which was the object of hearing, was used as a unit for written or spoken language. Today it has come to mean a word, but originally it was employed to mean the language of unit which was progressively subdivided into *vākya* or sentence, *pada* or word, and *varṇa* or letter. The world was thought to be made up of five elements, viz. *śabda*, *sparśa*, *rūpa*, *rasa*, and *gandha*: but in attempting to explain it, it was reduced to one (or in some cases more) or two elements, by means of certain symbolic representation. When it was reduced to *śabda,* it was called language. It is the language which became the most powerful means of expression, and gradually people began to study the notion of language.

Normally question like 'What is the nature of language?' and 'What is it for an expression to have a meaning?' began to occupy the minds of philosophers of many different schools of thought. The logicians based their account of meaning on the consideration of single letters. They believed that the relation that exists between a word and its 'meaning' is only conventional. The words are formed arbitrarily from letters; and the letters are formed from still smaller parts. The meaning of a sentence is thus just a sum of the meanings conventionally assigned to parts which are the smaller than letters. In their theory of philosophy, these logicians can be compared roughly to the logical atomists of the present-day; but it is not their metaphysics which is of real and direct importance in the theory of meaning. This was definitely rejected by other schools of thought like Mīmāṁsā and Vedānta, though its logic and theory of meaning were accepted. It is, therefore, interesting to trace the development of logicians' theory of meaning.

No one will deny that words are symbols. But when the Indian logicians say that the meanings are conventional, they are treating letters, words, and sentences as if they were names or rather proper names. Let us take the word 'Oslo'. The logicians hold that not only is the word 'Oslo' a name of some entity, but also each letter like O, S, L, and O is the name (of a certain entity). Fortunately, however, they do not specifically insist that corresponding to each name there has to be some entity. Had they said so, the word 'Oslo' would be a queer continuation of symbols jointly and separately standing for some entities of which the symbols are names. But though such a theory does not seem to have been actually developed by the logicians, the philosophers belonging to the Mīmāṁsā school of thought did go so far; and by implication it can be asserted that the logicians subscribed to such a theory.

The logicians thought that words are the names of certain entities and the relation that exists between the *word* and its meaning is the relation that exists between a name and the *bearer of a name.* The word, in other words, denotes, and that which it denotes, is the denotatum. If it is a proper name like Henry or Devadatta, it denotes a single individual: if it is a common noun, it denotes a certain range. But in either case it denotes and does not behave in any other way.

It is, of course, true that, when we talk of the meaning of words, we do mean that the words are symbols standing in a certain relation to an entity and that the relation may be conveyed as the relation of the object and its name. A proper noun has no meaning except one given in the above sense. If a thing has two proper names, one proper name can be used as a meaning of the other proper name. It is in this sense that meanings are given in dictionaries. Similarly, just as one thing may have two names, so two or more things may have one name. It is a common noun and it behaves like, say, surname. Similarly insofar as the words are symbols, their meanings undergo changes as the usages change. The logicians, therefore, held that the relation between words and meanings are arbitrary and conventional; meanings can change and are, therefore, in some sense temporal in character.

But this is surely only one kind of meaning. The grammarians, therefore objected to the theory of meaning propounded by logicians. They distinguished sentence meaning from word meaning, a use of word from the usages of words, and pointed out that in many cases there may not all be a bearer for a name word. When we talk of the meaning of a sentence, we cannot say that a sentence is either a name or a symbol of an entity or idea. The theory of the Indian logicians, at least as it comes down to us, failed here. They simply applied the theory of word meaning to sentence. Meaning, according to them, was a relation of a name and its bearer. Therefore, the sentence which is a combination of words must also ultimately be a name. The meaning which a significant sentence has was, for logicians, only artificially given and was intrinsically arbitrary and conventional.

The philosophers of the Vyākaraṇa (Grammar) school distinguished between the meaning of a sentence and the meaning of a word. In order to aviod confusion, they used two different words to distinguish the two. Thus, they used three cardinal terms: (1) '*artha* or meaning', which stood for the meaning of the word as well as of the sentence; (2) '*vākya* or the denotatum', which stood in relation to name words; and (3) *vākyārtha* or *vākyasphoṭa* which stood for the meaning of a sentence. The meaning of a sentence, they argued, is not a list of entities standing in relation to words. Had it been so, a list of a few names such as cow, horse, man, elephant, would be a sentence. Or a mere list of words, nonsensical in nature and not having any syntax, e.g., 'A thing action the shape of a pot' would be a sentence. But, evidently, this is not so. A word in a sentence stands in a very peculiar relation to the other words, which is expressed in Sanskrit as *sākāṅkṣā*, expectant. This peculiarity of a sentential meaning is very clearly brought out by

Ryle, and it would be quite useful to see how he looks at things. Ryle writes:

> First, if every single word were a name, then a sentence composed of five words, say 'There is a prime number' would be a list of five objects named by these five words. But a list, like 'Plato, Aristotle, Aquinaas, Locke, Berkeley', is not a sentence. It says nothing true or false. A sentence, on the contrary, may say something about someone thing—which is true or false. So the words combined into a sentence at least do something jointly which is different from their severally naming and several things that they name, if they do name anything. What a sentence means is not decomposable into the set of things which the words in it stand for, if they stand for things. So the notion of having meaning is at least partly different from the notion of standing for.

It is clear that the philosophers belonging to the Vyākaraṇa school knew perfectly well that a sentence meaning and the word meanings did not belong to the same category. But at a later date, four unfortunate things happened. (1) The three words especially introduced by these philosophers were indiscriminately used. (2) The word for sentence meaning was used to convey the general idea of meaning and *eight* varieties of meanings were recognised by later grammatical philosophers. The technical word was thus indiscriminately used. (3) The word for sentence meaning itself was regarded as a name word standing either for some non-existing unreality or for the ultimate reality, viz. *Brahman*. (4) The word for meaning became the word for object.

The philosophers of the Vyākaraṇa school rightly pointed out that a sentence cannot be formed by putting several words in a machine and pressing meaning out of them just as we press oil out of oilseed. A sentence cannot be further split up into parts, without destroying the meaning of the sentence. Though words are used in a sentence, when they are so used they do not refer to their bearers. Bhartṛhari, the last great exponent of the philosophy of grammar*

* In the tradition of Pāṇini, Kātyāyana, and Patañjali.

(fifth century AD), says that even a proper name like Devadatta, when used in a sentence, does not have any meaning of its own apart from the sentence.

In recent times, the distinction between reference and sense has been much emphasized, but it can be seen that when the grammarians talked of word meaning and sentence meaning or a *vākya* and *sphoṭa,* they were essentially pointing out a distinction of the above kind.

Bhartṛhari was the last well-known philosopher in the tradition of the philosophy of grammar, and his contribution to the theory of meaning is significant. It will be worthwhile, therefore, to consider his theory in somewhat detail.

He begins his discussion by saying that *śabda* and *artha* are not different. In the very first verse in the *Vākyapadīya* he says that the *śabda* can be compared to the ocean and meaning to the waves of a sea. Just as waves are not different from the sea, similarly, *artha* is not different from *śabda.* By *śabda* is not meant the 'sound pattern' which is termed by Patañjali as the quality of *śabda*. In the second verse he further explains this point. Though they (i.e., *śabda* and *artha*) are known to be one, on account of certain peculiar nature of the meaning, they appear to be different. The meaning is not an entity, but appears to be an entity. In the 13th verse he says that rules of meanings are determined by the rules of *śabda,* i.e., how we use *śabda*. In verse 23, he talks about the *constant relation* between *śabda* and *artha*. In the 24th verse he says that (when a sentence is broken into parts) we get two kinds of words — those 'which are explanatory' and those 'which refer to something'. Verse 47 says that which is originally conceived by mind is 'put in the meaning' (i.e., perhaps meaning is the intention of the person who uses the words). These meanings, so to speak, are objectified in a sound pattern. Verse 48 tells us that the sound pattern is, however, not the real *śabda*. Verse 49 distinguishes between *sphoṭa* and sound, i.e., the meaning of the word (or the real word) and the sound (or the body of the word). The sound pattern gives us the 'meaning' as well as the sound pattern. When we use words which are explanatory, we do not refer to their 'denotata' (*abhidheya*), at least in a straightforward sense. Verses 55 and 56 tell us that meaning is different from denotation. "Every word does have power (*śakti*); but that is when the words are considered separately" (verse 56). The words do not denote entities if there are no entities corresponding to them, but it is not true that words get meanings on account of their reference to existence (verse 66). Even a word which has a reference to an entity points out a certain entity only when it is used in the nominative or possessive case. (Thus, a proper name *X* will stand for *X*, only if *X* is already existing, otherwise it would be proper name of a fictitious entity. Similarly, in the expression, the King of France, it is 'of France' which gives meaning to the expression.) He continues that though in a sense words do not exist apart from letters and a sentence apart from the words, the *avayavas* (letters and words) do not have meaning apart from the sentence. The sentence, therefore, has a meaning as a whole. That we are required to separate it into different parts is really on account of the nature of language expression. Just as a number becomes meaningful only when you take into consideration the whole series of different numbers instead of various digits, similarly though every letter or word is different, the sentence behaves as one unit when it is meaningful.

Bhartṛhari then gives us the psychological reason why we regard meaning as a kind of substance — a pseudo-substance. It is, he believes, on a mode of analogy. If there is a smell, we believe that there must be a bearer of this smell, and so we begin to think that meanings require a bearer (verse 99).

Next, he refutes the theory that the words are molecules and the letters are atoms, that a sentence is merely a collection of words, just as a cloud is a collection of moisture particles (verse 111-14). He then concludes that, apart from its meaning, language or speech is like the corpse.

The Sanskrit language has nothing resembling prepositions. But the nouns and adjectives take cases. Thus, even if a word or name is used in a sentence, it does not always mean the same thing. The meaning of a word appears differently according as it takes different case suffixes. Dividing a sentence into parts is a good trick. But, in fact, neither a language unit (*śabda*) not its meaning can be split up into parts. Again, to say that every part of speech refers to something like a proper name is also not correct. Bhartṛhari, for instance, says that it is possible to have a significant sentence, without any reference whatsover to an existent. Letters which are made up of parts do not point out anything; similarly, a sentence may become meaningful even though it may not be referring to anything that exists. Any adjective or an adjectival, or what is now known as a descriptive, phrase need not exist. The adjective follows the noun. But, if the noun does not stand for any entity, the descriptive phrase too would not denote anything. Words like *pītāmbara* and *candramauli* are illustrations. (The adjectives, however, tend to become nouns. *Pānīya* with literally means drinkable, has come to mean water; *prīyaṁvadā*, which means one who talks beautifully, has become a proper name of a lady. When, however, the adjectives become proper names, they lose their meaning.)

According to the philosophy of grammarians, the relation between language (now being translated as *śabda*) and the meaning must be permanent or constant. This led to much controversy between the logicians and the philosophers of language. It appears that the controversy is based on a certain confusion of ideas which is essentially verbal and due to several factors. In the first place, the grammarians use the word *śabda* rather loosely. It stands for the sentence as well as for the word. In fact, they had realised this difficulty and had also used two other words, *vākya* for a sentence and *pada* for a word. But their loose use of the word *śabda* subjected then to a very severe criticism from the logic school. But, it can certainly be said that, while criticising the grammarians, the logicians have never cared to understand the distinction which the grammarians have drawn between the word meaning and the sentence meaning and between the word symbol and *śabda*. *Śabda* is for a grammarian language unit: and the 'meaning' is used only in relation to 'sentence' by the grammarians. It is, therefore, necessary to note that, when the grammarians say that the relation between *śabda* and its meaning is constant, they are not ignorant of the fact that the relation between the word symbol and its bearer is conventional, and as the usages change, the meaning of word symbols also change. It appears that, like the logicians, the grammarians also hold, that the language is essentially symbolic and that symbols in themselves have no meaning. The grammarians also make a distinction between natural symbols like 'cow' and the artificial symbols like *a*, *b*, *c*, *d*. But whether a symbol is natural or artificial, it is still a symbol and that it would still be possible to use another symbol instead. The different synonyms suggest this. In the *Mahābhāṣya*, a treatise on the foundation of language and grammar, Patañjali himself says this in unequivocal terms. "When a son is born, the parents name him Devadatta. The name itself does not mean anything. Its use gives it a meaning. Other persons also begin to use it and the name begins to point a certain form of flesh and blood." Therefore, to discard the theory of the grammarians that the relation that exists between *śabda* and meaning is constant on the ground that word symbols are conventionally given, does not appear to be sound.

What, then, is the sense in which the relation between *śabda* and its meaning is constant? There are two things to be noted here. The first is that the grammarians distinguish between *śabda* and its sound pattern. The sound pattern is called the quality of *śabda*. It is this sound pattern which takes the form of a symbol. If the sound pattern is distinguished from *śabda*, what does *śabda* stand for? Secondly, though the grammarians talk the language of relations, they make it clear that there are no two entities, *śabda* and *artha* (or meaning), and a relation *R* between them. *Śabda,* then, cannot be distinguished from meaning, and meaning is not the name of any entity. *Śabda* and meaning, then stand for *operations*, and nothing else. Though it is convenient to distinguish between *śabda* and its meaning, it is just a 'trick' or, to quote Bhartr̥hari, a 'tyranny' of language. It will be interesting to translate here a passage from Patañjali, "How do we know that *śabda* and its meaning are constantly related?" "From what appears in the world (i.e., on account of its use, practice or employment),we do not try to create words; we only employ words without distinguishing them from meaning. When the means and the end are different, we get the meaning and try to utilise it for achieving an end. A person who works with a pot goes to the house of a pot-maker, and says: 'Prepare a pot; I want to make use of it.' Words cannot be manufactured in the same way by a grammarian to be used by someone else. The meaning, words, and their use are indistinguishable. It appears that to regard meaning as a separable entity or the name of an entity is nonsense, once you distinguish between the sound pattern and *śabda*." And, though it cannot be said whether the theory of meanings held by the grammarians is correct, it appears to be full of possibilities.

This true nature of *śabda* (i.e., the meaning) is called by the grammarians *sphoṭa*. The theory was, so it is said, developed by Vyāḍi, in his work called *saṁgraha*. But, unfortunately, this work is lost. Patañjali uses the word *sphoṭa* only once, but since it is not a synonym of *artha*, people doubt whether Patañjali used it in the sense of meaning. There is, however, evidence in Bhartṛhari that he used it to convey the sense of meaning.

Let us summarize our results. The grammarians made a distinction between meaning of words and meaning of a sentence. Words and their meanings stand in most cases in a relation of name and the correspoding entity, and such relation is not meaning in strict sense of the term. When the words form part of a sentence, they play a different role; it is the sentence as a whole which is meaningful. Such a meaningful unit of language is indistinguishable from meaning. Neither language nor its meaning is an entity. They are simply operations.

Such a theory of meaning which is technically known as the theory of *sphoṭa* was, however, subjected to severe attack by every other school of thought. We have seen that the logicians' attack was really based on certain misconceptions and we need not consider it again. But the attack of Mīmāṁsakas was two-fold. In the first place, they quoted from scriptures, the meaning of which is really ambiguous. Secondly, they asked a question about the word *sphoṭa* or meaning. There must be an entity corresponding to each word. Thus, they thought. So if the *sphoṭa* was to be meaningful, there has to be corresponding entity. As Kumārila Bhaṭṭa suggested, if we accept *sphoṭa* we are accepting the existence of *sphoṭa* (This, of course, involves an ontological fallacy). Some held that since there cannot be any corresponding entity, the concept of *sphoṭa* is meaningless. (They perhaps thought that *sphoṭa* was different from 'meaning' and was mysterious in character.) Śrīdhara held that like the flower in the sky the concept of *sphoṭa* is improper. The

Vedāntins went a step ahead. They accepted the concept of *sphoṭa* and also the logic of Mīmāṁsā. Thus they said that *sphoṭa* was identical with the Absolute. The theory of meaning propounded by the grammarians was thus given its death blow.

It was really unfortunate for Indian philosophy that the theory of meaning proposed by the grammarians was thoroughly misunderstood and subjected to severe criticism and was ultimately discarded under the influence of Mīmāṁsā and Vedānta. For it appears that the grammarians made a substantial contribution to the theory of meaning, though naturally one cannot be sure whether they conclusively settled the issue.

8

The Concepts of Duḥkha, Tṛṣṇā and Vaira as found in Dhammapada

TODAY Buddhism has become a very rich scholastic philosophy. This is perhaps due to the fact that it had to fight out orthodox philosophies of India like Pūrva Mīmāṁsā, Advaita Vedānta, Sāṁkhya and Nyāya-Vaiśeṣika. But, it is also due to the fact that great logicians, metaphysicians and Sanskrit Paṇḍits like Diṅnāga, Dharmakīrti, Nāgārjuna, Asaṅga, Vasubandhu, Dharmottara, etc., embraced Buddhism and created methodology, logic and metyaphysics which could potently fight out the orthodox schools of India on the one hand and Jainism on the other. Nevertheless, it must be acknowledged that Buddhism started with certain codes and prescriptions of conduct, what men ought to and ought not to do, what is generally beneficial to man and what is not. Although I have used the word 'code' in the above sentence, in the first stage, this code or canonization was only oral; perhaps for a very long time the code of these practices remained only oral, and must have arisen from what Lord Buddha had said along with certain parables or stories from time to time. We do not have any direct writings of Buddha. We have only to depend on oral tradition,[1] which of course, is rich with truths. All these sayings were ultimately developed and systematised into Buddhist theory.

These prescriptions and parables are found in different Buddhist literature, *Tripiṭaka* being traditionally the earliest. Of these

1. That the tradition should be only oral is not Buddhist speciality. All our traditions were originally oral only.

Tripiṭakas, *Dhammapada* is a very small part of what is known as *Suttapiṭaka*. But even then *Dhammapada* has become extremely important both from the point of view of the theory and practice of Buddhism. All this early literature is in Pāli. But now we also find that there are Prakrit, Burmese, Tibetan and Chinese versions of *Dhammapada*. In addition, an hybrid version of *Dhammapada* is also found. Pāli *Dhammapada* is a collection of 423 *gāthās*. Some of them, of course, find place in the other versions of *Dhammapada*, but some of them are also missing from other versions. These *gāthās* must have been instantiated with certain parables and stories. This is clearly seen from the Chinese version of *Dhammapada* which abounds in such parables. However, it is possible that in oral tradition of India each prescription was substantiated by some stories. *Jātaka*, for example, is one such book. But several stories are found in *Majjhima Nikāya* and such other literature.

While studying *Dhammapada* some forty years back, I had a feeling that early Buddhism, stated a problem which was essentially social and which in a way was not dwelt upon by other schools of thought. I also had come to the conclusion that Buddhism aimed at educating culturally the common man keeping before him the aim of happiness and prosperity. It may be remembered that *bahujanasukhāya bahujanahitāya* is a Buddhist motto. No other philosophy of Indian origin seems to have tackled the social problem, the Buddhist way and through rational approach. Buddhist aphorism, *saṁghaṃ saraṇaṃ gachhāmi* is a clear indication that we must submit to the will of the group of wise men, the will of *saṁgha*. Buddhism did prescribe individual discipline; but that was because the individual discipline was a necessary element in social behaviour.

The Buddhists begin their enquiry with *duḥkha* or misery. It may be borne in mind that it is not 'my' misery but the human misery with which they are concerned. Sāṁkhya also talks of misery. It is not material to me which is the earlier doctrine. But I must point out that they are two different doctrines. Buddhism, talks of *duḥkha* in terms of relation between one man and another. The *gāthā* in the *Dhammapada* (=*Dhp*) clearly indicates this:

nahi verena verāni sāmmantidha kudacanaṃ |
averena ca sammanti esa dhammo sanantano | |

—*Dhp*, 5

Sāṁkhya talks of *duḥkhatraya* — *duḥkhatrayābhighātāt jijñāsā tadabhighātake hetau.*

The *vaira* or enmity cannot exist between a man and an animal. It clearly shows a relationship between man and man. Buddhism also talks of *karuṇā* which is evidently different from individual *duḥkha* but is nevertheless a kind of *duḥkha*. It is definitely a state of mind which has sadness as an element. It mentions *ahiṁsā*[2] in the *pañcaśīla* but there it does not necessarily indicate an attitude between man and man. The relation between man and animal may also be indicated by this.

Dhammapada means 'a step of *dhamma*'. It is concerned with the diognosis of (human) nature, the misery and how to get over it. What kind of misery or *duḥkha*, was in the mind of Lord Buddha? *Duḥkha* is an ambiguous word. It means both physical pain and misery. That which cannot be destroyed has to be borne by us. This is the case with the physical calamities or pains. But this is not necessarily so with miseries which are mental and social.

Lord Buddha also talks of *sukha*. He says:

upasanto sukhaṃ seti hitvā jayaparājayaṃ —*Dhp*, 201

susukhaṃ bata jivāma yesaṃ no natthi kiṃcanaṃ

—*Ibid.*, 200

We who have nothing, how *happily* do we live! Thus, he not only talks of *duḥkha* but also talks of *sukha*. It is from this point of view what he calls *dvādaśa nidāna* has to be looked at.

Let us see how Buddha formulated the problem of *duḥkha* and built up his theory of *dvādaśa nidāna*. The word *duḥkha* is

2. That early Buddhism should not mention the word *ahiṁsā* except once in *Dhammapada* verse is certainly strange enough. But in order to distinguish themselves from the Jainas and the Hindus of the cult of *Gītā* and Yoga the Buddhists must have sustained themselves from using it.

ambiguously used. As pointed out above it may mean pain or it may mean misery. In the story of Gautama Buddha, when he went from his palace to the court, he came across an old man, a man suffering with disease and a dead body. Perhaps, some of these *duḥkha*s can be classified under pain and are individual *duḥkha*s. But when one begins to talk of misery one also transcends the individuality of *duḥkha*s and considers them in social context. For whether conscious or unconscious, misery presupposes a certain communication amongst men. It also presupposes self-consciousness and awareness of man's suffering. This misery, again, may be of two types. Suppose *A* is prosperous and *B* is jealous of *A*'s prosperity. Here is a situation where we will find that *B*'s misery is due to *A*'s properity and *B*'s knowledge of *A*'s prosperity. What our seers have enumerated under the category *saḍripu* — *kāma*, *krodha*, *moha*, *lobha*, *mada*, *matsara* — these *duhkha*s (or the generatiors of the *duḥkha*s) can be classified under the first. But all these *duḥkha*s will, of course, be social. This is also the case when we want something but do not get it.

There will be another category of *duḥkha*s also. *A* is in misery and *B* notices this misery. Suppose *A* is starving and *B* is unhappy on the account; *B*'s unhappiness is due to sympathy for *A*. *B*'s misery is of a different kind, different order. It is dependent upon and generated from *A*'s misery. Such misery is called *karuṇā*. *Karuṇā* is a cousin of misery. There is inbuilt sadness in it. There is indeed a difference between *karuṇa* and misery that arises through *kāma*, *krodha*, *lobha*, *moha*, *mada*, *matsara*, etc. *Karuṇā* has strength to reduce misery, to remove the misery of others. *Karuṇā* also presupposes certain order of self-consciousness. But this order of self-consciousness is far higher than, and different from the self-consciousness which is required when man is under the spell of *kāma*, *krodha*, *lobha*, or even fear. Unlike *karuṇā*, the misery arising out of jealousy, etc., increases misery. But both these require a social context and it can be seen from the context of sermons and parables that Buddha definitely had social misery in his mind. Buddha's problem of *duḥkha*, therefore, is of a different kind from the one about which one talks in Sāṁkhya philosophy. Sāṁkhya says, *duḥkhatrayābhighātāt jijñāsā tadabhighātake hetau*. What are these *duḥkhatraya*s? They are *ādhibhautika*, *ādhidaivika* and *ādhyātmitka*. In a sense, they also have a social context. For man is a social being. But the social context of these miseries does not seem to have been taken notice of, by the Sāṁkhya system. That is why Sāṁkhya talks of *kaivalya* or loneliness. It is individualistic and having no social significance. Buddha does not talk of such purely individualistic *duḥkha*s. Of course, in a way all our social *duḥkha*s are *ādhyātmika duḥkha*s, they are concerned with our awareness and have a reference outside the concerned individual. But sometimes *ādhyātmika duḥkha*s seem to be projected outside this world. The *duḥkha*s about which Buddha talks are concerned with this world, concerned with society. This is clear from *Dhammapada* verses 197, 198, 200 and 201.

It is very interesting to see how Buddha talks of *duḥkha* or misery in *Dhammapada*. He says, "O, Bhikkhu, misery is a prime truth, birth is misery, ailment is misery, death is misery. A relationship with disliked is misery, and the *viyoga* of the liked is also misery." But Buddha does not ask the question as to why misery arises in this world, or what the cause of misery is. In the fashion of a physician he wants to diagnose several aspects or dimensions of misery and calls them *dvādaśa nidāna*. In fact, Buddha does not, like Mrs. Rhys Davids, say that *pratītya-samutpāda* was the law of causation. I would like to point out that when Buddha talks of *dvādaśa nidāna*, he is, in fact, talking of twelve symptoms. *Nidāna* is a medical term for diagnosis. *Avidyā*, for example, is one of these twelve. We have seen that Buddha says that misery arises due to *avidyā*. *Avidyā* means ignorance. It is one of the necessary conditions for the manifestation of misery. (It also develops through *saṁskāra*, i.e., through culture.) *Avidyā*, it must be remembered is an epistemic category. It is not a negation of knowledge. Awareness is as much implied in *avidyā* as it is in *prajñā*. As a matter of fact the whole development of the human world is two-fold. Either it develops through *avidyā*, i.e., through belief system or it is developed through *prajñā*, i.e., through knowledge system and through *saṁyama*, i.e., through control and *saṁkalpa*, i.e., determination. As we have seen earlier, Buddha refers to both these epistemic concepts, *avidyā* and *prajña*, and also to the concepts of *saṁyama* (control) and *saṁkalpa* (determination).

Why does misery arise? The basic answer is, because man has *vedanā* developing into *tṛṣṇā* (blind appetites); *avidyā* and *saṁskāra* help the continuation of growth of this *tṛṣṇā*. For so long as human being is living and so long as he is not controlled rationally by *prajñā* and by *saṁyama*, there is no possibility of *duḥkha-nāśa* or *sukha* or *nirvāṇa*; for there would be neither *tṛṣṇā-kṣaya* nor *tṛṣṇā-nāśa*. Buddha in verses 190, 191, and 192 talks of four noble truths. Two of them are concerned with misery itself. *Duḥkha* and *duḥkha-samudaya*, and the remaining two are concerned with control of *duḥkha* and the eight-fold path (*aṣṭāṅgika-mārga)* by which the *duḥkha* can be controlled. This path of control of *duḥkha* is called *mārga* and consists of eight constituents, proper reason (*samyak prajñā*), proper determination (*samyak saṁkalpa*), proper speech (*vāc*), proper action (*karmānta*) proper *ājīva*, proper *vyāyāma*, proper *smṛti* and proper *samādhi*. It means that misery can be controlled if one follows proper discipline. Buddha also tells us here that misery is concerned with transitoriness or *anityatā*. The base of misery is, *tṛṣṇā*. It is the development of *sparśa* and *vedanā*, through *avidyā*. *Sparśa*, *vedanā* and *tṛṣṇā* (partly) are the constituent conditions of misery. *Avidyā* and *saṁskāra* are its epistemic conditions. *Prajñā* supplies such a focus. The *vedanā* becomes *tṛṣṇā*. It takes the form of enmity. It arises in our blind desire to have more and more.[3]

Buddha tells us that *sparśa* and *vedanā* are two important concepts which cannot be got rid of if a man is living. He is bound to have sensation and feelings. But very soon these sensations and feelings take the form of appetites and desires and attachment. Through all these, man develops a world of his own. He wants to get rid of miseries; but what happens is exactly the opposite, *tṛṣṇā* starts controlling the man and once this happens, instead of getting rid of miseries, he gets more and more involved in miseries. The only way, therefore, to get rid of miseries is through the *aṣṭāṇgika-mārga*, the eight-fold path. This leads to peace. But rational efforts

---

3. It is the same appetite which has developed into Imperialism. Man wants to preserve his mental empire everywhere and so unless one becomes mentally anti-imperialist one cannot get over the misery which in social sphere takes the form of *vaira* or enmity.

have to be made in every respect in order to be on the right track. Instead of *avidyā* controlling one's feelings, one must now be controlled by *prajñā*. Instead of *saṁskāra*, you must now have *saṁkalpa,* i.e., will to do. You must not only have the will, you must also speak it out and communicate it to others. It must also develop into action. It must continue throughout your life. This must be like an exercise. This must be like a memory. This must be like a *samādhi*. Only then can the social misery be controlled.

Although Buddha talks of twelve-fold diagnosis of *duḥkha*, to my mind three of them *sparśa*, *vedanā* and *tṛṣṇā* as pointed out above, are basic. In fact, the only difference between *sparśa* and *vedanā* on the one hand and *tṛṣṇā* on the other is that *tṛṣṇā* gives us not just a fact of experience but a tendency to have *vedanā* or *sparśa*. *Tṛṣṇā* indicates a tendency, a disposition, manifesting itself from time to time, of a certain kind of feeling, of our not having something or others having something. On account of *avidyā* and *saṁskāra*, this concept of our owning or possessing something develops. One starts having a fixed idea of possessing something and this is what is called *āsakti*, this is also *parigraha*. This naturally requires an epistemic state. The person who has *vedanā* would be conscious of what he wants and also conscious of what others should not have and he alone should have. But this is not rational awareness. It is blind and to indicate this Buddha brings in the (epistemic) factors of *avidyā*. This tendency develops and becomes complex on account of the social habit which is called *saṁskāra*. *Sparśa*, the sensation and *vedanā* the feeling thus get transformed into emotional dispositions and tendencies. And if these dispositions and tendencies are to be got rid of, one must know that the basic *sparśa* or *vedanā* cannot be got rid of. It can only be controlled and this control must also have awareness as a constituent. But such an awareness will be rational awareness. Buddha, therefore, brings in the factors of *saṁyama* and *prajñā*. These are again the epistemic factors though of a different kind. It must be remembered that *saṁyama* is also determined by *prajñā*. And when *saṁyama* plays its part, although the *sparśa* and *vedanā* have developed into *tṛṣṇā* due to *avidyā*, *tṛṣṇā* starts withering away. But for this withering away, one more epistemic factor has to be necessarily thought of. And this is the factor of 'will' which is at the back of *saṁyama*. This 'will' is indicated in Buddhist theory by *saṁkalpa*. So just as through *avidyā* and *saṁskāra*, *sparśa* and *vedanā* grow into *tṛṣṇā*, similarly through *prajñā* and *saṁkalpa*, *saṁyama* is established and it leads to the decay of *tṛṣṇā*. Thus, when *tṛṣṇā* decays although the basic *sparśa* and *vedanā* remain, they do not develop into hate of others and selfishness for oneself. Of course, this *saṁkalpa* cannot merely remain as *saṁkalpa*, it has to be brought into practice, it has to be expressed, it is to be practised with devotion as an exercise, it has to be continuously remembered. Because of this Buddha also talks of *vācā*, *karmānta*, *ājīva*, *vyāyāma*, *smṛti* and *samādhi*. Just as *dvādaśa-nidāna* gives us the diagnosis of *duḥkha*, similarly *aṣṭāṅgika-mārga* gives us the steps in the cure of the *tṛṣṇā* or *duḥkha* itself.

Let us begin with the concept of *vaira* or social misery. How is it to be understood? First, it is a relation between two or more terms. Secondly, the terms of this relation must necessarily be men, that is, self-conscious beings. There cannot exist a relation of *vaira* between two trees or two animals other than men. Again, this relation though asymmetrical in logic appears symmetrical in practice, perhaps due to *ajñāna*. That is, if there is a relation of *vaira* between *A* and *B*, then the counter-relation between *B* and *A* will also usually be the relation of *vaira*. So in practice, i.e., in human world it would not be one-sided necessarily. For if *A* has a relation of *vaira* with *B*, then in this human world it would be usually found that *B* has also the same relation with *A*. That such a relation must naturally be between two self-conscious beings is clearly indicated in the very first verse of Pāli *Dhammapada*.[4] It points out this unambiguously when it says that mind is the source of all human attitudes and action. 'It persues man's behaviour and generates *duhkha* in the same way as a wheel of a cart follows the steps of an ox.'

Buddha's solution to the problem of *vaira* has also to be understood properly. Buddha wants to tell us that we should recognise that if *A* has enmity with *B* it is not necessary that *B* should have enmity with *A*. In fact, it is a recognition of this fact which is going to reduce or abolish enmity altogether and bring

4. *Manopubbaṅgamā dhammā*. . . etc. *Dhammapada* 1.

about peace. The fifth verse in *Dhammapada* is very eloquent in this regard. It says, enmity does not end enmity. It is the non-enmity on the part of one which would end enmity.

It is against this concept or tendency of *vaira* or enmity that Gautama the Buddha is protesting or reacting. He is pleading for *avaira* (or *avera* in Pāli). 'The *vaira* cannot end *vaira*' it can be ended only with *avaira*. And this is possible because, as a matter of fact, *vaira* is not a symmetrical relation. *Vaira* seems to be the psychological or natural tendency, *avaira* seems to be the human answer to it. In *Dhammapada* it is clearly stated that those who do not give abode to such thoughts as 'he has abused me', 'he has beaten me', 'he has conquered me' from them the *vaira* withers away. In *Tripiṭaka* there is a story of the people from two (different) *gaṇarājya*s; one of them was Śakya *gaṇarājya*. A dispute had arisen between the kingdoms on the question of the right to own, possess or use some river water. The dispute grew so intense that almost every man and woman on each side appeared on the scene with the determination to exterminate the other. Hearing about the dispute Lord Buddha appeared on the scene and said. "Can the fight between you bring peace to this holy land? Will your problem be settled if you report to fight? The waters of the river are for the use of both. If you start quarrelling about the river waters, you will only kill one another and no one will get the water for which you are quarrelling?" It is only when by some sustained thought you get over the concept of *vaira* and refuse to quarrel then alone the quarrel comes to end. If there is a quarrel or *vaira* between *A* and *B* then both *A* and *B* must give up *vaira*. If this is not possible then wisdom must dawn either on *A* or on *B*. Then *vaira* would be futile. In such a case, the situation would be very interesting: '*A* wants to quarrel, but *B* does not want to.' He would not just submit to the other as the *kapota* submitted to *śyena* in the *Mahābhārata* story. He would now 'fight' with non-violent means. He would insist on what is today known as *satyāgraha*. That *vaira* does not end *vaira*, is *satya*, an eternal truth and one has to insist on it. The teaching of *Dhammapada* was not only the teaching of Buddha, it was also the teaching of Christ and Gandhi, if the import of this teaching is properly understood. If somebody slaps you on one cheek, give him the other, Christ said. This was certainly not a case of cowardice or weakness; this was a case of strength. Gandhiji did the same thing. When he was awakening the Indian masses he asked the revolutionaries whether their handgrenades or revolvers, could bring about freedom and peace to India. Ultimately peace comes by converting others' heart. This was the message of Buddha when he said.

> *nahi verena verāni sammantiha kudācanaṃ* ।
> *averena ca sammanti esa dhammo sanantano* ॥

What Gandhiji called, *satya* was for Buddha the *dhamma*, then human nature.

Lord Buddha talks of *sukha* or happiness. He says,

> One who has given up *vaira* can happily live amongst those who are still inhaling the concept of *vaira*. How happy all of them would be if all of them had given up the concept of vaira.
>
> — *Dhammapada*, 197-201

Although *avaira*, non-enmity has to be distinguished from *ahiṁsā* or non-violence, the basic concept of affection or kindness must be at the back of both *ahiṁsā* and *avaira*. That is why Buddha, when he talks of *pañcaśīla,* talks of *ahiṁsā*. It is the basic element in every individual and has a potentiality to end enmity. But Buddha's philosophy seems to be basically concerned with human relations. This is very clearly seen if we try to understand the verses 203 and 204 in *Dhammapada*. In 204, he says health is the great gain, satisfaction is the great wealth, trust is the great relation (of binding one man to another) and *nirvāṇa*, i.e., complete extinction is the greatest happiness. Now one can easily see that barring health, everything else is really of social nature. Both in the hands Jñāneśvara and Gandhi the concept of *ahiṁsā* is magnified. Jñāneśvara, for example, says: *āni jagāciyā sukhoddeśe kāyāvācā mānase, rāhatane te ahiṁse, rūpa jāṇa*. But Buddha does not seem to philosophise this concept of *ahiṁsā*.[5]

5. It may be interesting to contrast the concept of *vaira* with that of violence (*hiṁsā*). *Hiṁsā*, too, requires two beings such that one is the agent and the other is acted on. It is possible that the *vaira* may end

All *duḥkhas*, we have seen, are basically mental and because they are mental, and belong to the human world, it is possible to get rid of them. The *duḥkhas* originate in relation of one man to another. They arise from my reaction to what others have and what I do not have. It is clearly indicated in the 3rd and 4th verse of *Dhammapada — akochhi maṃ avadhi maṃ ajini maṃ ahāsi me.* So long as one has an ill-will towards others, one is not going to get rid of *duḥkhas*. But if we are able to control them, man's *duhkha* can whither away.

ye taṃ no upanahyanti vairaṃ tesu upasammati. (*Dhp*, 4)

One who does not give abode to such thoughts as 'the other has abused me', 'the other has beaten me', 'the other has conquered me', alone can get rid of the *vaira*. Thus the *duḥkha* which arises in human mind always arises in contrast with others' state of affairs. It is a relationship of me with others and, therefore, the *duḥkha* which Buddha talks of is a social evil, social *duḥkha*. This *duḥkha* is not of the nature of pain, it is of the nature of *vaira* or hatred. *Sparśa* and *vedanā* which have already grow into *tṛṣṇā* take the form of *vaira* when one finds that one does not have what one wants whereas others have it. The problem of *duḥkha* which Buddha raises thus belongs to the human world. Buddha thinks that if I know that my life itself is transitory and that I would not be able to possess anything beyond a certain time I would easily understand that if somebody hated me it did not mean that I should hate him too. So long as I begin to hate somebody when he hates me, the hate grows, the hatred grows. When it dawns on me that I need not hate somebody when he hates me, the hate decays and ultimately vanishes. Recognition of this is the recognition of the fact that *X* hates *Y* is not symmetrical relationship, that is, the counter relation. '*Y* hates *X*' need not necessarily be true. And that which is not

---

in *hiṁsā*. But *vaira* is a mental relation where both the relata of the relation have capacity to be agents. Each one can be violent to the other. Further this violence is also due to well developed self-conscious act, although it may not be desirable. If an animal reacts to a certain action by man and kills him even then the situation cannot be regarded as that of *vaira*. *Vaira* further requires a prolonged trendency to behave in a particular way towards each other.

necessarily true can and has to be realised. One must also know that the opposite of hatred, (for example, friendship) is a symmetrical relation. If I am a friend of *B* there cannot be a friendship between me and *B* unless *B* is also my friend. So the only solution for the elimination of *vaira* is the inculcation of friendship. Friendship also requires awareness as a constituent. But this awareness is not of the nature of *avidyā*. It is a conscious awareness, not a blind one. *Duḥkha* in human world thus can be got rid of only by invoking friendship, only by invoking love of others, only by compassion for others, for other's misery, and not by hatred. One can easily see that this message of Buddha is very pregnant with truth even today.

Today we are on the brink of destruction. Each one is living in the shadow of atom-bomb. Great powers are manufacturing atom-bomb and common man has to live continuously in an atmosphere of fear generated by the atom-bomb. How is this problem going to be solved? Is it going to be solved by creating more atom-bombs? If one party wins and the other destroyed, will the problem be over? The answer is no. The great Mahābhārata war is an instance of it. Pāṇḍavas and Kauravas fought this great war to become the rulers of Hastināpur. What happened in the end? Only five Pāṇḍavas, Draupadī and Subhadrā remained on Pāṇḍavas' side and Dhṛtarāṣṭra and Gāndhārī remained on Kauravas' side. Pāṇḍavas could not even rule over the people over whom they wanted to rule. Lord Buddha very correctly says:

jayaṃ vairaṃ pasavati dukkhaṃ seti parājito ।
upasanto sukhaṃ seti hitvā jayaparājayaṃ ॥ —*Dhp*, 201

Victory gives rise to *vaira*. The man defeated sleeps in agony or misery. It is only one who has gone beyond victory or defeat can sleep happily. The story of Aṅgulimāla is very relevant in the context wherc Buddha proves that love, fearlessness and absence of enmity can alone change the world. This is the only solution to the world problem. "Only one who is able to transcend the concept of victory or defeat can reach the State of happiness and perfect peace." (*Dhp*, 179 and 291).

It is of significance here that after discussing the concepts of *duḥkha* and *sukha*, Buddha also gives the criterion for deciding which is a good act and which is a bad act. According to him, if the action does not lead to repentance or lamentation then that action can be regarded as good. It is certain that this criterion is also social, and it is forgetting of this criterion which has brought about misery today even in international sphere. Let us take the case of atom-bombing Hiroshima and Nagasaki. Perhaps, at the time of bombing the Americans were not aware of what they were doing, but after seeing the havoc that had taken place even they must have been shocked. They must have had repentance and would lament for what they had done. Thus, bombing with atom-bomb would never be justified.

According to Buddha the misery or *duḥkha*, the basic truth, has several constituents. First as suggested above it is mental, i.e., belongs to the human world. Naturally, that which belongs to the human world must be of the nature of correlation between two or more human beings or it might be a correlation between the natural world and the human beings. To me it appears that the concepts of *sparśa* (and *vedanā*) suggest this contact. *Sparśa* gives us the relationship of either man or the natural world to human beings. It suggests a sensation of some kind of cognising element which brings about this contact. But the *sparśa* does not merely remain *sparśa*, it evolves into some kind of feeling which is suggested by the word *vedanā*. Both *sparśa* and *vedanā* have epistemic element in them and this is very clearly stated in *Dhammapada*, when it is pointed out that all miseries are *mānasika* or mental. This, of course, means that miseries may be all epistemic or they may arise due to interaction with natural things although epistemic elements would be their accompaniment. But if *vedanā* had been the only element in misery then it would have been only momentary. It should in fact be momentary. But due to its epistemic nature, that is due to *avidyā* it appears to be continuous and grows in the fashion of foetus. This *vedanā* takes the form of appetite and a blind desire to get more and more. It is not just one *vedanā* which controls human beings, it is *vedanā-vaipulya*, it is the multitude of *vedanā*, which gives us a feeling of length in time and is the beginning of the problem. Although this is of the nature of misery, man has a desire to possess it. It is colourful, it is tasteful and man feels a strong aptitude to have it. This element is called *āsakti*. Jainas call it *parigraha*. But what is important to understand is that all these are element of ego. The ego itself is of the nature of epistemy and on account of the feeling of continuation the ego begins to act as something permanent. My identity is marked by a continuity in time, and my ego becomes a proto-universe. If these are number of men then naturally their different aptitudes will determine the relation amongst them and the most dominant ego will rule. This concept of ego is called *ātman* and the Buddhists have tried to disown the *ātman* by bringing in the concept of impermanence — *anityatā* — *kṣaṇikatā*. But the fact is that a human being is continuously under the epistemic spell which creates an impression that the ego is constant and our desires are also constant. Thus, in this pseudo constant-world the *sparśa* and *vedanā* tend to become continuous and 'persecute'. The continuous tendency that I should have something is suggested by the word *tanhā* or *tṛṣṇā* and, therefore, it would be adequate to say that our miseries in which we get lost have their origin in, *tṛṣṇā*. This tendency of *tṛṣṇā* must have been called 'interest' sometimes , and each individual may have his own interest. If the interests are conflicting then sometimes it may take the form of violence or at least enmity — *vaira*. If the self-interest becomes a common interest the it would result in friendship or *maitrī*. This common interest may also be due to two things. It may become a more developed *tṛṣṇā*, not of one man but of group, one may remember the word *mamatā* in *Bhagavad Gītā*. In that case the nature of misery would remain as it is. Or one may transcend one's ego and look to others' misery with compassion and sympathy. This would take the form of *karuṇā*. *Karuṇā* itself is like misery but it has capacity to make others' misery bearable and reduce one's own misery also. It is a recognition of the fact that there are other beings. When this dawns on man he has already transcended the selfish universe and is now looking at the universe from objective point of view. This is again due to awareness. But this awareness is of a different kind. It is no more *avidyā*, it is now *vidyā* or *prajñā*. When *prajñā* dawns on us, one begins to look on *tṛṣṇā*, *vedanā* and *sparśa* in a different way. The feeling that I should want more and more no longer exists. I am not controlled by the appetites; *prajñā* now begins to control the appetites. This is what is called *saṁyama*. That something has to be controlled gives us one more factor in the analysis, the factor of *saṃkalpa*. There is a determination to do something. Without such determination the *tṛṣṇā* cannot be reduced to mere *vedanā* which *ipso facto* must continue all the while with its temporal length reduced to a point. One cannot get rid of *vedanā* but one can get rid of *tṛṣṇā*. To be get rid of *tṛṣṇā* is to able to be get rid of *duḥkha*, to be able to get rid of *vaira* (enmity), the cause of social misery. This removes the multiplicity (or *vaipulya*) or the attachment of ours to the things. *Prajñā* removes this *āsakti* or attachment.

In Chinese version of *Dhammapada*, there is a story of a King and Lord Buddha. I would like to end my paper with that story. Once upon a time there was a brāhmaṇa King. To-miseay, by name. The King thought that by distributing the precious treasure to people he would be able to remove their misery and so he invited them to his court. He asked each one of them to take handful of precious stones. The king had forgotten that the worldly wealth was of the nature of attachment and was the very embodiment of misery. Lord Buddha thought that it was necessary to make the King understand the shortcoming of such kind of distribution. Lord Buddha assumed the form of a *brahmacārin* and went to the spot. The King gave him due respect and requested him to ask whatever he wanted. The *brahmacārin* said, he had a desire to build a house (He had a *vedanā* for wealth) and, therefore, he wanted a few jewels. The king said that he could gladly take them. The *brahmacārin* took a few jewels, went a few steps but came back and put the jewels back on the heap. The king asked him as to why he did it. The *brahmacārin* replied. "O King, this handful is indeed enough to enable me to build a house. But if I build a house, I would also want to have a wife and then these jewels would not be enough". (The *vedanā* is now getting multiplied into *tṛṣṇā*). On this the King asked him to take a few more jewels. The *brahmacārin* took more jewels, again went seven steps and came back and put the jewels on the heap. The king again enquired as to why he did so, Lord Buddha in the form of *brahmacārin* replied, "These might be enough to provide me with house and wife, but would not be sufficient for me to maintain the house-hold." King on this asked him to take some more treasure. *Brahmacārin* accepted the King's offer, went a few steps and again returned. And when questioned by the King replied: "These would not be sufficient for the maintenance and welfare of children." The king, therefore, asked him to take the whole heap of the jewels. On this the *brahmacārin* appeared in the form of Lord Buddha and said that attachment and increase of wants would indeed be "the over accumulating mass of sorrow and pain that resulted from the worldly life". Increase of wants would grow in increasing progression and would never bring peace. Our wants or *tṛṣṇā* must not be allowed to increase wildly. This would only 'make vice resemble virtue and love resemble hate' (creating such confusions is the function of *avidyā* and removing such confusions is the function of *prajñā.*) Prosperity cannot be brought by borrowed help or gifts from other men or from abroad. One must curtail one's wants and cut the coat according to the cloth available.

9

Buddhism and Change

WHEREAS early Buddhism is associated with the doctrine of perpetual flux, Advaita Vedānta is associated with the opposite doctrine that Reality is one and unchanging. The Advaitic doctrine lays stress on the authority of the Vedas. The nature of the argument of Advaitism finally in this: Reality (or *Brahman*) is one because the Vedas say so. The diversity that appears to us is, therefore, unreal because it is inconsistent with the Śruti. The logical argument employed by Advaita is thus either negative in character or it is only a supplementary *pramāṇa*. Buddhism on the other hand wants to discard Śruti or for that matter any authority as a *pramāṇa*. In spite of such differences, Buddhism in the history of thought, gradually came closer and closer to Advaitic thought and influenced the thought of philosophers like Śaṅkarācārya as is evident from the criticism levelled against him as a Veiled Bauddha (*Pracchanna Bauddha*). What is the reason for this? I believe, among other things, two important tendencies in Buddhistic thinking are responsible for this somersault of Buddhism. The first of these is the hidden platonic tendency in Buddhism. The second is the confusion between Metaphysical and Ethical points of view. It is my object in this paper to trace some important doctrines common to all forms of Buddhism and to show how the two tendencies referred to above are involved in those doctrines.

The first such doctrine is that everything is impermanent (*sarvaṁ anityam*). This is the first seal of *mudrā* of Buddhism. Buddha also held that 'everything is suffering' (*sarvaṁ duḥkham*). If we carefully examine the stories that are associated with Buddha's name, before he actually left the palace, it would be clear that he was absolutely convinced through his own observations that the whole world was full of misery. He could get over this problem of misery or suffering when, through penance, he realised the transient character of reality. Thus, for Buddha the two propositions 'that everything is suffering' (*sarvaṁ duḥkham*) and 'that everything is impermanent' (*sarvaṁ anityam*) are correlated. And although Buddhism, in the early stage, was mainly concerned with the ethical problem, namely that of suffering, still it presupposed the metaphysical problem, that everything is impermanent. A reference to a few parables in the *Dhammapada* will make my point clear.

The first parable relates that Śakra having on one occasion been conceived in the household of a potter, as the offspring of the female ass that turned the mill, the ass, overjoyed at the prospect of progeny, kicked her heels up, and broke all the pitchers and pots which the master had made. On this, the man, taking a stick, belaboured the beast to such a degree that the newly-formed foetus was destroyed and the prospect of offspring cut off. On this occasion Buddha repeated these lines. "Whatever exists is without endurance, and, hence, the terms 'flourishing' and 'decaying'. A man is born and then, he dies. Oh, the happiness of escaping from the condition! For, the life of men is but as the earthen vessels made in a potter's mill; formed with such care, they are all destined to destruction."[1]

Similarly, on another occasion, Buddha spoke to Prasenajit, the king who had come back after finishing the funeral of the queen mother: "There are four things, O Raja, which form the first still now have been the causes of constant anxiety and fear to men — the fear of old-age, of disease, of death, and of grief consequent on death. Alas ! the life of man is but as the perishing things we see around us; to-day they flourish, tomorrow they are gone. *Just as the waters of five rivers are ever flowing on without cessation day and night, such is the case with man* — his life is ever ebbing away." "As the waters of a river ever hasten in and flow away, and once gone, never

1. This is taken from the Chinese Version of the *Dhammapada*, translated by Samuel Beal, published by Susil Gupta (India) Ltd., Second edn. 1952, Section I, p. 13.

return, such is the life of man. That which is gone knows not any return."[2]

Similarily, on a third occasion, Buddha seems to have said: "Such is the fate of all *that lives*; it is thus it flourishes for a moment and then dies."[3]

The above examples bring out the fact that Buddha believes that everything is impermanent, everything is momentary, and everything has a duration. It is because of this tenet that Mrs. Rhys Davids says:

> According to Buddhist, there is no being, there is only a becoming, the state of every individual being unstable, temporary and sure to pass away. Everything, be it a person, a thing or a God, is, therefore, merely a putting together of component elements. Further, in each individual, without exception, the relation of its component parts is eternally changing and never the same for two consecutive moments. Putting together implies becoming, becoming means becoming different, and becoming different cannot arise without a dissolution, a passing away, which must inevitably at some time or other be complete.[4]

Impermanence is a fact and as a fact it is self-evident. But why is it that all things are impermanent? The answer that Buddhism gives is very interesting. It is due not to what we ordinarily call a causal law but due to *pratītya-samutpāda* or what I should like to call, the law of objective sequence. The operation of this law is dependent upon certain conditions and, therefore, the law is known as the law of dependent origination[5] — that being present this becomes. Of course, the Buddhist concept of 'cause' is many a time confused with our ordinary concept of cause.

This impermanence is of three kinds:[6]

2. *Ibid.*, p. 14.
3. *Ibid.*
4. *Early Buddhism*, pp. 56-57.
5. For the discussion of *pratītya-samutpāda* see ch.4 of this book.
6. Yamakami Sogen: *Systems of Buddhist Thought*, Calcutta, University, pp. 8-10.

(a) Impermanence of life period

(b) Momentary impermanence

(c) The Principle of Impermanence.

The impermanence of the life period can be easily understood. For, we ordinarily regard the same man as living between the period of his birth and death. By the words attributed to Buddha, 'where birth is, death will come' a particular variety of continuity or becoming is recognized and this is in keeping with common sense. "Death is a change of a body into four great elements: earth, water, fire and air." We experience such impermanence every now then; it is self-evident.

But this impermanence also presupposes momentary impermanence. Everything is undergoing change; every moment or rather a thing is an aggregate of such changes.

Of course, there does not appear any contradiction between the first kind of impermanence and the second one. The second one represents only another order of existence. The histories of things, like tables and chairs, and beings like Rāma and Lakṣmaṇa represent one order and in modern thought we call it macroscopic order. On the other hand, the momentary impermanence represents microscopic or atomic order. And it is only by making such a distinction that the confusion about the nature of physical things can be avoided. Impermanence of life period gives us immediate experience of duration and momentary experience gives us an experience of flow. All this is in keeping with the facts of experience. Buddhism is the doctrine of Becoming in this second sense, i.e., in the sense of momentary impermanence. Impermanence in the first sense gives it a latitude for holding a common sense belief that there are permanent (i.e., permanent in a relative sense) bodies. But these permanent bodies, looked at from a particular angle, will be only nothing but change. It is in this sense that Buddhaghoṣa says that strictly speaking the life duration of a living being is exceedingly brief.

> Just as a chariot wheel in rolling rolls merely at one point of the tyre and in resting rests only at one point, even so the life of a living being endures only for the brief period of our

> thought and as soon as the thought has ceased, then being, too, is said to have ceased. Thus the being of a past moment has lived, but does not live nor will it live; the being of a future moment will live but has not lived nor does it live; the being of the present moment does live but has not lived and will not live.[7]

But the momentary impermanence according to the Buddhist view also presupposes another order of impermanence, viz., the principle of impermanence or *śūnyatā*. "This doctrine of *śūnyatā* has been sometimes criticised as the doctrine of Void. But it must be noted that *śūnyatā* is not another name for Nothingness. It does not mean 'emptiness' either but means the principle of perpetual change occurring at every step in this phenomenal world." It is a principle which itself does not change but makes change possible. *Śūnyatā* is thus quite positive in 'meaning', though it does not have any bearer. It connotes though it is not a name of any substance or an entity or *dravya*. It is in this sense that Nāgārjuna in his *Madhyamaka-śāstra* says that a person who is able to understand and use the concept of *śūnyatā* understands everything and one who is not able to use the concept of *śūnyatā* does not understand anything. To interpret *śūnyatā* as something else, sometimes void and sometimes mere transitoriness, is due to confusion. For, it is neither of the two.

However, it is extremely difficult to formulate such a principle of Universal Impermanence which is to be thought of a logically prior to the concrete happenings of change. But, the Buddhist philosophy thinks that it is necessary to recognise such a principle, as without it ultimate impermanence or change would be inconceivable. Such a position evidently smacks of deducing the process of change from one *a priori* principle, just as the Hegelians try to deduce existence from Reason; one step ahead and we shall have to say that *śūnyatā* is the real nature of things that are conditioned, and if, *śūnyatā* is nothingness everything will be nothing. If we do not understand the principle in this way, a metaphysical way, we shall have to regard it as a formal canon of Logic like 'Dictum de omni et nullo' where the events happen

---

7. H. C. Warren, *Buddhism in Translation,* Harvard University Press, Cambridge, Mass, 1986, p. 150.

according to the law but where the law has not got the potentiality of creating the events. Now, in both these ways it is not necessary to postulate the law of 'Universal Impermanence'. When we say that everything is changing, we need not necessarily presuppose a principle that change alone is real. In postulating such a principle it appears that Buddhists have a hidden belief that the principle (or law), which is not of temporal process, exists in some sense and is more real than the temporal process itself. Somewhow or other it is assumed that *śūnyatā* is a name of some ontological state. If so, Buddhists like Vedāntins use the word 'existence' in two different senses: (1) first, in the sense of experience or a fact, and (2) secondly, in the sense of 'eternity'. As soon as we equate eternity with existence, transitory existence ceases to be existence and the momentary existence is rejected, and we have to fall back upon some formal reality like that of 'Universal Impermenance' which itself does not change and which is of the nature of *Plato's Idea.* Thus, acceptance of such a principle either leads to Hegelianism or Platonism and is a complete refutation of the philosophy of Change, for, in so doing you objectify 'Change', make it a static principle and rob it of 'the flow or succession'. Change or *śūnyatā* thus objectified becomes a permanent entity. Again the eternal principle of change does not seem to be a self-evident principle in the sense that the principle exists 'first' (in a non-temporal sense) and, therefore, changes conform to it. Rather such a principle may merely be an induction from experience. And a recognition of a metaphysical principle of change may not be necessary. Further, if the above principle of *śūnyatā* is taken to be *a priori*, then Buddhism would involve certain immutables over and above change — a natural contradiction to which it has led. It would mean that in order that impermanence be possible the principle of impermanence must be permanent and universal.

It appears to me, however, that Buddhists hold that this is a kind of logical principle according to which deduction takes place and is presupposed by the first and second kind of impermanence. If 'Socrates is mortal' is the conclusion of a syllogism, it cannot be a valid conclusion unless all men are mortal or rather unless all *M*s are *P*s. The deduction becomes possible because there is a specific correlation between *all Ms are Ps* and *S is P*. Similarly, Buddshists think that for a proposition to be true it must be supported by or presupposed by a formal proposition (or a canon of all changes). The first two kinds of Change — Universal Impermanence of life period and momentary impermanence — seem to be in time or temporal in Nature. The principle of *śūnyatā* on the other hand does not seem to be in time or temporal in character. Now, as already pointed out, such a postulation is not necessary. The whole world may exhibit a form of change. But such a change may merely be contingent and, therefore, it might not be necessary to deduce it from a certain Universal *a priori* principle.

But even if such a principle is postulated it should be strictly logical principle, i.e., it should only suggest certain use and should in no way suggest either a physical thing or a metaphysical entity. It should not suggest any existence, but should suggest only 'meaningfulness'. But as is well-known a transition from a logical to metaphysical point of view is common and it is change in point of view which creates some pseudo-entities, *śūnyatā* being one of them. In later Buddhism, particularly after Nāgārjuna, this shift from the logical to the metaphysical point of view has taken place.

Like *śūnyatā*, Buddhism also accepts *nirvāṇa* as another category. This I believe is a vlaue catagory and should not stand for existence. It need not denote any reality. It only suggests a 'not yet' state and does not suggest 'is' state. But, to confuse an ethical category with some sort of ultimate reality is quite common and both Indian and non-Indian systems have done so on several occasions. Thus, Nāgasena conceived *nirvāṇa* as an ontological category and considered it as a substratum of changes as ocean is a substratum of waves or *vivarta*. On account of this changeover to the metaphysical point of view the two originally non-metaphysical categories of *śūnyatā* and *nirvāṇa* were combined and were ultimately unified. Perhaps, as the original meaning of both these terms suggest, Gautama the Buddha wanted to use them in a non-denotative but non-negative sense. But in the course of history either these terms were regarded as negative and representing void or they were regarded as some existent either in the ordinary or in the Platonic sense.

Let us now examine another tenet of Buddhism, viz., *sarvam anātman*: 'All that is, is without *ātman* or soul'. What is the meaning of this tenet? It is alleged by Buddhist philosophers that even Śāṅkarācārya failed to comprehend its real import and so 'malinged it to condemnation'. Let us, therefore, see what the Buddhist mean by *anātmavāda*, or the doctrine of no-soul. According to them, Buddhism accepts two sorts of *anātman* or non-ego. The first is the denial of subjective *ātman* or a personal Ego, and the second is the denial of the objective *ātman* or 'the Ego of the *dharma*s or the phenomenal world'. By *ātman* is meant a permanent substance or a Unitary principle which does not change and which endures in spite of the changes of qualities or mental states. Therefore, it follows that the existence which is eternal (*ātman*) cannot be implied by the world which is ceaselessly changing. A Buddhist would ask: 'why should we assume such a substance, whether mental or physical?' One might answer that unless a substance is accepted the qualities would have to stand independently. Qualities or *dharma*s require a substratum, and mental states presuppose a unity of apperception — a mind which synthesizes different mental states into one. But a Buddhist world discard it as a dogma. He would ask: Why do you suppose that such a permanent substance is necessary? After all you can never be aware of a physical substance or a mind. You can only be aware of certain aggregate of qualities or *saṁghāta*. Why then suppose that there is any physical substance at all? Or, for that matter, even a mental one? Why not suppose that the aggregate, i.e., *saṁghāta* is itself the substance, mental or physical? The Buddhists, therefore, come to the conclusion that the substance is not in any way different from five *skandha*s analogous to what are called sense data to a very great extent. Buddhist theory, then, may lead to some sort of logical atomism like Russell's . The Ego or substance which is merely to be inferred is, thus, denied and our assumption of such an ego is regarded merely as our prejudice. As soon as ego is denied the world is reduced to momentary states (*sarvam kṣaṇikam*) and is corroborated by the first principle that everything is changing, *sarvam anityan*. It is true that Buddhists believe in four different kinds of (permanent?) atoms. But, either this might be a piece of thinking at tangent to the thinking of *sarvam anātma*, or by some confusion and through the Vaiśeṣika school it might have entered the philosophy of Buddhism.

However, as this world is perceived as ceaseless flow it leads to a further principle, *sarvam santānam* (Everything is duration or continuity). But, it must be remembered that this continuity exists without a uniting principle. Buddhism states that this continuity exists without a uniting people. *Pratītya-samutpāda* postulates this. This continuity is perceived in two ways: (1) by *pravṛtti vijñāna*, where a physical thing is perceived as enduring, and (2) by *ālaya vijñāna*, where mind is perceived as enduring. Thus, the four tenets of Buddhism viz., *sarvam saṅghātam*, *sarvam anātmam*, *sarvaṁ kṣaṇikam*, and *sarvam santānam,* provide a ground for the theory that Change is real. (There are of course passages in Buddhist literature which point out that 'The Tathāgata sometimes taught that the *ātman* exists', but, as Nāgārjuna points out, such a doctrine was taught only when he wanted to impart to his audience the conventional doctrine.)

But like *śūnyatā* or *nirvāṇa*, the doctrine of no-soulness also gets inverted and permanent ego in the form of *mahātmatā* is brought back by a backdoor. There is a passage in Asaṅga's *Mahāyāna-Sūtrālaṅkāra-Śāstra* which recommends "to the aspirants to Buddhahood to look upon the universe as a mere conglomeration of conformation, *saṁskāra*, devoid of an *ego* and fraught with suffering, and to take refuge from the bane of individualism in the mightily advantageous doctrine of *mahātman* — great soul of universe." "Thus Buddhism not only acknowledges the permanence of the noumenal ego, but actually enjoins its adherents to train themselves in the manner as to be able to attain union with *mahātman*."

Sometimes we also find the word *paramātman* used for *mahātman*, and *mahātman*, *paramātman*, and *anātman* equated. Sometimes we also find the expression *tathāgata-garbha* used for *mahātman*, etc. Thus, Buddhism again brings back the conception of non-changing reality by a backdoor. '*Anātmatā* or no-soulness', thus, becomes a denial of an individual soul but suggests that there is one binding principle of the whole universe which may be called *mahātman*. What can this principle be except the principle of *śūnyatā* or the principle of *śūnyatā* cum *nirvāṇa*? It appears that intitially the concept of *tathāgata-garbha* or *paramātman* or *mahātman* has at least a superficial similarity with the *Brahman* of Advaitins. But when *parmātmatā*, *śūnyatā* and *nirvāṇa* get united and ontological status is given to them they become almost identical with the *Brahman* of the Advaitins.

In short in Buddhism, concepts like *śūnyatā*, a logical concept, *nirvāṇa*, an ethical concept, and *mahātmatā* or *anātmatā*, a metaphysical concept, get mixed up and the result is that Buddhism has to believe in two kinds of realities: (1) that which is ceaselessly changing, and (2) that which is beyond this change, that which is eternal. Buddhist philosophy thus begins to suppose that the conditional existence, that is empirical and which can be described in sequences and series, alone is in flux. But beyond this there is *nirvāṇa*, *śūnyatā* or *mahātman* which is almost like the *Brahman* of the Vedāntin which is eternal and absolute. The ethical ideal is regarded as a higher reality and it is prescribed to everyone to attain this reality. Buddhism thus paves the way for doctrine like that of Vedānta.

There is, however, still a problem about the lesser reality. There cannot be two realities one less real and other more real. Either the lesser reality must be got rid of or Buddhism would have to be regarded as a doctrine of dualism. The history of Buddhistic thought tells us that under the leadership of Nāgārjuna Buddhism decided to regard the world of change as illusory and accepted *nirvāṇa* as the only reality. *Nirvāṇaṁ śāntam* was thus interpreted as a metaphysical proposition and was regarded as the only 'Calm', Calm being a kind of reality.

The acceptance of a *nirvāṇa* as ultimately real impelled the followers of Buddhism to accept the illusory status of the world. This was done, as in Nāgārjuna, by identifying *saṁsāra* with *nirvāṇa*.

10

Jīva and Ajīva[1]

JAINA philosophers talk of *jīva* and *ajīva*. Is it a division, a category distinction or an abstraction? Do *jīva* and *ajīva* exclude each other? Or are they abstractions from experience, and so just the concepts and not existences?[2]

If we look at experience at macroscopic level it will be clear that the world consists of *jīva* or the animate and things different from *jīva* or the inanimate. This is the case of a division of the world on a certain principle, or *fundamentum divisionis*. Such a division would not suggest that the life or *jīva* had no spatio-temporal

---

1. I have based my study particularly on the Jain texts like (1) *Samaya Sāra*, (2) *Pravacana Sāra* (3) *Bhagavatī Sūtra* and (4) *Tatvārtha Sūtra*.

2. Before we proceed further it may be pointed that it was the custom in ancient India to give a list of concepts but the list was not necessarily exclusive and several concepts mentioned in the list were overlapping. Bharata, e.g., gives a list of *rasa*, *bhāva*, *abhinaya*, etc., but the concepts mentioned in his list are neither exclusive nor exhaustive. Similarly, the Vaiśeṣikas mention nine *dravyas* — the *mahābhūtas*, the Space and Time and *manas* and *ātman*. It is difficult to assume that Space and Time and the *bhūtas* exist independently of one another and that they are not overlapping. It is difficult to imagine *pṛthivī*, *āp*, *tejas* or *vāyu* or *ākāśa* without spatial or temporal dimension. I understand that when the Vaiśeṣikas give this list they treated *pṛthivī*, *āp* etc., as also their forms, Space and Time as belonging to one list of investigations. The Jainas similarly could give a list of what is traditionally known as Jaina *padārthas* and amongst them could be *jīva* and *ajīva*.

aspects, nor would it suggest that it had no material aspects. It would, e.g., be possible to imagine two kinds of matter, one having life and the other without life. This is what is, for example, said in the *Caraka Saṁhitā*, *asmin arthe sarvaṁ dravyaṁ pāñcabhautikam, cetanāvad, acetanañ ca.*[3] But on such a division the living and the non-living things or substances will both have some common properties which are spatio-temporal. For, whether something is living or non-living, it would primarily be material and located in space and would be just real, one that can be experienced.

Sometimes, however, we may classify our experience into life and otherwise and such a classification would easily he ambiguous; for, one could mean by it either the classification of real things or one could mean by it a classification of concepts, a case of mere abstraction. It is further possible that we might confuse, between the division of things and classification of concepts and in that case we might be doing what is known as abstraction but thinking that we are dividing (or classifying) the things in the world. In this case the confusion would arise due to the fact that we would be treating concepts and things on par, the images of things and concepts succeeding each other in such a quick succession that one is mistaken for the other. When Descartes, e.g., thought of extension and consciousness as substances he was, as Spinoza later suggested, talking of attributes or was merely abstracting, i.e., distinguishing extensional and consciousness aspects of experience, but was thinking that he was dividing (or classifying) the substances into two. But dividing substance, having extension into living and non-living substances, is quite different from classifying the concepts of extension and consciousness (without extension), and then thinking that consciousness without extension was one kind of substance and extension was another kind of substance. In experience we do come across the living beings and non-living things. But, however, minute a living being may be our experience always tells us that it is always determined by extension. That we are not able to see the extension of it by our naked eyes does not prove that there is no extension determining these substances. One has to admit that the language, a *aṇoḥ aṇīyān*, etc., is the language of extension or space. The problem which arises here is that how there can be a *saṁyoga*

— an external contact, between something that is extensional and something that is extensionless. People of various schools including Jainism must have noticed this difficulty and that is why the concept of *liṅga-deha* or *kāraṇa-deha* must have been introduced. It goes without saying that *deha* suggests that although consciousness was different from body it still had extension. But if this is admitted it is a tacit admission of the fact that *jīva* and *ajīva* was a division of matter, i.e., existence having extension, into non-living and living, and from this it would follow that Jaina philosophers were primarily concerned with dividing (or classifying) the world into extensional but conscious and extensional and non-conscious world, and not into extensional and non-extensional world. My contention is that in a physical analysis or division it is never possible to divide the world into something that is extensional and non-extensional. When we try to talk of extensional and non-extensional and also identify extensional with non-conscious or *ajīva* and non-extensional with conscious or *jīva* we are, as a matter of fact, abstracting, conceptualizing, logicizing and only mistaking a logical analysis for physical division.

Of course, a problem would arise here: When we are talking of living being we know that it is determined by birth and death. In a state after death consciousness or livingness disappears and it makes us think that it has gone away. We forget that 'has gone away' is a metaphor and if it is not used in a metaphorical way it would only belong to the language of space. But the fact is that we simultaneously hold the belief that (*a*) it belongs to the language of space and (*b*) it does not belong to the language of space. We simply overlook that to hold two such beliefs becomes possible because they are held in two separate chambers of consciousness without any communication between them. Of course, one will have to explain the phenomenon of exit or vanishing of life. But saying that life is a separate substance and it goes away at the time of death is not offering a real explanation of the pheneomenon. Space and a thing in space cannot be separated from each other. From this if someone suggests that they are two things and they only come together by some external contact it would be incorrect. Similarly if there is green leaf and if later on it dries up it would be incorrect to say that green qua green itself has gone somewhere else. When a revolving wheel stops it does not mean that the movement is taking rest somewhere. Vanishing is not equivalent to going somewhere else just as existing together of space and a thing in space is not equivalent to external contact or *saṁyoga*. A better explanation would be to say that (1) space and a thing in space are one phenomenon, (2) greenness and vanishing of greenness of leaf is another kind of phenomenon, (3) Revolution of wheel and stopping of its movement is a third kind of phenomenon, and (4) death of a living being is a fourth kind of phenomenon. One need not explain the one in terms of the other. But unconsciously one commits this mistake and fluctuates between the process of dividing (or classifying) and conceptualizing. Perhaps a better explanation of Jaina category would be possible if we understand *jīva* and *ajīva* as a division of existents, say matter, on the principle that one is animistic and the other is not. One has to remember that the process of dividing, enumerating, counting or sometimes even classifying things is of one kind and categorising of things is of another. You cannot divide, enumerate, etc., unless things exist in their own right. Of course, conceptually you can even give concepts the status of a thing and then count (as you do when you count categories). But primarily this process belongs to things which exist in their own right. On the other hand, when you distinguish different qualities or characteristics you are not separating the independent things, you are abstracting them, and such abstractions are neither in space nor in time; they are not existing, nor living, they are just concepts.

A problem, of course, would arise about the relationship of such concepts to reality. Concepts in logic do not require a bearer or substratum, but if they are to be real then they can be real only in relation to some substratum which is real, i.e., these concepts should be such that they must be capable of having a form which is a form of existence, a form of life. This form of life or existence makes it possible for us to think that the concept has existential relevance. Take, e.g., the case of sweetness. In order for sweetness to have significance in life it will have to go with something and to talk of a thing we will have to talk of space, time, and substance. Space, time, and substance, so to say, provide a medium for the concept of sweetness to be real. The process by which we concretise a concept is the process in which we supply medium for the concept to exist. And this according to me is the Jaina concept of *astikāya* — a body for its existence, a form of existence. This form of existence will naturally vary according as the concept in its concretised form is dynamic or not, and accordingly the *astikāya* concept also will be modified into *dharmāstikāya* and *adharmāstikaya*, etc. But the point that I am making is that when a Jaina philosopher tries to conceptualize and abstract, he rather talks of *dharma* and *adharma*, both of them being characteristics (*adharma* is also characteristic) and when he talks of concrete things he talks of *jīva* and *ajīva*. One can easily see the distinction between *jīva* and *ajīva* on the one hand and *dharma* and *adharma* on the other.[3]

In the light of what has been said above, let me now try to understand the theory of *jīva* and *ajīva* as understood traditionally by Jaina thinkers. In doing this, it will be my object to remove the contradictions or inconsistencies in the theory and present the theory in a consistent form. Thereby I might be able to show that the theory of *jīva* and *ajīva* is, in fact, concerned with a division of certain matter which is divided on the basis of animate and inanimate only.

First, Jaina philosophers think that both *jīva* and *ajīva* are *dravyas*.[4] Of course, *dravya* is that which has got certain characterstics. But they think that all *dravyas* are spatial in character. Even time is spatial in character for them. Space seems to be the common characteristic of all *dravyas* or things. They use the word *pradeśa* to denote spatiality of a thing. They bring in an important notion here: The notion of *ākāśa*. They divide *ākāśa* into *loka ākāśa* and *aloka ākāśa*. *Loka ākāśa* is the space wherein the things exist and activity takes place. But the *loka ākāśa* is encircled by a limiting line (may be imaginery) beyond which there cannot be

---

3. At a later stage, however, he must have made a distinction between *jīva* (as a concept) and *jīva* (as *āstikāya*). Similarly, he must have made a distinction between *dharma* and *dharmāstikāya*, etc.

4. I am aware that the Jainas use the word *dravya* where a Vaiśeṣika would use the word *padārtha*.

any activity nor can there be any existence of things. It is on this line of demarcation that Jaina philosophers imagine that there are *siddhaśīla*s and think of them as abode freed souls. The freed souls simply cannot go beyond this line because as soon as they are free their activity comes to an end. Beyond this line there is only empty space. It is empty space not because there is nothing in it but because there cannot be anything in it. All things of different kinds, therefore, exist only in *loka ākāśa*. It must be remembered that the empty space in *loka ākāśa* is different in kind from the empty space in *aloka ākāśa*. There is, however, a difficulty which may be pointed out here. Everything which exists is *astikāya*. However, *kāla* is not an *astikāya* though it exists in *loka ākāśa* only. How to conceive of *kāla* as not *astikāya* and still in space is in fact a problem. Therefore, I think, it is necessary to think that the term *astikāya* does not simply indicate a thing but it means, as Jaina philosophers rightly assert, a medium introduced like Kant's schemata to make up for the relation between concepts and things. But if we think this way *jīva* and *jīvāstikāya* would be two notions and not one. *Jīva* would be the concept of *jīva*s and *ajīvāstikāya* would be an actual *jīva* having extension. This will not only be true of *jīva* but for all *dravya*s. In ordinary language we do use the word *jīva* in these two senses. This would also explain why *kāla* is not *astikāya*, for the concept of time does not require any other medium in order to be significant. Time itself is such a medium. It is not bound to space in the manner material things are bound to space. Thus, only those concepts which require spatiality in order for them to be significant, and have a form of existence would alone be *astikāya*. *Astikāya* would also thus mean the body or medium of a concept which makes the concept exist and cease to be merely a concept. I feel that at some stage Jaina philosophers must have confused between the concept of *jīva* and the actual *jīva*. It need not be added that the concept of *jīva* is a logical notion whereas *jīva* (or *jīvāstikāya*) is an empirical existence.

Let me now understand how the Jaina philosophers think of *jīva* which is a *dravya* and so which exists in its own right. And here comes a very significant notion of the Jainas. First they think that the *jīva*s are *ananta*s — infinite. They also think that the *jīva*s are *asaṁkhya pradeśa*s. *Pradeśa* here means space and by the statement *jīva*s are *asaṁkhya pradeśa* what is meant is that different *jīva*s can have different spatial dimensions. What is admitted here is that the existent *jīva*s are spatial in character. Again, if there is a living child, then the *jīva* of that child has the same extension as the extension of the body. If the child grows the *jīva* also grows for there is no part of the living body which is unconscious. The *jīva* is regarded as a life-coat for the body. It is a cap or a gown which covers every part of the body and is co-extensive with it. This *jīva* is not ordinarily separable from the body. When it becomes *mukta* then like the left-skin or scale of the serpent and the serpent, which can be separated, the *jīva* and the body are separated. The *jīva* in the context of the living body is continuously growing but a *mukta jīva* would not occupy that part of the body where there are empty spaces or hollowness. Thus, in the case of a *mukta jīva* there may not be a one-to-one correspondence between the extension of *jīva* and the body, and the extension of the *mukta jīva* may be smaller than this body.

The most important and common sense element in the whole theory of Jainas is this that they agree that consciousness or *jīva* cannot exist without space. But this is possible only if *jīva* and body are inseparable. But inconsistently with this belief they also believe that at the time of *mukti*, the *jīva* and body can be separated. It is like taking out a cap of a fountain pen and keeping it away from the fountain pen. In the case of fountain pen, both the fountain pen and its cap are material. But can there be a spatial form which exists and has no material characterisation? It is almost like thinking that there is a form of fragrance as a quality without any material bearer. It is like the Cheshire cat in "Alice in the Wonderland", which goes away leaving its grin behind. Can there be spatial layer of consciousness without a material body? To think of such layer is in fact to think that consciousness is also material though different from the material body which is non-living. It is holding two belief-systems together in two different chambers. Jaina philosophers were toeing the common sense so long as they were thinking that the *jīva*s had *pradeśa*s. But to think of the *jīva*s along with *pradeśa*s without body, i.e, *deha,* is to mystify and liquidate the common sense. It is the mistake of not distinguishing between vanishing of the phenomenon and separation of the two independent phenomena.

This paradox can be dissolved only if we regard that there are living spatial phenomena and non-living spatial phenomena such that both of them have some material substratum. While interpreting Jaina theory it is the common sense, which we have to depended upon. The common sense tells us that matter is to be divided into living and non-living and is not to be abstracted into matter and non-matter. But in such a case it is redundant to say that there are two bodies one living and the other non-living and that the living body is super-imposed of the non-living one. Spatiality, it is insisted, is a property both of living and non-living. In the process of abstraction spatiality would also be abstracted. Perhaps for this reason people talked of *kārmika-deha*. Unless *karma* had spatiality and material properties it could not be attached to *jīva* at all. But this common sense stand of the Jainas is given up when they bring in the *mukta jīva*, and like other systems of Indian philosophy add to confusion and become more or less like traditional Sāṁkhya or traditional Advaita.

11

Philosophy of Kundakunda

ELĀCĀRYA Kundakunda is recognised as a great philosopher of the Digambara Jain tradition. By writing works like the *Samayasāra, Pravacanasāra* and *Pañcāstikāya* he has, in fact, enriched Indian philosophical thought. In Jain mythology there is a story of one *Rohiṇī*, the moral of which is that our wealth should be increased. This is true of knowledge, too. The philosophical wealth of the Jains is the heritage of our culture and should not be confined to the ranks of the Jain community alone. If it spreads beyond these bounds, it would have wider philosophical significance. From this point of view, the translation of the *Pravacanasāra* by Dr. Tagare should be welcomed. Kundakunda wrote this book, as well as his other works in Śaurasenī Ardhamāgadhī, and so was beyond the reach of scholars who were not conversant in it. In this chapter, I propose to examine the philosophy of Kundakunda in the light of what Tagare has said.[1]

---

1. Tagare, in his introduction to the book, considers the four different aspects of Jain philosophy in four different parts. In the first part, he gives the history of Jain philosophy. He points out how the Jain and Brāhmaṇical cultures were entangled in the development of philosophical history. In the second part, he discussed the life and literature of Śrī Kundakunda. Here he also discusses the background theory presupposed by Kundakunda. In the third part the philosophical concepts of Kundakunda, are discussed and in the fourth, he furnishes elaborate notes on the commentaries on *Pravacanasāra.* Tagare also gives the complete text of the *Pravacanasāra* in the next part. In addition to the original Śaurasenī text, Tagare also gives its Sanskrit version. For all this scholarly effort Tagare has to be congratulated.

Jain scholars hold that their culture, the Śramaṇa culture, is (historically) earlier than the Brāhmaṇical culture. The sculpture of the bull in the excavations of Mohenjo-Daro is, by one interpretation, taken as a symbol of the first Jain *tīrthaṅkara* Ādinātha Ṛṣabhadeva. There is a mention of one Ṛṣabhadeva in the *Ṛgveda*. The Jains identify him with their Ādinātha Ṛṣabhadeva. There is also a legend that the very name of our country, Bhārata, is derived from the name of emperor Bharata who was the eldest son of Ṛṣabhadeva. This story is also found in the *Bhāgavata Purāṇa*. In the *Mahābhārata*, perhaps this story goes by the name of Jaḍabharata and obliquely refers to the story of emporer Bharata of Jain legend. One thing is certain: the name Bhārata or Bhāratavarṣa, has no reference to Bharata the son of Duṣyanta and Śakuntalā around whom the story of Kālidāsa's *Śakuntalā* develops. There is, indeed, a high degree of probability that the name Bhāratavarṣa or Bhārata refers to the Jain emperor Bharata. From this, it is possible to conclude that the Śramaṇa civilisation may be contemporary or even earlier than Brāhmaṇical civilisation, and one need not dispute that this civilisation had an independent origin and development. However, the similarities found in Jain and Brāhmaṇical philosophy could be either independent or borrowed from each other.

What has been borrowed from whom? Dr. Tagare discusses this. It may be pointed out that just as there are points of similarity on several counts between Brāhmaṇical and Jain civilisation, there are points of similarity between Brāhmaṇical and Buddhist civilisation, also. I have a feeling that the original and early growth of Brāhmaṇical civilisation can be seen in, and traced to, the Pūrva Mīmāṁsā philosophy and the rituals that have come down to us (through Pūrva Mīmāṁsā). Of course, today's Brāhmaṇical civilisation is not an unadulterated picture of Pūrva Mīmāṁsā thought and practice. The influence of Uttara Mīmāṁsā on the present Brāhmaṇical civilisation cannot be ignored. The influence of Uttara Mīmāṁsā means the influence of *jñāna-mārga* on philosophical thought. This tradition of

---

However, it does not mean that every interpretation of Tagare and the views that he propounds would be accepted entirely by other scholars. Tagare's strength lies in the fact that it would make other people think about the problems raised by Kundakunda.

philosophical thought is as much perceived in Buddhist and Jain literature as in the Upaniṣads. This tradition of the development of ideas could either be due to mutual communications of thought, or could have arisen independently. If the origin of Jain civilisation is traced back to Ādinātha Ṛṣabhadeva, it would carry nearly five to six thousand years back. In that case, it is earlier than Buddhist civilisation, but it cannot be definitely stated that it is earlier than the Brāhmaṇical civilisation. When one tries to trace the roots of history in the uncertain past, one can never assert one's propositions positively or with certainty. The only thing one can definitely say is that whatever is seen in Brāhmaṇical philosophy today is due to the synthesis or superimposition of Advaita philosophy on the ritualistic Pūrva Mīmāṁsā. The present Advaita opinion, as dipped or blended in the *karma-kāṇḍa,* has been so universally accepted that questions about the original Advaita doctrine and the source of this doctrine, whether Buddhist, Jain or Vedānta, can no more be legitimately asked. This Brāhmaṇical doctrine which has come down to us and the Jain doctrine propounded by Kundakunda in the *Samayasāra*, and *Pravacanasāra*, etc., have quite a good deal of similarity in form. Whether this similarity is really fundamental or is only superficial must be decided by experts of the subject. Tagare seems to think that Brāhmaṇical thought is earlier, and that it has influenced the Jain philosophy.

According to Tagare, there is a further similarity in Brāhmaṇical, Jain and Buddhist philosophical thoughts or ways of life. Acccording to him, these three varieties of thought are basically concerned with practice, leading to *mokṣa* or 'liberation'. A question that would arise here is, who originally thought of liberation? Every traditional paṇḍit thinks that the practice leading to *mokṣa* or is the fundamental part of his theory. I am doubtful of it. *Mokṣa* or 'liberation', according to me, is basically and directly related to man and his practices, his way of life. I do not think that liberation is directly connected with the philosophical theory. There need not be any logical relation between them. Suppose a man who has a desire to know reality succeeds in his desire and knows reality. Why should such a realisation lead to his liberation, at least in the traditional sense of the term? To know that the nature of reality is such and such should not enable man to liberate himself. To know reality cannot even have a far-fetched relation to liberation. At the most, by knowing the laws and nature of reality he might understand that life is without an ideal, without purpose and is *viphala*. But to know that life is purposeless and unsuccessful, or is bound to be so, has nothing to do with the traditional concept of *mokṣa*. If we regard *mokṣa* as a purpose or ideal, shall we also regard *vaiphalya*, if it is a necessary consequence of our search, as our ideal? Furthermore, if we are concerned with the development of an individual, how can we start with the presumption that everything is meaningless, purposeless, illusory or *mithyā*. As a matter of fact, the concept of 'fruitfulness' or 'purpose' is basically related and really concerned with the concept of *dharma*, or 'practice'. In this concept of *dharma*, it is not implied what the nature of *Brahman* or *viśva* is; what is really implied is what a man should do, what a man should strive for, what is his 'should' or 'ought'. In this empirical world of ours, there is also a phenomenon called 'desire' or 'will' and unless it is accepted, what we should do or what we ought to do does not become meaningful. In the very word *jijñāsā,* also, the concept of 'will' or 'desire' is latently present. Suppose we say everything is *pudgala*, or if we analyse the whole world into categories such as substance, quality, action, universality, particularity, *samavāya* or *abhāva* or in the alternative, if we divide or classify the world into *jīva* and *ajīva* or *jīva*, *pudgala*, *dharma, adharma*, *āsrava*, *saṁvara*, etc., how will this kind of knowledge lead to *mokṣa*? In a way, it is true that to know this is to know our nature. And to know the nature of ourselves, or *jīva,* is also our end. But this kind of end does not seem to be the same as the end indicated by *mokṣa*, at least not in the traditional sense of the term.

What I feel is that man's practice and thought process sometimes tread independent paths, and only after sometime do they combine, with the result that we create a false causal chain, such that we begin to think that thought is the cause of practice and /or *vice versa.* There is, of course, an important reason for this kind of genesis or process. It is only by selecting certain atoms of thought from practical life that man creates his theories, doctrines and philosophy. I feel that it is from the practice, or *ācārāṅga*, part of the Jains that, with some kind of nationalisation, the philosophical categories of *jīva*, *ajīva*, etc., are introduced.

In man's pursuit of knowledge, he does not (or should not) play with the concept of 'truth'. However, bitter the truth may appear, he has to accept the truth and nurture it. It is in such a nurturing of truth that the analysis of objects or the cosmological analysis of the Bauddhas, Sāṁkhyas, Naiyāyikas, Vaiśeṣikas or Vedāntins takes form. Why is the doctrine of *mokṣa* superimposed on this analysis? I do not understand how it is thought that as soon as we have the proper understanding of the nature of the world, our knowledge will automatically lead to heavenly happiness or bliss, and that man will gradually shed worldly unhappiness or misery. I do understand that the concept, of 'Heaven' is intimately connected with 'desirability', and is compatible with our notions of 'happiness' and 'desirability'. I also understand that this concept of 'Heaven' is the kith and kin of the concept of *preyas*, or that which is relished by us. But when we think of *mokṣa*, we go beyond the concept of both *preyas* and *śreyas*. It is the concept of *niḥśreyas,* not *śreyas*, and it is not the concept of 'worldly prosperity' or *abhyudaya*. I do not understand why we mingle the concept of 'worldly prosperity' with the concept of *niḥśreyas*. If at all any such mixture has any significance, it is only historical and not logical or theoretical. But this happens because we forget to distinguish between *niḥśreyas* and *śreyas*. Basically, the concept of *śreyas* has its origin in *kāma* or *kāmapuruṣārtha;* the concept of *niḥśreyas* is primarily concerned with the withering away of such *kāma*. Unfortunately, a commom man does not distinguish between *kāma* and *mokṣa*, and starts understanding and explaining *mokṣa* in terms of *kāma* only. We, therefore, begin to feel that even *mokṣa* belongs to the same category as 'paradise' or 'Heaven'. In the Jain *Mahāpurāṇa* this is positively seen. But in different *śāstra*s of Indian origin, also, this concept is interpolated. 'Why should one learn mathematics?' 'For the attainment of *mokṣa*', is a the answer given. 'Why should one do *dharma*?' Again the answer is the same. 'Why should one marry?' For attaining *mokṣa*. 'Why should one read the *Kāmasūtra*, a treatise on sex?' The answer is ditto. 'Why should one learn grammar?' Again it is answered, 'For the sake of *mokṣa*'. Either way it is a contraction or a caricature of the concept of *moskṣa*. Since the concept of '*mokṣa*' became elliptical and rounded in this way, the differences between the concept of 'Heaven' and *mokṣa* or *śreyas* and *niḥśreyas* were almost ignored, and *mokṣa* was regarded as the supreme purpose of every worldly discipline, by the Indian common man and elite alike.

It is through the symbiosis of such ways of thinking that the concept of *mokṣa* arose and became the royal concept of all walks of life, and started dominating philosophical and religious thought. In Jain philosophy, too, the fundamental problem which was concerned with the nature of things, or world, thus, receded into the background, and *mokṣa* as *śreyas* (not *niḥśreyas*) eterned the arena of *dharma* and culture by the back door, enveloping the whole of our philosophy. It is from this point of view that the *Pravacanasāra* could also be regarded as a treatise, discussing and analysis the *mokṣa-mārga*.

It is necessary to discuss one more point. Of the several Jain sects, the Śvetāmbara and the Digambara are the most important. On account of the differences in sects, their philosophical or social thought also became differenrt. For example, the Digambaras think that a woman cannot be liberated. Of course, such a belief was in the cultural atmosphere of the time. That is why there is a reference to such a belief even in the Buddhist literature. In the Buddhist *Saddharmapuṇḍarīkasūtra*, such a belief finds a place. Perhaps on this account, the Digambaras did not agree that a woman could be a *tīrthaṅkara*. Thus, whereas the Śvetāmbaras accepted that there was a woman *tīrthaṅkara* called Malli, the Digambaras insisted that the name of the *tīrthaṅkara* was not Malli but Mallinātha. It may be pointed out that in the language of the culture in which our civilisation grew, the use of the first person singular was masculine. Until the concept of 'feminity' does become explicit in language, there is no feminine grammar. When I do something, when I eat, drink or play, it is never thought whether 'I', the user of the language, is a man or woman and, therefore, the feminine gender is never used. Perhaps because the very concept of *mokṣa* is connected with 'me', that is the first person singular, the concept of *mokṣa* was never discussed in the context of 'woman' and perhaps it is on this account that it might have been thought that a woman was incapable of being liberated. If a woman can have a proper concept of 'reality', it is absurd to think that she is not capable of understanding the concept of 'liberation'. Nevertheless, such a concept did arise in ancient India.

In his foreword, Tagare also tries to prove that Mahāvīra was a brāhmaṇa. This is not impossible. Historically, brāhmaṇas were in the fore-front of social revolts and movements. The founder of the

Vīraśaiva sect, too, was a brāhmaṇa. But it is unimportant to prove whether Mahāvīva was a brāhmaṇa or not. I shall, therefore, turn to philosophical issues raised by Kundakunda, and discuss the principles and doctrines emerging from Jain culture. Such principles and doctrines are: *jīva-ajīva*, *dharma-adharma*, *pañcāstikāya*, *guṇa-paryāya*, *āsrava*, *saṃvara*, etc.

In all his works, such as the *Pañcāstikāys*, *Pravacanasāra* and *Samayasāra*, Kundakunda discusses the concerned issues, and Tagare also refers to them. It cannot be denied that the basic object of Jain philosophies is to create categories of phenomena in the world. By adhering to division by dichotomy, they talk of *jīva* and *ajīva*. It should be carefully noted that in Jain thought *jīva* is of the nature of *dravya*, or 'substance'. They talk of *dravya* as always having *guṇa* and *paryāya*. It means that as soon as we think of the concept of *dravya*, we have to think of several particular *dravya*s. Here the problem will arise whether the word *dravya* stands for a class or for a common noun denoting a common substance, and whether a particular *dravya* should be regarded as a collection of all particulars. It appears to me that there has always been a confusion between what we call 'division' and what we call 'classification'. When, for example, we regard *dravya* as a class concept and not as a collectivity concept, we are using the word *dravya* in the way Nyāya philosophers use the word *sāmānya*. But while using the word in this way, we forget that we are only making an abstraction of something that is concrete. If *dravya* is to be regarded as something concrete and existing (in time), and if it is to be known in a perceptual process, it cannot be an abstraction. In that case, it will merely be a collection of different particulars. And it is only in such a case that each particular *dravya* or *dravya paryāya* will be meaningful. If we regard concepts as abstraction and belonging to our imagination, then the particulars coming under that class (and the class itself) will not give us a relation between two existentials. Either both of them will be imaginary or the class concept will be imaginary and the particulars will be concrete and existing. But if the class concept is imaginary and just conceptual, what is the nature of their modes? If the modes are to be existential particulars, then the original substance also would have to have all the characteristics of the modes (including the existence and concreteness). If the mode has space as a characteristic (and *pradeśa* has been regarded as such a characteristic by the Jains), then the substance, also, would have to have the characteristic of space. It is only under these conditions that the substance can be divided into *paryāya*, or mode. Thus, the primary substance, or *dravya*, cannot be understood as a concept and *prayāya*, as something existing. But somehow, it is so thought. However, to do this is to adhere to some form of magic. The very moment we use the word *paryāya* and the word *dharma* in the context of 'substance' or *dravya*, we are , in fact, using the world *dravya* or sunstance' as a collection of all *paryāya*s or 'modes'. It is in such a context that we should understand Jain thought in respect to *jīva* and *ajīva*. As soon as we regard *jīva* and *ajīva* as concepts, we are likely to get trapped in the logic or magic of the word 'concept'.

Let us see how we use the words *sajīva* and *nirjīva* or *ajīva*. They express an actual experience. But we also talk of *jīva* without body or body without *jīva*. One is something mysterious, the other is matter without consciousness. The abstracted *jīva* gets existential import or concreteness on account of the prefix *sa*°. *Sajīva* means that which has *jīva* (that may mean body, substance, etc.), and *ajīva* or *nirjīva* means that which has no *jīva*. In such use, the concept of 'space' is not integrated with the word *jīva* but is connected with 'that' which has got *jīva*. It is clear that in this use of the word *jīva*, *jīva* is not regardeed as something concrete, a concrete substance. The Jain use of the word *jīva* is different from this. This division, or even classification (but not abstraction), of which the Jains thought is of the *astikāya padārtha* (things which have existential or spatio-temporal body). Time is the only exception to this. Time is existing but it has no body indicating existence. When we divide things that exist or even classify them, we do it on the basis of two principles: one is the principle common to both, and the other is the one which distinguishes one from the other. According to the principle of division, the common element is known as *fundamentum divisionis*. What is the common element between *jīva* and *ajīva*? Jains are clear on this point. Space or boundedness by space is, according to them, the common point. It means that the Jain use of the word *jīva* is to be compared with the use of *sajīva* by other Indian philosophers. These other philosophers, as a matter of fact, use *jīva* as a characteristic, or at least use it as something other than 'substance' or *dravya*, although they may say that it is a substance.

It must be realised that place or space cannot be separated from the *jīva* in the Jain theory. *Jīva* and *pradeśa* are inseparable. They can only be distinguished in the conceptual process. The area of extension of *jīva* may become less or more but it can never be reduced to zero.

It must be recognised that this concept of *jiva* is different from the concept of *ātman* of other *darśanas*. It is, for example, not comparable to the concept of *ātman* of Vedāntins of Nyāya philosophers. The *jīva*, for Jain philosophers, is a concrete living particular. This concrete particular, they say, is also all-knowing, omniscient. The word 'omniscient' is ambiguous. Literally, it means 'one who knows everything'. But the use of the word has to be properly understood. Is it to be understood as one knowing everything that exists collectively and simultaneously, or is it to be understood as one who has ability to know anything and can know whatever he wants to know, whenever he makes an effort to do so? The second interpretation depends upon the ability and potentiality of the knower and does not mean that the knower has actually known everything. Similar is the case in regard to the word *sarva*. Is it to be understood as 'whole' or 'all' or 'any' or 'every'? These four English words have different shades of meaning. The word 'all' is used sometimes in the sense of 'every' and sometimes in the sense of 'any'. When we say that all men are mortal, we have in our mind a distributive use of the word 'all'. We have to say that each and every man is mortal. We are not concerned with the wholeness, or collectivity. We are not concerned with the class man. When the Buddha says, *sarvam duḥkhaṃ,* what he means is that every single and differnet experience is full of misery. On the other hand, when the Upaniṣads say *sarvam khalv idaṃ brahma*[2] what is meant is not just that each and every thing is Brahman, but it also means that everything collectively is Brāhmaṇa. The improper use of the words lead to confusion. This is illustrated in the different uses of the word *sarva*. Kundakunda defines *dravya* as *guṇaparyāyavat dravyaṃ*. When we talk of this *paryāya*, we mean that it is an *aṃśa*, that is, having each and every characteristic of *dravya* except the equality in extent. This is what is called the *aṃśāṃśi* relation. This is also indicated in Spinoza's use of the word *modus*. The relation between *dravya* and *guṇa* is not of this kind. One *paryāya* can be

---

2. *Chāndogyopaniṣad,* III.14.1.

separated from another *paryāya*. But both the *paryāyas* belong to the same level although their extent may vary. On the other hand, *guṇa* and *dravya* cannot be separated from each other although they can be distinguished. They do not belong to the same level.

Just as the Jain philosophers divide the world into *jīva* and *ajīva*, in the same way they give the division of *ajīva* into *pudgala*, *dharma*, *adharma*, *ākāśa* and *kāla*. I have a feeling that although I have used the word 'divide', the word 'divide' is not very appropriate here. Perhaps the most appropriate model for explaining this division is to be found in the *pratyāhāra* division of Pāṇini. Perhaps this kind of division may be called inclusive division. In Pāṇini's *pratyāhāra*, only the first and last letter are given, and they include all the letters in between. Take, for example, *pratyāhāra aṁ*. It stands for the letters *a, i* and *u*. On the other hand, if you take the *pratyāhāra ak,* it stands for *a, i, u, ṛ,* and *ḷ* ; i.e., it includes the previously expressed letters *a*, *i*, and *u* and also *ṛ* and *ḷ*. If we take the *pratyāhāra ik,* then the letter *a* will be excluded. A similar thing, I think, has happened in the Jain list of *dravyas*. When we talk of *jīva*, I think, it does not exclude a reference to *pudgala*, *dharma*, *adharma*, *ākāśa* and *kāla*. In fact, I feel such a reference is intended. If there is no reference to *pudgala* in *jīva*, *jīva* will be merely an abstract notion. Similarly, if there is no reference to *dharma*, *adharma*, *ākāśa*, *kāla* or 'time', even the *jīva* will be an abstraction. In the same way, if we take *pudgala* from the list of *ajīvas*, *jīva* would be excluded, but there should certainly be a reference to *dharma*, *adharma*, *ākāśa* and *kāla*. It may also be pointed out that when we use the word *dravya* in the Jain context, the use of the word is not comparable to the contemporary use of the word in Indian languages. In the pure concept of *kāla* or 'time', there will be no reference to *pudgala*, but when we use the word *pudgala*, it would and should necessarily have a reference to time. Time seems to be just a pure substance which does not include anything else. And *jīva* seems to include in it in some inseparable way the whole range of *dravyas* from *jīva* to *kāla*. All these *dravyas* will naturally have *paryāyas*. They become possible on account of spatial characteristics. Pure time would have no *paryāya*, for time is not determined by space.

We must also know the meaning of *dharma* and *adharma* in the context of *dravya* in Jain philosophy. In the first place, this use of the word has nothing to do with the use of the word in Jain ethics or in

Nyāya philosophy. Like the word *dharma, karma* is also used in different ways. Jains use the word *dharma* here as the cause of motion or mobility. The word *karma* is used as motion by the Vaiśeṣikas. In Jain philosophy the cause of this motion is *dharma*.[3]

It is a *dravya* and so behaves like *jīva* and *pudgala,* but is somewhat like *apūrva* or *adṛṣṭa*. Even *adharma* is to be understood in a similar way. It must be clearly undestood that in this context, the words *dharma* and *adharma* are not used in the sense of 'desirable' and 'undiserable'. *Jīva* has also the characteristic of *ākāśa. Akāśa* is usually used as that of which sound is the quality, symptom or cause. But for Jains, *ākāśa* does not mean this. Jains use it in the sense of 'space'.[4] *Ākāśa* means *avakāśa,* i.e., space. It is that which can be occupied by *pudgala* or *jīva,* etc. Such an *ākāśa* is known as *lokākāśa.* This is distinguishable and different from *jīva*, *pudgala*, *dharma* or *adharma*, but like the other four it is also positive (i.e., not abstract) and entity-like. However, the entity-likeness (can it be called mass?) or the capacity to occupy, in this case, is different. *Ākāśa* can contain *jīva*s and *pudgala*s, but *jīva* and *pudgala* can contain only as much *ākāśa* as their volumes occupy. For such existence (in a non-conceptual or non-abstract way), capacity to occupy becomes important, significant and relevant. *Kāla*, or 'time', does not have this capacity although it is positive, non-abstract and existent. This is how only *jīva*, *pudgala*, *dharma*, *adharma* and *ākāśa* become *astikāya*, i.e., having dimensions, whereas *kāla* does not become *astikāya.* We use the words 'is' in different ways, as for example, 'the concept is ', 'space is', 'a thing is', 'imagination is'. In all these cases 'is' signifies different things. I, therefore, think that in Jain philosophy, *astikāya* should be taken as that where the spatial parameter of occupation can be employed. In fact, the concept of *astikāya* is like Kant's concept of 'schemata'. Kant's categories behave like objects when they are associated with space and time. This is explicated by schemata.

Jains also use the term *alokākāśa.* This could mean either, (1) where there is space but nothing to occcupy it or (2) where there is space but no entity can occupy it. On the second alternative, it will be

3. But the Jain use of the word *karma* is different.
4. Vedāntins also use it in this sense when they use such words as *maṭhākāśa* or *ghaṭākāśa*.

like a logical space where nothing can *actually* exist. On the first alternative, it would simply mean the empty *ākāśa* not occupied by objects. For movements of things such an *ākāśa* is necessary; otherwise there would be no motion. But when we say that the liberated *jīva*s go to *siddhaśīla* (on the boundary of *lokākāśa*), the word *ākāśa* is not used in the entitative sense. It is used as a logical concept, although these words from spatial language like *śīla* and *akāśa* are also used in context. When the word *ākāśa* is not used in the logical but in the physical sense, *ākāśa* unoccupied by entities will also be *alokākāśa*. For how would that *ākāśa* unoccupied by entities be known except through imagination? From this a question can be asked: in what way is *ākāśa astikāya*? Or how is *ākāśa* known to sense-organs and mind? One can, perhaps, answer by saying that *ākāśa* is *astikāya* because it has the ability to contain other *astikāya*s. It centainly has extension, although its shape cannot be specified. Everything that is pervaded by space is also pervaded by time. But that which is pervaded by time need not be pervaded by *ākāśa* or for that matter by *jīva*, *pudgala*, *dharma* and *adharma*. Therefore, in the case of time, whereas we can say that it exists, we cannot say that it has extension or mass, which is a necessary condition for *astikāya* things. In the case of time, we cannot say that time is an entity like a table or chair, so it is not *astikāya*.[5]

Perhaps this may help us to understand the proposition that *jīva* is *astikāya*. If a *jīva* is without body, it would be abstract and would not belong to the category of entity according to Jains. For it is only the body which has the characteristics of space. No real object will be spaceless. Thus, in Jain concept, there would be things occupying space and time, and there would be space, and there would also be time. But if one talks of *jīva* without a body, that *jīva* would be merely conceptual and only notional. A *living being* cannot be separated from body. It is possible that the 'volume' of the body of *jīva* may undergo variations. For example, if a certain organ is amputated, the volume of the *Jīva*, also, will become less. The amputated organ will be lifeless. *Jīva*, *śarīra* and *ākāśa* can be distinguished, but in reality they cannot be separated. Thus, the concept of *jīva* is to be distinguished

5. For Nyāya philosophers, *kāla* or 'time' is the substratum of all entities, *sarvadharaḥ kālaḥ*. But Jain argument is different.

from the existent *jīva*. In the same manner, the body will be different and the space will be different, although they would overlap. But whether it is *jīva* or *śarīra* or *pudgala*, it would be measued in terms of 'space' only. But this is not so with time. Time is not dependent on any of these and even then, it is not conceptual. We can, therefore, say that time 'is' but we cannot say that it is spatial like *ākāśa*, or entitative like *jīva* or *pudgala*.

According to Jain philosophy, there are varieties of *jīva*. Once we accept *jīva* and what we call *mahābhūta*s are inseparable, the *astikāya jīva*s could be classified under *pṛthvī-astikāya*, *ap-astikāya*, *tejas-astikāya* and *vāyu-asrtikāya*. By permutation and combination, we could think of *jīva*s belonging to more than one *mahābhūta*. But there would not be a separate category of *ākāśāstikāya jīva* only. It is important to note that *pṛthvī*, *ap*, *tejas* and *vāyu* are *mūrta-dravya*s. It really means that these have spatio-temporal characteristics, that space and time are implicit, inbuild in them. But once we recognise that there are *jīva*s belonging to each *mahābhūta*, we will have to say that there are *astikākya jīva*s belonging to *pṛthvī* only, *tejas* only, *ap* only and *vāyu* only. And once we say this, we will have to conceive of *jīva*s which exist in different temperatures, in different motions, etc. Jains have propouned such a theory. Ordinarily, when we think of *jīvas* we do understant that they exist in certain temperatures only. It would not be proper to think that some kinds of *jīva*s exist in higher temperatures, for example, on the sun. But it is also true that some *jīva*s are comfortable within the range of a certain temperature. We, for example, say that certain vegetations are tropical, certain vegetations are polar, etc. Different trees and shrubs grow in different temperatures and climates. But from this we cannot conclude that there would be certain vegetables which will grow in darkness or on the Sun.[6]

What is the explanation of *dharmāstikāya* and *adharmāstikāya*? Once we regard *dharma* and *adharma* as the causes of motion and 'static' respectively, they cannot be conceptual and will have to be *astikāya*, and, perhaps, will have to occupy some *pradeśa*s, or space, however minute it may be. 'Yellowness' and 'humanity' are conceptual,

6. However, when we think of *tejas-astikāya*, certain insets included under tropism (photo-hortism) may come to our mind.

but when we say that they exist, we have to think of them as characteristics existing in some actual space and coordinating with something actual. Such spatial characteristics which ar^ grounds for motion and 'static' are known to us in terms of 'length' and 'breadth'. Perhaps it is on this account that the Jains thought of *dharmāstikāya* and *adharmāstikāya*. But adequate information is not available in the Jain scriptures or books on this point.

It is necessary to consider the Jain concept of *dravya* more elaborately. On first impression, it appears that the Jain concept of *dravya* is akin to the Vaiśeṣika concept of *padārtha*. But this looks like a superficial resemblance. For Jain thinkers first talk of *jīva* and *ajīva*, and under *ajīva* they include *pudgala*, *dharma*, *adharma*, *ākāśa* and *kāla*. This division and inclusion of *dharma* and *adharma* in this scheme misleads people. For in ordinary usage, *dharma* and *adharma* are not substantives but are qualities.[7] Here they are used only inthe sense of *dravya* or 'substance'. One must not forget that even the word *guṇa*, which ordinarily stands for 'quality', is sometimes used, for example, in Sāṁkhya, as a substantive. The three *guṇa*s of *prakṛti* are not qualities of *prakṛti*. They are constituents of *prakṛti*. In a similar way *dharma* and *adharma* in this context stand for substantives. Since the word *dharma* is also used in the sense of 'quality', or in Jain literature 'characteristic', it is natural to think that *jīva*, *ajīva*, *pudgala*, *dharma*, *adharma*, *ākāśa* and *kāla* are categories and not substances.

Another reason, also, may be adduced for thinking so. Once we classify and divide the world into *jīva* and *ajīva*, we are likely to think that this is a conceptual analysis of things. For in our ordinary concept of *jīva* it is something having no spatial qualities, something miraculous, and not having length, breadth or thickness. It is different from *pṛthvī*, *ap*, *tejas vāyu* and *akāśa*. Although we claim it as a thing, we use it more or less as a concept. For example, when we talk about a common man, i.e., man as a universal, we know that such a

7. There is a substantive — like use of *dharma* when we use *dharma* in the sense of 'religion', 'duty' or 'law'. But such substantives are abstract in nature and are not on par with *jīva* and *ajīva*. In fact, even in Jain philosophy, the words *dharma* and *adharma* are used in this sense in other places and in another context.

universal man never exists. Almost in the same way, we think of *jīva* in the body as a ghost in the machine. Once we regard *pudgala*, the physical consituent of *ajīva*, as the basic element in our scheme, we unconsciously regard *jīva* as secondary and treat it as something mysterious.[8]

Such misleading thoughts may breed the idea that this Jain thought is of *padārtha* or 'categories'. To think that *jīva*s are totally different from *ajīva*s is incorrect. *Ajiva* is not just a negation of *jīva*; *ajīva* and *jīva* are things which have something in common although they are different. *Jīva*s possess all the characteristics which are possessed by *pudgala*, *dharma*, *adharma*, *ākāśa* and *kāla*. They are different from the rest because the characteristics of *jīva* are successively eliminated, one by one in *pudgala*, *dharma*, *adharma*, *ākāśa* and *kāla*. In Jain thought, *pradeśa* is common to both *jīva* and *ajīva*, and consciousness is present in one and absent in the other, that is *ajīva*. Thus, for Jains *jīva-dravya* is not something abstract; it is not to be understood as just consciousness. It is, first, a thing or an entity having consciousness. *Jīva* is equivalent to *sajīva* of other philosophies. *Jīva* is a *sajīva-dravya* and other than *sajīva-dravya*s are *ajīva-dravya*s. It is like Pāṇini's *al* which includes all letters from *a* to *ḥ* inclusive of all vowels and consonants. *Jīva*s are, first, existents and therefore, they are *dravya*s. *Dravya*, therefore, gives us a division of existents like *jīva* and *pudgala* which is *ajīva*. They exist in their own right and they have the characteristics of *dravya*s which *dharma*, *adharma*, *ākāśa* and *kāla* also have. Only they do not have consciousness, which characterises *jīva*. *Dharma* and *adharma* are the *dravya*s which can be classified as (1) those having motion and (2) those having staticness. They would be like inertia, but what exactly they are is not explained by any Jain thinkers from Kundakunda onwards. It is said that Bhadrabāhu had thought over the same, but since his writings are not available today, we can do nothing except imagine what he thought.

There is a difference, however, between the motion of *jīva* and that of lifeless *pudgala*. Unlike the motion of *pudgala*, the one of *jīva* can be self-propelling. It can be *karma* or 'action'. Jain thinkers

8. Perhaps this has made Jain thought vulnerable insofar as *dhrauvya* and *nityatā* are concerned.

propound that action is also made up of action-atoms. These action-atoms must, therefore, be living atoms. The *pudgala*s have atoms but they are not action-based. So, in order for *pudgala*s to a have movement, the force of some other outside agency is required and they have to be in an orbit. Again, their motion will have to be expressed or exhibited in some kind of medium. It may be noted here that this process must introduce a medium such as ether, which physicists had for sometime introduced in physics. Ether was regarded as some kind of physical existent which supplied a medium for light-rays. In the same way, Jain philosophers thought of medium both for *pudgala* and *jīva*. Today when scientists send rockets to outerspace, we know that they break the layer of atmosphere, and proceed. But earlier scientists believed that nothing could break the cover of atmosphere. Even today, rockets have to overcome obstruction while passing through the atmosphere of space. This obstruction is either of the magnetic field or gravitation. We must know that ordinary light-rays cannot pass through cetain obstructions, but through these obstruction X-rays can pass. It means that different media-tracks are required for different kind of things. What is true of motion is also true of a static state. Today, man has succeeded in breaking an atom, but the process of breaking an uranium atom is different from that of breaking an hydrogen atom. An atom cannot be broken in an ordinary way. It means that the processes by which we can break different kinds of atoms differ.

The process of motion forms a kind of obstruction to non-motion. This obstruction can be removed by a certain process. Due to similar thinking, Jain thinkers must have thought that the cause of motion and the cause of non-motion must be some kind of ultra microscopic *dravya*s, or 'elements', and called them *dharma* or *adharma*. But, however, minute and microscopic these elements may be, they are positive and have to be in this world, that is in *ākāśa*, and have to pervade some space, maybe some kind of theoretical, geometrial space. As we go to micro things and, thence, to the so-called 'thingless' vacuum, we require real lenght, breadth, etc. Maybe they are infinitesimal, but they are not imaginary. It means that just as *pudgala*s are not absent in *jīva*s, or just as *dharma*s or *adharma* are not absent in *pudgala*s, similarly *avakāśa* or *ākāśa* is not absent in *dharma* and *adharma*. The Jain concept of *ākāśa* is of this type. This *ākāśa* is of two types: one is *lokākāśa* and the other is *alokākāśa*. In *lokākāśa* everything (from *jīva* to *adharma*) is existing, i.e., pervading and, therefore, they all have the properties of *ākāśa*. According to Jain philosophy, *jīvas*, whether liberated or unliberated, are still pervading; therefore, they pervade in *ākāśa*. They believe that liberated souls exist in the final limiting core of such *ākāśa*. This may be part of the poetry of metaphysics of the Jains. But all these *jīvas* and *ajīvas* exist in *lokākāśa*; without *ākāśa* neither the motion nor the non-motion can be generated. For motion and non-motion, like *dharma* and *adharma*, also presuppose *ākāśa*. But once we build a fence around this *ākāśa*, we have also to talk of something which is outside the limits of the *ākāśa*. This is the *alokākāśa* of the Jains. It is not just a poetic fancy. It is like a counter set (of a set) in mathematics. But no *jīva*, *pudgala*, *dharma* or *adharma* crosses the limit of (*lok*)*ākāśa*. All these *dravyas*, on account of their mass, whether macro or micro, have a body, and since they have a body, they are regarded as *astikāya*. All these elements, from *jīva*, motion (*dharma*) and non-motion (*adharma*), presuppose endurance, which is not possible without time and so, all of them are in time. Time means edurance, but it is not pervasive. All these *dravyas* that the Jains thought of are realities; they are not imaginary; they are not concepts. This is a thought about *dravya*, and about categories.

While thinking of the classification of *dravyas* as given by Jain thinkers, we come to understand the things, the nature of things as given by them. They had kept before them the physical matter as a paradigm. They say *dravya* is *guṇa-paryāyavat*. They also speak of beginning, permanence and destruction as the states of *dravya*. In the case of physical things alone, this is possible. We can class them into one class. *Pṛthvī*, *āp*, *tejas*, *vāyu* and *ākāśa* can be regarded as *paryāya* or 'modes' of this *dravya*. If we take gold, then the different ornaments of gold can be regarded as modes or *paryāya* of gold, i.e., we can think of one basic elements and its many modes. But how can we apply this concept to *jīva*? If we regard different *jīvas* as *paryāya* of *jīva*, then the particularity which is at the back of *jīva* is destroyed and instead of talking of the plurality of *jīvas*, we would have to talk of one living element. In Oriental thought, the Advaitins and in Western thought, Spinoza, have thought of such a kind of substance. But once we think of such a basic conscious substance, I am doubtful whether we can make the division of such a *dravya* into *jīva* and *ajīva*.

Similarly, regarding the concept of *jīva-dravya*, if we posit the state of permanence along with birth and destruction, then, as in the case of 'matter', we will have to assure that one permanent *jīva* would continue to exist even after particular *jīva*s are destroyed. This *jīva* would be permanent and immortal and also one. Thus, we are led to unitheism or unispiritism—*ekeśvaravāda* or *ekātmavāda*. Whether or not both these trends have arisen in Jain philosophy will have to be examined. Such a question did arise before Nyāya philosophy, and relying on the concepts of *ādhāra* and *ādheya* i.e., 'substratum' and 'superstratum', *ātman* was regarded as *ādhāra* and every characteristic of *ātman* was regarded as quality, *guṇa* or *ātman*. But if we now regard *dravya* as basic and *jīva* and *ajīva* as its *paryāya*s, shall we regard *jīva* as dependent on *dravya*? If we do not think so, then we will have to regard *guṇa* as a constituent entity following the Sāṁkhya style. But a further problem would arise if we think of *jīva* as entitative and *ajīva* as merely dependent upon it. Jains have accepted a plurality of *jīva*s. Are we to regard them as *dravya* or *paryāya*? If we regard them as *dravya*, what will be their *prayāya*s? And if they are *paryāya*s, are we to regard a combination of all these *jīva*s as one *jīva-dravya*? But, in such a case, where is the plurality of *jīva*s? We will have to think that at sometime the individuality of different *jīva*s would evaporate and a new individuality of the combination will come into existence. But when will this happen? Again, if we regard that the *jīva*s are infinite, then the question would arise whether we can postulate two caterories—*jīva* and *ajīva*. Spinoza's theory of pantheism gave rise to plurality of monads in the philosophy of Leibniz. If we regard *jīva*s as infinite and think that on account of their *karma* they belong to differnt species, then *jīva*s would be a class name. In that case, a combination of all *jīva*s could not be regarded as one *jīva*. The question is whether the classification of *dravya* and *paryāya* could be properly applied to *jīva*s. Either Jain philosophers should give an answer to these questions or they should say the concept or *dravya* cannot be applied to *jīva*s.

Nayavāda is another important doctrine in Jain philosophy. *Naya* means point of view. We know that according to Jain philosophy this point of view is of seven kinds. But we must think of the theory on two different levels; one would be the ontological and the other would be the epistemological. What is the real nature and status of the world? It could be one point of view. How do we get knowledge of the world? What is it, to know it definitely and positively? How do we get to know the world? This will be the second point of view — the point of view of epistemology or axiology. It will be the *vyavahāranaya*. Śaṅkarācārya has said that *vyavahāra* comes into existence on account of copulation of *satya* and *anṛta*. But it is not correct to say that it would be complete and comprehensive knowledge of *vyavahāra*. In Jain literature, we get the story of an elephant and the seven blind men. In *naya* theory, also, there are seven (i.e., many) alternatives of *dravya* and we get seven *paryāya*s. When *dravya* occupies a certain space, we get its knowledge gradually by combining the knowledge of the parts. Similarly, since *dravya* is in time, we regard that it is subject to past, present and future. But we can also think of *dravya* without consideration of the past and future. Thus, *vyavahāra* also can be considered from different points of view.

In Jain philosophy, the basic classification is in terms of *dravya* and *paryāya*. The two points of view indicated are known as *dravyārthika* and *paryāyārthika* (*naya*). These two *naya*s will have to be again tested on the touchstone of *niścaya* and *vyavahāra*. This will give rise to three *naya*s: *niścaya-naya, vyāvahārika dravyārthika-naya* and *paryāyārthika vyāvahārika-naya.* From the point of view of *niścaya-naya, vyavahāra-naya* is unreal or invalid, but from the point of *vyavahāra,* it is true. Thus, we get three folds: *sat*, *asat*, and *sadasat*. Tagare pointed out that Gosāla Maṅkhaliputta was trying to comprehend reality in these three modes and it is from this kind of thinking that he could posit three modes: *dravyārthika*, *parayāyārthika* and *ubhayārthika.* These *ajīva*s were known as *trirasika*. Tagare pointed out that from these *sat*, *asat* and *sadasat* came the three *bhaṅga*s: *syād astī*, *syān nāsti* and *syād astī ca nāsti ca*. I differ from Tagare. We will have to think here as to what is meant by *kevala-jñāna*. I believe that the Jain *kevala-jñāna* is comparable to *turīya-jñāna*, the *turīyāvastha* where the difference between knowing and being is compeletely annihilated. This kind of *jñāna* is certain knowledge. No *syād*, *vikalpa* or possibility is involved here. Such certainty is of two kinds, positive or negative. The knowledge which is neither positively certain nor negatively certain falls in the category of possibility, and, therefore, the *bhaṅgas* which will fall in the category of possibility will be totally different from knowledge either positive or negative. In the case of liberated man having *kevala* knowledge, these possible alternatives will be totally absent. They will be relevant only in the case of a practical man or one who desires *mukti*. So, although in *niścaya-naya* and *vyavahāra-naya* the word *naya* is common, still the word *naya* in these two usages is not of the same order. There can be seven (several) vaireties of *naya* belonging to the subclass of possibility. Therefore, we must try with sympathy to comprehend the Jain vision of *paryāya* in relation to possibilities. All these possibilities are true, for they give us (partial) knowledge of reality. Here arises the problem of expression: instead of saying that a particular thing *is* this, one could say that a particular thing *could be like* this. We could also express this in the form 'it can be of this kind', 'probably or possibly is of this kind'. If we assert that something *is* so, then that it *is not* so will be its contradiction. But 'possibly that thing is not so' is not the contradiction of 'possibly this thing is so'. Both these expressions could be different modes of one and the same truth. And all these different modes or alternatives can be collectively true (or collectively false) and again, although all these *paryāyas* or 'altenatives' could be known to us, it is not necessary that we should be able to express them in language. They could, therefore, be *avaktavya*, or 'inexpressible'. We must remember that the meaning or intension of *syāt* and *tavya* is the same. Both mean possible. So from *asti*, *nāsti* and *ucyate* we get seven alternatives: *syād asti*, *syān nāsti*, *syād asti ca nāsti ca*, *syād avaktavyaḥ*, *syād asti cāvaktavyaḥ*, *syād nāsti cāvaktavyaḥ* and *syād asti ca nāsti cāvaktavyaḥ*. All these are modes of knowing or knowledge. But in addition to these modes, we have to accept two more which are implicitly in Jain thought and expressed by them elsewhere under the name of *niścaya-naya* (positive and negative); knowledge of certainty is not a knowledge of *paryāya*, 'mode' or 'substitute'. So, in the epistemological framework there will be seven substitutes or possibilities. But in logic, in addition to the seven possibilities, there would be two certainties[9] expressed by certain truth and contradiction. If we have to put the Jain modalities in a logical format, we will have to add the *niścaya-naya* in two modes, positive and negative, and make it a format of nine. The two certainty alternatives act like the limiting posts in the game of *kho-kho*.

Jain philosophers have, in this context, used the three technical words: *bhaṅga*, *naya* and *syāt*. They are not identical in meaning; they are three different concepts and have a role to play in Jain thought. But many a time, Jain philosophers have used these words loosely and this has given rise to certain confusion. Some modern interpreters have used *syāt* to explain possibilities; some people used it in the sense of 'value' which is at the back of many-valued logic. When the word 'possibly' is used, many Jains think that it is not a proper word and that it expresses doubt. It certainly has a shade of doubt, but this shade points to something positive. For the two alternatives, complete certainty and complete contradiction, have been already eliminated. Some people regard that the word *syāt* is also used for expressing the seven points of view. This is because the words *bhaṅga* and *naya* are supposed to be alternative words for expressing the same ideas. Let us examine these words.

The word *naya* is used for expressing different points of view. For the Jains, the points of view can be only two, primarily, *vyavahāra-naya* and *niścaya-naya*. In *vyavahāra-naya* is reflected man's viewpoint to look at the world, whereas the *niścaya-naya* is cosmocentric in focus, self-luminous. Thus, the *niścaya-naya* leads us to ontology, whereas the *vyavahāra-naya* belongs to the sphere of epistemology. Ontology is not concerned with different viewpoints; there is always only one. There cannot be different possibilities as in *vyavahāra-naya*. But man can have different points of view, concerned with our knowing, our understanding. They are not concerned with being. For being is being. Here one could remember the Vedic *mantra*, *ekaṃ sad vipra bahudhā vadanti*. *Sat* is only one, *vipras* express it in different ways. Expressing (*vadanti*) is concerned with knowing. In knowing or expressing, one can commit mistakes also, so there will always be alternatives, true, false, or neither.

9. 'Certainty' is to be distinguished from 'necessity'.

Such knowledge in the technical language is *dharma-jñāna* and not *dhārmī-jñāna.* But even though something is related to *dhārmī*, its knowledge will be merely the knowledge of characteristics, and again, every *dravya* has its modes and is also subjected to birth, continuation and destruction. So even here it will be subjected to few alternatives like *naigama* and *saṁgraha.* Similarly, on account of our difficulties and complexties in knowing, there will be alternatives like *ṛjusūtra, śabda, samābhirūḍha, evaṃbhūta*, etc. These will be human points of view. A point of view may be different from other points of view. But even in the same point of view there could be different shades. On account of these differences in the same *naya* or 'point of view', people must have used another word caled *bhaṅga*. These *bhaṅga*s were in the beginning only three, and the *naya*s were only two. But from these *bhaṅga*s emerged seven *bhaṅga*s and they gave rise to seven points of view. All these points of view need not be completely exclusive of one another. So when one thinks of whether or not they are completely exclusive, the theory of *syāt* can be understood satisfactorily. In *syādvāda*, also, there are seven *bhaṅga*s. The 'seven' seems to be very prominent in Jain thought.

Let us take the first proposition, *syād asti*. We must first know that this proposition is about *dharma-jñāna* and know further that it is concerning its predicate. So its logical form would be '. . . *syād* . . . *asti*'. We have to keep the subject place open, for it would have to be filled in by some *dharmī.* Some *dharma* could be specified, for example, between *syād* and *asti.* One could put the word, e.g., rose in the first blank, and the word *śubhra* or *mṛdu*, etc., in the second blank. This will be a characteristic; it will be objective in nature, and the position is kept vacant not on account of our not knowing its nature but rather on account of there being a possibility, or probablity. It should also be known that although existence is not a predicate, existence is not completely bereft of predicateness, for in order for the predicate to be predicate, its first essential is that 'it is'. So the real propositional format of *syād asti* is: 'Some χ is (perhaps, probably, possibly) ρ'. If we take another propositional format *syān nāsti*, then it will be 'Some χ is (perhaps, possibly, probably) not ρ'. It must be known that in such a format the sign of negation changes the status of ρ without affecting the status of the predicate. In the above case, the scope or jurisdiction of the negative sign is over ρ

only. But if the predicate is to be negated, then it has to be negated by 'is not'. In that case, the negation operator would have scope over 'perhaps' or 'possibly' or 'probably', and negated proposition would be: 'Some χ is not (perhaps/ possibly/ probably) ρ'. And this is different from 'Some χ is (perhaps/possibly/probably) not p'. If we merely take the words *syānnāsti*, we might be misled to think that *nāsti* denies the subject, but it is not so. *Asti* and *nāsti*: these words do negate each other. But when qualified by *syāt*, they do not so behave *syād asti* like the adverb of *astī*. Again, they are not concerned with the subject in any way. Thus '. . . *syād asti* and . . . *syānnāsti*' can go together, for the subject is thereby unaffected. The same will be the case in regard to *asti* and *avaktavya* and *nāsti* and *avaktavya*. A thing may exist but it is not necessary that it should be expressed. So *syād asti*, *syānnāsti* and *syād avaktavyaḥ* — all these can go together. Thus, all seven *bhaṅga*s are compatible with one another and do not contradict. It means that although some of them may not be true, the truth value of the compound proposition is always true; it is compounded by the truth function *or*, and so, if one of the alternatives is true, the whole expression would be true. This is so because of the modalities. No proposition in this scheme is really negative. The Jain logic should be studied in this way. Only in this way can justice be done to the *syādvāda* of the Jains.

Finally, it is necessary to point out that the loose use of expression is not uncommon to Jain thinkers. The words *dharma* or *ātman* can be cited as examples of such loose use. Since *dharma* and *adharma* are used by Jains in the classification of *dravya*, they sould have struk to it. But in the beginning of the *Samayasāra*, too, Kundakunda sometimes used the words *dharma* and *adharma* in the way Mīmāṁsā uses them, that is, they are used with ethical connotation. This is equally true of *ātman*. As a matter of fact, the words *jīva* and *ātman* do not have identical status. Primarily, *ātman* is a pronoun like 'I', and is the first person singular. But gradually, the use of the word was extended and it became a noun. This has happened in all systems of Indian philosophy. Even a great philosopher like Kundakunda is not an exception. *Ātman*, *jīva*, *puruṣa* in fact, have different status. But they were used as if they were synonymous. So although the Jain philosophy is different from that of Vedānta, gradually Jain thought was combined with it.

12

The Grammar of Indian Moral Concepts

I HAD once asked a question whether there could be philosophy or for that matter any reflective study if the human race were dumb, and I had replied that in such eventuality (*i*) it would be difficult to convey our thoughts to others and (*ii*) sometimes it would be even difficult to form our thought ourselves. For, thought does require some models and relations connecting the models and it is not possible to have them without translating them into linguistic forms. Language thus comes to perform a very important aspect of any theory and how the different concepts in a theory are used, becomes the task of grammarians. One difficulty in regard to language, however, is that the words on account of misuse sometimes become meaningless, sometimes they become obsolete and sometimes they become degenerate and sometimes they are also used in different senses, i.e., new uses come into being. All such things distort the word meanings and obstruct the growth of theory. Patañjali, the author of the *Mahābhāṣya*, while discussing the purpose of grammar has said that grammar may be preserved for preserving logic, the *Āgamas* and for making the language pithy and clear and unambiguous. But inspite of the warning given by Patañjali, Sanskrit language and the thought within it, is obstructed and, therefore, today we do not know how some of the concepts I am going to discuss below were meant to be handled, when they were introduced in the grammar and *dharma* literature. What is true of words, it must be remembered, is also true of suffixes which give us different forms of the words in their different uses.

Vyāḍi, an important Sanskrit grammarian whose works are lost except in some fragments quoted by others, said that although there appear to be a large number of verbs (and verbs indicate some kind of *kriyā* or action), the verbs can be properly classified under two heads only. Therefore, there are two and only two verbs. They are: *as*, 'to be' and *kṛ*, 'to do'. In fact, these two verbs are pointers to the fact that the reality is also of two types, the one which is, *sattā* and the other which is created by man, imposed on the earlier reality by some kind of symbiosis. Its *samavāyī-kāraṇa* is the reality that is given and its *asamavāyī-kāraṇa* is supplied either by the dynamic aspect of the reality or by *kartā*, in this context, the man.

To the classification of verbs given by Vyāḍi I would add one more verb, viz., *bhū*. In the strict sense of the term *as* does no give us an action, it only represents the existence, the eternal present, it has neither the past nor the future. But the reality has ability to get transformed, it has a dynamic aspect. The concept of reality is not that of just being, it is also that of becoming and it is suggested by the word *bhū*. Its face is like *as*, but its behaviour is like *kṛ*. That is why all the future forms of *as* take the form of *bhū*. *As* will not become *aśiṣyati*, it only-becomes *bhaviṣyati*. So far as the past tense is concerned, perhaps *as* and *bhū* will behave alike and, therefore, *abhavat* and *āsīt* would perhaps mean the same. But in their *vidhi* forms they would behave differently, *astu* and *bhavatu* suggest different patterns of behaviour. Like *bhavati*, *bhavatu* also suggests its possibility of being in future time. *Astu* merely suggests o.k.ness. We would be able to translate *astu* by the phrase, 'well, O.K'. *Bhū* does not really point out to something that actually is and, therefore, it becomes an ideal verb for suggesting action and for being used in optative moods. Sanskrit grammarians sometime say that *bhū* is a form of *kṛ, bhū iti karaṇe dhātuḥ*. But although sometimes the root *bhū* is used in the form of *kṛ*, the action suggest by *bhū* and the action suggested by *kṛ* are different.

It may also be pointed out that in the strict sense of the term Sanskrit grammar does not talk of tenses. They have used one common word for expressing both the tenses and the moods. The word they have introduced is *lakāra* and they are of two varieties, one is called *laṭ-lakāra* and the other is called *laṇ-lakāra*. But under *laṭ-lakāra* comes *loṭ* which is generally translated as imperative and under *laṇ-lakāra* comes the two *liñs*: *vidhi-liñ* and *āśīr-liñ*. It perhaps means that with *laṭ-lakāra* goes either some kind of necessity or certainty and with *laṇ-lakāra* goes some kind of freedom (but of course this hypothesis will have be tested). But these two forms give us two moods, one is imperative and the other is optative, and, thus, make a way for prescriptions or law-theories and desirabilities or end-theories.

Like the verbal forms of *liñ* and *loṭ*, grammarians have also used or discovered participles with the ending in *ya, tavya* and *anīya*. They also fall in two groups, the *pratyaya* in *ya* is either *yat,* or *nyat* and the *pratyaya* in *tavya* is either *tavyat* or *tavya*. The *sūtras* being *yat nyat* and *tavyat tavyaniyaraḥ*. Grammarians normally consider the linguistic forms with these affixes added to them as conveying an order or command or the freedom to act to the hearer or reader. This seems to be ambiguous. In the first place an order or command or even freedom to act will be only with regard to the verbs which convey action and, therefore, will be some form of the verb *kr̥*. *Bhū* being of the form of *kr̥*, these *ya, tavya* and *anīya* could be affixed to them. Thus, form *bhū* by adding word *ya* will become *bhavya*, by adding *tavya* it will become *bhaviavya* and by adding *anīya*, it will become *bhavanīya* (though the form *bhavanīya* is not in use). Form *kr̥* the forms will be *kārya*, *kartavya* and *karaṇīya*. To me it appears that *tavya* suggests some kind of necessity, some kind of compulsion and, therefore, *bhavitavya* stands for fate having no other alternative and *kartavya* stands for duty having a *must* about it. *Bhavya*, *kārya* and *karaṇīya* do not seem to have any kind of compulsion suggested by their use of meaning. But grammarians like Pāṇini or *vārtikakāra* like Kātyāyana, *bhāṣyakāra* like Patañjali or other great grammarians in the tradition from Bhartr̥hari to Bhaṭṭojī Dīkṣita do not seem to have discussed these points which are philosophically important and which would give us optative forms or imperative forms. Perhaps on account of the usages which became current from time to time the original distinction might have been erased. This, e.g., happens in the case of *vidhi*. Originally, *vidhi* in *vidhi-liñ* suggested some kind of freedom. But when such *vidhis* became connected with rituals, although they were requisitions and were not in the form of orders or commands, they acquired the sense of obeying. The optatives became latent imperatives. Thus, the *vidhis* are classified under five sub-heads (1) that which must be normally obeyed or *nimantraṇa*, (2) that which has a permission to act according to one's choice, (3) that which is a kind of a request or *adhiṣṭa*, (4) that which is of the nature of persuasion, *samprasana,* and (5) a request, *prārthanā*. The first four types are compressed into one expression *pravartana* or making one to act. Or one could also say that the first four types are only the expansions of what is meant by *pravartana*. (*Padmañjarī* on *Kāsikā*, *Pā*. 3.3.161). The next *sūtra* of Pāṇini 3.3.162 is *loṭ ca* which means the verbal ending *loṭ* also conveys the meanings conveyed by *liñ*. This suggests that *liñ* and *loṭ* became interchangeable (at some point of time) without affection the meanings. The next *sūtra* 3.3.163 of Pāṇini says that the *kṛtya* suffixes *tavya*, *tavyat*, *amiyar*, *yat*, *kyap* and *nyat* although six are virtually three as far as the tangible forms are concerned and are used to convey (1) the meaning of order — *praisa*, (2) permission to act according to one's choice — *atisarga* or *kāmācārānujñā*, and (3) indication of the time to act — *prāptakatā.* It means that *tavyat* forms one group, *aniyar* forms another and *yat*, *kyap* and *nyat* form the third. The *sūtra* 3.3.169 of Pāṇini further tells us that *kṛtya* suffixes also mean 'to deserve'. He also states that these suffixes can be used to convey the force — necessarily or the cover oblige (*Pā*., 3.3.171).

Pāṇini further tells us that *kṛtya* affixes can be used to mean 'to be able to' (*Pā*. 3.3.172). The *liñ* and *lot* can also be used to mean desirability (*Pā*., 3.3.157). Pāṇini goes further and says that when two statements, the meanings of which are connected as cause and effect are to be made (i.e., a conditional statement) even with regard to a past act the *liṅ* can be used, e.g., had the teacher been there we would have read (*ādhyāpakaś cet āgacchet adhiyāmahi*).

Thus, according to grammarians the *liñ, loṭ* and the *kṛtya pratyaya*s can be used to indicate many moods and tenses of an act, viz., (1) order, (2) command, (3) obligation, (4) freedom to act, (5) request, (6) requisition, (7) reminding of proper time, (8) entreaty, (9) desire, (10) ability, (11) necessity. But in usage, especially with regard to enjoining, religious or moral acts generally the words with *liṅ*, *loṭ*, *ya* and *tavya* are formed. Pāṇini himself says that in Vedic language *loṭ* is used in the sense of the *liñ* — *liñ arthe loṭ* (*Pā.*, 3.4.47). It means that these concepts were regarded as different but later, on account of usages the distinctions were obliterated. However, one can peep through them and see how these different suffixes stood for different concepts. It may be added that Mīmāṁsakas, Naiyāyikas and others accept this position of the grammarians regarding the linguistic form of the order or enjoining.

Śabara in the *Pūrvamīmāṁsā sūtra,* 4.3.3 has made a very significant remark while explaining the *vidhi* and linguistic form which conveys it. He quotes a verse which prescribes that the *liṅ* form of the root *kṛ* or *as* (to be) and the *tavya* suffix connote a *vidhi* or enjoining

evaṃ hi padavākyārthanyāyavidaḥ ślokam āmananti:
kuryāt kriyeta kartavyaṁ bhavet syād iti pañcamam ।
etat syāt sarvavedeṣu niyataṃ vidhilakṣaṇam ।। 4.3.3

The form of *vidhi* when translated into English may roughly mean: 'One shall do', 'It should be done', 'It ought to be done', 'It should be so', 'It ought to be so'.

I have pointed out earlier that according to Grammarians the affixes *yat*, *nyat*, *tavyat*, *tavya* and *aniyar* and *loṭ* (imperative) and two forms of *liṅ-vidhi* and *āśīr* suggest varieties of senses. At least some of them may suggest command, order, prescription, suggestion, request, desire or expression of volition. I may also point out here that except the overt command every other *vidhi* is, in fact, optative in form and is not a case of command. We will have to say that the varieties only suggest weaker and stronger forms of optatives. The ethical theory according to me, comes out of the blending of two concepts: (1) desiring and (2) owing (that is our debt to others). When the second concept dominates it gives us two forms, (1) obligation where the domination is from within and (2) command or order where that domination is from outside. In the case of obligation, i.e., where the source springs from within, it is an outcome of freedom. Where it is a command the freedom part gets lost. But unless the order or command is just mechanical and accepted without understanding (where freedom would not be a constituent), all other commands which are consciously accepted, freedom will be playing its part and so a command will be also a kind of optative.

Perhaps this is what is suggested by Śabara. It will be a case where the desirable end takes the form of law perhaps as in the case of Kant. In fact, even in some of the dialects of Marāṭhī and Gujarātī languages there is a form of command which expresses a request, e.g., in Varhādī dialect we say *karjo*. The affix *jo* softens the order which otherwise would have been expressed by just *kara* — do. But the softened order suggests that the person to whom the order is given, has to accept it after understanding the order and has to execute it only after the order has been made his own and is to be executed as if it is his own initiative. Thus, when one says *kārya* using the termination *yat* or *nyat*, it means just desirable to do. When one says *bhavya*, it merely means desirable to have it. But when one says *kartavya*, the desirable part starts vanishing and the possible alternatives lapse in the background and the only alternative that remains is that he has to act although the act has not begun. But when one says 'do' then one has not to question 'why' but one has only to act on the order. It will thus appear that there is also a difference between *tavya* and imperative. I may also point out that there is a difference between *loṭ* or imperative and the two *liṅs*, the *loṭ* (imperative) sometimes acting like *liñ*.

The difference among these different moods and attitudes must be understood at psychological and philosophical level. We have to understand the moods which result in action. They are either due to our desires or they are due to commands from the superior. But our desire itself may take the form of commands and in that case we will say that it is our conscience or it is a categorical imperative and the like. The fact is that our action is either due to the internal source or the external and this is because man is not alone. He lives in society, i.e., has social relations with others and has also to react to the environment. Left to himself he could be free and desire anything and do anything perhaps in his mental space. But his freedom is continuously being curtailed either on account of the environment or on account of the interaction with the other's freedom and his own understanding that the other's freedom is as free and valuable as his own. He, therefore, rationally curtails his freedom. I, therefore, feel that man's behaviour has two poles: One is the pole of his freedom to another is the pole of his owing to others, i.e., *ṛṇa*. And on the scale of freedom and *ṛṇa* he adjusts his behaviour and in this adjustment arise the ethical norms as I said earlier by contrast. The successive and accepted adjustments are becoming norms and values. In Western ethics we learn desire-based ethics and ought-based ethics. In both these freedom plays a very important role. This part of freedom is exhibited according to me by universalising 'desires'. I have pointed out elsewhere the relation that exists between the desired and the desirable. G.E. Moore has said that the relationship between the desired and the desirable is not comparable to that which is seen and visible and that which is heard and audible. But I want to suggest that the verb 'desire' does not behave like 'see' or 'hear'. It is an expectation verb, it is some kind of expectation-achievement verb and not an episodic verb and, therefore, its logic is different. When I desire, the object of my desire is always desirable to me. Even when someone wants to murder, he desires so, because he thinks that it would be desirable to murder, that murdering would be valuable. In Sanskrit expression it would mean that it is *iṣṭa* at that time. But it is not *iṣṭa* because it does not lead to further *iṣṭa* consequences, he is not able to universalise his desire. A desire always is an individual desire but it becomes desirable only when it could be the desired end of everyone. That is, even in the case of desire theories the hypothesis is not based on solipsism. It has to take into consideration that there are other beings in the world, that there are other agents of action and to do this is to curtail one's freedom, is to accept the dictum that everyone owes everyone else. That is, desire theories are potentially ought theories and ought theories are also potentially desire theories, for they are based on the concept of freedom or *icchā*, *svatantratā*. All these again are possible because the man or the agent of action not only knows but also knows that he knows. Not only is *jñāna* possible but *anuvyavasāya* and *pratyabhijñā* are also possible. (In the *Yogasūtras*, Yoga is described as *nirodha* of *cittavṛtti*. This *nirodha* begins even in the case of an ordinary man and acts in all the situations). Basically, therefore, all ethical theories have in the background optative moods and this is what is expressed by Indian grammarians like Pāṇini and Mīmāṁsakas like Śabara.

Let us consider the two sentences: (1) 'You must do it' and (2) 'I must do it'. The first is perhaps an advice and may be even a covert or hidden order. If it is a hidden order, then it could be rephrased into 'do it'. Can the second 'I must do it' be rephrased into 'do it'? I am doubtful, i.e., it cannot be an expression of order, at least it is not an expression of order. Sometimes one does order oneself. But in that case its form would be 'You do it'. Like the case of self-consciousness 'I know that I know', here also the first 'I', is now ordering the second 'I' and says 'do it', i.e., 'You do it'. 'I' takes the role of both 'I' and 'you'. When you say 'You must do it' there is indeed some force. That force is an external force. When I say 'I must do it', it has some internal force. This internal force is known as *codanā* in Indian philosophical literature. 'You must do it' can be an advice and as an advice it will be a form of optative and if it is stronger still, it would take the form of an order. An optative can pass into an imperative or order or *vice-versa* dependent on the force that is has. It may take the form of request when it is weak and order when it is strong. But whether it is weak or strong, it is a form of imperative, and is primarily in the second person. Do it or must do it: this form of verb must usually go with you, not with 'I', the first person or he, she, it, the third person. But the grammarians while declining the verb forms also give the first person and third person forms of imperatives. *Bhavatu* and *karotu* are the imperative forms and go with third person. *Sahanā vavatu sahanau bhunaktu saha vīryaṃ karavāvahai* or *bhavatu bhavatām aśīrvādaiḥ vadhuvara maṅgalam* are such forms. The second clearly indicates that although the imperative forms are used, it is really a case of *āśīr liṅ*. The first is also an indicative of *vidhi*. But in both these *āśīr* and *vidhi* forms it is imperative mood, i.e., *loṭ* is used. Thus, the Sanskrit grammarians use only one scale, the optative scale, for explaining different moods from pure request to order through prescription, advice, etc.

In the sentence 'I must do it' the force is internal, it is an urge and should be called *codanā*. It is a psychological urge. The grammarians or the Mīmāṁsakas however do not recognise this internal urge. They say that it is the sentence 'do it', i.e., a sentence which is likely to 'start' (*pravartaka*) an action is *codanā*. Thus, to my mind the explanation they give of *codanā* is just mechanical. Such mechanical orders have transformed the theory of *codanā* into rituals. But fact remains that there is a difference between man and machine. Man has mind which manifests itself at least sometimes in the form of an urge. Unfortunately, the Mīmāṁsakas do not seem to have distinguished between the psychological state leading to action and expression of psychological state in language giving an order for action. The *kriyāpravartaka vacana* as a sentence leading to action will presuppose or will have in its background a psychological mood, an urge to do something which will take the form of 'I must do it'. I feel that when one 'must' (expressing a certain force) it goes with the first person pronoun or the *kartā*, i.e., when the potential action or the action likely to be initiated is the potential action of the doer himself. It gives us a primitive ought. The urge 'I must do it' should have its logical form 'I ought to do it'. If it is directed towards himself it will take the form of *kāma* and if it is directed towards others it would take the form of *dharma*. But in both the cases it will be a manifestation of *ṛṇa*, I owe; just as I owe . . . to others, I do owe to myself. This is later on recognised in *puruṣārtha*. But ordinarily it is not recognised, for I owe myself is a very special case of owing. I must primarily owe others. In fact, all shortcomings in the society, start on account of obeying the dictum that 'I owe myself alone'. It leads to egoism in philosophy, egotism in sociology. It brings about the concept of owning. 'I owe myself' leads to 'I own'. It leads to the concept of private property and becomes an assertion of my freedom. The verb 'owe' or its counterpart *ṛṇa* in Sanskrit must, therefore, indicate a direction 'towards the others'. And the ritualists seem to have made ample use of it either in the form of reinforcing ritualism or in some sense giving the philosophy of perpetuation of race. In the *Ādiparva* of the *Mahābhārata* there is a story of Jaratkāru. While wandering he goes to Pātāla world and he sees some living beings kept hanging. He asks them as to who they were. Reply comes 'We are your forefathers, father, grandfather, etc.' He asks as to why they were kept hanging. They reply 'You are keeping us hanging. You have not paid that which you owe us. We are, therefore, not getting an entry into heavens'. What was the *pitṛ-ṛṇa* which Jaratkāru had not paid? He had not married and had not produced a son. The *pitṛ-ṛṇa* seems to be the perpetuation of the family or the clan. But it comes from a *codanā* that '(you) must do it' and this comes from 'I must do it' which again is an expression of my urge to do it. To my mind the basic concept of urge is vitiated, when it is used in all such forms. But in its basic form it does give us the concept of ought. Our forefathers seem to have discovered it but they did not use it for developing a moral theory. But one thing follows from the whole discussion and the story that *codanā* ('I must do it') is a binding principle of society, when its meaning is 'I owe you . . . others'.

What is a duty or *kartavya* (*kr̥* + *tavya*)? We have seen that in its weaker sense it is an optative, a form of *tavya* and in a stronger sense it is a form of an order which is accepted. The concept of duty arises through the basic concept of owing and *svatantratā* or freedom (manifestation of self). When on account of man's own freedom he universalises that everyone has freedom and everyone owes everyone else, an intersection of each one's freedom in ideal space takes place and each one's owing others now takes a limited form, in that ordered canvas, and this accepted, either it is legalised or moralised, and then our owing *r̥ṇa* or obligation passes into duty so far as it has a relation to others (and it is imposed from outside).

Notes on Dharma and Vidhi

1. DHARMA, RTA AND ṚṆA

The word *dharma* which is obviously derived from the root *dhr̥* to support or sustain, is a very ancient one and has many shades of meaning, and is therefore, difficult to translate into any other language. It certainly covers 'religious ordinances of the *Veda*', 'fixed principles', 'rules of conduct', 'the privileges duties and obligations of man in different contexts and in different stages of his life'. To those who want to study the Indian views on morals and ethics, an understanding or the different shades of its meaning is essential. The Mīmāṁsakas, especially Kumārila, stretches the meaning of *dharma* to include all those means which are used to attain the highest merit. He defines, following Śabara, *dharma* as *śreyas* (highest merit); the acts of religious rites and the means employed for them are, therefore, considered to be *dharma*, inasmuch as they are *śreyaḥ sādhana* (*Śl. Vār.*, 13-14). Another word which is important next to *dharma* is *r̥ta* which generally means 'the course of nature or the regular general order in the cosmos' and signifies the concept of (moral) law in the universe. Closely connected with this word is *r̥ṇa* which generally means a 'debt', and used to signify man's indebtedness to his ancestors, teachers and society at large. It can, therefore, be briefly stated that while *dharma* is comprehensive of all moral laws, ethics, code of conduct and religious acts, *r̥ta* is logical concept underlying it and *r̥ṇa* suggest the obligation of man to make his life conform to *dharma* and *r̥ta*.

2. VIDHIS

According to various writers on the *Dharma-Śāstra*, the sources of *dharma* are the Vedas, the moral codes based on the Vedic teachings, the conduct of people who are by consensus, noble and least selfish and one's own satisfaction of conscience. The last two are elusive of any clear-cut definition and may be difficult to have universal application. The Vedic sentences and the moral codes prescribe the 'dos' and 'do nots', sometimes with explanations and reasons and sometimes pointing to some definite results. The linguistic forms used for these presumptions may be discussed in brief, so that the basic elements for understanding the prescriptions and the logic underlying them may not be missed. As the grammarians are the authority as regards to these linguistic forms let us consider their statements on this.

Grammarians

The verbal forms which end in *liñ* or *loṭ* and the participles with the ending in *ya*, *tavya* and *anīyar* are normally considered to be the linguistic forms which convey an order or command, or the freedom to act the hearer or reader. Pāṇini (3.3.161) states that the verbal ending *liṅ* conveys the following meanings: An order to be obeyed and not to be questioned (*vidhi*), requisition, though not an order or command, must be normally obeyed (*nimantraṇa*), a permission to act according to one's choice (*āmantraṇa*), an entreating request (*adhīṣṭa*), persuasion (*sampraśna*) and a request (*prārthanā*). The first four meanings can be compressed into one expression (*pravartanā*) or making one to act (or one can say that the four items are only an expansion of what is meant by *pravartanā* (*Padamañjarī*, on *Kāśikā*, *Pā.*, 3.3.161). The next *sūtra* of Pāṇini (3.3.162) is *loṭ ca*, which means the verbal ending *loṭ* also conveys the meanings conveyed by *liṅ*. This suggests *liṅ* and *loṭ* are interchangeable without affecting the meaning. The next *sūtra* (3.3.163) of Pāṇini says that the *kṛtya* suffixes (*tavya, tavyat, anīyar, yat, kyap, vyat,* although six, are virtually three as far as the tangible forms are concerned) are also used to convey the meaning of order (*praiṣa*), permission to act according to one's choice (*atisarga* or *kamācārānujñā*), indication of the time to act (*prāptakāla*). Another rule of Pāṇini (3.3.169) says that these *kṛtya* suffixes also mean 'to deserve', and further he states that these suffixes can be used in the sense of 'necessarily' or 'obliged' (3.3.171). Again Pāṇini gives the rule that the *liṅ* and *kṛtya* suffixes can be used to mean 'to be able' (3.3.172). The *liñ* and *loṭ* can also be used to mean 'desirability' (3.3.157) when two statements, the meanings of which are connected as cause and effect, are to be made (i.e., a conditional statement) even with regard to a part act, the *liṅ* can be used (3.3.156). For example, 'Had the teacher been there we would have read' (*adhyāpakaś cet āgacchet adhīyāmahi*).

Thus, according to the grammarians the *liñ, loṭ,* and *kṛtya pratyaya*s can be used to indicate moods and tenses of an act namely, order, command, obligation, freedom to act, request, requisition, reminding of the proper time, entreaty, desire, ability and necessity. But in usage, especially with regard to enjoying religious or moral acts, generally the *liñ, loṭ, ya* and *tavya* are found. Pāṇini (3.4.47) himself states that in the Vedic language (*chandasau*) *loṭ* is used in the sense of the *liṅ*. The Mīmāṁsakas, Naiyāyikas and others accept this position regarding the linguistic form of order or enjoining, following the grammarians.

Śabara in explaining the *vidhi* and the linguistic form conveying it, quotes a verse which prescribes that the *liṅ* form of the root *kṛ* (to do) or *as* (to be) and the *tavya* suffix connote an order or enjoining:

> *evaṃ hi padavākyārthanyāyavidaḥ ślokam ānanti —*
> *kuryāt kriyet kartavyaṁ bhavet syād iti pañcamam* ।
> *etat syāt sarvavedeṣu niyataṁ vidhilakṣaṇam* ॥
>
> — *Pūrvamīmāṃsā-sūtra,* 4.3.3

The form of *vidhi* when translated into English may roughly mean 'one shall do', 'it should be done', 'it ought to be done', 'it should be so' and 'it ought to be so'.

The Mīmāṁsakas on Dharma, Vidhi and Codanā

As the source of order or command on morals is to be found primarily in the Vedas, since the Smṛtis or treatises on moral conduct are only of secondary importance, because they derive their authority from the Vedas 'an examination' of the views of the Mīmāṁsakas on *vidhi* or order is essential. The *Pūrvamīmāṃsā-sūtra* defines *dharma* as *codanā lakṣaṇo'rthaḥ*. Śabara explains the word *codanā* as *pravartakaṃ vacanam*; the utterance that motivates the hearer to act — *lakṣaṇa* is interpreted as *pramāṇa*, authority. So it comes to mean that thing which has the authority of Vedic order is *dharma*. He also says that *dharama* is *śreyas* which is supreme satisfaction or bliss. Kumārila explains that *śreyas* is the satisfied condition of man. That is to be attained by the things, their specialities and acts (*dravya, guṇa* and *karma*). The authority for their being, for attaining satisfaction are the orders of the Vedic sentences which motivate man to action. Therefore, the things, their specialities and acts constitute *dharma.*

śreyo hi puruṣaprītiḥ sā dravyaguṇakarmabhiḥ ।
condanālakṣaṇaiḥ sādhyā tasmāt teṣv eva dharmatā ।।
— *Ślokavārtika*, *Codanāsūtra*, 191

But there are also Vedic sentences which refrain men from certain acts, although some sentences may enjoin certain acts. So it is necessary to accept that the Vedic sentences which are positive in enjoining some acts as well as those which are in negative form and refrain man from certain acts do come under the purview of *codanā*.

Kumārila has slightly modified the definition of *codanā* 'as the sentence motivating man to act' given by Śabara. He says that what is meant by Śabara is that *codanā* consists in the awareness of the persons hearing the Vedic sentences that should act or refrain from certain act:

pravṛttau vā nivṛttau vā yā śabdaśravaṇena dhīḥ ।।
sā codaneti sāmānyaṃ lakṣaṇaṃ hṛdaye sthitam ।
— *Ibid.*, 210b-211a

Pārthasārathī notices the shift in the meaning of *codanā* and states that 'awareness is also *codanā* as the word *dhīḥ* indicates. He further quotes a verse to support this view. The verse means that the utterance which causes the knowledge in the hearer in the form 'I shall do' is meant by *codanā*; or it can also be the knowledge which results in activity:

pravarte'ham iti jñānaṃ yena śabdena janyate ।
sā codanocyate yad vā pravartanaṃ phalāmatiḥ ॥

Further in order to accommodate the statement of Śabara that *codanā* makes one know of the past, present and occurring in future, Kumārila says that the word *codanā* in this statement is to be taken as 'an utterance' (*śabda*) not a particular utterance alone (*śabdaviśeṣa*) which induces activity. Pārthasārathī clarifies this view of Kumārila and points out that since every utterence is valid as it generates a knowledge (in the hearer) *codanā* which is also an utterance can be valid in generating a knowledge of *dharma* which is beyond perception and reasoning:

tenaivaṁ bhāṣyārthaḥ codanāyāḥ prāmāṇyaṁ
dharme. kutaḥ? śabdasya hi sarvasyaiva
jñānajanakatvena prāmāṇyaṃ sambhavati.
śabdacodanā. Tana asyāḥ sambhavati
atīndriya'pi dharme prāmāṇyam iti.

Prabhākara differs from Kumārila in interpreting the passage of Śabara explaining the nature of *codanā*. He asserts that the interpretation of the *Codanā-sūtra* should only refer to those Vedic utterances which order an action. The natural question here is how can there be validity for the *mantra*s and *arthavāda*s which do speak of an action to be accomplished but merely make statements of some facts? Prabhākara answers this question by stating that these statements of facts are also connected with the order for action and, therefore, they get validity. Śālikanātha, the faithful commentator on Prabhākara further elucidates that the word *dharma* in the *Codanā-sūtra* is intended to convey only the Vedic meaning (*dharamśabdaś ca vedārthamātraparaḥ*).

Now the question is which is the part of the Vedic utterance in a sentence that conveys the meaning, order, etc.? *Codanā* or *vidhi* as we have seen above stands for both the utterance and the meaning of order which it conveys. Here the Mīmāṁsakas themselves hold different views. We shall examine the views of Kumārila and Prabhākara, one after the other.

Kumārila Mīmāṁsakas

Kumārila Bhaṭṭa has made two statements regarding the meaning of *vidhi*, i.e., the grammatical forms ending in *liṅ*, *loṭ*, *ya*, *tavya*, etc., which have given room for interpreting his views on the subject in different ways. Both the statements are often quoted by his followers and the writers on other schools of philosophy. The first statement is:

> *abhidhābhāvanām āhur anyām anyām eva liṅādayaḥ*
> *arthātmabhāvanātvanyā sarvākhyāteṣu gamyate* ||

We may analyse this by taking the stock example. There is a Vedic utterance *yajeta*. This consists of two parts, grammatically. The root *yaj* and the suffix *ta*. *Ta* is the form of *liṅ* which means order, command, permission, etc. *Liṅ* as well as all other *la* forms (such as *laṭ*, *liṭ*, *laṅ*, etc.) suggest an action. That is to say they are verbal forms. Therefore, *liṅ* implies two things, (1) that it is a verbal form and (2) it conveys order, etc. So, Kumārila says (in the above quoted verse) that *liṅ*,etc., mean *abhidhā*. This *abhidhā* is not to be confused with the *abhidhā* accepted by all as a function of word in denoting its primary sense; so it called *abhidhā-bhāvanā*. This is the exclusive function of *liṅ*, etc., and different from the significatory function which is common to all words. This *abhidhā* motivates man to act and, therefore, it is called *bhāvanā*, which literally means a particular operation or activity of an agent which conduces to the coming into being of the result. In *yajeta*, the *ta* element which is *liṅ*, signifies motivation to activity and the act is here *yāga* (giving away oblation to the deities), which is the meaning of the root, *yaj*. As *liṅ* is also a verbal suffix it signifies an effort or volition (*pravr̥tti* or *kr̥ti*) as all verbal suffixes do. Thus, the *bhāvanā* significant of *liṅ* gets itself related to the volition (*pravr̥tti*), the significant of the verbal suffix through *yāga* (the meaning of the root *yaj*), by force of *yogyatā* or contextual compatibility, as the *yāga* is a means to achieve the desired end (*svarga*,etc.). This capacity of *liṅ* to motivate a person to activity is a called *śābdī bhāvanā*. Why? When a person utters imperative or order form, the hearer understands that he is motivated to action by the former. Here the motivation is in the form of a desire in the utterer. This can hold good in the common parlance, between man and man in a community. But with regard to the Vedic sentences this cannot hold good. For, the Mīmāṃsakas do not accept an utterer of the Veda. They hold that the Veda is 'beginningless' and they do not accept God or Īśvara who could have uttered the Veda at the beginning of the creation. So, for the Mīmāṁsakas, the *śabda*, here the *liṅ* itself has got the power to motivate; it is not a desire on the part of an utterer. Hence, it is called *śābdī-bhāvanā*. This *śabdī-bhāvanā* has its object in the *ārthī-bhāvanā* which is the significant of all verbal suffixes, namely the volition (*pravṛtti*). Thus, we find that the Mīmāṁsakas have transferred the 'desire' or 'feeling' of a person who orders another to the linguistic element *liṅ*, which is a verbal suffix.

Another statement of Kumārila was thus:

śreyaḥ sādhanatā hy eṣāṁ nityaṁ vedāt pratīyate.

This means that the Vedic passages convey the idea that whatever is ordered by them, leads to supreme satisfaction. This has been interpreted by some of his followers to mean that the significance of *vidhi* (or *liṅ*) is *iṣṭasādhanatā*, a means to achieve the desired result. A knowledge of it motivates man to act.

The Prābhākaras have a different view about *vidhi*. According to them the *liṅ*, etc., which are called *vidhi*, signify an injunction or command. It is directed to a person who hears the utterance. So, the person who hears the *vidhi* forms understands that he is commanded; and then acts. This command is called by the term *niyoga*. This injunction of *niyoga* in order to establish its own existence, requires a person who understands that he is commanded to act. Another expression for *niyoga* is *kārya* (is to be done). This is also *apūrva* as it is not known by any other means, but the Vedic order. Thus, the words *niyoga*, *kārya* and *apūrva* are almost synonyms, as they by different ways of description signify the same thing. *Niyoga* (order) refers to the person; *kārya* (is to be done) to the act (*yāga*) and *apūrva*, the intermediary new element which leads to the result ultimately at a different time. For *yāga* is an act of giving away, as has been already mentioned.

Svarga or heaven, the result, is to be achieved only after a long time. Thus, *apūrva* makes it possible to relate the act the result of which takes place in different times.

Maṇḍana

Maṇḍana Miśra, a renowned Mīmāṁsaka and independent thinker of eighth or ninth century has written a monograph on the subject of *vidhi*. The work is named *Vidhi-viveka*. He discusses the various theories and views advanced by Kumārila, Prabhākara and their followers, and others. He challenges the view of Kumārila that *abheda* is the meaning of *liṅ*, etc., and it is *vidhi*. He says it is a simple presumption and it is not conveyed by the utterance (*śabda*). So it cannot be the significance of *śabda*. He sticks to the point that if the utterance directly motivates action it will be a *kāraka* not a *jñāpaka*, and, thus, the fundamental nature of the function of *śabda* as *ajñāta-jñāpaka*, illuminating something which is not formerly known will be violated. Next he turns to the Prābhākaras and shows that their theory of *niyoga* is untenable. He puts this question: 'Is this *niyoga* (the awareness that I am commanded) which is obtained through the utterance, the meaning of the whole sentence or a particular word? It cannot be the first, for all agreed on the point that the sentence-meaning is obtained through individual word-meanings. It cannot also be the second, because a word-meaning requires syntactic relation, with other word-meanings in order to convey its meaning. This means, it requires something more that the words for its coming into being and this position violates the accepted rule *ananyalabhyaḥ śabdārthaḥ*. Another defect in the Prābhākara view is that it does not take into account the fact that *niyoga* can be only the function of a *niyoktṛ*, who must be a sentient being. As the Mīmāṁsakas do not accept any being responsible for the Vedas, the theory of *niyoga* gets a clean cut at its root. He finally comes to the conclusion that nothing but the knowledge that a particular act is a means for achieving the desired end (*iṣṭasādhanatā jñāna*) can motivate man to act. Therefore, the significance of *vidhi* in the form 'This is a means to achieve the desired end', and its knowledge motivates action. This position was acceptable to older Naiyāyikas and the later Grammarians like Koṇḍubhaṭṭa (*tasmāt iṣṭasādhanatvam eva pravartanā* (*Vaiyākaraṇa-bhūṣaṇa-sūtra*).

Naiyāyikas

Naiyāyikas have also interpreted *vidhi* as they also profess to have accepted validity of Vedic passages. Gautama states 'that which ordains in *vidhi*' (*vidhir vidhāyakaḥ* — *Nyāya-sūtra*,2.1.63). It refers obviously to the Vedic utterances and Vātsyāyana clarifies it by saying that this *vidhi* is the *Brāhmaṇa* portion of the Vedas (*ayaṁ vidhiḥ bhāhmaṇabhāgaḥ*). Vātsyāyana further elaborates that the word *vidhi* is found used in both senses, namely, the utterance (*śabda*) that enjoins something and its meaning, namely, 'the knowledge that this is a means to achieve the desired end'. The sentence that ordains is *vidhi*, it is also *codanā*. *The* meaning of it is either an 'order' or a 'permission' (Vātsyāyana on 2.1.63). Udayana, the celebrated Nyāya-Vaiśeṣika teacher has made use of this *vidhi* as an additional proof for establishing the existence of God. His argument is that if *vidhi* in the Vedic passages make man act, the passages should have the intended meaning to that effect. Intention is a mental mode of a sentient being. So we have to accept that the Vedic passages make us act, as they are intended by the utterer of such sentences to make us act. This utterer can be none but a thoroughly trustworthy person. As there can be no hundred per cent trustworthy person among the mortals, God is to be accepted, otherwise there will be no meaning for the Vedic passages. Udayana uses a very sharp imagery to convey this idea: This *vidhi* impregnated with the intention to motivate itself shows that the *śruti*-maiden has connection with a person, just as pregnancy assures a girl's contact with a male (*garbha iva śrutikumāryāḥ puṃyogaṃ darśayati*). The later Naiyāyikas brought in two more meanings besides *iṣṭasādhanatā* on the significance of *vidhi*. *They* are (1) the knowledge of the possibility of achieving the result by human effort and (2) that the achievement of the result does not involve great calamities which are unwanted. As Maṇḍana remarks, both these conditions need not be recognised as the significance of *vidhi* as they are known by common sense based on our experience. The more modern Naiyāyikas have, therefore, made it in this way. A *vidhi* normally conveys the idea that some act is a means to attain a desired end; but in certain contexts it also signifies the capability of the effort to achieve the result and in other contexts it may also imply that there are no undesirable calamities following the action.

In this way they have also affirmed the necessity of accepting *vidhi* as *iṣṭasādhanatā*.

Three Functions of Vidhi

The Mīmāṁsakas and others have accepted three types of *vidhi*s depending upon their different functions. There are some injunctions which convey a new information or order as to act in a particular way which is not got through any other means of knowledge. This type of injunctions are called as *apūrva vidhi*. The second type is restrictive injunction (*niyama-vidhi*). In this there are two alternatives of which one is ordered to be accepted. The third type is preclusion of one alternative when both are equally contextual.

The stock examples of these three types of injunctions given by the Mīmāṁsakaṣ are shown below. The injunction 'one should perform a *yāga* if one desires of heaven' (*svargakāmo yajet*) is and example of *apūrva vidhi*. Here the fact that *yāga* is a means of heaven is not known by any other means of knowledge except this Vedic passage. For obtaining rice for the sake of cooking it with the ultimate objective of making it an oblation to deities, there is an injunction, which is in the verbal form *loṭ*, 'He shall pound the paddy'. This is an example of *niyama-vidhi*. To obtain rice from the paddy what is required is to remove its husk. This can be done ordinarily by pounding it with a pestle or even by removing the husk from each grain with one's nails. So two or more alternatives are possible to obtain the rice. This injunction *vrihimāva-hanti*, therefore, restricts the possibility of removing the husk to the act of pounding (*āvāhanana*). The example for the third type is 'Five five-nailed animals are to be eaten' (*pañca pañca nakhāh bhakṣyāḥ*). This is not really a positive injunction as eating flesh is already established by men's appetites. Nor is it a restriction (*niyama*) as one can eat the flesh of five-nailed animals as well as of the other animals at the same time to satisfy one's appetite. It prohibits the eating of the flesh of animals other than the five-nailed animals. So, although in the form it is apparently an injunction as the word *bhakṣyāḥ* ending in the suffix *ya* is used, its function is prohibitory. The discussion on the *vidhi*s of these three types has been carried out by several writers beginning from

Kumārila up to Appayadīkṣita who has entirely devoted one monograph for this purpose (*vidhirasāyanam*). The discussion throws much light in interpreting many Vedic and secular injunctions, in the *śrutis* and the *Dharma Sāstras,* which have been of much help to the lawyers who have to interpret the legal implications of acts and statutes.

An understanding of the *vidhi* and its meanings and nuances is very necessary to understand and evaluate the concept of Indian Ethics. The examples of these different types of injunctions (*vidhi* forms) orders, permission, options, etc., may be drawn from the *Brāhmaṇa*s, and classical literatures, like, epics, Purāṇas and popular fables like *Pañcatantra.* Some *vidhi* forms are given below:

The Vidhi Forms

kuryān (bhavān), kurutat! (*bhavatā or bhavataḥ*)
kartavyam. (*bhavataḥ* or *bhavatā*) *kāryam.*
(*bhavataḥ* or *bhavatā*) *karaṇīyam. itas tati*
(*hotā*). *ādadhāti (bhajamānaḥ*).

You should do that. You are obliged.

You must do that.	You are expected.
You can do that.	You are ordered.
You may do that.	You are commanded.
You ought to do that.	(It is) Your duty.
Do that !	Your obligation.
You have to do that.	

13

Māyā-vāda

A Critical Examination of the Theory of World-illusion in Post-Śaṅkara Period

THE word *māyā-vāda* may have many meanings. In its wider application it may mean the whole theory of Advaitism and may thus include all the cardinal doctrines of Advaitism, such as the reality of *Brahman*, the illusoriness of the world, and the relationship between *jīva* and *Brahman* on the one hand, and *māyā* and *Brahman* on the other. In its more restricted sense, however, *māyā-vāda* may mean only the doctrine of the illusoriness of the world. In the present essay I proposed to discuss *māyā-vāda* in this restricted sense. In this connection I will consider the following questions: (1) Why is the world of our perception to be regarded as illusory? (2) Can it be intelligibly held to be unreal? (3) What is the cause of this world-illusion? Or is it without any cause? (4) If the cause of the world-illusion is an entity other than *Brahman*, what is the relation between the two? I shall begin by stating the answers which Advaitism gives to the above questions, and then examine whether the answers can be maintained justifiably.

However, before proceeding with the subject proper, it is necessary to point out that Advaitins regard Upaniṣads as the first and last authority for their doctrine. The authority of the scriptures as a means of knowledge must not be challenged. And, in fact, many supporters of Advaitism assert that it seeks only to give clearer expression to the truth which is already contained in the scriptures. It is, of course, true that Advaitism does not rely simply on Śruti but also adduces arguments in favour of its thesis. But Śaṅkarācārya, the greatest teacher of the doctrine has clearly said that argumentation is never conclusive[1] and may lead anywhere. But if Śruti is to be the last authority, then it is clear that the doctrine can neither be maintained nor refuted on the grounds of pure reason. But philosophy is a rational enquiry into the nature of Reality; so as a student of philosophy I shall confine myself solely to the rational part of the doctrine. There are, indeed, reasons to doubt whether the scriptures can be regarded as the final authority to decide what is and what is not.

(1) Thus, within the scriptures themselves three kinds of passages are found. Some of them definitely advocate the theory of Advaitism. But some are definitely against it. And there are other passages which are more or less indifferent and can be interpreted either way. Now, the question that will naturally arise is, which passages are more reliable. But the scriptures cannot themselves decide this issue. Many interpreters of the *Vedānta Sūtras*, taking their stand on the scriptures have arrived at conclusions which are altogether different from those of Advaitism. Under these circumstances it would be better not to adduce any scriptural testimony for maintaining any theory.

(2) Secondly, if it be said that Śruti (but not perception or reason) is the only valid means of knowledge, then all our philosophical thought is likely to end in utter scepticism. Even scriptural texts would be of no use as a means of knowledge unless they be heard, and, thus, perceived. If so, perception too, along with scriptures, becomes a source of knowledge. If perception does not give correct knowledge at any time, how can the scriptural texts? To the extent we believe that the scriptures give us true knowledge, perception must also be admitted as a valid means of knowledge.

Let us now consider why the Advaitins think that the world of perception is illusory. The reason why they think so is that according to them there is only one reality which is a differenceless, changeless, and attributeless consciousness or *Brahman*. It follows that if there be only one reality and if that reality be *Brahman*, then the world

1. *Tarkāpratiṣṭhānāt*, Cf. *Brahma-Sūtra*, Śāṅkara-bhāṣya.

cannot be real unless it is supposed to be identical with *Brahman*. But how can the world of multiplicity, difference, change, and attributes be identical with the attributeless *Brahman*? Hence, this world must not be real.

Still, it cannot be denied that the world appears, unreal though it be. What is the ground of this appearance? If there be any ground it must be *Brahman*. For, *Brahman* is the only reality that there is. But though in this way *Brahman* is the ground of the world-illusion still it cannot be regarded as its cause. If something is the effect of some other entity which is real, then the effect cannot be regarded as unreal; and if the world is the effect of *Brahman* then it would automatically follow that the world has the same order of existence as is enjoyed by *Brahman*. But this would imply two realities. Besides if *Brahman* be the cause of the world then it cannot be pure. So *Brahman* should not be regarded as the cause of the world.

Nevertheless, *Brahman* is the ground of the world appearance. That is, *Brahman* may be regarded as giving birth to the world of diversities without itself undergoing the least change in its nature. In our ordinary experience we meet with illusions where one entity appears in the place of another. In such experiences we find that the illusory thing does not affect the nature of the reality in which it appears. Thus, we may see a snake where there is really a rope. But the appearance of the snake does not change in any way the actual rope. The appearance of the world in *Brahman* is to be understood in a similar way.

For proving the illusoriness of the world the advocates of the doctrine usually give the following four arguments[2]: The world is illusory, (*i*) because it is an *object of knowledge*, (*ii*) because it is *non-intelligent*, (*iii*) because it is a *whole* made up of parts, i.e., because it is created, and (*iv*) because the things of the world are *limited* in

2. Cf. *Advaita Siddhi* —

   (*i*) *Prapañco mithyā dṛśyatvāt.*

   (*ii*) *Prapañco mithyā jaḍatvāt.*

   (*iii*) *Prapañco mithyā paricchinnatvāt.*

   (*iv*) *Prapañco mithyā aṁśitvāt.*

respect of (*a*) space, (*b*) time, and (*c*) one another. The arguments may be expressed syllogistically thus:

Major premiss

> Whatever is an object of knowledge, whatever is non-intelligent, whatever is made up of parts or created, and whatever is limited is illusory, just as the silver which is seen in the place of a shell is illusory.

Minor premiss

> The world is an object of knowledge, is non-intelligent, is created, and is limited.
>
> ∴ The world is illusory.

Now it seems clear enough that there is no formal fallacy in the above syllogism and as soon as we admit the major premiss, the conclusion inevitably follows. Nor does the major premiss seem to be untrue. No fallacy of 'illicit major' is involved here unless it be a fact that some object of knowledge or some non-intelligent thing, etc., is real. But are there not things which are objects of knowledge, or are non-intelligent, etc., and are still real? For example, an objector may urge that 'a pot' is an object of knowledge and still everybody knows that it is real. Hence, it may be said that there is an undue assumption in the major premiss. But is it really so? When the point at issue is whether the whole world is illusory or not, no particular thing in it can be accepted as real, and pointed out as an exception to the major premiss. We can speak of only four kinds of things using the word thing in a most general sense in which it includes even a 'patent absurdity'. These four things are: (*i*) the *ātman*, whose existence is not doubted by any of the disputants; (*ii*) the empirical world; (*iii*) the illusory, like the silver which is seen in the place of a shell; and (*iv*) a 'patent absurdity' like 'the son of a barren woman'. Now of these four things there is no dispute about the three things, viz., the *ātman*, the illusory, and the 'patently absurd'. There is a dispute only with regard to the status of the empirical world. Besides the empirical world, there is only one thing, namely, the illusory which is an object of knowledge, and is non-intelligent, etc. Thus, once it is argued on the basis of the method of 'Presence and Absence'[3] that whatever is an object of knowledge, whatever is non-intelligent, etc., is illusory, no fault with the argument can be found out. For, no one can show to the contrary. Of the possible four 'things' in the world the remaining two, viz., the *ātman* and the 'Patently Absurd' are neither the objects of knowledge, nor non-intelligent, etc. So once it is asserted that whatever is an object of knowledge, non-intelligent, etc., is illusory there is nothing in the world on the basis of which we can argue that something is an object of knowledge, non-intelligent, etc., and is still real.

It has been pointed out in the above section that *māyā-vāda* makes a distinction between the 'illusory' and the patently absurd. According to it, though the world is illusory still it is not an absolute non-entity like the 'son of a barren woman'. 'Illusory' is a category by itself, which, though it has the same ontological status of unreality, is not describable as real or unreal. In fact *māyā-vāda* grants some reality, even to illusions. We cannot assert that an illusory object is unreal. For, it is actually perceived in the same way as any other object is commonly accepted as real, such as a pot. Nor can it be regarded as real. For, with the rise of the right knowledge, the illusory no longer appears to be where it was formerly seen. The fundamental difference between real perception and the illusory perception lies in this that the former is un-contradicted and uncancelled, while the latter is contradicted and cancelled. Thus, the object of illusion is describable as neither real nor unreal. It is indeterminate or *anirvacanīya*. The world too, which is an object of cosmic illusion has a similar status.

Let us now pass on the question: "What is the cause of this world-illusion?" An illusory object, though ultimately unreal, still appears to us. So there must be some cause for its appearance. There must also be some cause for veiling the real object or the substratum of the illusion. By the law of parsimony, these two causes may be supposed to be one. The Advaitins names it as *māyā, avidyā*, or *ajñāna*, which itself is to be positive in nature, and has

---

3. *Anvaya* and *vyatireka*. Sometimes the method of agreement and difference is supposed to be the same as the method of *anvaya* and *vyatireka*. But it is not so.

the power of concealing the real from our sight and manifesting false appearances. This *ajñāna*, it is argued, is certainly not the mere absence of knowledge. For, from mere negation of an entity, nothing positive can be produced. This ignorance, too, like the world, or any other object of illusion, is regarded as indeterminate, i.e., neither real nor unreal. It cannot be regarded as real; for, if it is real, then the ignorance would be either a different reality from *Brahman*, or it would be a part or an attribute of *Brahman*. But on Advaitic philosophy neither of the alternatives can be maintained. If *ajñāna* is a real part or attribute of the substratum then the true knowledge of the substratum would involve the knowledge of the ignorance also, and the ignorance would not be destroyed even when the true nature of the substratum is known to us. So *ajñāna* is not real. Nor can it be said to be unreal. For, this *ajñāna* is able to bring about effect, viz., that of veiling the substratum and showing up an illusory appearance there. Neither the act of veiling nor the act of showing an appearance can be supposed to belong to the substratum. Hence, we have to admit as their cause a positive entity, which has been named as Ignorance. This positive entity, therefore, cannot be unreal. Thus, *avidyā* is neither real nor unreal. This being an entity which is neither real nor unreal cannot be supposed to affect the non-duality and changelessness of *Brahman* which is absolutely real. So the Advaitins think that the fourth question which was raised in the beginning of the essay, viz., about the relation between *Brahman* and the Ignorance does not arise.

The arguments which an Advaitin adduces in favour of this positive entity, *ajñāna*, are chiefly based on the consideration of the following: (1) our experience of it in waking life and deep sleep, and (2) our experience of illusion. As I have considered arguments based on the experience of illusion in the above section, in this section I shall confine myself only to the arguments following from our experiences in waking life and deep sleep. It is argued that unless Ignorance be something positive in nature we cannot properly understand judgements like (*i*) 'I am ignorant'[4], (*ii*) 'I do not know the meaning of what you say'[5], 'I slept happily and did not know

4. *Aham ajñaḥ.*
5. *Taduktam artham na jānāmi.*

anything',[6] etc., which we make about ourselves from time to time. Ordinarily one would interpret ignorance as the negation or absence of knowledge (*jñānābhāva*). But if *ajñāna* be a mere absence of knowledge, then, the knowledge (*jñāna*) would be the *pratiyogin* of *ajñāna,* i.e., *ajñāna* would not be intelligible without reference to knowledge. So the experience of ignorance as expressed in the judgement 'I am ignorant', would include also the experience of knowledge. But when I have an experience of knowledge it cannot be said that I have no knowledge or that there is absolute absence of knowledge in me. That is, if ignorance be equivalent to absence of knowledge the experience of ignorance would be impossible. And yet we do have the experience of ignorance. So, ignorance cannot be the same as absence of knowledge. Similar conclusion follows from the statement: 'I do not know the meaning of what you say'. Like the previous statement 'I am ignorant' this statement also should be thought to give us the knowledge of 'positive ignorance'; otherwise the difficulties and contradictions which arose in the case of the statement 'I am ignorant' would also arise here. The same conclusion follows from a consideration of the experience of deep sleep. Immediately after getting up from sleep, a person says, "I had a sound sleep and did not know anything". Now the Vedāntin says that, by the statement 'I do not know anything' we should mean that he knew ignorance. 'I did not know anything' seems to be a case of past experience as it refers to the period when the person was sound asleep. Thus, it cannot be the case of an actual experience. Rather this seems to be a case of memory. But there can be a memory only of positive experience and not of a mere absence of knowledge. Thus, 'did not know anything' must be referring to some actual experience at the time of deep sleep. But here as we have no remembrance of any particular experience, 'I did not know anything' must be a memory of the ignorance itself.

It may be objected that in the deep sleep there is a complete absence of all consciousness; and when a person says, he did not know anything he is referring to this complete absence of all knowledge. Thus, it may be said that the absence of knowledge is not known by memory but by inference. But can 'I did not know

6. *Sukham aham asvapsam na kiñcidavediṣam.*

anything' be justifiably held to be the case of inference? If it is a case of inference, then, it must either be on the basis of the absence of memory at the time of the deep sleep, or on the basis of a universal proposition. But 'I had a sound sleep and did not know anything' does not seem to be a case of absence of memory. For then he could not have said: 'I had a sound sleep'. On the contrary this seems to be a case of memory. Again this does not seem to be an inference from a universal proposition. For, in order to assert a universal proposition, "wherever there is a sound sleep, there is an absence of knowledge", a person must independently know at least one instance of deep sleep, where there is an absence of knowledge. When any instance to this effect cannot be found by any other means, no universal connection between deep sleep and the absence of knowledge can be asserted. And unless there is a universal connection or *vyāpti* between the deep sleep and absence of knowledge 'I had a sound sleep and did not know anything' cannot be a case of inference. Thus, because the judgements like 'I am ignorant' or 'I had a sound sleep and did not know anything' cannot be satisfactorily explained if we mean by ignorance, a mere absence of knowledge, ignorance, as a positive entity has to be admitted.

So far, I have tried to give a fairly reliable account of the theory of *māyā*. But can the theory be maintained in the form in which it is stated above? I think it cannot be justifiably maintained. Let us examine the theory at length.

Positive Ignorance

The conception of positive ignorance as the cause of the world-illusion, has been variously criticised by various philosophers. And I think, even from the standpoint of Advaitism there seems to be no reason for positing a cause for the world-illusion. If a person tries to explain the world-illusion on the principle of causation and posit ignorance as the cause of it, the matter will not end here. As 'Ignorance' is not one with *Brahman*, the question that will naturally arise is: What is the cause of Ignorance? And there would not be any satisfactory answer to the question. It is true that in order to meet this difficulty Advaitism posits Ignorance to be beginningless, but still the logical difficulty remains unsolved. Further if Ignorance to be the cause of the world-illusion, that is the relation of *Brahman* and Ignorance? If *Brahman* by itself without the help of any other agency could bring about ignorance, it should be able to bring about also the world-illusion without the help of any other cause; and then there would be no necessity of positing Ignorance as the cause of the world. If, however, Ignorance be an effect which is real, then *Brahman* would not be only reality and there would be a dualism.

The arguments which are put forward to show that we have a knowledge of Positive Ignorance, are also not conclusive. Expressions like 'I am ignorant' do not mean that I have the knowledge of ignorance. It means that I am not omniscient and do not know everything in the world, though I might be knowing something. Similarly, about the deep sleep. The question is whether in deep sleep we have simply a pure consciousness, or the knowledge of ignorance, or a rudimentary vague consciousness, or a complete absence of consciousness. It is true that a man does say that he slept happily and did not know anything. But what is the analysis of the expression 'Did not know anything'? One can use such an expression when one has a knowledge of ignorance and then remembers it; or when one has a complete absence of knowledge; or when one has some knowledge but does not remember it. Now the precise meaning of the expression 'did not know anything' can be settled only by analysing the phenomenon of deep sleep; and this is a matter of experiment. The view, however, that is generally advanced, nowadays, is that even in what is called the state of deep sleep we have some rudimentary consciousness or a very vague knowledge of objects. Now if the above analysis be correct, then, the expression, 'did not know anything' may mean 'do not remember anything', and that is the end of the matter. Similar is the case with the statement 'I do not know the meaning of what you say'. This sentence cannot mean that I have the ignorance of what you say. It means that I know that you are saying something. I also know that what you say has a meaning, but I do not know what that particular meaning is. It is, thus, clear that even when we use ignorance in the sense of absence of knowledge, it stands neither for a state which is absolutely devoid of knowledge, nor for a state of positive ignorance. It may be admitted that a person cannot strictly be said to know a state of absence of knowledge, unless we have the state of knowledge. But there is no harm, if, after we have the knowledge of an entity, we refer to the previous state in which we had no knowledge of it, as a state of the absence of the knowledge of the entity. There is, thus, no necessity of supposing *ajñāna* to be something different from the illusion itself.[7]

The Three-fold Division of Real, Unreal and Illusory

The category of 'illusory ' plays a great part in the theory of *māyā*. But this category is regarded to be different from both the real and the unreal. Thus, as we have seen, according to *māyā-vāda* there would be three kinds of entities. On what basis is this three-fold division made? What is the *fundamentum divisionis* of this distinction? It seems two different principles are employed here. The distinction between 'real' and 'illusory' is made on the basis of the principle that the knowledge of what is illusory is cancelled, and what is real is not cancelled. On the other hand the distinction between 'unreal' and 'illusory' is made on the principle that what is an object of perception cannot be unreal. For, it is clearly said, "How can an object of illusion be unreal when it is actually given to us?" Now it is clear that if a division like real, unreal and illusory is to be made it should be according to one principle and not two. If two principles are employed simultaneously then the division cannot be exhaustive and there is likely to be a fallacy of cross-division.

Let us examine the principle according to which 'illusory' and 'unreal' are distinguished. The principle is that *what is an object of perception cannot be unreal*. Now what does this principle imply? Why cannot the object of perception be unreal? The only possible answer to such a question is that so long as it is perceived it exists, or is actually there. But to say that a thing exists is the same thing as to say that it is real. So whether the principle is correct or not, the distinction between unreal and illusory is a distinction between unreal and real; and if this is so, then the division is made according to the principle *that which* is *perceived is real*. Whether this is a right principle or a mere prejudice one would not think of making distinction of illusory and unreal without some such presupposition.

7. Cf. ajñāna, Prof. G.R. Malkani's article.

However, what I want to point out is that if this is the principle which is presupposed by *māyā-vāda* then it cannot be rejected later on; for, it would mean a shifting of the ground. But, in fact, *māyā-vāda* wants to prove just the opposite of this, viz., *that whatever is perceived is unreal*. It seems to me that there is a plain contradiction between the two positions and if we start with the one we cannot end with the other.

Even if we accept the other principle of division namely whatever is uncancelled is real, we shall not get, as a result three things called real, unreal and illusory. Instead, we shall have only two things namely real and illusory. The unreal that is the patently self-contradictory cannot be connected with this principle at all. For, it is neither cancelled nor uncancelled. It is held that nothing but what appears can be cancelled; but the self-contradictory never appears.

Nor can we formulate a single principle of division by combining the above two, so as to get the division of real, unreal and illusory, which will be accepted by Advaitism. For according to the proposed combined principle, 'that which is perceived and is not cancelled' would be real; 'that which is perceived, but is later on cancelled' would be illusory; and, 'that which is neither perceived, nor cancelled' would be unreal. Now, of these three definitions Advaitism may accept the definition of the 'illusory'. But Advaitism cannot accept the definition of the 'real' and unreal, for it goes against its very thesis. According to *māyā-vāda* the 'real' is neither perceived nor cancelled. But according to the above principle of division, it is the definition of 'unreal'.

It seems then necessary for *māyā-vāda* not to make any distinction like real, illusory and unreal. There should only be two categories real and unreal. And this division can easily be made without employing the above two principles. These two principles are only common sense tests for deciding whether a certain object is real; and the theory of *māyā* ought to reject them if it has to give a consistent philosophy. It is true that there seems to be a different order of existence between the contradictory like a square-circle and an illusory object like silver which is seen in the place of a shell. In a later section I shall try to account for the difference. But from the standpoint of *māyā* this difference is really irrelevant. According to *māyā-vāda* the contradictory as well as the illusory are both, in the last analysis, unreal. And so, *māya-vāda* should better make a distinction between real and unreal on the basis of some other principle.

Māyā theory of illusion — In *māyā-vāda* the world is declared illusory on the basis of commonly accepted experience of illusion. Let us, therefore, see whether the Advaitin's analysis of illusory experience is correct. When I see silver in the place where there is really a shell it cannot be said that I know silver for the first time in my life. It is indeed true, that when a person has a wrong perception of silver he has no memory of having seen the silver before. But is it necessary to have this memory? Even in the case of veridical perception, when a person sees a certain thing for a second time, he need not be conscious of the fact that he had seen it before. And still the fact remains true that he had seen it. Perception is not a simple, but a complex process, whether it be illusory or veridical. To think that perception involves no memory or conception is wrong. As Kant pointed out long ago, perception without conception is blind. Modern Psychology, therefore, regards every perception to be an instance of 'apperception'. So it is quite plausible that even when I think that I have the perception of silver, the silver might have been supplied by my past experience of it, and, thus, it is possible for me to see silver where it does not actually exist. That is, unless we recognise that there is silver somewhere we cannot possibly have an illusion of silver.

I now come to the second point in the theory of illusion. It has been seen that what is regarded as an illusory object is real somewhere and at sometime. Thus, if there is an illusion of silver, silver must be real. But, further some other thing ought to be real if I am to know that a certain perception is illusory. How is a person able to distinguish between the real and the illusory I need not consider just now. I shall simply take it for granted that a person is able to distinguish between the illusory and the real. Silver is illusory because the shell is real. We, thus, conclude that the illusion of silver implies the reality of both the shell and the silver at some place or other. Further, they must belong to the same order of existence. The silver must be a part of the same world of which the shell is a part.

Here a difficulty arises. In front of me there is only a shell. Silver is somewhere else. How then is it that I see silver in the place of the shell, unless there be illusory which is neither real nor unreal? My answer is that the above difficulty is based on the notion that perception is a simple process in which one has simply to receive what is given from outside and nothing to add of one's own. Modern Psychology tells us that this notion is mistaken. In a perceptual process what is given from outside is a very small datum and on the basis of this datum we construct our objects. Now it may sometimes happen that several objects have some common datum. If only this common datum is sensed while perceiving one such object, our perception of it is likely to be illusory, unless we correctly interpret it. In all cases of perceptual illusion some common datum will be found. Where, for example, silver is seen in the place of a shell, the visual data of silver and shell are the same; and so long as some other datum is not sensed the shell may appear as silver. That a perceptual process involves a good deal of intellectual interpretation, can be seen in cases of 'Complication'— as for example, when observing a piece of ice, one says that it looks cold. In such cases there is an immediate inference from one datum to another. Had there been no interpretation of the datum one should not be justified in saying that the block of ice looks cold.

In a previous section I have pointed out that there is no difference between calling a thing illusory and calling it unreal. Still, the nature of the illusory object seems to be different from that of the contradictory. How to account for this difference? I shall take three examples and try to contrast them with one another. I have already examined the first, namely, the case of illusory silver. The other two examples which I shall consider are those or 'pink rats' seen by a drunkard and of things like a square-circle or a barren woman's son.

The illusion of pink rats is also perceptual in nature. But, there seem to be important differences between the experience of silver which is seen in the place of a shell and pink rats. In the instance of illusory perception of silver, we experience a thing which though it does not exist where it is perceived to be, still, exists somewhere. Further, while in the first case there is a perceptual datum which is misinterpreted, in the second there is no such datum. This means that, while the latter is mainly imaginary the former has some basis in actual perception. Secondly, unlike the illusion of silver which is seen in place of shell, a 'pink rat' illusion consists in bringing together by imagination two separately existing entities (*i*) pink (colour) and (*ii*) rat. Now what makes the pink rat illusion perceptible? It will be admitted that a strong imagination generally takes the form of images and if the images are compatible they may exist together. This is what has happened in the illusion of pink rat. A rat is a thing which has a colour, though it is different from pink. Thus, by imagining some other colour say, pink, instead of its natural colour one can arrive at the image of the pink rat. Though we do not come across pink rats we know that if we paint a rat with pink colour, it would appear pink. That is how the illusion of pink rats becomes possible. But just as by strong imagination we can bring two or more compatible things together, and make one composite thing like a pink rat, so also we can bring together two or more incompatible entities, e.g., a square, and a circle. Now these two entities do have a separate existence. But they cannot exist together. It is owing to this that the square-circle is not real. Moreover, it is not possible to perceive it because each of its constituents excludes the other. Hence, the perception of the square-circle is not possible. But though its perception is not possible, it is not in any way different in nature, from the illusory silver or a pink rat. One is, therefore, justified in concluding that there is no difference between the 'illusory' and the 'unreal'.

To summarise the results of our enquiry regarding an ordinary experience of illusion, in the first place, I should say that though an experience may be regarded as illusory, the object of the illusory experience cannot be unreal or non-existent. Secondly, an experience can be regarded illusory only on the basis of some other real experience. There is no sense in calling an experience illusory, if one is not able to distinguish between an illusory experience and a real experience. One could deny reality a certain thing, only if one could assert some other thing to be real. Thirdly, the illusory object as well as the object on the basis of which the illusory object is regarded as unreal, should have the same order of existence. And again, there should be some common datum between the two.

Let us now in the light of these results, consider the thesis that the whole world is illusory. If the distinction between the illusory and the real is essential to the understanding of an illusory experience, shall we be able to say, that the whole world is illusory? If the experience of the world is false, it must be only on the ground that some other experience is true. An Advaitin may object at this stage, "yes, the experience of this world is false because, some other experience, viz., the experience of *Brahman*, is true". But then, the question that would arise is, whether the *Brahman* has the same order of existence as the world; for, we can have an illusion of the world, in place of the *Brahman* only if the *Brahman* and the world have the same order of existence. Further, one would like to ask, "What is the common datum (which is needed in order that there should be an illusion), between the *Brahman* and the world?" Unless these two questions are satisfactorily answered, one cannot declare the whole world as illusory.

But, further, can we on the basis of our ordinary illusory experience, declare the whole world to be unreal? We can judge an experience to be illusory only on the basis that the world is real. Can we, then, declare the world to be illusory on the basis of such illusory experience as those of silver in a shell. I venture to say that we cannot. But the argument given for the illusoriness of the world is of this very type. We may formally put it in the following manner; *X* is illusory because *Y* is real, and *Y* is illusory because it is similar to *X* in many respects. Now, such an argument appears to be quite fallacious on the face of it. But, this in substance, is the argument which declares the world as illusory.

There seems to be one more difficulty involved in the illusoriness of the world. In an ordinary illusion, the so-called illusory object is real, though, of course, at a place and time other than that in which it is perceived to be. We have seen that we can have illusion either of some real thing or of a composite thing made up of parts which are real. Now, if the world is really illusory, it must be either itself real somewhere, or it must be made up of some real parts. But in either case the reality of the world is admitted somewhere and at sometime.

The Advaitin may reply that for an illusory perception it is not necessary that the illusory content should be real; it is enough if there be a previous cognition, true or false of the same content. It is, thus, thought that as everyone has the knowledge of the world, the illusion is possible. But one would ask: how could one have the previous knowledge of the world if the world be not real at all? The reply may be: because, though the world is illusory, still, it is beginningless. But still the question remains: If this beginningless world is illusory and, therefore, unreal, how could there be an illusion of it for the first time? To say that the world is beginningless is no answer to the above question; it is simply avoiding the issue.

Thus, it seems that on the basis of the ordinary illusion we cannot argue the illusoriness of the whole world. On the contrary there is every reason to believe that the world may be real. According to Advaitism, non-cancellation of an entity is a test of its being real. By cancellation (of an entity) is meant a cognition which asserts that something is false and that it did not exist in the past, is not existing now, and will not exist in the future. Non-cancellation is just the opposite of this. Now an illusion is cancelled by a later perception; but the knowledge of things like pots and tables is never cancelled in that way. These things may be nonexistent at sometime or place. But it can never be denied that they are real where and when they exist. It is sometimes contended on behalf of Advaitins that a thing which has a beginning and an end is unreal. It would appear, however, that this is no *a priori* truth. It is true that a Vedāntin would argue, that though things like pots and tables are not cancelled by any of our perception, still they are cancelled by reason, and that when a person has self-realization, things like pots and tables which constitute the world, are cancelled even by perception. We, however, need not consider the case of a man who attains self-realisation. Because, one cannot have a self-realisation unless one is intellectually convinced of the illusoriness of the world. We must, therefore, see whether there is an intellectual cancellation of things like pots and tables. We have seen that, because we cannot argue the illusoriness of the world on the basis of an ordinary illusion, there cannot be an intellectual cancellation of the world. Thus, when there is a positive evidence in favour of the reality of the world and none whatsoever in favour of its unreality, the world is definitely not illusory. We can, then, conclude that what are supposed by Advaitins to be characteristics of an illusion such as objectivity (*dṛśyatva*), non-intelligence (*jaḍatva*), limitation (*aṁśitva*), etc., are not the characteristics of an illusory object only. They may be characteristics common to both a real and an illusory object. So if we try to argue the illusoriness of something on the basis of these characteristics then, the arguments will involve the fallacy of 'Undistributed Middle'.

Two more arguments are likely to come from the side of Advaitism:

(1) If pure consciousness is real how can there be any other reality? If there be some other reality then there would be a real relationship between the two. And insofar as there is a real relationship between the two, the two realities would make one whole. I need not go in criticism of this view for want of space. But such a view seems to be a mere consequence of the prejudice that the real must be only one having no other to it, . . . a prejudice which has its source in such passages of the Upaniṣads as, "O, Soumya this was in the beginning one having no other".[8]

(2) It may be said that *māyā-vāda* is not a theory; it is a state of fact. Whatever explanation we try to give of the world it is sure to end in contradiction. I shall make only three passing remarks on such a position.

(*a*) It is doubtful whether we cannot give any satisfactory explanation of the world. Even if all attempts made for explaining the world, have failed hitherto, still it is possible that someone in future may be able to explain it satisfactorily.

(*b*) If our categories are inadequate to explain the world we ought to evolve other categories through which we may be able to explain it. But because the categories in terms of which we try to explain the world are inadequate, we should not conclude that the world is illusory.

---

8. Cf. *Chāndogya Upaniṣad.*

(*c*) Even if we are not able to give a satisfactory explanation of the world, we cannot prove the illusoriness of the world unless the proposition "What cannot be satisfactorily explained is unreal" is true. But such a proposition does not seem to be self-evident. Nor are there reasons to support it. We can then say that the illusoriness of the whole world does not seem to be quite intelligible.

Is it then a non-significant proposition to say that the world is *mithyā*. That the world is *mithyā* does not seem to be quite a non-significant proposition, and indeed, a person does feel that the world is *mithyā* on some occasions, when, e.g., he is greatly disappointed or when he is in great miseries. But it seems to me that when we say that the world is *mithyā*, we do not mean to say that it is nothing at all, or that it never existed or will never exist. What we mean to say is that the World is not 'good'; it is not 'valuable'. Thus, that the world is *mithyā* seems to be a value judgement and not an ontological judgement; and insofar as it is a value judgement it seems to me to be quite intelligible and may also be more or less probable, though whether actually it is so is extremely doubtful. Thus *mithyā* seems to me to be an ambiguous word having two meanings: (1) illusory, (2) valueless. It seems it was primarily intended to be used in the second sense; but on account of confusion between the two meanings it was interpreted in the first sense and an ontological theory was devised in conformity with that sense. That by the proposition, that the world is *mithyā*, an ethical sense was intended can be seen even in Śaṅkara's writings, like "the world is valueless or *asār*".[9] If we suppose that the word *mithyā* is used in the ethical sense and if we look at the whole theory from an ethical point of view it becomes clearer. For example, it seems difficult to imagine how there can be different grades or degrees of reality. But certainly there can be different grades or degrees of value. Thus, it seems quite possible, that empirical reality (*vyāvahārikī sattā*) may be more valuable than the illusory (*prātibhāsikī sattā*) and the ultimate 'Reality' (*pāramārthikī sattā*) more valuable than the empirical. But we should not be able to say

9. *Asāraḥ khalu saṁsāraḥ.*

that the so-called 'Ultimate reality' is more real than the empirical one.

It is, of course, likely to be said that the distinction between ethics and metaphysics is not ultimate and what is real is also good, and what is good is also real. I shall not enter into this controversy here but shall simply state in the words of Prof. G.E. Moore, that from no metaphysical proposition an ethical proposition can be derived. One cannot say that something is good *because* something is real. If one tries to give such a reasoning then one is committing what Prof. Moore calls a *naturalistic fallacy*.[10]

In the conclusion it may be said that we have tried to understand the reasons usually given for regarding the world as illusory and we have also tried to see if this thesis can be defended, but ultimately we have found that the illusoriness of the whole world is an unintelligible doctrine, hard to believe and harder to defend. However, we found that though the doctrine that the whole world is illusory seems to be unintelligible, the doctrine that the whole world is valueless does not seem to be quite unintelligible though its truth is doubtful. That the world is valueless may be the intended meaning of the proposition that the world is *mithyā*. We then conclude that *māyā-vāda* as a metaphysical doctrine is not acceptable. If it be acceptable at all, it must be interpreted as an ethical judgement about the world. But even, as such a judgement of value, it is not free from doubt. To those, however, who claim that it is a metaphysical doctrine, we answer:

> If the world be a phantom as thou sayest,
> A splendid figment and a prodigious dream,
> To reach the Real and the True I shall make no haste,
> More than content with the worlds that only seem.

10. 'Cf. *Principia Ethica*, chapter 1.

14

Śaṅkara on Prescriptive and Descriptive Sentences

THE question whether Śaṅkara had any specific Philosophy of Language is to be distinguished from whether he had made use of certain aspects of the Philosophy of Language for establishing his thesis. One is not sure, whether any specific theory of Language like the theory of *apoha* or *sphoṭa* can be attributed to Śaṅkara although he raises several important issues relevant to the functioning and Philosophy of Language, for example, in a sense in his philosophy he gives a critique of language and maintains that by language we are not able to comprehend reality. He would, for example, quote from Upaniṣads and *Bhagavad Gītā* sentences like *vācārambhaṇaṁ vikāronāmadheyaṁ* and *yato vāco nivartate.*

Of course, he accepted the authority of Śruti and especially made use of sentences from Śruti and Upaniṣads in particular, for establishing his thesis that the reality is one and unqualified and the world, as it appears to us, has the statue of *nāma-rūpa* only. For this purpose he used certain aspects of the theory of language for interpreting certain sentences from Śruti. For example, he refutes the interpretation of Śruti as given by Jaimini, namely that the Vedic sentences are prescriptive or imperative. But from this one cannot say that other functions of language like that of commanding and prescribing are ignored by Śaṅkara. Since the problem before Śaṅkara is only a theoretical one, i.e., of knowing *Brahman* those aspects only in the theory of language which are concerned with naming, and describing or identifying seemed to be more emphasised by Śaṅkara. In asserting his thesis it is certainly true that Śaṅkara does not explicitly prescribe certain practical norms except *śravaṇa*, *manana*, *nididhyāsana*. But prescribing practical norms does not come in the purview of Śāṅkara's philosophy. It is true that Śaṅkara challenges the *kriyārthatva* meaning of the entire Vedas. But this is not the same as challenging the *kryārthatva* meaning of *any* sentence. The problem before the Pūrva Mīmāṁsakas was a practical one and a practical problem is concerned with action or prescription. The question 'what you are to do and what you are not to do' thus, assumes significance. Naturally, actions and performances become your primary objectives and prescriptions and injunction become relevant. For this purpose a *pramāṇa* or means of knowledge either becomes irrelevant or if it becomes relevant becomes relevant, in a secondary way only. What is important in practical life is to find out the authority for action. Naturally, this authority of action is either your own authority or the authority of a person whom you respect as authority. Thus, the viewpoint when you are concerned with practical life is entirely different from one when you are concerned with the theoretical enquiry, i.e., where you are concerned with knowledge along. This attitude will naturally be reflected in language. In practical enquiry the sentences which become relevant are the sentences which are concerned with *codanā* or inducement to action and not with either naming or description, since your objective in *dharma* and not *Brahman*. This concept of *codanā* becomes explicit in what is stated by Pūrva Mīmāṁsakas as *vidhi-vākyas*. These *vidihi-vākyas* are of the type —

> *jyotiṣṭomeṇa svargakāmo yajeta; pañcapañcanakhāḥ bhakṣyāḥ; aharaha saṃdhyām upāsīta etc.*

What the Pūrva Mīmāṁsakas insisted on was that only such sentences in Śruti are significant which indicated *vidhi* or prescriptions primarily. Sentences which do not give the prescriptive or performatory sense are useful only secondarily and only when they assist the original thesis of *codanā* or *vidhi* sentences. Such secondarily significant sentences are supposed to give only *arthavāda*. In the theory of the Mīmāṁsakas the descriptive sentences are either non-significant or are only subservient to prescriptive and performatory sentences. Perhaps in the enthusiasm to interpret the Vedas as commending a pattern of behaviour to man the Pūrva Mīmāṁsakas had gone only too far and perhaps created a feeling that there is nothing in the Vedas which is primarily descriptive or concerned with names, etc. Śaṅkara criticises this position and focuses our attention on sentences in the Vedas which point to existence or identity. He, thus, makes use of sentences like *ahaṁ brahmāsmi, sarvaṁ khalu idaṁ brahma, tat tvam asi, so'ham, rasovaisaḥ* and the like. All these sentences are in fact not of one type and they as a matter of fact require different explanations in the philosophic grammar. But in Śaṅkara's logic all these sentences are significant and also have one common point viz., they prove false the viewpoint of the Pūrva Mīmāṁsakas that the Vedic language is *primarily* prescriptive. For this purpose Śaṅkara, of course, makes use of one aspect of the *naïve name theory* of meaning. If there is a thing we may *ostensively* know it, name it and describe it. *Brahman* according to him is such a thing. It is a *bhūṭa vastu*. Thus, if it is to be named or described or communicated in some sense, it will always be in a linguistic form that is in indicative mood and present tense. The above quoted sentences like *ahaṁ bṛahma asmi* also presuppose this name. Theory of language though only indirectly. But it must be borne in mind that it cannot be specifically said that Śaṅkara completely disregarded the prescriptive of performing function of language or Jaimini ignored the descriptive or naming function of Language. Jaimini, for example, very clearly states this at the beginning of the second *pada* of the first *adhyāya*,

> *āmāyasya kriyārthatvāt ānarthakyam atadarthānām* (1-2-1); *na pūrṇatvāt* (1-2-21) *uktaṃ tu vākyaśeṣatvam* (1-2-22)

Here Jaimini considers *other than* prescriptive meaning of sentences. But on the whole the problems before Jaimini and Śaṅkara are different and since both of them want to rely on the evidence of the Vedas, language has to assume different roles for them, prescriptive for Jaimini and descriptive for Śaṅkara, for it is primarily on these roles of language that their philosophy depends. It is true that 'What is the meaning of the Vedas?' Is the problem both before Jaimini and Śaṅkara. But Jaimini had taken for granted that the subject of the Vedas was *dharma* and *dharma* he defined as that the object of which is will or inducement to act *codanā lakṣaṇārtho dharmah*. Thus, although Jaimini classifies sentences into *vidhi-vākya, arthavāda* or *praśaṁsā*, still the primary meaning of the Vedas for his is only prescriptive, performatory or injunctive. It is against this view that Śaṅkara raises an objection. He grants that *Brahmasūtras* are nothing but the garland or collection of the sentences from the Vedas-Upaniṣads-Vedānta *vākya kusuma grathanārthatvāt sūtrānām.*

And for the interpretation of the *sūtras* one would have to take into account the rules of the linguistic and logical syntax — *vākyārtha — vicāranadhyavasana nirvṛtta — brahmava — gatiḥ na anumānapramāṇāt pramāṇāntaraninṛtta*. But Śaṅkara emphasises on the 'objectivity' of Brahman —*manu bhūta vastutve brahmanaḥ.*

However, the syntax or grammar of descriptive sentences, particularly when the object of description is existent is different from the grammar of other kinds of sentences. Śaṅkara states this by saying:

> *tatra evam sati yathābhūta brahmātmaviṣayam api jnānaṃ na codanātantraṃ. tadviṣaye liṅgādayaḥ ṣrūnamaṇā api aniyojya viṣayatvāt kuṇthībhavanti upalādiṣu prayukta kṣurataikṣṇyādivat. antyānupādeya vastu viṣyat vāt.*

He specifically states that the knowledge of something which exists in its own right (*yathā bhūtam*) cannot be dependent on anybody's will, desire or impose. This is also true of the knowledge the object of which is *Brahman* or *ātman* which exists in its own right. Śaṅkara here points out that even sentences which appear to have prescriptive structure may sometimes have only a descriptive function. The sentences like *ātmā vā re dṛṣṭavyaḥ* or *śrotaryaḥ mantavyaḥ*, though apparently appear to be perscriptive have primarily a core which is essentially concerned with ostensive definition. The sentence which says, 'you should see, etc.' really presupposes a sentences which are grammatically in subjunctive mood are really concealed indicatives. They really emphasise on knowing or indicating the *ātman*. In its expanded form the sentence of the form, *ātmā vā re dṛṣṭavyaḥ* could be *so ayam ātmā, sa dṛṣṭavyaḥ*. Unless the word *dṛṣṭavya* is needed only in a figurative sense. That it should be seen or cognised could be merely the idiomatic expressions for saying that the *ātmā* is such and such. One can easily contrast the expressions like *yajeta* against *dr̥ṣṭavya yajeta* does not presuppose a prior existence *yajña* or sacrifice or for that matter of anything else. It is concerned with something is *possible* but which is not *actual* at that particular moment. But this indeed is not the case with regard to something which is to be cognised. The framework is which *dr̥śa* becomes significant is entirely different unless our perception is illusory. Something can be perceived only if the object of this perception already exists. Knowledge is not something which will manifest itself even in the absence of something of which it is knowledge solely on account of the performance of the Vedic rituals or man's will. It is as futile as to cut a stone with a knife. However, sharp it may be it is only the knife which will lose its sharpness in this process. In the same way if we try to find out reality or *Brahman* merely through prescriptions, individual will or impulse, we will never succeed in our effect. The language which states about the existence or *Brahman* is and must be descriptive and indicative because *Brahman* exists in its own right and on its own account.

The same point is elaborated by him further by taking into consideration the different aspects involved in knowing Śaṅkara, e.g., contrasts knowledge (perceptive knowledge) with mental processes. 'Knowing' for him is not a process, not to say that it is not mental. He, thus, contrasts 'thinking' with knowing 'Thinking', he says 'is very different from knowledge'. It is dependent on one who wants to think. If someone does not want to think or think otherwise no one else can control him. Thinking is thinker dependent. It is not so with knowledge which is dependent on things as they are. Thus, it is not possible to create or uncreate knowledge at one's own will. It is entirely governed by the thing of which it is presentation. It is neither dependent on the knower nor on his impulse or will. Thus, knowledge is very different from mental processes. In fact, it is knowledge only and not a process (*jñānam eva etat na kriyā*) (*nanu jñānam nama mānasī kriyā . . . jñānam eva etat na kriyā*).

This knowledge, being the object of *Brahmasūtra*, when we translate this knowledge into linguistic form, the form of the language would be only descriptive and not prescriptive or injunctive. This is indicated by Śaṅkara in his commentary on *Athāto Brahmajijñāsā*. He writes, *abhyudaya-phalam tu brahmavijñānam na ca anuṣṭhānāntarapekṣam. bhavyaśca dharmo jijñāsaḥ na jñānakāle asti puruṣa vyāpāratantratvāt. iha tu bhūtam brahma jijñāsyam nityatvāt na puruṣavyāpāratantram. codanā-pravṛttibhedatca. ya hi codanā dharmasya lakṣaṇam sa svaviṣaye niyuñjana eva puruṣam avabodhayati eva kevalam avabodhasya codanā janyatāt na puruṣo avabodhe niyujyate. yathā akṣārtha sannikarṣeṇa arthavābodhe tadvat.*

Knowledge of what to do and what not to do leads to prosperity; this is dependent on one's performance or skill. The *vijñāna* of *Brahman* leads to *niḥśreyas*. It does not dependent on some other kind of performance. That impulse which is the definite characteristic of *dharma* makes the individual know the impulse itself. On the other hand, the impulse to know *Brahman* makes the individual now. But since cognition alone is the product of that impulse it does not make the knower the object of this impulse. (Since the impulse is merely to know it leads the knower to know), just as a thing is known on account of the contact between the eye and the thing.

This very attitude of Śaṅkara is further confirmed in the grammatical-philosophical analysis of the compound *brahma-jijñāsā*. He writes, *brahmanaḥ it karmāṇi sasti na śeṣe*. The word *brahma-jijñāsā* is to be understood not in the sense we understood the phrase 'the horse of a king'. Here, there is relation between the owner and the owned. That is, it is a relation between two substantives. Nor is it to be understood in the sense in which we understand a 'rafter of a house', where though both the words 'rafter' and 'house' have independent existence, they together form a whole and exhibit a relation between a part and a whole. The phrase *brahma-jijñāsā*, does not point out any such relation. *Jijñāsā* is only a grammatical substantive. As a matter of fact logically it is a verb and points out a relation between a verb and its object. Śaṅkara is here pointing out that the verb 'know' or 'to desire to know' is a transitive verb and behaves like a transitive verb. Thus, in the phrase *brahma-jijñāsā* the object of *jijñāsā* is *Brahman* and it is the object of that alone which it the object of inquiry. It is needless to say that such an inquiry is bound to be descriptive and objective or non-subjective.

Śaṅkara points this out again and again by using the word *vastu-tantra*. He defines *vastu-tantra* in the following way:

> *na hi sthānau ekasmin sthanurva puruṣo anyova iti tattva jñānamam bhavati. Tatra puruṣo anyo va iti mithyā jñānam, stnānureva iti tatvajñānam vastu tantratvāt. evambhūta vastu viṣayanan pramānyam vastutantram. tatra evam satī brahma-jñānam api vastutantrameva bhūta vastu viṣayatvāt.*

When something is a pillar the cognition that it is a pillar or a man is not tantamount to veridical knowledge. That it is a pillar alone will be veridical on account of the existence of a pillar. Thus, the prior existence of the object of knowledge makes the knowledge objective. In the same way the knowledge of *Brahman* too is objective.

If the knowledge is objective in character, and its expression descriptive and if the Vedas describe knowledge than at least some part of the Vedas will be concerned with descriptions and the indicative sentences in the Vedas would be meaningful. In such a case Jaimini's thesis that the sentences in the Vedas are one and all perscriptive stands repudiated.

While advocating the thesis that in the context of knowledge the meaningful language must be descriptive and in indicative mood Śaṅkara, however, tries to point out that even an indicative sentence may have non-indicative secondary meaning, function or use. For example, when someone says 'it is a rope and not a snake', the sentence may not just be an indicative sentence, its structure is indicative but it may tells us that we need not be afraid of *it*. *(Rajjuriyam na ayam sarpaḥ) iti vastumātra kathane api prayojanasya dṛṣṭatvāt*. Thus, while refuting Jaimini's thesis about the interpretation of the Vedic sentences Śaṅkara also points out that language may have more functions than one and even an apparently descriptive sentence may behave as a hidden prescriptive sentence and may induce people to action.

In Śaṅkara's philosophy there are several points which are important from the standpoint of linguistic philosophy. We shall mention here two points which are interesting. While trying to prove that the world is *mithyā* and *Brahman* alone is real he very skillfully makes use of the concept of name. He compares the world with 'name' and in establishing his thesis he incidentally brings to light many interesting points about the concept of name. World and *Brahman* are only like a name and bearer of a name. There is only a false identification between the two. Thus, he draws a distinction between a thing and its name. A name is *mithyā* because it is different from the thing and arbitrarily given to it. It is not integral to the thing. Nevertheless a name is useful, without a name it is difficult to communicate. So although a name does not have an ontological status it is not nothing or *asat*. When Śaṅkara uses the model of name for the explanation of the world he definitely has in his mind a theory about the relationship of a name and a thing. A yet another point of linguistic and philosophic significance is emphasised by Śaṅkara when he talks of *tādātmya* or what is wrongly known as identity relation between *aham* and *Brahman* or between *tat* and *tvam*. The first shows the *tādātmya* between the subject and the object, the second shows *tādātya* between things. Śaṅkara evidently does not want to say that *aham* and *Brahman* are identical. The shadow and the thing of which it is shadow are not identical although they cannot be separated from each other. If we say that A is identical with B then A and B must not be different things. B must be A. This can be logically put thus: $A = B$ if $A \subset B$ and $B \subset A$. The *tādātmya* relation of Vedas, therefore, is different from the identity relation. Nevertheless the sentences describing *tādātmya* relation will fall under the general structure of descriptive sentence. (Although they may not always be descriptions proper). Now the descriptive sentences or sentences in indicative mood may indicate some relation between the subject and predicate. But this relation may not always be of one kind. And by emphasising that the sentences like *aham brahmāsmi* or *raso vai saḥ* exhibit *tādātmya* relation it can be inferred that for Śaṅkara the relation between the subject and the predicate is not of one kind. This should help in determining the varieties of descriptive sentences.

In short although Śaṅkara is not primarily interested in problems pertaining to the theory of language for their own sake he makes very valid and important points in his philosophy which are relevant to the Philosophy of Language.

15

Vedāntic Theory and the Practical Vedānta of Swāmī Vivekānanda

PHILOSOPHICAL problems arise due to the curiosity man has about the world which surrounds him right from his birth. He perceives the world, locates several men like him in the world. He see several living creatures in the world who are partly unlike men and he also sees things in the world which are neither like men nor like other creatures. He observes the phenomenon of death. He realises that after death the body becomes more or less like the 'material' things in the world. When he looks at material things he is able to classify them, categorise them. Finally, he also tries to locate his own place in this world and assesses his status. I think, all philosophical problems arise out of such observations and give rise to different philosophical thoughts, religious, scientific, metaphysical or moral. In short the investigations arising out of such observations are concerned with man's relation to the world. It may take different forms like, Pūrva Mīmāṁsā, Sāṁkhya or Vedānta or Advaita Vedānta. But on this scale at one end is Pūrva Mīmāṁsā and at the other end is Vedānta (of different varieties). By Pūrva Mīmāṁsā I mean a philosophy which starts with rituals, gives common sense explanations or entertains common sense beliefs about death, thinks of souls, other worlds like heaven and hell, entertains beliefs like immortality of souls, some kind of causation related to his action, etc.

But such a way of thought is likely to have its reactions also and we find them in the Vedānta Philosophy. This Vedānta Philosophy (particularly of Advaitic variety) became the most accepted philosophy in India, for the last several hundred years. Of course, it would be incorrect to think that the Pūrva Mīmāṁsā lost its ground. The rituals either in the original or changed form began to participate in our life and were largely syncretised with Vedāntic thought. Nevertheless on the theoretical side Vedānta systems of thought were generally accepted by most people and dominated our life. It was concerned with the interpretations of Upaniṣads, and so was regarded as orthodox philosophy. To my mind it appears that in order to understand the basic tenets of Vedānta particularly the Advaitic, it is necessary to understand the background, at least the logical background, which has given rise to Vedāntic way of thinking. This background is supplied by Pūrva Mīmāṁsā. The main tenets of Pūrva Mīmāṁsā are the following:

1. The Vedas must be accepted as infallible.
2. The Vedic sentences basically give us prescriptions and injunctions, i.e., what we must do and what we must not do. These prescriptions and injunctions at least for the members of the higher class are centered around the rituals connected with sacrifice.
3. Man must always act. For, action is prescribed in the Vedas.
4. A man who is living is a compound of two parts — the body and the soul. Our soul being the agent of action has freedom and responsibility to act.
5. The soul exists in its own right (contrary to this it is also believed that soul requires somebody to act).
6. The action exists in its own right and modifies or gears the soul to action. The circuit of actions is not complete during one's life period. So the soul and action exist beyond death, therefore, in order to fulfil the actions or suffer the consequences of action, the soul takes rebirth.
7. It also has to pay for the actions in the other world. Heaven and the hell are such worlds.

8. Each action or the object of the action has a deity and a man must please the deity through sacrifice. It also takes for granted inequality in society thanks to *karma* and provides a justification for *cāturvarṇya* and also for *jāti-vyavasthā*. It would naturally believe in many souls which would remain as souls. And so philosophy would either be the philosophy of the society of men or the philosophy of the society of souls.

In a way Vedānta in general and Advaita in particular, joined Sāṁkhya and Buddhism in raising a banner of revolt against this system. The Pūrva Mīmāṁsā school thinks that there are several souls. Advaita points out that each soul gets identity only so long as it is limited by a certain body. It illustrates this from the example of *ākāśa,* we can talk of particular space in particular pots, but spaces are not many. It is only one space limited by different pots. So also different *jīvas* cease to be *jīvas* as soon as they are considered in the context of the whole reality. Advaita Vedānta suggests that when we are talking of consciousness or *caitanya* we cannot talk of *jīvas*. It is not possible to talk of this *caitanya* and that *caitanya*. As soon as we begin to talk of *caitanya* the individuality which characterises *jīvas* is lost. In fact, there is a subtle inconsistency involved in talking of *jīvas*. The plurality of *jīvas* we get, on account of what Sāṁkhya calls *ahaṁkāra*. This *ahaṁkāra* determines the identity of *jīva* from within but if a third man is to know the *jīvas*, there must be specificness of the *jīvas* knowable to the third man. To me it appears that this cannot be done unless the third man knows or imagines spatio-temporality regarding the *jīva* and this is not possible in regard to a *disembodied jīva*. It is difficult to imagine a disembodied *jīva* and so when we so imagine, we somehow imagine it with some kind of 'ethereal body' and this is really inconsistent with our own assumptions. What we do is, to isolate the consciousness from the usual body and then supply another body to it. A better hypothesis, therefore, is to think that when the body is destroyed the individuality itself is destroyed. This may happen either at the time of death or when the *liñga-deha* or subtle body is destroyed. But when the body is destroyed will the consciousness persist ? Here, Advaita resorts to another kind of argument. It is based on *satkāryavāda*. If consciousness is experienced as effect then it must also exist as cause. It cannot come into existence as an accident. It must be there right from the beginning. So even after the individuality is lost it must be (potentially) present. In fact, it, the consciousness must institute the cosmos. Furthermore, what we call individuality itself may be a play of consciousness. When we talk of individual consciousness, consciousness is taken as something that is subjective. When the individuality is lost and a position is taken that consciousness still persists, whether such consciousness can exist without spatio-temporality is a question. To me it appears that Advaita is not clear on this point. That is, it could allow spatio-temporality and even matter occupying space and time in their thesis. The matter can be charged with consciousness. In fact, like the quantum physics the reality could appear as matter from one point of view and consciousness from another. It is not the body that is denied to consciousness, it is only some gross body which gives self-consciousness that is denied. Not that it does not come into existence but that, that which comes into existence, perishes. The self-consciousness comes into existence but 'perishes' into the ocean of consciousness, liquidates itself into the ocean of consciousness. The self-consciousness in a body gives you subjectivity. It is this realisation that the subjectivity eliminates itself into the cosmos (i.e., in the consciousness that is objective) which gives you the thesis that I am *Brahman*, or *ayam atma brahma* or *prajñānam brahma*. This realisation is equivalent to saying that I am not, the *Brahman* is. There is no identity between I and *Brahman*. 'I' simply does not exist when there is a realisation that there is *Brahman*. Saṅkarācārya in *Satpadī* has very clearly stated that *taraṅga* is *samudra* but *samudra* is not *taraṅga*. This means that a self-conscious being cannot be without body, that it is the self-conscious being who can have aspirations which can be mundane or supra-mundane. It is with these aspirations that the concepts of *karma*, *dharma* and *svarga* are connected. It is with this that the concept of birth and death are connected. If this self-conscious body is denied or if it is realised that the self-conscious body comes into being and is destroyed in the course of time all problems which Pūrva Mīmāṁsā raises would vanish. This I think is the main thesis of Uttara Mīmāṁsā. Sāṁkhya aids this thesis for it is in

Sāṁkhya that *puruṣa* or consciousness is taken out of what they call union of *prakṛti* and *puruṣa*. When *puruṣa* is taken away from *prakṛti* it is no more *jīva* and such *puruṣa* cannot have any aspirations of either doing anything or achieving anything. Both *karma* and *karma-phala* are denied to him, for they are of no significance to him. The concepts of *svarga* and *naraka*, as also birth and rebirth, become redundant. Nevertheless these concepts take their shelter in the Uttara Mīmāṁsā and also in Sāṁkhya and Buddhist doctrines. This makes the whole thing complicated and no clear view is arrived at. It should be remembered that the naïve uncritical belief of a common man is, that there is a disembodied soul, although it is accepted that such a disembodied soul also has a microscopic body. This belief is perpetuated and presupposed in the Pūrva Mīmāṁsā thinking. Sāṁkhya points out that we can legitimately accept disembodied consciousness as a concept existing in its own right, because consciousness or sentience is a fact of experience. But such disembodied sentience would be only inactive. This is indirect admission that when we distinguish body and consciousness or matter and consciousness we have started or initiated the process of abstraction. But to say this is not to say that consciousness or sentience is unreal. Whatever is experienced in the form of effect must be potentially present as cause also or in the form of cause also. There is a difference between sentience or *purusa* of Sāṁkhya and *jīva* of a tiny or micro-living being. A *jīva* cannot exist unless it is a complex of matter and sentience, for, it is this complexity which gives it self-consciousness or consciousness or self-identity. It is this argument which is carried forward by Advaita. Instead of using the word *jīva* they prefer using the word *ātman*. *Jīva* is an empirical existence. It is not segregated from body. Perhaps when one talks of *jīva* the emphasis is on sentience. But it should not mean that the sentience exists in its own right. Each *jīva* is limited by certain limit and is comparable with space, limited by certain pot. The model is of *ghaṭavacchinna ākāśa*. This limitation gives it its identity. But the sentience, like space, is real. It is to be presupposed as real and would constitute the very nature of reality or *Brahman*. Sentience is not *mithyā*. The ontological status of sentience is not denied in the context of *Brahman*. But its manifestation in the form of individual is different from the general status of sentience. It is not regarded as a function of the body, nevertheless, it is regarded as inseparable from the body so long as the body exists. But when the body perishes, the separate existence of the individual sentience also perishes although the sentience as such does not perish. This position does not allow for the persistence and influence of *karma* over either the sentience or the individual beyond a certain point. The sentience when it is manifested as a complex takes the form of awareness and so paves the way for epistemology. Cārvāka would differ here on one point. He is likely to say that sentience does not persist beyond death for it is the function of the body, function of the four *mahābhūta*s when they came together in a unique and particular way. But both Cārvāka and Advaita should agree that in a living body the function of the sentience should be epistemic and sentience should act as agent, behave as agent and controller of the body. Everything that the body does would appear now as being directed by the agent and in a way, though in a limited way, the function of the *jīva* and the function of this agent would be similar. This agent would be called *ātman* or *ahaṁ* and he should be responsible, along with the several other *ātman*s for the construction of *māyā*, the 'human' universe. This agent would never have a cognition that it dies although as a matter of fact it does perish and so if one is not careful enough, the trap for identifying the *ātman* with *jīva* would always exist. To me it appears that this has happened again and again and so *ātman* is, many a time, confused with *jīva*. But the concept of *ātman* is not the same as that of *jīva*. What *ātman* indicates is merely the *sākṣitva*, *ātman* is merely the linguistic expression of that *sākṣin* which means mere presence of sentience.

The embodied sentience, that is man, asserts his freedom over the universe, makes further constructions over the universe. These constructs or constructions begin with naming and continue with more and more elaborate and complicated forms. The variety, however, is characterised by the same sentience namely, the *Brahman*. And if sentience is accepted as the general feature of this universe then the real stuff of all this universe will be sentience. But in its appearance it will look otherwise. This difference will be partly due to sentience taking a form other than that of sentience, or due to man's giving it different form. Now it is possible that the nature may be matter characterised by sentience or the nature may be sentience itself, though it is very queer to understand it in this sense. It is easy to understand or misunderstand matter characterised by sentience as sentience itself. But one thing is certain, if Vedāntic position is accepted the sentience cannot be eliminated and it also will have to be admitted that man will give it different forms. This would be *loka-vyavahāra*. This will be the combination or copulation of *satya* and *anṛta* and will be the extended reality, the social reality, which in its own right will be nothing but the sentience or the primordial stuff with which we have started. In a sense we could say that the primordial stuff is real and all constructs over it are unreal, because although there is a potentiality in the original stuff to take these forms, the forms are only constructs of man. They are real forms but they could be regarded as appearances and then it is possible to think that the whole world that is constructed is *māyā* or illusion. Whether this was originally intended by Advaita or not, in one of its interpretations such a position has been taken. Constructions could be imaginary and real and one would have to distinguish between the two, nevertheless both these will be constructions. What is important to note is that whereas it is possible to think of *jagat* or constructed world as *mithyā* or illusory, it is never possible to think of *ātman* as *mithyā* or illusory. It is always real for, it is non-different from the primordial stuff. Its individuality alone is unreal, but *ātman* as such cannot be unreal, for finally it is *Brahman* the primordial stuff. In the constructs themselves there are several belief systems playing part. The belief system of birth and death cycles and *karma* is one such of belief system. The belief system with which we live and communicate and transact with others or try to educate other is another and the belief system connected with dreams and supernaturals is still another. That in our life several belief systems arise does not mean that they have the same status. Some belief systems are to be disposed of instantaneously and some belief systems are required to be retained for our communication with others. If we discard the belief system which lays emphasis on heavens, *karma* and rebirth it does not mean that we have simultaneously to discard all belief systems.

Although all epistemological investigations begin with and

presuppose consciousness or sentience as an element in experience, the world that is experienced cannot be denied. What can be denied is that consciousness qua consciousness is a separable unit in the complex that is the experienced world. How can consciousness as such exist unless it has some form either comparable to the form of matter or energy, is the problem? What we experience is sentient matter and not sentience. But once you make sentience as separable form the other part of the experienced world it is easier and possible to think that the other part does not exist and what exists is the sentience alone. The argument for holding such a view is that if matter can exist in its own right, why cannot sentience exist in a similar way? In fact, it is this argument which has been forwarded or is supposed to be forwarded by all idealists including even the epistemological idealists who take for granted the knower as independent of the body. This is also the argument attributed to Advaita. The question, however, is whether such sentience qua sentience can exist without space and time, i.e., without spatio-temporal properties. Even those who talk of sentience qua sentience have to supply some kind of microscopic spatio-temporal body for such sentience. But once you start with the argument that sentience can exist without a body then you can also regard the world as a nebula of sentience and you can further hold that at some stage spatio-temporal and material properties emerge from sentience and limit the sentience. It is this limitation which may give rise to a manifest self-consciousness which is only potentially present in the sentience, that is although existing, it is only in a hidden form. Once you make this assumption you are thinking of sentience as a whole. You cannot think of sentience in a pluralistic manner, that is just as a materialist thinks of matter as a whole, as a common substance, similarly you are thinking of it as a whole. This concept of sentience is justified by man's concept of a whole. Imagine that the world consists of several inseparable elements, one of which is sentience. As soon as you think of a whole which cannot be separated into several independent parts you have no alternative except thinking that the world is sentient, i.e., sentience is characterised as the whole. Once we assume that the world is a unity it is natural to think that the world is sentient and that it appears to be manifold on account of spatio-temporal limitations, i.e., *samvṛtatva* or *paricchinnatva*, which also is one of the manifestations of sentience itself. But instead of having unitary or holistic concept of the world if you think of the world as a name for the manifold then it is possible to think of a variety which may consist of both sentient and non-sentient elements, and the sentient element would not be segregated from its spatio-temporal body.

However, once you accept sentience as an element in the world or once you accept the world as manifestation of sentience you have already paved the way for epistemology not only of knowledge but also of beliefs. You have accepted that it is possible for you either to construct or imagine some belief system particularly when you go further away from reality. You thus construct a theory about *karma*, think that it must always be active such that one *karma* must tend to some other *karma* and *karma* requires an agent to perform *karma*. Therefore, the agent of *karma* must also be immortal, that it must exist beyond the point of death and, therefore, the rebirth must be possible and that there must be heavens and hades. All these are make-belief systems. If you are self-conscious, through knowledge you can know that they are make-belief systems. And once you know that they are make-belief systems, they would simply evaporate. But so long as you are ignorant of their make-belief character, it would go on haunting you as real. Our social beliefs perpetuated by Pūrva Mīmāṁsā are of this make-belief nature. These naïve beliefs are shattered only when you know that you, as a knower, are capable of creating them. That which is created by our make-belief can be destroyed by further knowledge. If something is a part of physical reality it cannot be so destroyed by knowledge. I think, the main propositions of Advaita theory tell us that propositions of Pūrva Mīmāṁsā are only of our own creations, of our make-belief system. Of course, while asserting this, they create certain other make-beliefs, viz., that world is a unitary whole, that the world is an illusion, i.e., everything is a make-belief. And somehow *karma*, *jīva*, etc., though believed to be make-belief still persist as real beliefs in some other chamber of our mind and peep into Uttara Mīmāṁsā system. On account of such further beliefs, I should think that some of the basic and important propositions of Advaita Vedānta are lost to us, and we again fall in the trap of Pūrva Mīmāṁsā which starts controlling our mind. In fact, this has already happened. We as Vedāntins have accepted all beliefs of Pūrva Mīmāṁsā and in addition have accepted that the world is an illusion. This has paved the way for our inactivity. In fact, neither Pūrva Mīmāṁsā nor Vedānta teaches us to become inactive. Śaṅkarācārya has said, *yad yad karma karomi tad tadakhilam śambho tavaradhanam.* Whatever, I do, O Śambhu, is your *ārādhanā* (Prayer). But in practice Advaita philosophy became a license for inactivity and a manifesto for Nihilism. It had to be rescued from this aberration. Swāmī Vivekānanda did this by —

(1) emphasising on the one-ness of the universe,

(2) by regarding man — a common poor man (*daridra-nārāyaṇa*) as an incarnation of God, and

(3) to work for the prosperity of man and the society as the duty or *dharma* of everybody.

He emphasised that man can be liberated only in this world and that he has not to wait for the other world for the achievement of his goal. The world is not illusory, it has only a beginning and an end. Thus, he says: a theory may be 'good indeed'. 'But how are we to carry it into practice? If it be absolutely impracticable, no theory is of any value whatever except as intellectual gymnastics. The Vedānta, therefore, . . . must be intensely practical. We must be able to carry it out in every part of our lives . . . the fictitious differentiation between religion and the life of the world must vanish'. (*Practical Vedānta*, part I, p.1. Lectures delivered in London on 10 November 1896). And again he writes: "Inactivity in the sense of passivity cannot be the goal. Were it so then the walls around us would be the most intelligent; They are inactive" (*ibid.*, p. 3. He says, "The Vedanta teaches men to have faith in themselves first" (*Ibid.*, p. 6). That would, indeed be knowing the *ātman*. He writes: "The Vedanta teacher", that "the actual should be reconciled to the ideal, the present life should be made to coincide with the life eternal. . . . You must always remember that one central life of Vedanta is this Oneness" (*Ibid.*, p. 10). "Never think, there is anything impossible for the soul" (*Ibid.*, p. 27). He also talks of oneness of body and mind: "The ideal of dual or treble existence comes from reasoning on insufficient data . . . but such perception never really exists. The perception is either of the body or of the soul. . . . Try to think of yourself as a soul, a disembodied something. You will find it to be almost impossible. . . . This shows that whatever exists is one." (*Ibid.*, p. 83)

And again in the famous speech before the Parliament of World Religions in Chicago on 19 September 1893, he explains: "Non-dualistic Vedanta speaks of two souls, as it were; the real soul and the apparent soul, the Universal and the individual. . . . The real soul which is the same as Brahman. . . . The apparent soul is the one with which we deal in our daily practical life, which identifies itself with the body, senses, mind. . . . In reality there is only one Existence". (p. 189, Chicago Address — From his works).

All this clearly shows that Swāmī Vivekānanda tried to reformulate the Vedānta Philosophy by reconciling the theory with practice. He had realised that Philosophical problems are concerned with how man looks at Reality. For, all our enquiries whether theoretical or practical, point to only one thing, "What is man's place in the world, Reality." What is necessary to realise is that man always creates a second reality on the reality that is given. (In fact, he, himself, is a constituent (*aṁśa*) of this reality). You may call it *māyā*. But it is not a phantom or a dream. It is certainly a fabrication, but a fabrication in the sense the real, manufactured things are fabricated in the factory. It is the world which is shared by all living beings. Man is a part of the world that is given. But in the process of understanding the world, he begins to separate himself from other men and the rest of the world. Thus, he not only creates physical, architectural and engineering designs but also creates social and political organisations, cultural patterns and economic and financial systems. There is communication between one man and another and what we call the world of beings is really the world of understanding superimposed on the physical world. Of course, one does not always realise this superimposition. A young child living in Bombay, for example, may think that the buildings which he sees are like the mountains or the seas given to him when he comes into this world and he may also think that the lifts, escalators, radio-sets and televisions are as natural things as pebbles from the sea-shore. To know that they are different requires a deeper understanding of the world. And on this understanding depends man's deeper or superficial relation with the world. The second world is the social reality. Man creates this reality using the material from the natural reality. It has, therefore, to be accepted, respected. It may be in the first type, man may simply reconstruct the natural reality and bring into existence buildings, bridges, escalators, etc. When he uses principles from natural reality to introduce things entirely new, the like which could never be there in the natural reality such as electric bulbs, radio-sets, television, etc., it is of the second type, where it is the creation of man's ideas and takes the form of poetry and art, it is of the third type. Ethical theories and political systems, literature and art and aesthetic appreciations — all these are the instances of the third. This is the second order world. This is what we call civilisation and culture. This has a beginning, existence and end.

Vedānta tells us that this second order world is to be reconciled with the first order world. That is Advaita.

Swāmī Vivekānanda emphasises on this Advaita or oneness of the world, on the harmony that exists underlying the apparent diversity of this world. Ignoring Swāmījī's message will result in grave consequences for the human race. Now ecology tells us that atmosphere, the vegetation and the animal world together create harmony in the world. If we do not realise that the whole universe is one then the balance would be upset, lifted, the harmony would be lost, the plague of pollution would destroy us. If this is not to happen the Advaita of the universe has to be recognised and with it man's oneness with the universe also has to be accepted. That would be practical Vedānta. The concept of Practical Vedānta, which Swāmījī initiated in the nineteenth century would provide a valid philosophy for 21st century, and for several centuries to come.

16

Paryāpti Relation

PARYĀPTI is a very peculiar concept introduced by Nyāya Logicians to explain in particular, the theory of Natural Numbers. In order for explaining relation known as *paryāpti-sambandha*, it will be necessary to explain the concept of number in general and the concept of number for Nyāya in particular. When we talk of Natural Numbers like one, two, etc. (or even zero) we think of them as abstractions. That number 1 is an abstraction, can, of course, be 'verified' in the sense that it can be indicated by pointing out to a thing. Oneness or uniquness is properly and peculiarly connected with *one thing*. When we use the phrase 'One thing' we use the word *one* as an *adjective* of a thing. But just as *one* can be treated as adjective of a thing can 'two' be treated as adjective of two things? What are *two* things? Is it a unity of *two in one-thing's*? And if they are so, do the two *one-thing's* come into existence on account of the contact (*saṁyoga*) of two *one-thing's*? Do the two things which are kept at distance, (that is, separated in space) have a contact or *saṁyoga*? It will be very difficult to envisage the things, *A* and *B* (or even *C* and *D*) to be separated in space (or time) and still to be regarded as joined together by the relation of *contact* 'R'. What would happen if the distance between *A* and *B* grows less or more? Apparently when we talk of two or three or four, that is, when we talk of numbers, we are evidently talking of *plurality* and not of unity. It is in this plurality that collectivity gets some how involved. But this 'collectivity' is not 'unity'. Thus, words like *some* or *many* or even words like platoon, company, army (or *chamu* or *senā*) signify something different from what the words like one or unity signify. It means that when we use these words we mean thereby a group separated in space and/or time and do not mean by them a unity. Numbers like 2, 3, 4, are not wholes (or organic wholes). There is a discreteness about them. We can significantly use the words *all* and *some* but we cannot in the same or similar way and sense say that the Number two is *one number, one whole.* Manyness (and not one-ness) is the essence of it and *saṁyoga* or contact would ignore this important characteristic of numbers from 2 onwards. When I talk of 2, 3, 4, it is not a relation of parts and a whole where *two separate ones* or *three separate ones* are parts. The concept of quantity preserves in it the manyness of its constituents. It is not a relation of *avayava* and *avayavī* where the *avayavī* is a product and where the characteristics of *avayavī* are different from the characteristics of *avayava*s taken separately. Philosophers might say that a number 2 or 3 is still a unity, although its plurality is preserved. He might, for example, say that when we talk of number 2 or number 3 although two ones or three ones are not connected to each other or one another by the relation of contact directly, they (two or three ones) are still connected by the relation of contact through one common support, or subtratum. It is like a peg-stand where the pegs appear separate and still they form a unity. One need not have an objection to accepting this kind of model although one may say that in such a model the distance between one peg and another may he varied and also the substratum on which the pegs have their stand may merely be conceptual or imaginary.

The problem, however, does not end here. When we talk of Numbers we talk of 1, 2, 3, etc., and in ordinary language we talk of two + two (2 + 2), two × two (2 × 2) and so on. But strictly for the Nyāya philosophers two, three, etc., are not numbers. It is not *ekam*, *dvi*, *tri*, *catur*, that are the numbers. They are not *guṇa*s or adjectives as we think when we talk of *two* (*things*), *three* (*things*), etc. The numbers for them, are *ekatva, dvitva,* etc., But this makes the position more complicated. If *eka* or *dvi* is not a number what is it? Nyāya philosophers would, in all probability, answer that one is a *dravya* or substance and on the basis of this primitive concept say that what we call other numbers, 2 or 3, is a peculiar combination of substances or *dravya*s. This is because they cannot think of abstraction except in the form of *guṇa* or (*sāmānya*). Thus, whenever we talk of 1 we have before us one thing, one house, one elephant, one table and so on. Since *one* and the thing (when we say, one thing), cannot be separated from each other, substanceness (concreteness) which is the characteristic of 'one thing' is attributed or transferred to 'one'. Thus *one* becomes the 'name' of the thing. Only it is not a proper name for it does not denote the way a proper name denotes. But like a common name it is given to a (any) thing. Unless we understand Nyāya theory in this way we, indeed, cannot proceed further. The logic of calling '1' a thing is like this. We see a man named *X* and we know he is both *X* and a 'man'. We see another man *Y* and we know that he is *Y* and 'man'. Similar is the case of the man *Z*. *X*, *Y* and *Z* are treated as proper names and the name 'man' is treated as if it was a surname. Both the proper name and surname are names of substances. In the same way in the case of 1 chair, 1 table, 1 phone, etc., table, chair, phone, etc., are proper names and *one* is a common noun for it commonly fits the things individually. Of course, in ordinary language, that is in the language of common man, we would regard one as an adjective. Let us understand the following case. We see a person 'Hari'. We say he is a man. By that we mean that Hari is an individual belonging to the class man. We see 'Rām'. We also say that he is a man, that is, he belongs to the class of Man. Rām is a member of the class Man. In this way we begin to think ordinarily that number (or particulars) belongs to 'one' particular class. But when we say that different individuals like Rām and Hari belong to the class man it is a different notion from the one when we say that a thing like chair, table or telephone (when taken individually) belongs to the class 'one'. They (chair, table and telephone), if taken together do not belong to the class *one*. 'One' does not seem to be a class to which these different objects belong. It is difficult to say why they should not? Different men belonging to the class 'man' and different individual thing belonging to 'class' one do not appear to be on par.[1] But just as we talk collectively of Man, that is use the word man in plural number similarly we can also talk of one in plural number as in the phrase 'these ones', etc. From this it is only a step further to think that *one* and a *concept like man* belong to the same category. By far-fetched logic one could perhaps say that *all the individual*

1. I would not say that number is a class. But Russell did think so.

things in the world separately belong to the class one. It may be noted however, that Indian Logicians use the word *jāti* or *sāmānya* in the sense of characteristics and not in the sense of collection of each particular. So when they talk of *jāti*, they could talk of characteristics. Thus, if they talk of man then they would talk of *manuṣyatva jāti* or class 'manness' and not of *manuṣya jāti*. *Jāti* as such cannot be used in plural numbers. If there are ten men we can talk of man in plural. But we cannot talk of *manuṣyatva* or manness in plural. That is why we have to use expressions like 'the *jāti*, manness is on the *adhikaraṇa* man'. A class of men is formed by the collection of men. The collection functions as substance. It is a collection of different substances. The common characteristic does not function as collection.[2] It rather functions as an abstraction. That is why when we have to explain the activity of counting we have the notion of collectivity in background. If we try to find out the common characteristic of ten thousand men we perhaps get the characteristic 'man', but we will not get the characteristic, crowd, or army, or *sabhā*. So it is to be recognised that concept *one* cannot be treated as a characteristic. Perhaps Nyāya Logician had this kind of Logic in their mind. They could not think of 'one' as a characteristic. Although in ordinary language we use the word *eka* as a characteristic, they thought that it was not a proper adjective and, therefore, they regarded it as quantity or *saṁkhyā*. It is perhaps on account of our use of the word 'adjective' in the sense of quality that such a thing happens. They think that we can talk of *ekatva* and not *eka* as a *guṇa* or quality. The anomaly is that in ordinary language we do not talk of *oneness man* or *ekatva manuṣya,* but talk of one man. Nyāya Logician thought that although we talk of *one man*, *one* in the phrase, *one man* really stands for *oneness*. Here I would like to make a suggestion. Once we recognise that the finding out of the characteristic is a different kind of activity from finding out that it is one, that is a quantity, we should also realise that there must be categorial difference between a chair and a characteristic like

2. The word *jāti* or *sāmānya* is used as characteristics and collection in different traditions. The notions, class, concept and universals are used in ambiguous way. Perhaps they are used both in a denotative and in a connotative sense. Perhaps the word group is used in denotative way only.

redness and one. In fact, even the *one* would be different from oneness. Nyāya Logicians have themselves recognised this. What they have not recognised is that it is not *oneness* but *one* which is connected with quantity. *One* may have one characteristic, *oneness* but in our day-to-day life, when we count, the measure of our counting is *one* and not *oneness*. There is a sense in saying that one is a name of a thing. It is a general name, common name or a surname. When we talk, e.g., of a chair, its particularity is unique. It is different from other chairs or things by its uniqueness. It may have other characteristics in addition. If we ignore all these characteristics still its uniqueness would remain. It is still a *viśeṣa*. Another chair or another thing may also have all these characteristics. But all these characteristics may be ignored and still two 'ones' will be different. 'One' seems to be a subtratum on which particularities can be superimposed. In other words we can say that the notion of *one* gives us the most general form of particularities. When we talk of one thing its particular characteristics are omitted but its specific organic characteristics are retained. This can be argued in the following way. There is a particular horse. It may be white, red, tall, fast and so on. If all these characteristics are ignored even then we can think of its parts. Its special characteristic of figure, for example, is not eliminated. It is on account of this characteristic of figure that we get a characteristic *one* which gives the horse uniqueness and concreteness. This concreteness is given up; when we talk of oneness or horseness. We can think of dividing the horse into parts. But we cannot think of dividing the horseness into parts. The same idea can be stretched further, when we talk of integers and fractions. Just as a horse can be divided into parts in the same way we can think of 'one' divided into parts. Thus, we can think of 1/2, 1/3, 1/4, etc. The old Nyāya, like Aristotle, had distinguished between form and idea or concept. It can now be seen that when we talk of *one* we talk of form and not idea or concept. It will be desirable to revive the old distinction, and say that number is concerned with *ākṛti* and not with *jāti*. When the concept of *ākṛti* was given up, they had to explain *ākṛti* in terms of *jāti* and, therefore, they had to resolve to concepts like oneness. Thus, when *one* was regarded as a substance *oneness* was regarded as a *guṇa* and so they had to bring forth the concept *onenessness*.

If we have to explain the number-theory in the modified form taking into account the constraints of Nyāya ideas we will have to make a few modifications. Numbers like 1, 2, 3, will now stand for *ekatva, dvitva*, etc. That is *eka, dvi, tri* will not be equivalent to one, two, three. Similarly, *ekatvatva, dvitvatva*, etc., will have to be translated as oneness, etc., and not by onenessness, etc. This is because the English words 1, 2, 3, have a shade of abstraction which *eka, dvi*, etc., do not have, at least for Nyāya Logic.

Before proceeding further it must be clear that for Nyāya Logician all the Numbers except the Number 1 is due to *apekṣā buddhi* (expectant intention). The significance of this observation is to be understood clearly. In the first place it means that the analysis of the number one, (viz., (1) thing,) is not the same as the analysis of the number two (viz., (2) things, etc.). When we talk of 1, (1) thing '1' is a quality of one thing. The quality or *guṇa* '1' (oneness) exists by the relation of *samavāya* on the substratum of (1) thing, that is the quality '1' has the same kind of relation to the thing as the quality, e.g., red, has to it. This relation exists even if there is no one to perceive it, but the relation of two onward, to things is not of this kind. It arises through *apekṣā buddhi*. That is in the absence of any sentient being to perceive this relation, it would not exist. These relations are perceiver—(knower) dependent relations. It is a clear admission of the fact that Numbers from 2 onwards are only epistemic. Although there may be plurality, we understand the plurality as collectivity.

To understand any combination of plurality as gestalt, is dependent on the percipient mind. It really means that although the quality one may exist in the substratum of a thing the quality 'two' exists on the substratum of *ātman* or *manas*. The situation is thus more complex. If there are three things say *A, B* and *C* then *A* will have a quality *one*, *B* will have a quality *one*, and so also will be the case with *C*. But if there is an observer *O* he would be able to observe '(*A* & *B*) or *A, B* and *C* together. And in this observation he will combine each one together. In this togetherness emerges the concept of number 2 or 3 (*dvitva* or *tritva*). It means that *dvitva* or *trivta* is not possessed by things *A* and *B* or *A-B-C* in their own right. They are superimposed on the things by the observer or the knower, Numbers beyond 1 'exist' only in the epistemic world. It is clear then that the relation of 2 (*dvitva*) to two things cannot be either the relation of *saṁyoga* or *samavāya* which for Nyāya Logician are ontological relations. It is a case of, to use Aristotle's terminology, a kind of 'separable accidents' which arises in the world of knowledge. To use the Advaita terminology it is some kind of, '*Japāsphaṭika nyāya*'. When we talk of four things having fourness (*caturatva*) it will be the quality *caturatva* which in one sense (epistemic) belongs to each thing separately and to all the (four) things collectively, but in another sense we should be able to say *eko caturvān* or *caturcaturvān*. But as Late Kurundkar Shastri said this awareness would exist only for a moment and that too would be of the nature of pastness (*āsīt*) for the awareness would depend on the percipient mind. It is the percipient mind which can think of the gestalt of the several things whether they are actually combined by contact or are separated by spatiality or temporality. This explains how we can talk of crowd, army and so on. Such a notion of possessing both collectivity and distributivity would allow the discreteness, that is the essence of number. For when we are talking of the number 4 we are not talking of a whole that consist of four parts and which are joined together either by the relation of *saṁyoga* or *samavāya*. A part and whole relation would not allow for the discreteness of the parts. In a whole made up of parts, parts lose their identity as parts. When we talk of any number say 4, its elements do not lose their separate identity. Thus, if we are to talk about a whole of four parts, we are able to say that the whole has 4 parts. We thereby mean that we are able to count the parts separately, and still each part is not separate and independent so long as it is a part of the whole. This is not the case, say, with any number other than number 1.

A Nyāya Logician, while explaining such phenomenon would say that there are things (even the plurality of course, is due to *apekṣā buddhi*). He would not regard *eka* as *viśeṣaṇa* or quality. It would merely be the form of each thing. Ordinarily when we talk of numbers, we talk of them as if they are adjectives (quality) of the things. A Nyāya Logician would here employ *ekatva* and not *eka*. Though it would look very artificial, in his language there would not be *eka-vastu*. There would be *ekatva-vastu*. Since in this language *ekatva* is the quality, it will have to have a characteristic in the same fashion as red has characteristic redness. He will then say that the quality *ekatva* has the *jāti, ekatvatva*. This *jāti* is possessed by every substance. Now through the *apekṣā buddhi* he will also talk of *dvitva* or two, *tritva* or three, etc. So from this he will have the knowledge of the *jāti*, *dvitvatva* and *tritvatva*. Strictly speaking they will not be *jāti*s because they do not have existence in ontology. They will be rather *upādhi*s. These *jāti*s and also characteristics *dvitva*, *tritva*, etc., will belong to things collectively without losing their separate identity. We will thus say that *dvitva* will be possessed by *dvi*, meaning thereby *dvau vastūni* or two things. The *vastu* does not inhere *dvau*. Similarly, when two things are comprehended together they are not necessarily connected together by way of contact. To recognise this peculiar relation Nyāya Logicians introduced the concept of *paryāpti*. The discreteness of numbers can be retained only if we set an order in them. Thus '4' would not mean a collection of '4' but would mean '1-1-1-1' independently and also together that is *one* could be counted up to *fourth* place. One can easily see that *fourth* is an ordinal Number. Without going into details, I may say that by distinguishing *paryāpti* from other relations, Nyāya Logicians have brought forth or given a place to the concept of ordinality in Number theory.

17

Nyāya Logic and Epistemology

TRADITIONALLY Indian philosophy is classified into six orthodox systems, Nyāya-Vaiśeṣika, Sāṁkhya-Yoga, Pūrva Mīmāṁsā and Uttara Mīmāṁsā, and some unorthodox systems, namely Buddhism, Jainism, and Cārvāka. This kind of classification is inadequate, for, in the first place in addition to the systems mentioned above there are some other systems, e.g., the school of philosophy of Grammar. Secondly, when philosophical writers said that they belonged to a particular system, it was not the case that they did not criticise the earlier writers or deviate from the views of their predecessors. However, in this chapter I am restricting myself only to the problems of knowledge and logic and here it does not appear to me that there was a separate theory of knowledge for each system although the writers of each system made some significant contributions to certain problems in the general area of logic and knowledge.

Epistemology

In the context of Indian philosophy although we talk of the problem of knowledge, there are, in fact, varieties of problems and not one. The problems are related, but one blanket theory of knowledge may not answer all the problems. When I say 'I have knowledge of the table', or that 'there is a flower-pot on the table', the problem concerning this kind of knowledge is different from when I say that, 'I have knowledge of *Brahman*'. The problem connected with the knowledge of *Brahman* is entirely different from the problem connected with the thing like a table or a flower-pot on a table.

Again, when I say I have knowledge of a class of objects or a concept of knowledge of the absence of something, the problems connected with this kind of knowledge are again different from knowledge of concrete objects. When we have knowledge of concrete objects, this knowledge itself can be divided into definite and indefinite knowledge, or determinate and indeterminate knowledge. And the theories concerning them may not be of one kind. Then again, two different problems may face us. The first, how do you get knowledge? The second, what is the justification of knowledge?

At the outset it should be made clear that when the different systems of Indian philosophy talk of knowledge, they are not primarily concerned with every problem about knowledge. Pūrva Mīmāṁsā which is concerned with what should be done and what should not be done, was not interested in the problem of knowledge as such, in the sense that the problem of knowledge is, for example, concerned with knowledge of a table. But in later Pūrva Mīmāṁsā, the problem of knowledge assumed importance and theories of knowledge were hotly discussed. In Sāṁkhya or Yoga, the problem of knowledge is not primarily important. But when we begin to ask questions about the self, we somehow or the other get involved in the problem of knowledge. This problem assumes importance in Śaṅkarācārya also. In a knowledge situation there is a subject and an object. The characteristics of the two are opposed to each other. But one may suppress the one with the characteristics of the other. This is what we do, to a certain extent, when we are supposed to know. But we go further and attribute the characteristics of the subject to the object and *vice versa*. This, of course, would be a fallacy. But the philosophic problems of knowledge, according to Śaṅkarācārya, arise on account of 'identifying' the subject with the object or *vice versa*.

Let us try to formulate the questions one by one. How do we explain the knowledge that there is a table or a flower-pot on the table? The first thing that Indian philosophy generally assumes is that knowledge is a kind of relation and it is an irreducible relation. It cannot be reduced to, or analysed into anything else: this is what the philosophers of Nyāya school would term the *viṣaya-viṣayī-bhāva* or the epistemic relation between the subject and the object. Unless you accept a *viṣaya* and *viṣayin* or the subject and object and a certain peculiar relation between them, you cannot explain knowledge. This peculiar relation cannot be classed under any other kind of relations. One relatum of this relation is *viṣayī* or the knowledge and the other relatum is the object of knowledge. The *viṣayī* as if holds the *viṣaya*, the counterpart of object in epistemic world in its grip. This relation is to be distinguished from the *tripuṭi* or knowledge triad known as *jñātā* or knower, the thing that is known or *jñeya* and knowledge or *jñāna*. The knowledge is related to the knower by an inseparable relation, termed *samavāya*. For, a knower can always possess knowledge as his property. This is how the Nyāya philosophers regard knowledge as the quality of the soul and the quality is uniquely and inseparably related to the subject. But unlike other qualities this quality, namely knowledge, does not entirely belong to the knower, but is also related to the thing, or the object of knowledge. And this is expressed by *viṣaya-viṣayī-bhāva* or the relation between *visaya* and *viṣayī*. The knower (we can use the word *ātman*) is the *āśraya* or the complex of *jñātā*, *jñeya* and *jñāna* is not the same as the complex of *viṣayī* and *viṣaya* and this complex of *viṣayī* and *viṣaya* is not the same as the subject and object, although Western philosophers have so used them. It is this relation which distinguishes knowledge from desiring, expecting, feeling and so on. Knowing is a transitive verb and (for its existence) it as much depends on the object of knowledge as on the knower. This peculiar complex in the theory of knowledge is known as the knowledge triad consisting of the knower, the known and the knowledge. And I believe that it is universally accepted by all schools of Indian philosophy.

It will be interesting to point out that, according to Śankarācārya, knowledge is not a mental process or act like feeling or desiring. It is not something that a knower does. Finally, it is the thing that shows itself. It is *vastutantra*. This attitude is more or less accepted by philosophers of different schools. It is only because of this that finally a thing is known as a thing. If we do not regard knowledge as relation and merely regard knowledge as a quality only because *A*'s knowledge is *A*'s knowledge and is not shared by *B*, and *B*'s knowledge is *B*'s knowledge and is not shared by *A*, then we will have no other alternative except accepting the representative theory of perception. It is the acceptance of the relational theory of perception and the recognition that the subject-object relation is peculiar and unique that makes the Indian theory of knowledge of almost all varieties, a non-representative theory.

Indian theory recognises that there is a knower and the object of knowledge but the psychological act of perceiving gives us only qualities of the object. Psychologically speaking, we cannot assert the existence of the thing once we proceed from our sensations. And it is a known fact that illusions do occur. But in order to distinguish illusions from veridical knowledge we are actually going beyond sensations. It means that we are inferring the objects of knowledge from our sensing them. Otherwise we would not have noticed silver at the place of a shell, water at the place of hot sand, and two moons in the place of one. Here perhaps one of the points which Indian philosophers would make is that psychological illusions presuppose some direct perception. We would not be able to have an illusion of two moons, unless we have the real, veridical perception of the moon.

Indian philosophers would not be satisfied with the kind of explanation the British Empiricists or the philosophers of the Sensum School would give of perception. When I say I perceive a certain object, is it merely a theoretical relationship between me and the object or is some practical relationship also involved? Is it not the case that the object is 'known' by me as the object in practical activity, in my using or handling the object? Starting from mere sensations we would never be able to distinguish a thing from the qualities of that thing. Perhaps it would be correct to say that a physical object is given to us not in the theoretical knowing of that object but in the practical relation which that object holds with the knower. This practical relationship goes beyond the relationship of knowing which is only secondary to the practical relationship. We realise that here is an object, although we may not know it through knowing. When I hold a flower-pot in my hand, it is not merely the sense of a flower-pot, nor a construct out of sense; we hold a thing in our hand and, whatever explanation we may give, for our practical purposes it is a thing that we are holding. Thus, when I have knowledge or when I assert that there is something, it is a kind of motor activity on my part, and not merely a sensory activity which gives me knowledge of a thing.

If knowledge of an object is distinguished into knowledge of a thing and the knowledge of the qualities of thing, the knowledge of the thing is not given to us by the senses, though it is given in the presence of sense-knowledge. The knowledge of qualities and relations on the other hand is given to us by the senses. This presupposition of a thing and its justification is called by Buddhists *arthakriyā-kāritva*, and by Nyāya philosophers *saphala-pravṛttitva*. *Artha* is an object and the existence of an object is proved by the behaviour of the object itself. I do not perceive or describe the object; the object shows itself. The object shows itself in my doing, in my activities. In order to explain this action or 'do-ness' Indian philosophers, particularly of the Nyāya School, think that, even in the act of our perceiving, the object of our perception and the one that perceives 'touch' one another.

Superficially this looks absurd; but, since the object of perception or the thing is not given to us in our senses, we must be discovering it, as a blind man does, by touch. A perception is supposed to be a conjunction, a touch of two substances. Without a touch perhaps it would not be possible for us to know a thing. So even when we perceive by our eyes a thing at a distance, the philosophers of Nyāya (and following them all Indian philosophers) say that our eye goes and touches the object. What perhaps they want to say is that some peculiar kind of action is involved in the act of perceiving. This action either accompanies perceiving or it is a part of it. Now, to say that my eye goes and touches the thing is absurd unless it is figuratively used. Modern optics tells us that through light it is the image which falls on the retina. But two important points arise here: (1) When the image falls on the retina the perceiver must be catching it. The 'doing' activity cannot be totally ignored, and (2) even though in perceiving a thing we act at a distance, the contact between the thing and the eye cannot be disregarded, e.g., if we put an opaque curtain between the eye and the object perception is prevented. It means that though there is a condition for light falling on the retina, it is prevented on account of the curtain. It means that there is not contact. The 'doing' part and the 'touching' part in the Indian theory of perception are intimately related. They convey something quite important. The only thing that is necessary to remember is that words like touch or doing are used figuratively, only to explain something on the basis of analogy.

Thus, when a perceiver perceives, he perceives a thing or a substance and through the sense-organs he senses the qualities, etc., of the thing or substance. How a perceiver perceives a thing — a bare thing — is not explained but is taken for granted as a datum. But this is always done in the presence of sensing or experiencing. The first requisite of a perceptual experience is that it must be a kind of contact, and the metaphysical presupposition of this epistemological process is that there cannot be a kind of contact except between two things. Thus, both the object of contact and the subject are taken for granted as things. This interesting theory is developed by the Nyāya philosophers in its full aspects. But though it has not been clearly worked out by philosophers of other schools, it appears to me that this was in the background of their philosophic or epistemological thinking too.

Let us work out the details of the Nyāya theory of perceptive knowledge. They say that we have perception through six different ways. They would say that there are six different kinds of *sannikarṣa*. The first and the basic *sannikarṣa* is, of course, that of 'touch' or contact. If *X* perceives *Y* then *X* is a substance and *Y* is also a substance, and both *X* and *Y* touch each other (either through the touch or through the eyes). It is because the two substances *X* and *Y* touch each other that a perception arises. Of course I have already explained above that this touch is to be understood not always as a physical touch but rather as the absence of non-contact; for if there is an absence of contact then no perceptive knowledge would be possible. But when we say we have knowledge it is never knowledge of the bare thing or substance. It is always a determinate specific knowledge. That is, it gives a particularity to that piece of knowledge, and it is always distinguished from other things. It is printed on the background of other unspecific things. Suppose I am seeing a radio set before me. Then it will not be correct to say that I am seeing a bare indeterminate thing. My object of perception is characterised by radioness and certain physical qualities of that thing like size, shape, cover, etc. A Nyāya philosopher would say that one 'guesses' the knowledge of the qualities through the senses, because the qualities belong to the thing and always belong to the thing. If I say I have knowledge of the qualities, I am a step removed from the knowledge of the thing. It is not the case that I have knowledge of the qualities and then I construct those qualities into some kind of a hypothesis about a physical thing. The qualities are permanently related to the thing. (I am doubtful whether this last part will be finally acceptable to other schools of Indian philosophers.) Thus, when I have knowledge of the qualities I have first the knowledge of the thing and then the knowledge of the qualities; because the qualities belong to the thing. I have thus knowledge not of qualities but as qualities belonging to the thing. The qualities belong to things by a permanent relation; that is the qualities inhere in the things. The knowledge of the qualities is, therefore, through the contact of the thing and through the permanent relation between a thing and the qualities. This is termed as knowing through *saṁyukta samavāya*.

On the basis of the knowledge of the thing, however, we will not be able to discriminate one particular thing from other particular things. A thing is discriminated from other things on account of its being of a particular class. When I say I see a cow, I have already circumscribed, limited my knowledge by drawing a line of demarcation between a cow and other things. In Western philosophy and logic a class is supposed to be a special kind of thing and the members of the class belong to the thing. The class is as if made of these members, although at some stage the concept of a class is regarded as different from the sum-total of all its members. In Indian logic and philosophy perhaps a similar concept of class might have existed in the very beginning. But very soon and in the quite early development of Indian Philosophy the concept of class underwent a change. Class was regarded not as a collection of things but as a common characteristic which is shared by all particulars to which we apply the term class. Thus, the class 'cow' doesnot mean a group of all individual cows. But it means the characteristic 'cowness'. Thus, we will have to change the usual usage of saying that this particular cow belongs to the class cow. We will rather have to say that the class characteristic cowness exists in an individual cow. Thus, to refer to the earlier example of a radio set, there will not be a class of radio sets, rather we will have to say that the radioness exists or belongs to a particular thing. It should, however, be noted that the extensional concept of class continued to exist in the inferential theory (see inference).

When we talk of a perceptive situation we not only talk of the class characteristic but also of the particular characteristics or qualities. When I see a flower, I do not merely see the thing with the class characteristic for flowerness. I also notice the colour; we may characterise that flower as having a particular colour; say, for example, red or rose or the like. This particular characteristic which belongs to the colour is explained by the Nyāya philosophers by what they term as *saṁyukta samavāya*. The qualities too have a class characteristic and the explanation of this knowledge will be a step removed and the model suggests that a quality inheres in a thing and the class characteristic of a quality inheres in a thing and the class characteristic of a quality inheres in the quality. In Nyāya language this is known as *saṁyukta-samavāya*.

The above theory, however, will not explain the perception that is concerned with hearing. The Nyāya philosophers think that hearing is of the kind of a sound and this sound is a quality of ether. Since ether is all-pervasive, when a certain sound is produced it belongs to the whole ether. The auditory organ, so it is thought, is also ether and so the sound becomes a quality of this particular ether, the ear. This is how the sound produces similar sound waves in the ether and man is able to hear.

When one perceives an object, one is, so to speak, drawing a line of demarcation between that object and the other objects which he does not perceive at that time. Similarly, when someone does not perceive a particular thing at that time, someone perceives that someone does not perceive an object at that time. According to Nyāya philosophers, this means that, just as we have knowledge of positive things, similarly, we have knowledge of the non-existence or absence of things. The Nyāya philosophers think that the non-existence is also known through perception. Philosophers belonging to other Indian schools do not accept this contention of the Nyāya philosophers. They say we have knowledge of the absence of a certain thing by a special faculty of knowing, viz., the faculty of knowing the absence.

It is difficult for anybody to say that all we perceive is actually the case; illusions cannot be ruled out. How then do we distinguish illusions from veridical perception? If sometimes we can have illusion, how can we be sure that we do not have an illusion at any particular or all the time? The Nyāya philosophers start with an empirical outlook. There cannot be an illusion according to them unless that of which it is an illusion already exists or existed and was perceived. Thus, if we have an illusion of water in a place of hot sand, the water must exist and be perceived somewhere and sometime. Similarly, if we have an illusion of a snake, then the snake must exist somewhere. Sometimes we do have illusions like the illusion of a hare with horns or pink rats; but the illusions of the hare with horns or pink rat is possible because the pink rat, for example, is a composite object consisting of two simples, the pink and the rat and, therefore, we can, by joining these two simples, get an illusion of a pink rat. We can also talk of a barren woman's son because it is possible for us to conjoin the words like barren, woman and son. But in the strict sense of the term we can never have an illusion of a barren woman's son.

The Nyāya philosophers take it for granted that an illusion always presupposes a real veridical perception. To take the stock example, they would say that we do see sometimes that there is silver where there is only a shell. But when we ascribe silverness to the shell this is so because we know that there is silver; we have a memory of silver; we must have seen the silver in the goldsmith's shop and we must be aware of the usual qualities of silver. Thus, when we see a shell, on account of the similarity of the usual sense of the shell and the silver, we can mistake the shell for the silver. The mistake is only with regard to the qualities and the class characteristics of those qualities. But there is never a mistake about the substance to which the qualities belong.

To a great extent this empirical point of view is accepted by philosophers of the Vedānta and Mīmāṁsā schools. One school of Mīmāṁsā accepts the contention of Nyāya. The other slightly differs from it. But even if it differs this school of Mīmāṁsā says that there is, in fact, no illusion; there is only the knowing of the elements in an illusion, because the wholes that we construct out of the composite parts are not the usual wholes. To consider the shell-silver illusion, a philosopher belonging to this school of Mīmāṁsā will say that the shell is real and the silver is also real. But the whole of the shell and the silver is not real because the object that is shell belongs to one whole, the object that is silver belongs to another. In an illusory perception we are bringing together the parts of different wholes and combining them in one.

The Philosophers of Advaita Vedānta raise very interesting issues in regard to the ordinarily accepted illusory phenomenon. If we consider the case of an illusion like perceiving a snake in place of a rope, they will say that it is difficult to verify whether something is actually a rope or a snake. For the only criterion, according to them, is whether you actually perceive something. When you perceive a snake at that moment, say at time t_1 you are actually perceiving a snake. Suppose at time t_2 you have perceived a rope instead of a snake; we have a tendency to believe that the snake was unreal and the rope was real. This is what is termed in Indian philosophy as Bādha. And all our common sense behaviour is based on this. But let us analyse the situation further. At time t_2 we have seen a rope and, therefore, we infer that what we have perceived at time t_1 was illusion. Now, there are several possibilities here. One possibility is that there was actually a snake and it disappeared; another possibility is that there was a snake and it turns itself into a rope at time t_2; a third possibility is that there was indeed a snake and it does exist even at time t_2 but it went somewhere out of our sight and when we were perceiving a snake at time t_1 the rope also existed there, but was unnoticed. All these theoretical possibilities cannot be entirely denied. It may be argued that it is against common sense to think that the snake turns itself into rope the next moment or the snake disappears the next moment and a new thing called rope comes into existence. In the common sense world we do believe in the permanence of things. But as a matter of fact it is this permanence which is challenged by the Advaita (Vedānta) philosophers. What we call permanent is not permanent according to them. In this world we assume that a thing continues to be the same: a table continues to be a table at time t_1, t_2, t_3, t_4, etc. But it is difficult to conclude that it will continue to be a table all the time. Sometimes the table may break; it may be burnt and so on.

Ordinarily we believe that if a thing has existed for sometimes then it would continue to exist. If the sun rises for all these days, then it will rise tomorrow. If I deliver a lecture on every Wednesday, then I would continue to deliver a lecture on Wednesday. The logicians base their arguments on the belief that what continues to exist will continue to exist. But this is indeed fallacious. If I lecture on every Wednesday, then the correct conclusion would be that there will, at least, be some Wednesday when I would not lecture; for I may be no more. The Advaita philosophers make use of this. They say there is no reason to suppose that there is a distinction between the 'illusory' snake which exists for one moment and a thing belonging to common sense world which exists for a much longer time. Whether it is an illusory snake or a permanent thing in the common sense world, it has both a beginning and an end. And, therefore, there is some time when something did not exist and there is a time when something would be no more. Thus one, cannot say that if a thing exists for four moments, it is more real than a thing which exists for one moment. Nothing can, therefore, be verified on the basis of greater length of time.

Although perception may be regarded as simple and something non-composite, we can distinguish in it several elements. For example, when we say we perceive something determinate, our knowledge of the thing is always determined by a certain characteristic which, so to say, limits this knowledge. According to Nyāya philosophy this characteristic is related to the thing of which it is a characteristic by a certain relation. This concept of Nyāya has come to be accepted by almost all schools of India philosophy. The concept of characteristic, however, is only relative. For example, if we are perceiving a blue pot then the pot will be reported as a thing and blueness its characteristic. But if we are talking of a pot alone, then potness itself is the characteristic which limits the otherwise non-determinate knowledge of the same *X*. Indian philosophers, therefore, distinguish two kinds of perceptive knowledge — one that is determinate and the other that is indeterminate. No one really has this indeterminate knowledge any time. But because we distinguish between things and qualities or characteristics, and also between the knowledge of things and the knowledge of the characteristics of things, the ancient Indian philosophers somehow jump to the conclusion that knowledge of things qua things, is not only distinguishable from what we call knowledge — the composite knowledge, but also that the bare things are separately and independently known or perceived. From this they further conclude that the bare things must be 'perceived' a moment earlier than the composite or determinate object. They, thus, distinguish between the knowledge of the bare things and the knowledge of the qualities. This last part, I think, is a muddle; for here Indian philosophers confuse between (1) the logically distinguishable and the physically separable and (2) also confuse that which is logically prior as temporarily prior. This knowledge of bare things is named by Indian philosophers of almost all schools as *nirvikalpa* knowledge — or knowledge without any construct.

There are, however, differences amongst Indian philosophers about the status and relations between the two kinds of knowledges, *nirvikalpa* and *savikalpa* or determinate knowledge. The Buddḥist (excepting perhaps those belonging to *yogācāra*) think that in the first moment of our perception (and by this they, in fact, mean visual perception) we have knowledge of bare things. These bare things they term as *śvalakṣaṇā* — that which defines itself or that which exists in its own right. Here, of course, comes the Buddhist metaphysics that what exists in its own right is just discrete unconnected moments, although the moments together would form a series or continuum. The Nyāya philosophers on the other hand would take a realistic position. Just as from a long distance a thing is only vaguely perceived and the parts or qualities of the things are not clearly distinguished and they become clearer and clearer only gradually as we approach the thing, similarly they also think that in the first moment we have knowledge of things qua things and in the subsequent moment only we come to have determinate knowledge. This is some kind of a compromise between Locke's position about qualities and the position of the naïve realists. But in the case of Nyāya there is no mental construction or projection when there is determinate knowledge. The knowledge of a thing and determinate knowledge are only two stages of the act of perceiving, the stage of determinate knowledge being only later, deeper or clearer. This analysis is again based on Nyāya metaphysics, for they believe in the objectivity of the substance-quality model. The qualities according to Nyāya are not mind-dependent although they are substance-dependent; they exist objectively, although on account of the muddle between logical and temporal priority, philosophers belonging to the Nyāya school think that in the first moment of its existence a thing is a bare thing and the qualities which are otherwise inseparable from the things are born only the next moment of the existence of things.

The position of the Sāṁkhya school of thought is rather interesting in this respect. I shall indicate two important features of its theory. What we call knowledge arises only when *prakṛti*—matter (the nature or the *natura naturata*) and consciousness fall in each others' shadow, due to the criss-crossing of cosmocentric and anthropocentric points of view. Things (including the self) are distinguished on account of the ego or egoness or *ahaṁkāra*. When a table is distinguished from a chair, it is due to nothing else except my intellect and my ego. From the cosmocentric point of view there is no distinction between a table and a chair. Both of them are only *prakṛti* or matter. Thus, the distinction between a table and a chair is as much due to me or my ego (*ahaṁkāra*) as my distinguishing myself from other men.

Another feature which one can bring out in the Sāṁkhya theory of knowledge, although perhaps by speculation, is the distinction between *tanmātra* and *mahābhūta*. *Tanmātra* is what exists in its own right and *mahābhūta* means its magnification (I believe in knowledge). Corresponding to our five organs of sense there are, so it is speculated, five pure objects of sense (or sense data); they are pure data or objects of sound, touch, vision, taste and odour. Whether these are to be called objects of sense I am not sure. And why these should be an independent object of each sense is also a matter of metaphysics. However, the Sāṁkhya position can be interpreted in two different ways: (1) One can take *tanmātra* as the object of one sense and then distinguish it from perception which, though it may primarily be due to one sense, is more complex in the sense that it includes the data from other senses. According to the Sāṁkhya theory of *pañcīkaraṇa* in each of the objects of perception the object of one sense is dominant although the objects of other senses also form part of the thing perceived. (2) On the other interpretation it would mean that *tanmātra* is something which exists in its own right; but, when it is subjected to perception, it is perceived as a *mahābhūta* — *mahābhūta* signifying some kind of phenomenal reality.

The position of Advaita in this respect would be very similar to that of Buddhism. The philosophers of Advaita would distinguish between knowledge of bare things and determinate knowledge. Like the Buddhists they too would hold that it is the first kind of knowledge which gives knowledge of reality; the other kind of knowledge would merely give knowledge of phenomenal reality. However, since their presupposition is that, Reality is one without the other, this would include knowledge of 'reality along with the person who knows'. This will have the form — 'I along with the rest of the reality'. Such knowledge can never be had by perception. For in perception reality is always broken into the knower and the known. Advaita, therefore, holds that this knowledge is attained through some kind of intuition which is to be distinguished from perception. Advaita philosophers hold that at some stage this knowledge is obtained through Vedic sentences.

It will now be clear why a Vedāntin of Advaita thought thinks that knowledge of *Brahman* is of a different kind from knowledge of empirical things, although it is similar to it and so known as knowledge. First empirical knowledge presupposes the duality of the knower and the known. Unless the knower separates himself from knowable objects (the rest of the world) no knowledge of the empirical type is possible. Such knowledge is always characterised by some limitation; for by assumption it is not knowledge of the whole. The whole will include the knower also, whatever be his status. This cannot be the case when we are thinking of perception; and, if inference is also based on perception, it will not be possible even by inference. Knowledge of the logical form 'I am *Brahman*', then, cannot be had through perception through which we have knowledge of ordinary things. One would 'know' it intuitively when the duality between the knower and the known is eliminated and when he no more knows it but becomes it.

Perhaps the scriptures may give rise to it and intuition may be hastened on account of *upamāna* where what happens in perception is reverted. When we know that something is Yak (if it is based on *upamāna*), it is first given by description and then confirmed by comparing this description with the object of perception. Knowledge of *Brahman* also follows the same model. But there would be a difficulty in the last part of the process. *Brahman* cannot be finally perceived as the object *of upamāna*, as for example, the Yak, can be perceived. For, as pointed out earlier, knowledge of *Brahman*, being knowledge of the whole will require the elimination of the subject-object relationship. How can such knowledge be possible? The Advaita Vedānta says that this relation is broken in the practical relationship, when the logical form is no more 'I know *Brahman*' but when it is 'I am *Brahman*'. It is not knowing, as knowing requires quality, it is being itself and so the duality is undone. In fact, this is in keeping with the pragmatic attitude of Indian philosophers towards knowledge. How does one know that a thing is a table? From a distance it merely appears like a table. It is only in the practical use that it is confirmed as a table. The confirming of knowledge is living with it. And this is also true of knowledge of the whole or *Brahman*. Knowledge of *Brahman* is not something that is theoretical. It is not knowledge at all. It is only *Brahman*, and categorising it as theoretical, etc., does not arise.

The philosophers of the Nyāya school seem to have a similar concept of intuition. They are pluralists and atomists. But one cannot have knowledge of the atoms in perception. They, therefore, think that there is another kind of perception or rather intuition. They give it the name *alaukika pratyakṣa* (an extraordinary perception) and think that it is by this that one acquires knowledge of atoms. Knowledge of classes or generalities is also through extraordinary perception only. When one sees a table, for example, one does not see merely a particular table but sees the whole class of tables. This is due to extraordinary perception. The later Nyāya philosophers have elaborated this concept of extraordinary perception still further. They think it is of three kinds: (1) Not only knowledge of concepts or classes but also the relations between classes or concepts is had by this kind of extraordinary perception. They give it a name, *sāmānya-lakṣaṇā-pratyāsatti* (an extraordinary perception through which general concepts are given). (2) The other kind of extraordinary perception is called *jñāna lakṣaṇā*. It is the same as what modern psychology terms as pre-perception or complication. Logically its form is that of analogy. One perceives one thing, but it immediately gives rise to another perception. One perceives a thing of sandalwood (at a distance). But (on account of memory) he connects (without specifically being conscious) it with fragrance. This connection is immediately perceived, although it is not an ordinary type of perception. (3) The third type of extraordinary perception is known as *yogaja-lakṣaṇā-pratyāsatti*. There has been a good deal of confusion about this concept amongst Indian philosophers. Often it is confused with the super human powers by which the *yogīs* are supposed to know all the particulars in the past, present and future. But the definition of *yogaja-lokṣaṇā-pratyāsatti* merely tells us that through this perception one is able to perceive empirical generalisations and a connection between particular and empirically general notions.

There is one small point which deserves our attention. While discussing the problems of perception, perception is described as knowledge arising out of contact of the object with some sense. These senses are classified as external and internal. The five organs of sense are regarded as external senses. But there is an internal sense (*manas*) too. Pleasure, pain, etc., are directly known through *manas*; but *manas* is also employed to know external objects. Although *manas* has been usually translated as mind, understood in the technical sense, *manas* does not mean mind. It is more akin to the nervous system. Ultimately the object of knowledge is related to *ātman* or the self (psyche) through the sense-organs, external and internal. Therefore, it is the *ātman* alone which is the knower in the ultimate sense of the term.

There is yet another important point connected with the general discussion of perception. In perception, as we have seen there is a contact between the sense-organ and the object of knowledge. Knowledge is supposed to be possible because it is thought that both the object of knowledge and the sense-organ are made of the same material. Thus, the eye is supposed to be made out of light, the ear out of ether and the organ of cutaneous sensation out of air primarily. The metaphysical presupposition is that knowledge becomes possible on account of the similarity between that which is known and that by which it is known. All that is known by our vision is thus made up of light and all that is known by hearing is made up of ether. The so-called mystical perception of the Yoga system makes use of this concept. It is alleged that ether is all-pervading; so, if the power of the ear could be increased through concentration, then one's ear could be used to hear any sound anywhere. Our ear will act like a wireless receiving station and one could adjust it according to a wavelength. Similarly, if the power of the eye is increased one could see any object which has the capacity to be visual. Perhaps this would go against the modern theory of light and I need not try to defend it here although people may try to defend it using the notions of reflection and refraction.

When an Indian philosopher talks of the problem of knowledge he also talks of the sources of knowledge and gives it the name *pramāṇa.* The followers of different systems give different sources of knowledge and grade them on a scale of merit. On this scale perception is usually accepted as of prime importance. All other sources of knowledge generally presuppose knowledge by perception or perception, at least, plays a significant role in the process. The Cārvāka school, representing an extreme type of empiricism, even goes further and rejects all sources of knowledge except perception. This helps them to reject causation, the unity of self, etc. The importance of perception is recognised even by the adherents of Advaita Vedānta like Śaṅkarācārya in respect to empirical knowledge. He said in his commentary on the *Bhagavad Gītā* that even if one thousand Śrutis tell us that fire is cold it cannot be accepted, for it is contrary to experience.

Logic

Until now we have generally discussed problems connected with perception. The other important sources of knowledge are *anumāna* or Inference, *śabda* or Authority (also language), *upamāna* or knowledge by comparative description, *arthāpatti* or semantical implication, and *anupalabdhi* or knowledge by non-existence. All these, in one sense or the other, fall within the scope of logic and I shall now proceed to deal with them.

The word *anumāna* (inference) literally means that which follows already existing knowledge. The word knowledge also needs to be properly understood. For ancient Indian thinkers a form of knowledge is not knowledge. Thus 'two and two make four' or 'All *M*'s and *P*'s, All *S*'s and *M*'s, ∴ All *S*'s and *P*'s' which gives the form of the first figure syllogism is not knowledge; knowledge must give information and that information is knowledge only when it is true. It must never be ignored that inference is a means of knowledge. The conclusion in the inferential machine gives this knowledge part and is jointly implied by the premises. It already exists in the premises and is carried through the premises to the conclusion.

The knowledge part in inference is called *anumiti* in Sanskrit logic. Although *anumiti* differs from knowledge obtained through other sources of knowledge, inasmuch as it is obtained through a different source, as knowledge it has the same knowledge content or characteristic as knowledge obtained through other sources. However, we will have to distinguish between *anumāna* or the inferential structure that leads to knowledge and *anumiti* or inferential knowledge. The inferential structure is empty. Only if it is filled in with information is it able to pass that information to the conclusion. The inferential structure, however, is regarded by logicians of all schools as infalliable. Validity is a necessary characteristic of this machine, although truth may not be. This structure is known as *anumāna* only when truth is a characteristic of the premises so that it becomes a characteristic of the conclusion also. The empty machine, which has the ability to be a carrier of knowledge, is only a construct — *vikalpa* — according to the Buddhists (and other logicians) and is, therefore, neither concerned with truth nor with falsity (but is simply concerned with formal validity).

This peculiar view of (inferential) knowledge is largely responsible for the peculiar development of Indian logic. First, nothing is knowledge unless it is particular (or singular). A sentence of the form 'anything is *x*' is not knowledge. It should not be 'anything' but 'this definite thing'. Secondly, it should not be '*x*' but some definite thing or characteristic. Whereas 'anything is *x*' is not knowledge, 'this is a blue pot' is knowledge. Even in perception it is only when the perception is definite that it is regarded as knowledge. A cognition of the form 'this is either a pillar or a man' is not knowledge. And this concept of knowledge is carried even in the region of inference. Thus, the conclusion of the inference must necessarily be singular (particular). It can be easily seen that in order for the conclusion to be singular-particular, the premises also must have the core or singularity-particularity although it may not be visible always.

One cannot have knowledge that is characterised by particularity-singularity unless it is based on experience. The premises of inference then must be (1) either particular empirical propositions or universal propositions based on empirical observation. It is necessary to ascertain further that they are actually based on empirical observation. That is, it must be asserted that there is at least one instance of the universal premise or *vyāpti vākya* as it is called in Sanskrit. Unless this is done one will not know whether the general premise has an empirical basis or whether it is empty.

It is stated above that the conclusion and premises of the inference machine must be empirical propositions, but the inferential machine is not basically of the linguistic form or nature. It is only when it is for communication that it takes the linguistic form. So the inferential model that is linguistic (*parārtha* — for others) is to be distinguished from the basic inferential machine that is non-linguistic and which exists for oneself (*svārtha*). Some people tend to call it a psychological process of inference. But it is necessary to remember that it is not psychological in the sense that trains of ideas are psychological.

These presuppositions have had very important repercussions on the development of the Indian theory of inference. First, inferential knowledge is bound to be probably only and would never have absolute deductive certainty. Secondly, a universal general premise will be only probably and will not carry with it absolute certainty. In fact, the history of Indian logic tells us that earlier there was no general premise in the inferential model at all. The inference model was only analogical. *A* has *P*, *S* also is like *A*, ∴ *S* also has *P*. It is only gradually that the premise '*A* has *P*' grew into 'All (or every) *A* has *P*', and *S* was brought under *A* as a member of the class of *S*. (It appears to me that when Indian philosophers talk of the general premise they use a concept of a class suggested by *vyāpti* exactly the way it is used in Western logic.)

It should, however, be noted that the general premise in Indian logic is never a proposition with a bare universal form. It is always accompanied by an instance. This would make sure (1) the possibility of predication and (2) ensure a (probably) particular conclusion, which would be impossible if the universal proposition had been empty. Again the kind of subsumptive relation which holds between a class and a sub-class is not accepted by Indians as inference. It does fit in the accepted norm that knowledge must be particular-singular; a relation between a class and a sub-class is only general. (A class or a sub-class cannot be an instance of a class in the sense that a particular is an instance of class.) Thus, Indian logic will not have all those moods and figures which arise in classical Aristotelian logic. It will also not give merely the relations of implication. Indian logic of inference is rather, to use W.E. Johnson's terminology, applicative. Not that subsumptive relations are not dealt with in Indian logic. But they are not called inference. They are regarded as simply rules indicating the relations between a class and a sub-class or *vyāpya-vyāpaka-bhāva*. Thus, one could easily say that wherever there is potness there is earthness, and wherever there is earthness there is the characteristic of having odour; therefore, wherever there is potness there is the characteristic of having odour. But this is not regarded as inference.

Indian inference is sometimes called Indian syllogism. I think this is a mistake. It does not have the syllogistic form although, if one means to bring it about, one could. It will be worthwhile to note that the form of inference in Indian logic is that of controversy and, therefore, it should be better called dialecticism and not syllogism. The form of inference that has come down to us as a form of inference for others (*parārthānumāna*) is not that of three propositions, the major premise, the minor premise, and the conclusion — but that of five sentences required in the dialectics for convincing others.

The first is the enunciation of the position or the proposition to be proved. The second is the statement of the reason which would imply the enunciation. The third is a statement of an instance which is similar to the proposition of enunciation. In the course of history, the concept of concomitance between the middle term and the major term developed out of this instance by subjecting it to generalisation and came to be known as universal relation or *vyāpti*. The fourth states that the enunciated proposition is similar to the instance with which the claim is supported. In the course of time, however, the relation of similarity was replaced by that of application of the universal proposition to the case under consideration. And in the final stage this concept was identified with *parāmarśa* or comprehension. A discussion about this concept will follow. The fifth is the conclusion. This is the same as the proposition which was enunciated.

It will be proper to recall that in the earlier days of logic there were not only these five parts of arguments, which are mentioned above, but there were in addition five parts, making the total of the parts of argument ten. Thus, it will be clear that the form of argument of inference is not that of a syllogism, but that of controversy or debate. That the five-part argument was not in the strictly logical form was clearly brought out by the Buddhist logicians Diññāga, Daharmakīrti and Dharmottara who said that only two parts representing premises and a conclusion were enough for the argument.

Before we proceed further it will be necessary to point out that although I said that according to Indian logicians inference proceeded from the general to the particular, Indian logicians would not allow any syllogism of the form 'All men are mortal', 'Some Greeks are men', ∴ 'Some Greeks are mortals' as inference. For inference must always be characterised by definiteness. When Indians talk of particularity they only mean singularity.

It is important to point out here that there is yet another difference between the Indian and Greek syllogism. From negative premises no affirmative conclusion can be drawn according to the Greek technique. But in Indian logic there can be a negative premise and an affirmative conclusion, and a conclusion can also be drawn from two negative propositions. This is so because (1) Negation has a very different significance in Indian logic. Being primarily empirical, Indian logic does not allow any negative entities. And in the final stage even non-existence was loosely understood as some form of conceptional existence. If we say that wherever there is smoke there is fire, then we say this because we have actually seen smoke somewhere and so there will be fire. Modus ponens is thus allowed. But modus tollens will have no place in Indian inference except for confirming the universal premise, by adhering to contra-positive or *tarka*. And here too, the objective is not to prove something negative. The sole aim of Indian logic is to prove the positive concomitance between the middle term or the reason and the major term. In a sense it will not be very correct to say that the Greeks did not draw positive conclusions from negative premises. In a weak disjunctive syllogism from $p \vee q$, the conclusion p is drawn only by denying p, and p is drawn by denying q.

In the logical literature of India there is an allusion to three kinds of inference. In one book (*Aphorism of Vaiśeṣika*s) there is a reference to the fourth one too. But the theory of inference that is actually developed is of only one type. It is only the deductive one and is usually termed *sāmānyatodṛṣṭa* or seen from the class or general characteristics.

Starting from these basic concepts, Indian logical theory developed in different ways. Since the inference proceeds from the class characteristics, the concept of class was profusely discussed. The earlier logician did not accept anything except the natural class. The same object could not be classed under A and class B. So also they did not accept the unit class. The later logicians, however, took the connotative view of the class, thought that classes need not have physical existence and depended on how we understand them. In fact, they thought that classes were concepts, and we can think of them conceptually, even if there was not a member of the class. A half-man-half-lion, or Narasiṁha as it is called, they said, is either a case of unit-class or a case of null-class.

The basic pattern in which a thing was conceived was that of substance quality. Indian logicians conceived the structure of inference and of propositions too in the same way. The subject of a proposition was supposed to be the substratum, and the predicate superstratum. Similarly, the form of the inference was that if on one substratum there were two characteristics always present then we could say that there was a concomitance between them. Thus, by bringing the substratum under a bigger class in which the substratum under consideration is a member, one could say that the member substratum would have a concomitance of those qualities. When we say, wherever there is smoke there is fire, we only mean that on all substrata smoke and fire go together. Now if this is so, then this will also be true in the case of the mountain, as mountain is only one of the members of the substrata which has smoke and fire.

The substance-quality, or the substratum-super-substratum relation; however, takes us to the logic of relations, the application of which, in a sense, is a speciality of Indian logic. When we say that the table is brown, the table is a substance, and brown is its characteristic; table is the substratum, brown is its super-stratum. They are inseparable and Indian logicians state this by saying that brownness 'inheres in' the table. 'Inhering in' is a kind of inseparable relation. When we say that a 'table is on the ground', there is no doubt that the ground is the substratum and the table is the super-stratum. But the relation that is denoted by 'on' is not an inseparable relation and is quite different from the relation 'inhering in'.

Indian logicians think that for a complete understanding of the substratum and the super-stratum the kind of relation which holds between them must also be added. We have seen earlier that in inference we infer from the class of substratum to a member substratum. Whether it is a class substratum or a member substratum the super-strata are related to the substratum, by a certain specific relation. The rule of the inference is that one can infer the super-strata and the relation between the super-strata and the member substratum, if and only if, the relation which holds between the member substratum and its super-strata is the same as the relation which holds between the class substratum and its super-strata. Only in such a case can the conclusion be validly held.

One of the important problems is how does one actually infer, i.e., proceed from premises to the conclusion. Suppose p is a premise and q is the conclusion, then can one simply say $p \therefore q$ if p and q are unrelated, if p and q do not overlap or are un-correlated in one's conceptual framework. Perhaps it is necessary to state that $p \supset q$, in order to draw the conclusion q from the given premise. That is, mere p as a premise is not enough to draw the conclusion q. One also needs another premise $p \supset q$. The same thing is true in the Logic of Terms. One cannot really conclude that Socrates is mortal from the premises 'All men are mortal' and 'Socrates is a man' unless the two premises are held together, unless the relationship is established between men, mortal and Socrates. In Indian logic this was pointed out by the concept of *parāmarśa*. It acted like modus ponens and made room for the detachment of the conclusion. It also acted like the rule of transitivity. A parrot who says that there is smoke on the mountain and that wherever there is smoke there is also fire will not be able to draw the conclusion that there is fire on the mountain. The parrot only mentions concepts but does not use them. In using the concepts one is going beyond the coexistence of worlds. They become parts of one's experience and it is such experience which leads to inference. *Parāmarśa* of Indian logic tells us that two premises get fused in one experience and, thus, are able to imply the conclusion.

Although it was not there in the beginning, at a later stage the instance or example was developed into the universal concomitance. Earlier too, the reason (the middle term) was supposed to be identical in two instances, although the instances were different and particular. Indian logic was essentially empirical and, therefore, strictly speaking, there should not have been any place for implication. But the concept of implication did creep in. Whenever we say that wherever there is smoke there is fire, whether this statement is true or not we have already resorted to implication. And there is evidence that in Indian logic the concept of implication was made use of. According to the Buddhist logician, Dharmakīrti, the implication is (1) either based on the cause-effect relation or (2) is based on the relation between a class and its sub-class. Thus, there is smoke implies that there is fire; because fire and smoke are related as cause and effect. So, since the effect cannot be produced without a cause, if there was the effect then it follows that there was the cause also.

However, since Indian logic is essentially empirical, how to get a universal proposition becomes a major problem. Observation is the main method for such inductive generalisation. Usually counting many instances, or many types of instances (*bhūyo darśana*) is recommended. But it is also pointed out that whereas many instances may not prove, one instance may disprove, and sometimes even one instance may be enough to establish a necessary concomitance. If two things are found going together (*sahacāragraha*), there is a tendency to think that they always go together. If one thing is present but another is absent, then they are not related by necessary relation. On the basis of these primary processes one may get (1) whenever there is A, there is B — a positive argument and (2) whenever there is $\sim A$, there is $\sim B$ — a negative argument. On this basis a hypothesis A and B are necessarily related is formulated and it is confirmed or proved false by mean of *tarka*. *Tarka* is sometimes called a proof by *reductio ad absurdum* or a case of counter-factual. But in form it is very different from both these, and I should like to call it the conditional transposition. The proposition wherever there is smoke there is fire, is tested on the ground that fire and smoke are cause and effect. So if there was no fire then there would be no smoke. But there is smoke. So there must be fire. Formally the argument would take the following form:

> $(\sim q \supset \sim p). p) \supset q)$. This is of course equivalent to $(\sim q \supset \sim p) \supset (p \supset q)$ by exportation. And since $(\sim q \supset \sim p)$ is given $p \supset q$ will be proved by modus ponens.

While dealing with the theory of inference Indian logicians have also discussed fallacies. Fallacies are ultimately due to fallacious reason; whether it is a wrong reason connected with the other term, it really comes to be a wrong reason. Hence, Indian logicians attribute all fallacies to fallacious reason. They give requisites of good reason.

(1) The presence of reason in the member substratum.
(2) The presence of the reason is co-substratum.
(3) Absence of the reason from that which is the substratum of the opposite characteristics.
(4) Non-contradiction of stronger proof.
(5) Absence of counter-balancing of reason.

Absence of these conditions leads to the fallacies. (1) If the reason (middle term) is present in the substratum where the contrary of that which is to be proved (major term) exists, then the fallacy is called non-invariable relations (*savyabhicāra*). (2) If the middle term and the major term do not exist on the same substratum but if they are asserted together, then there is a fallacy called *contradiction viruddha*. (3) If reason is assigned for a thing which is really not concerned with the case under consideration, then it is called unproved or *asiddha*. (4) If by the middle term the opposite conclusion can also be proved, then the fallacy is called the real opposite or *satpratipakṣa*. (5) When the conclusion is cancelled or refuted later on by some stronger reason, then it is called Cancellation or *bādhita*.

It will be interesting to point out that in India an elementary system of modal logic was also constructed by the Jain logicians. They thought that in the world of matter of fact every attribute is compatible with every other attribute of a thing. So in this limited sphere the law of contradiction would not apply and to use modern language the only logical operator that is necessary is 'or' (*V*). On the basis of this they developed their logic of seven possibilities known as *syādvāda*.

Some schools of Indian philosophy recognise *arthāpatti* or semantical implication as an independent source of knowledge. It is independent inasmuch as the knowledge which arises is dependent on the meaning of the earlier sentences and not merely on the form of sentences as is the case in material implication, formal implication or inference. The argument from *arthāpatti*, however, has the form, $p \supset (q \vee r)$ and by modus ponens, by asserting p we get $(q \vee r)$ and then by denying q we get r (disjunctive syllogism). However, the consistency of the argument depends on the meaning of p and the meaning of $(q \vee r)$. Further $(q \vee r)$ must be the only alternatives which are implied by p. The usual instance that is given is the following:

Devadatta who is fat does not eat during the day. The conclusion is drawn that he eats in the night. The implied propositions are:

(1) One cannot be fat if one starves.
(2) One eats either during the day or during the night.

The detachment of $q \vee r$ from the original *wff* is due to the meaning of p and similarly the assertion of r after the denial of q which, although it depends on the form $(q \vee r)$, is obtained through the meaning of the original argument. The logicians of the Nyāya school regard it as a case of inference. But if inference is defined as an argument from universal major premises to a particular singular conclusion, then it is plain that a universal major premise is not required for proving the case. Even when one tries to supply the universal premise, it is only forced. I call it 'semantic implication' because the suppressed premises can be supplied only if we take into consideration the meaning of the argument; and it is only on the basis of the meaning that the conclusion is drawn giving rise to new knowledge.

Upamāna or knowledge by comparative description is also regarded as a source of knowledge by the adherent of most schools of Indian philosophy barring of course Cārvākas, Vaiśeṣikas, Bauddhas and Sāṁkhyas. Some people call this an argument from comparison. In ordinary perception the existence of the object of knowledge is not only presupposed, but is actually felt. The object is presented to you and description of the object arises from the object itself. However, if you perceive the object a second time, traces of the previous perception modify your second perception and you are able to recognise the object of perception. In psychology it is called apperception. If you see a table, for example, on two consecutive occasions, on the first occasion you may not know that it is a table; but once it is ostensively taught you that it is a table, on the second occasion when the table is presented to you, you would recognise it. However, even if the same table is not presented, but another table is presented, you would know that it is a table. That is, you are able to recognize different particulars under the same class.

In knowledge by comparative description or *upamāma* you are able to transcend this limit of one class. You are able to recognise the object belonging to a different class, although you have not seen it earlier. This is of course due to the similarity between objects of different classes and also due to the fact that the similarity has been earlier described to you. Knowledge by comparative description is like apperception except that the span of apperception is extended from the particulars within the class to the particulars outside the class. I perceive a cow. I am later told that a yak is similar to a cow and exists in the Himālayas. Although I have not seen a yak, when I see a strange animal which is similar to a cow and yet different from it, I recognise it as a yak even though I have not seen it earlier. It will be important to note that concept-formation also takes place in the same way. If I see a cow and know that it is an animal, even when I see a horse, I know it as an animal although it is not a cow.

Indian philosophers also recognise *śabda* as an independent source of knowledge. The word *śabda* is variously used to convey (1) ordinary language, (2) revealed language, and (3) an authority. The word *pramāṇa* is also vaguely used to convey (1) the source of knowledge and (2) the authority of action. It is plain that when we are talking of prescriptions or actions we are not conveying any information or knowledge in the straightforward sense. The sentences (1) Open the door, (2) Do not do this, or (3) Read a certain book, etc. do not convey information primarily. They are imperatives, although for the execution of these imperatives some elementary information is presupposed. Here the meaning of *śabda* is 'authority for action', although this authority for action does not convey information exclusively. In Pūrva Mīmāṁsā, the word *śabda* is used to convey such authority of action. But when *śabda* is used as a source of knowledge, it conveys knowledge because the language or *śabda* conveys information. The information can be clothed in language because someone has used this language to communicate this information. The information is regarded as reliable on the authority of 'that' someone, who is sometimes regarded as *āpta* or the competent person. He is supposed to be not interested in deluding us. I read in the newspaper that the astronauts have landed on the moon. I believed it and regard it as information because I took it that the news agency which gave this news was interested in giving correct and not false news. Similarly, I also believe that the newspapers which printed the news were interested in giving me correct information Of course, the authority of anybody and everybody is not accepted. The authority of a man is decided by some criteria. In one sense of the term then, when we talk of *śabda* as a source of knowledge, we mean the authority of a competent person.

However, the competent person conveys this information through language. Some religious men hold that God and Messiah sometimes reveal sacred information which also is in language. The Vedas, the *Bible* and the Koran are regarded as sacred books, and the language in those books is regarded as sacred and revealed. The truth of such revealed language is usually not challenged and is called in Sanskrit *alaukika śabda*.

But sometimes the information is conveyed in ordinary language and then the syntax and the semantics of the language become important. Indian philosophers have given various theories about language and its syntax. According to one, the *sphoṭa* theory, it is the sentence which is the primary unit of language. It is not the words which combine themselves in a sentence but it is the sentence which we break into 'parts of speech'. According to the second theory a sentence is made up of words; each word expects some other word till the sentence is complete. A word in itself could have many meanings, but in a particular context it is only the specific meaning of the word which is relevant. This is called competency. Again in order to yield the meaning, the different words must be proximate. If one word is uttered today and another is uttered tomorrow, it will not convey any meaning. However, the kind of syntax which Indians talk of is not a pure syntax; it is a composite syntax where the semantical part has also to be accounted for. Unless the intention of the speaker is taken into account the sentence will not yield any meaning and so will not be useful as a source of knowledge. In accepting language as a source of knowledge Indian philosophers give an elaborate analysis of language.

According to some systems of Indian philosophy a special source of knowledge is recognised for negative knowledge or the knowledge of non-existent phenomena. If a chair is not in this room I know it by perception according to the Nyāya philosophers. According to them the absence or non-existence (of a chair) is also known to me by the same sense-organs by which I know positive objects. However, philosophers of some schools argue that, there is a difference in knowing that a thing exists from knowing that it does not exist or is not present. If there is no horse in this room, I cannot know it by perception. Therefore, non-availability (*anupalabdhi*) is regarded as an independent source of knowledge, particularly by the followers of Pūrva Mīmāṁsā and Vedānta schools.

How do we know that the knowledge which is conveyed through these different sources is valid when we know that erroneous knowledge is made up of parts which are in themselves real. Thus, though the composite knowledge may be invalid, still, the units of knowledge cannot be invalid. This is the view which is advocated by the Mīmāṁsā schools and is known as the self-validity theory of knowledge. The Nyāya school believes in the self-validity of the inference-machine and tests the validity of other knowledge by this machine. Therefore, the Nyāya view is that no knowledge is valid by itself. The Buddhists think that things in themselves are only inferred by us. Although they are presented to us directly and are known to us at the first moment, due to our own projection and construction, our actual perception, consists of (1) actual reality, (2) our construction. Our macro-cognition then is not as a whole and so the validity of knowledge will have to be established and justified by something else. The Buddhist theory is sometimes known as the extrinsic validity theory of knowledge. That our knowledge is valid is a belief. Either we take it as valid in its own right or test its validity. Then that by which we test it as valid in its own right (or the validity of previous knowledge) is to be tested by further knowledge and this in its turn is again to be tested by further knowledge. This is what happens in Buddhism.

18

The Concept of Tarka

THE word *tarka* was technically used by Akṣapāda in *Nyāya-sūtra*s and Diṅnāga used it for the title of one of his books, *Tarkapraveśa*. Perhaps its non-technical use may be much earlier chronologically but from our point of view it is unimportant. In *Nyāya-sūtra*, *tarka* is given as one of the *padārtha*s along with *pramāṇa-prameya* but it has not been given the status of *pramāṇa*. This could be for one of the two reasons. It is possible that Akṣapāda might have thought that it was not an important concept like *anumāna* which is regarded as one of the *pramāna*. *Brahmasūtra* mentions *tarka* in this derogative sense — *tarko-pratiṣṭhānāt*. But it could also be used in a sense in which it is concerned not with rule of the system but by a rule which could control the system itself. In such use, it is accepted. It would stand for some meta-theory of logic and not for logic. It is certainly true that all those later writers who came after Udayana regarded it as something connected with logical system itself and was regarded as a kind of *āhārya* knowledge. Viśvanāth Pañcānana for example, gives three varieties of such *āhārya* knowledge. *Tarka*, was compiled with *saṁśaya* and *viparyaya*. *Viparyāya* is that which is completely illusory or even delusory. *Saṁśaya* means *doubt* and cognition of *saṁśaya* and its validity and its being varedical can be questioned. Thus, logicians have come to the conclusion that *tarka* also is of the same kind — i.e., is concerned with something other than knowledge. Some logicians even enumerate it under fallacies and regard it as of five kinds. Some give this number as eleven.

Let us see how has Akṣapāda described *tarka*. He says,

avijñātatveyārhe karṇotpattitaḥ tatvajña-artham uhaḥ tarkah. I think every word in this description is important. If literally translated this *sūtra* means as follows:

> When the meaning (or the object of meaning) is not known, in order for knowing the (reality or) the principle behind reality, when an argument is formed from the point of reaching its basic principle or cause, it is *tarka.*

This description, I think is really very eloquent. It gives us a base of theory on which all inferences, whether deductive or inductive, are established.

What is fundamental to logic? I feel that the fundamental notion behind all logical theory is implication. If we discard the principle of implication then it would be impossible to formulate logic itself. The later Nyāya Logicians who regarded *tarka* as important for the logical theory regarded it as some kind of counter-factual. Somehow or the other this interpretation is even today accepted by many logicians and the logic of counter-factual is woven around it. I differ from them and think that since implication is at the back of even counter-factuals the basic concept of logic is that of implication and it is this that is conveyed by *tarka.* Maṇikaṇṭha Miśra, a logician of Navya-Nyāya school, uses the concept of *tarka*, the way I use. This Maṇikaṇṭha was a contemporary of Śrī .Reghunātha Śiromaṇi.

But it must be granted that barring Akṣapāda and Maṇikaṇṭha Miśra, in Indian logical literature the word *tarka* is ambiguously used. In its one application it denotes the whole range of logic and is equivalent to *ānvikṣiki.* It is in this sense that it is used in *Manusmṛti*, *Mahābhārata* and *Bādarāyṇa Sūtra*s. It is in this sense that it was also used by the earlier Buddhist logician like Asaṅga and Vasubandhu. One of the logic texts which, thanks to Prof. Tucci, is now translated from Chinese into Sanskrit is called *Tarka-Praveśa.* That the word *tarka* is sometimes used in this exhaustive sense can also be seen from "The History of Indian Logic" by Śrī Vidyābhūṣaṇa. The word *tarka* is, however, used in a narrower sense also and some later logicians used it in this sense, making it subservient to *anumāna.* This is how some of the early logicians regarded *tarka* as of eleven types and some neo-logicians said that it was of five types.[1]

Perhaps the difficulty about the role and import of this word arises on account of the fact that it has not been included amongst *pramāṇas* or means of knowledge. In his commentary on the first aphorism Vātsyāyana states in unequivocal terms that *tarka* is not included amongst the means of knowledge.[2] Even in the text it has been mentioned separately. This separate mention of the word or its exclusion from *pramāṇas* is perhaps the reason why most logicians have misunderstood its real import and have categorised it as *bhrama* or false cognition. This also seems to be the case with Annambhaṭṭa, whose *Tarka Saṁgraha* has been accepted as a good manual of Indian logic. Whether it was the real intention of Annambhaṭṭa or not, what Annambhaṭṭa has written in *tarka* plays only second fiddle to *anumāna*. *Tarka* does not prove anything, it only lends support to *anumāna*. The definition of *tarka* given by Annambhaṭṭa, *vyāpyāropeṇa vyāpakāropaḥ* has been interpreted by recent writes on logic as a method of *reductio ad absurdum*. I, however, strongly feel that for the correct significance of *tarka* one has to go behind such a usage of *tarka*.

Let us examine the argument of Annambhaṭṭa. Annambhaṭṭa first classifies knowledge into *smṛti* and *anubhava*, of memory and direct experience. Then he subdivides experience into two, that which corresponds to a thing (*yathārtha*) and that which does not correspond to a thing (*ayathārtha*). There can be no doubt that what corresponds to a thing is a veridical experience. From this, one is likely to conclude that when an experience does not correspond to thing it is a false one. Here one is presupposing that there are only two truth values, truth and falsity. But when a person's experience does not correspond to a thing it may be either because the experience is different from the nature of a thing or it may be because the person in the strict sense of the term is not experiencing at all, but is having before him only the non-empirical conditions of experience. The first experience will be an illusory experience, the second experience will be what is now known as *a priori* knowledge, thus, *yathārtha* knowledge and *ayathārtha* knowledge need not

1. See notes on *tarka* in *Tarka Saṁgraha* edited by Bodas and Athaley.

2. *Tarka na pramāṇa-samrahitah*

correspond to veridical and illusory experience. They may be referring to two different varieties of knowledge itself. This fact will be clearer if we understand the method Annambhaṭṭa follows. Annambhaṭṭa divides the *ayathārtha* knowledge into three kinds: *saṁśaya*, *viparyaya* and *tarka*. Of these three kinds it is only the *viparyaya* which is illusory experience. To equate *ayathārtha* knowledge, which includes *tarka* and *saṁśaya* in addition to *viparyaya*, with the *viparyaya* alone would not be proper. Nevertheless Annambhaṭṭa himself has done it in *Dīpikā*, his own commentary on *Tarka Saṁgraha*. It is such a loose use of words which has been responsible for the miscarriage of the true import of words and concepts.

It will be interesting to see how the Nyāya logicians explain the theory of *yathārtha* knowledge which one gets by way of perception. In perceptual experience there is a conjunction or contact of (1) the *ātman* and the *manas*, (2) the *manas* and the *indriya* and (3) the *indriya* and the *viṣaya*. If *ātman*, *manas*, *indriya* and *viṣaya* act in a normal way the person would have true perception; that is what is called *yathārtha jñāna* or knowledge. In *ayathārtha* knowledge either some element in the perceptual apparatus may go wrong and so something which is not there may be seen[3] or one of the factors in the perceptual or knowledge situation may be absent. It may be that during the perceptual process, a white object may be perceived as yellow due to certain psychological reasons. Or the person while perceiving an object may be seeing only a common characteristic which the object he perceives has with other objects. This second alternative deserves a careful analysis. It may lead to (*a*) illusion and (*b*) doubt. (*a*) A person perceives a certain thing but does not specifically know what it is. This happens when the person sees only the sense or characteristics common to several things. In such a case he may mistake one object for the other (which is a case of illusion). (*b*) Or he may have indecision (which is a case of doubt). When a man sees a rope and mistakes it for serpent the situation gives rise to the first kind of mistake. When the person doubts whether the object of his perception is a pillar or a man it gives rise

3. As for example, when a person sees a yellow conch which is, as a matter of fact, white.

to the second kind of mistake. The second kind of mistake may again happen at the conceptual level. Or in a knowledge situation, the object element or the content of the knowledge may be altogether absent. In the language of Nyāya, in such knowledge situations there may not be the contact of sense (*indriya*) and the object (*viṣaya*). Such knowledge situation gives rise to the form of knowledge but not to the concrete particular knowledge as such; for the particular element that is required for concrete knowledge is missing. Such knowledge will not give any information but be a definite aid to the information or particular knowledge. It is such knowledge that is required in the case of *tarka*. It is this kind of knowledge which we presuppose in the *reductio ad absurdum* method too; but the assumption leading to *reductio ad absurdum* will only be a special case of such a knowledge. In such knowledge what is really necessary is to use the language of the Naiyāyikas, a conjunction of the *ātman* with the *manas*, but not the conjunction of the *manas* with the *indriyas* and the conjunction of *indriyas* with the thing. Thus, this special variety of knowledge cannot be regarded as illusory, at any rate, in the ordinary sense of the term. All our *ayathārtha* knowledge, thus, need not be illusory. Even if in one sense *tarka* is *ayathārtha* knowledge it should not follow necessarily that *tarka* is illusory in nature (*bhrama*). It would only follow that *tarka* is something non-empirical.

It is interesting to note the definition of *tarka* given in the *Nyāya Sūtras*:[4] *avajñātatve arthe kāraṇopattitaḥ tatva-jñānārtham uhaḥ tarkaḥ*. The translation of this aphorism given by Gaṅgānāth Jhā does not appear to bring out its real import. According to the aphorism *tarka* is the *ūha* of reasoning which is necessary for the knowledge (of the thing) when that knowledge (of the thing) has not occurred. But it is not in the ordinary way. It is *kāraṇopapattitaḥ* — that is, from the point of the cause of reason. To what does *kāraṇopapatti* refer? According to the procedural rules of aphorisms the context must be found in the previous aphorisms. The previous chapter deals with the nature of Nyāya and discusses *avayavas*. The *kāraṇa*, thus, refers to the *pañcāvayavī vākya* or *anumāna* or inference. *Tarka* is, then, that argument which goes to the root of

4. 1.1.40, *NS*.

anumāna and so is its pre-supposition or condition. If this is so *tarka* cannot merely be a secondary argument in support of *anumāna*, supporting *anumāna* though it would be.[5] It should be as it were an *avyakta* or unmanifest picture of inference. It appears to me that this particular function of *tarka* has been overlooked by commentators of *Nyāya Sūtra* and by many other logicians. What is pre-supposed by *anumāna*? From the *vyāpti* or concomitance of *hetu* and *sādhya*, a conclusion is drawn. The *hetu* is given to us in perception and the concomitance of *hetu* and *sādhya* is also given to us in perception. That is why an inference is supposed to depend upon perception.[6] It can be said that inference 'follows from' *vyāpti* or major premiss which contains terms given from perception. The relation can be expressed in terms of 'follows from'. Thus, this earlier perception, i.e., the terms of *anumāna*, in one sense, may be supposed to be the necessary precondition of inference; but evidently by *tarka* this is not meant; for a conclusion would not *follow* merely because some terms were perceived earlier. A conclusion simply *does not follow* if mere terms and nothing else are given. It also requires a certain principle or dictum according to which it follows. We must, therefore, in further analysis, distinguish 'follows from' from 'according to '. Unless there are particular terms a conclusion would not follow. But when we say that a conclusion is 'according to' a certain rule the presence of a term or terms would not be necessary. The form bereft of particular *hetu* or *sādhya* is also presupposed by every inference. This form which also can be regarded as a condition of *vyāpti* is, according to me, pointed out by *tarka*. *Tarka*-knowledge points to this invariable condition in all its varieties and implications. It gives the relation between *āpādya* and *āpādaka* in its *anvaya*[7] or *vyatireka* form. As has been pointed out earlier this knowledge cannot be *yathārtha* knowledge unless it contains elements of objectivity. Though pre-supposed by all inference, a bare dictum would not be regarded as something empirically real. It is interesting to note that even those logicians who have not thought of this particular nature of *tarka* nevertheless

---

5. *Kāraṇa* is defined as *niyatārtha-pūrva-vr̥ttiḥ*.

6. Refer 1.1.5, *Nyāya Sutra, atha tat-pūrvakam.*

7. See notes.

explain it in a similar way. They say that *tarka* is concerned with *āhārya* knowledge. *Āhārya* knowledge is defined as that knowledge which arises out of our desire even when the object is non-existent. That is, it is just an assumed or hypothetical knowledge. If we presume that there is no fire where there is fire it is a case of *āhārya* knowledge. *Āhārya* knowledge thus, is the bare form of knowledge without any reference to objectivity. It is conditional knowledge, where the condition obstructs the knowledge being objective. Such knowledge is indicated by *yadi tarhi* (if — then) or by *vā*, *āhosvit* (or). If the conditional part of this knowledge is represented by if — then it is clearly the knowledge of the implication which is evidently presupposed by any *vyāpti*. *Vyāpti* cannot be established merely on the basis of the knowledge that two things in the world are found to co-exist. Two chairs in a room may happen to co-exist but the knowledge of this chair and knowledge of that chair do not make for *vyāpti* relation between them. When it is said that there is *vyāpti* relation between a *hetu* and the *sādhya*, what is meant is that there is a relation of implication or some kind of dependence between them which makes the *sādhya* deducible from the *hetu*.

It is important to note that other logicians particularly belonging to the *nava-dvīpa* tradition, do not regard *tarka*, *sāṁśaya* and *viparyaya* on one level. Viśvanātha Pañcānana is clear on this point. It is, indeed, true that all these three varieties of knowledge can be classed under *āhārya* knowledge. But that is for different reasons. Any knowledge to be meaningful must have the class characteristic (*jāti*), the form (*ākṛti*) and the matter or the content exhibited (*vyakti*). *Tarka* and *saṁśaya* have the universal characteristic (*jāti*) of knowledge. This is how *āhārya* knowledge is classed under knowledge, but the *ākṛti* (form) and the *vyakti* (content) cannot consistently and in its own nature co-exists in *āhārya* knowledge.

In the case of *saṁśaya* the form is represented by ' . . . or . . . ' *This is a strong*[8] 'or' and is usually represented by both (*a*) ' . . .V . . . ' (*b*) '~(. . . and . . .)', though (*b*) is preferable. The matter as such which occupies the place of dots, gives us two or more independent propositions. Had this form not been present, we would have been

8. But the argument holds good in the case of a weak 'or' too.

able to assert two (or more) propositions. We would have, for example, been able to say that (*a*) there is a man and (*b*) there is a pillar. But the form ~(. . . . and . . . .) prevents this. The *ākṛti* becomes *pratibandhaka* to *vyakti* and so *saṁśaya* does not yield any information, unless the form of this kind of knowledge is broken by a stronger assertion like, it is not a man. On account of such an assertion the form of *saṁśaya* knowledge — *ubhayakoṭikatva* — is lost and in the residue (of the knowledge) the form and the contents become compatible.

What is true of *saṁśaya*, is equally true of *tarka*. In *tarka* the form of *ākṛti* is represented by if — then or *yadi . . . tarhi*. The two assertions act as *vyakti* or content. Had there been just these two assertions then they would have been held independently. But here again the form of *tarka* obstructs such assertions. For the second assertion (or the first negation) at least partially is dependent on the other. But that assertion on which the other assertion is dependent is only conditionally asserted. That is it is not really asserted. It is *āhārya* or can be withdrawn. Thus, the form of *tarka* takes away the informativeness of both the propositions. In ordinary language *tarka* or hypothetical proposition is stated in the form, if *p* then *q*. This creates a misunderstanding that q is dependent on *p*. Like the modern symbolic logicians, Indian logicians too point out that this cannot be so unless we assert a stronger implication between *p* and *q*. So the form of ordinary language if *p* then *q*, on logical analysis, turns out to be its contraposition — if not *q*, then not-*p*. It is the not-*p* which is dependent on not-*q* and it is only by implication if *p* then *q* follows from it. Indian logicians, therefore, recognise only, if not-*q*, then not-*p* as the real form of *tarka* and define it as *vyāpyāropeṇa vyāpakāropaḥ*. It, thus, has the form of assumed contraposition of the original proposition which indicates the *vyāpya-vyāpaka-bhāva*. The original proposition is, wherever there is smoke, there is fire. The *tarka* is, if there had not been fire, then there would not have been any smoke. In the original smoke is the *vyāpya* and fire the *vyāpaka*. In the assumed contraposition, non-fire or absence of fire is supposed to be *vyāpya* and non-smoke or absence of smoke is supposed to be *vyāpaka*. However, the contrapositive implies the original proposition $(\sim q \supset \sim p) \supset (p \supset q)$. It goes without saying that $(p \supset q)$ and $(\sim q \supset \sim p)$ are equivalent. In

Indian logic this rule is illustrated in the development of the theory of *tarka*. *Tarka* state that if there is no fire there is no smoke. But that there is smoke is empirically given and so it (the proposition) cannot be denied. And if the smoke[9] cannot be denied, by implication the fire[10] cannot be denied too. A positive relation between *hetu* and *sādhya* indicates a relation of *vyāpti* but not prove it. The negative relation that wherever there is no *sādhya* there is no *hetu* proves it. Thus, *tarka* indicates the relation which is presupposed by *vyāpti*. Ordinarily it may not be necessary to work out all these implications but when there is a doubt expressed the implication can be worked out. The neo-logicians expressed this by saying that *tarka* is of two kinds: *viṣaya-pariśodhaka* and *vyāpti-grāhaka*. If there is no fire there is no smoke. But there is smoke, which implies that there is absence of non-fire which implies that there is fire. This is an instance of *viṣaya-pariśodhaka tarka*. But if there is a doubt a further implication can be worked out. If the connection between smoke and fire is accidental then smoke will bot be produced out of fire. Here is the case of *tarka* which is *vyāpti-grāhaka*. This indicates that if two things are bound by cause and effect such that the effect cannot exist without the cause, then when the effect is perceived, the cause must be presupposed. Effect statements imply cause statements. It is this kind of implication which builds up the *vyāpti*. It is clear that *tarka*[11] indicates implication and points to the law of implication. On the other hand *vyāpti*[12] indicates the actual relation that exists between two phenomena. Thus, if there is such a relation between *Smoke* and *Fire*, then it means not only $S \supset F$ (*S*

---

9. This is the short form of proposition.

10. It appears to me, that *tarka* presupposed by inference was clearly recognised by Udayana and Gaṅgeśa. Following them Indian logicians have given a definition of *tarka* which consists of five elements. They are (1) ineffectiveness of counter-*tarka* (*pratitarkī parāhatatvam*), (2) assumed *vyāpya-vyāpaka* relation between the opposite of original *sādhya* and the opposite of *hetu* (*āpādya-āpādakayoḥ vyāpya-vyāpakabhāvaḥ*), (3) dependence of the opposite of original *sādhya* on the other (*apādyasya-parāniṣṭhatvam*), (4) pointing out the existence of the other (*parānukūlatvam*), and (5) having the status of assumption (*viparyaya-paryavasānam*).

11. Vide later section.

= Smoke; F = Fire) but it also means *that there is S*. Thus, *vyāpti* relation is of the form $(S. (S \supset F))$. This is clearly the relation of inference and points to the law of inference or what is sometimes called *modus ponens*. But clearly the law of inference presupposes the law of implication.

However, *tarka* or implication cannot be classed under *pramāṇa*s or the means of knowledge which give us the knowledge of objects. In Indian logic the conclusion of deductive inference is always singular, some particular S, say S_1 is P. The form of *vyāpti*, *parāmarśa* and the conclusion can now be made clear

Vyāpti — $(S.\ S \supset F)$,

Parāmarśa — $(S_1.\ (S(S \supset F)))$ and $(S_1 \supset S) \supset (S1 \supset F)$,

Anumiti — $(S_1 \supset F_1)$ or $(S_1 \therefore \mathrm{F})$

A Further Note on Tarka

I am criticised by a few friends for my interpretation of *tarka* (and *arthāpatti*). Without defending myself I may say that when I was reading Ancient and New Nyāya and also the Buddhist Nyāya the question that engulfed my mind was as to which basic idea guided the path of Indian Logic. I thought it was that of implication as in logics of other origin. In Indian Logic I found four important terms used, *nyāya*, *anumāna*, *ānvikṣiki* and *tarka*. Was any one of them used for implication? I brushed aside the word *nyāya* because it was used more for the philosophical system which discussed all *pramāṇa*s like *pratyakṣa*, *anumāna*, *upamāna* and *śabda*. (If one took into consideration other philosophical systems like Pūrva and Uttara Mīmāṁsā one would also have to add *arthāpatti*, *anupalabdhi* and sometimes *aitihya*). So, for the word *nyāya* was not useful. Although *anumāna* is directly concerned with inferential process, *anumāna* also does not convey the basic idea underlying Indian Logic, for *anumāna* is a name which is given to a process whereby from a *vyāpti* sentence we are able to come to a singular (concrete) conclusion which is true. *Anumāna* is, thus, regarded as *pramāṇa* (for it gives us *pramā*). It does not give us the concept behind such a process. This particular concept was described by Dharmakīrti as *hetu sādhya pratibandha sāmarthya*. It is a potency or power by which one could go from *hetu* to *sādhya*. One could tie *hetu* to *sādhya* in such a way that one would be able to arrive at some valid (but not necessarily true) conclusion. This, I thought, was the concept of implication. I was here not concerned with determining whether it was 'material implication', 'strict implication' or 'formal implication'. In actual *pañcāvayavī vākya* there would be formal implication. But there should be some general implication, of which formal implication would be one of the instances. I thought, such an implication was conveyed by the word *tarka*. The word *tarka* did not give us any actual information but as Akṣapāda pointed out, it was at the root of any inference. *Tarka* is a word which is used by adherents of every system whether Orthodox, Buddhist or Jain. There is one book called *Tarka Praveśa* written by Diñnāga where the word *tarka* is concerned with methodology. But here it is not equivalent to *anumāna*. Jains use the word *tarka* in the sense of *pramāṇa*. But in the early use of the term it was used for something which was not necessarily *yathārtha*. That which is *pramāṇa* gives us true (*yathārtha*) information or knowledge. So, Logicians belonging to Nyāya tradition made a distinction between *anumāna* and *tarka*. This tradition continued between Akṣapāda and Udayana. In Udayana and in later thought, we find that the usage did become current in Nyāya literature and even in textbooks like Annambhaṭṭa's *Tarka Saṁgraha* and Viśvanātha Pañcānana's *Nyāya Muktāvalī* and *Dinakarī*. So one could say that in the course of time the word *tarka* was used also for counter-factual. *Nevertheless it should be noted that counter-factual is also based on what in modern times is called implication*. In my preface to my book *A Modern Introduction to Indian Logic* I have mentioned this usage, but have still asserted that the edifice of Logic is based on 'implication' and, in Indian Logic this idea was supplied by the word *tarka*. I have already pointed out that Maṇikaṇṭha, (who was perhaps contemporary of Raghunātha Śiromaṇi) stated this in his *Nyāya Ratna*, and said that *tarka* is at the back of the theory of *anumāna*. I have also clearly stated how the word *tarka* was gradually adopted for expressing different thought and still, it remains a fact that in the beginning the word was used for expressing the idea of implication and that implication was the most fundamental concept in any Logic. That is why in the body of the definition of *tarka* they use the phrase — *kāraṇopapattitaḥ*.

The other word for implication is *āpatti*. When the word *tarka* receded into the background people made use of the word *āpatti*. According to me, they rightly thought that this *āpatti* was of two kinds. One was due to the formal structure and the other was due to the implication of meaning. When one says that *The fat Devadatta does not take food by day-time,* the implication is, that he takes food during night. There is a relationship between fatness and taking food. So, there is not only the basic implication, but also a second implication based on the words 'fat' and 'not taking food by day-time'. One could not be fat without taking food. What is true of *Pino Devadattaḥ divā na bhavantu,* could be true of *kr̥ṣo devadataḥ dimanabhuṅkte.*

My critics seem to have forgotten that meaning plays an important role in this kind of implication.

I may point out that I do not want to be dogmatic or fanatic. I shall also be happy if my friends and students, point out my mistake. But I believe that my thinking in this context is not incorrect. If one introduces or discovers another word for implication I have no objection. But one could not talk of Indian Logic and at the same time say that there is no concept like one of implication in Indian Logic.

19

Inductive Elements in Indian Logic

IN a way problems of Philosophy and Logic are expressions of the level of civilization. At present in India there are two kinds of people echoing two different kinds of attitude. There is a group of people who want to cash the past glory of India and assert that there is nothing which the present civilization has achieved. On the other hand, the other group of people wants to disbelieve that India had any achievement to her credit and even a legitimate achievement is regarded as fictitious. Thus, someone tells us that India logicians in the past had made considerable progress in the direction of induction and scientific method, people are likely to laugh at it. For we are given to understand that scientific method is a gift of Galieleo, Copernicus, Bacon, Mill, Jevons and others. But the fact is that ancient and medieval India people had really thought of scientific method and had given several formulations of it. In the *Nyāya-Sūtra* itself, there is a discussion about different kinds of hypotheses.

Hume's distinction between 'matter of fact' and 'relations of idea' was certainly very eventful both from the point of philosophy and sciences. For sciences are concerned with *matter of facts* and if they behave erratically and freely then there would be no *rules* and no uniformities, all sciences would be impossible. Ordinary men, Scientists and Philosophers alike, thus, make an effort to discover rules. In the natural and social phenomenon finding only rules means, if a certain phenomenon behaves in one particular way on one occasion it would behave in a similar way on successive occasions. This, in fact, is the problem of induction and probability. Not only the modern scientists and philosophers face this problem but the ancient and medieval Indian philosophers had to face this problem in their epistemological enquiry. For Indian philosophers the knowledge was always the knowledge of things, i.e., the knowledge of matter of fact. Later they did have to modify their stand to some extent when they accepted the *reality of universals.*

Nyāya, for example, did not accept any knowledge as valid and certain, uncritically. For them no knowledge can be regarded as *sui generis* or absolutely certain; in that case a doubt in respect of knowledge cannot be explained. Viśvanātha[1] states this point in unequivocal terms: *pramātvam na svatogrāhyam samśayānupapattitaḥ.* All knowledge can at the most be regarded as probable, as there is always a possibility of our existing knowledge being refuted by *vyabhicāra* or *bādha* or what Karl Popper would call, the principle of falsification.

A large part of epistemological and logical inquiry of Indian philosophy in general and Nyāya in particular, centres round the problem as to how one does arrive at a 'universal' proposition? This is what is termed as the problem of *vyāptigrahopāya*. They rightly distinguish *vyāptigraha* from *vyāpti*. *Vyāpti* is the invariable concomitance. *Vyāptigraha* is the knowledge of universal concomitance. *Vyāpatigrahopāya* is the method by which one may arrive at the knowledge of universal concomitance. The problem may be tackled at two different levels. It may first be suggested that one arrives at the universal concomitance or *vyāpti* by observing several instances. This is what is termed as *bhūyo darśana* by Annambhaṭṭa and several other logicians. By observation, on many occasions, of the fact that there is fire where there is smoke, one may arrive at the proposition that wherever there is smoke there is fire. But evidently there is a risk involved in such a hasty generalisation. Viśvanātha is quite apprehensive of this. He states in unequivocal terms that repeated observation is not a cause (of knowledge), since sometimes the apprehension of universal concomitance takes place even from single observation (instance) in case inconsistency does not suggest itself.[2] But sometimes doubt is not removed even by

1. *Bhāsa Pariccheda*, 136.
2. B.P.T. by Mādhavānanda, p. 226. Brackets mine.

repeated observation.[3]

Some logicians are very critical about the efficacy of repeated observation. They state that even if two things are observed as going together for hundreds of times even then contrary cases are observed.[4] Mere repeated observation of two things together does not entitle them to be related in a universal proposition. Viśvanātha following other logicians like Gaṅgeśa suggests a method which is very similar to the method suggested by Bacon and Mill. He suggests that there should be *vyabhicāragraha* and *sahacāragraha* to determine the *vyāpti* or the universal proposition. *Sahacāragraha* means going together. It should be equivalent to the Method of Agreement: if *A* and *B* are found together then that there is a connection between *A* and *B* and that *A* and *B* 'will' always be found together. Viśvanātha, however, expands the notion, and includes in it the negative agreement also. Thus, the method of *sahacāragraha* becomes synonymous with the Joint Method of Agreement and Difference. In Nyāya logic of deductive inference *vyatireka vyāpti* has a special meaning. If p is the *hetu* and q is the *sādhya*, then *vyatireka vyāpti* means, $\sim q \supset \sim p$. Universal propositions are stated in this form when *vyatireka vyāpti* is intended. But while discovering the *vyāpti*, i.e., when the *vyāpti* is yet to be known, it cannot be clearly grasped whether out of the two terms one is *hetu* and the other is *sādhya*. *Vyatireka* in *sahacāragraha* does not, therefore, mean the negation of the consequent and thereby the negation of the antecedent. For the antecedent-consequent relations are still not determined. The *sahacāragraha* relation then means any one of the following four cases:

$A . B$

$\sim A . \sim B$

B. A

$\sim B . \sim A$

That *vyatireka* has this meaning can be clearly seen from the

3. *yatra tu bhūyodarśanādapi śaṅkā na apaiti*, p. 490 SM.
4. *yatra pārthivatvam tatra lohalekhyatvam iti mārtikadā-ravādau bhūyodarśanasya śataśataśaḥ pravr̥ttasyāpi vajramaṇau bhaṅgadaśanāt, pārthivasyaivatasya loholekhyābhāvāt. Op. cit.*

way Udayanācārya uses the term in *Kusumāñjali*. For determining the *vyāpti* and causal relations he gives the rule: *yatsatve yatsatvam, yadabhāve yadabhāvaḥ*. This clearly indicates the above enumerated four cases. It should be noted that in the present context (1) and (3) and similarly (2) and (4) are identical, because they have commutative properties.

There would be a *vyabhicāra* or violation of this rule of any one of the following pairs appears:

(1) $A \,.\, \sim B$ (or their commutation)

(2) $\sim A \,.\, B$ (or their commutation)

Vyabhicāragraha prevents the above cases. Thus, it strictly maintains that if there is an absence of the one there must be an absence of the other:

$\sim A \rightarrow \sim B$

$\sim B \rightarrow \sim A$

[$\rightarrow$ = def. strictly going together or implying] This is a clear case of the Method of difference.

Let us take a concrete case and see whether these methods establishing *vyāpti*, agree with the implications that exist between *hetu* and *sādhya*. Let us suppose that the relation between A and B is established as a relation between *hetu* and *sādhya*. Let A be smoke and B be fire. Then under the above explanation:

(1) When smoke is observed in kitchen fire is also observed.

(2) When smoke is not observed (somewhere) fire is also not observed, e.g., in a lake.

(3) When fire is observed, with it smoke is also observed. (This will be the same as the first case.)

(4) When fire is not observed (somewhere) smoke is also not observed. (This case will be the same as the second).

Each pair in the above instances can be presented in the form of propositions and a pair of such two propositions does not go against the principle of material implication, whereby even if there is no smoke there should be fire. For the second instance is simply a case where smoke and fire do not co-exist. It does not tell us that they should not co-exist. Similarly the third instance does not tell us that if there is fire there must be smoke. It is simply a case where they co-exist. So the cases under *sahacāragraha* do not contradict the principle of implication. The one case of *vyabhicāragraha* (stated above as $\sim A \rightarrow \sim B$) tells us that it cannot be that there is A and $\sim B$. This is what the principle of implication (or strict implication) also suggests. The other case is, $\sim \Diamond (\sim A \,.\, B)$. This does not agree with the principle of material implication. But cases coming under this are cases of equivalence ($p \equiv q$) based on the one cause[5] one effect[5] relation; at least some universal propositions do follow this principle.

It should be noted that the word *upādhi*[6] plays a very important role in determining the *vyāpti* relation. *Upādhi* has been defined as *sādhya-vyāpakatve sati sādhana-vyāpakatvam*. It almost acts like a concomitant variant in determining the relation between the *hetu* and the *sādhya*.

However, by using the method of *sahacāragraha* and *vyabhicāragraha* the problem is only postponed a step further. As in the case of repeated observation, here too, a universal relation that binds the two entities is never given to us. This was recognised by logicians of the Nyāya school. So they employed the method of *reductio ad absurdum*[7] to prove the *vyāpti*. They tried to base the universal relation on causality. This was, in fact, not a new idea. Dharmakīrti an important Buddhist logician had suggested long ago that inference can be based either on *tādātmya* or *tadutpatti* — causality. Following Dharmakīrti, logicians of the Nyāya school tried to establish the *vyāpti* by using the notion of *tadutpatti*. There cannot be an effect[8] without a cause.[8] So from a given effect a cause can be inferred. Similarly, if it can be maintained that there is no cause[8] then there is no effect[8] can also be affirmed. Of the two

5. In Indian logic the words cause of *kāraṇa* and effect or *kārya* are used in a very loose sense.
6. The word *upādhi* is used in three different senses in Indian logic. See supra, chapter III, section *Upādhi*.
7. I feel *tarka* had another sense in the beginning (vide *Tarka*, chapter 18). But later the word was used in the above sense.
8. In Indian logic the words cause or *kāraṇa* and effect or *kārya* are used in a very loose sense.

instances that which comes later in time and is dependent on the earlier is regarded by these logicians as effect; that which comes earlier is regarded by them as cause. It is just to be noted that Indian logicians use the words in this way. They found that smoke is dependent on fire for its existence. This relation they termed as the relation of effect and cause. It is because of this that one can infer the existence of fire from the knowledge of the existence of smoke. So if the *vyāpti* is denied it would be tantamount to saying that we deny the special relation between fire and smoke and to logicians of the Nyāya school this appeared absurd. If smoke, they observed, is not a constant concomitant of fire then it cannot be dependent on fire for its existence. *Yadi dhūmaḥ vahni-vyabhicārī syāt, tarhi vahni-janyo na syāt.* This is what is known as *vyāpti-grāhaka tarka*. Their dictum in this context is that one can doubt so long as one does not face a contradiction (*vyāghātāvadhirāśaṅkā*) and to say that smoke is not dependent on fire for its existence contradicts our everyday experience.

The weak points in the Nyāya theory of universal proposition and inference were two: (1) they made inference and universal proposition depend upon causality; and (2) they made the concept of causality very vague and open to bitter criticism. Other schools of thought took advantage of this and Cārvākas, long before the rise of Navya-Nyāya, doubted the efficacy of *anumāna* as a means of knowledge. They pointed out that from any number of known cases one cannot infer anything about unknown ones. They doubted causality also, saying that causality is a generalisation from particular instances of cause-effect pairs. We only observe that this smoke is seen along with this fire. How can we jump to the conclusion that this would be the case every time? Such a statement is based on *vyāpti* which in turn is based on the causal relation. Thus, there is a vicious circle or *anyonyāśraya*. There is, in fact, no argument against such a perfect scepticism except this that even a sceptic cannot be a sceptic all the time without inconsistency. The Nyāya logicians had to consider the viewpoint of the Cārvākas. The Cārvākas could not be refuted on the basis of theory. The Nyāya logicians had to take resort to pragmatism. They argued if a universal connection is denied, say, between (some) smoke and (some) fire it would be impossible to explain the human tendency to search food whenever a man is hungry or search for fire whenever he is faced with smoke.[9] Causality is embedded in human thinking and is a postulate for human actions. In a way this is a refutation of the Cārvākas, but in a way it is not; for there is an implicit recognition of the fact that all empirical knowledge has a sense of uncertainty about it. Our tendencies cannot really decide anything though they may have practical value. *A* may be existing for several years. This does not mean that he would never die. From the fact that the Sun rises everyday it does not necessarily follow that it would rise tomorrow. The ultimate resort to pragmatic argument by the Nyāya logic for establishing *vyāpti* and causality is the recognition of the fact that it regards all empirical knowledge as only probable. It will be interesting in this context to point out that even the *vyāpti* of *dhūma* and *vahni* is not regarded by Viśvanātha as infallible. He writes: *manmate tu sāmānya-lakṣaṇayā sakala-dhūmo-pasthitān kālāntarīya-deśāntarīya-dhūm-vahni-vyāpyatva-sandehas-sambhavati.*[10] "According to me even if all smokes are presented to us, by the faculty of knowing universals, there is always a doubt that some smoke at some point of time or space may not be concomitant with fire."

The Faculty of Knowing Universals and Universal Propositions

For the Naiyāyikas a general proposition is known by a kind of perception or *pratyāsatti*. According to Nyāya logicians there are three kinds of *pratyāsatti*s, two of which — *sāmānya lakṣaṇā pratyāsatti* (*SLP*) and *yogaja lakṣaṇā pratyāsatti* (*YLP*) give us knowledge of the universals or universal connections. From what is written in the Nyāya texts I feel that *SLP* gives pure concepts and relations whereas *YLP* gives us the generalisations from experience. 'Yoga', means connection and here it means a connection between empirical particulars and the universals. Unfortunately even in some texts *yogaja* is confused with yogic. But as a matter of fact *yogaja lakṣaṇā pratyāsatti* has nothing to do with *yogī*s or *Yogaśāstra*.

---

9. *Tṛptyarthām bhojanasya dhūmārtham vahneḥ niyamataḥ upādānam katham syāt.* (*Dinkarī*, T.C.)
10. S.M. on B.P., p. 65/p. 280, Nirṇaya Sāgar edn.

So it need not be thought that the object of these two *pratyāsatti*s should be different and independent although the pure process of *SLP* could be distinguished in the complex.

The Nyāya logicians object to complete enumeration of instances as a step towards induction or *vyāpti*. They, in a way characteristic to themselves, raise an objection to the procedure of arriving at the *vyāpti* and then answer the objection. Annambhaṭṭa, the author of *Tarka Saṁgraha* and Dīpikā writes: *sakala-vahni-dhūmayoḥ asannikarṣāt katham vyāptigrahaḥ iti cet na. dhūmatva-vahnitva-rūpa-sāmānya-lakṣaṇā-pratyāsatyā sakala-dhūma-vahni-jñāna-sambhavāt.*[11] If it is objected that when there is no perception of every fire and every smoke there cannot be the notion of concomitance, the objection is not valid. It is possible to cognise every smoke and fire in the universe through the class notions of fire and smoke which are arrived at through the faculty called *sāmānya-lakṣaṇā-pratyāsatti*. Athaley's comment on this point is very interesting. He writes, "The objection shows that the Naiyāyikas clearly saw the error into which Aristotle[12] fell and they tried to escape from it in a way peculiar to themselves. The difficulty is two-fold. In the first place, there is the obvious impossibility of our observing all the particulars denoted by the class term (e.g., *dhūma*); and secondly, even granting that we have ascertained all the cases, how do we arrive at the general notion of *vyāpti*, comprising those cases but certainly distinct from them? Co-existence[13] of smoke and fire may be seen to exist in this case, and in that and in a third, and so on; but how do we get the super-added knowledge that it exists *everywhere*? The notion of *everywhere* is distinct from and additional to the totality of particular cognitions. The expedient by which the twofold difficulty is avoided by the Naiyāyikas is very characteristic. . . ."[14] Formation of *vyāpti* is certainly a process where one goes from *the* known to unknown as in the case of inference. But the Nyāya logicians "regard induction

11. T.S. (Dīpikā) Athaley, p. 38.
12. The remark about Aristotle may be overlooked as it is based on the nineteenth-century interpretation of Aristotle by English authors.
13. *Dhūma-vahni-sāhacarya.*
14. *Tarka Saṁgraha*, p. 260: Athaley.

not as an inference but as a kind of an extraordinary perception (*pratyāsatti*)".[15] This extraordinary perception is "the process by which after perceiving an individual thing such as a *ghaṭa* we at once cognise its *jāti*, *ghaṭatva*, by the law of association.[16] When two things are closely associated together, the perception of one necessarily leads to the immediate apprehension of the other. This is not an *anumāna* for there is neither *parāmarśa* nor any *hetu*. It is not also ordinary perception, because there is no *indriya sannikarṣa* or the contact of the sense-organs with smoke in all the cases."[17] This is what is called *pratyāsatti*.[18]

It appears to me that though the learned scholar has correctly grasped the problem of universal generalisation he shows certain confusion in his solution. Perhaps even the text like Annambhaṭṭa's may be responsible for this. He seems to have confused pure universal propositions with universal propositions which have an empirical basis. It is only the pure universal propositions which should be cognised by *the pure faculty of sāmānya-lakṣaṇā-pratyāsatti*.[19] As we have observed above the universal propositions with empirical basis are known by *yogaja-lakṣaṇā-pratyasatti*, although in it too *sāmānya-lakṣaṇā-pratyāsatti* should be operative insofar as there would be reference to *universality*. Let us try to analyses the problem presented by Athaley.

For the Nyāya logician *jāti* or *sāmānya* is a category by itself and is different from any particular substance which is its substratum. This is even recognised by Athaley. For he confesses that the totality of particulars is not a class of particulars. The knowledge of *jāti* is got through particulars. But *jāti*s continue to

---

15. *Ibid*., p. 261.
16. Sri Athaley's use of the phrase is unhappy; but it may be overlooked. This is not the law of association. It is a wrong tanslation.
17. *Ibid*., p. 261.
18. It is peculiar kind of perception. In addition to ordinary perception the Nyāya logic recognises three other varieties of perception They are *SLP*, *YLP* and *JLP*.

    I shall use *SLP* for *sāmānya-lakṣaṇā-pratyāsatti*, *JLP* for *jñāna-lakṣaṇā-pratyāsatti* and *YLP* for *yogaja-lakṣaṇā-pratyāsatti*.
19. The Nyāya logicians regarded to non-empirical knowledge as *dhārya*.

'exist' even if all particulars are destroyed. The relation of *jāti* to individual members can be compared to that of the whole to its parts with the only difference that when the parts are destroyed the whole is destroyed, whereas even when the particulars are destroyed the *jāti* continues to exist. The notion of *jāti*, thus, is not an empirical notion like that of the totality of particulars, which would lead to perfect induction. When a particular is cognised the notion of *jāti* is supplied *a priori*.[20] Without this notion of *jāti* there cannot be any cognition at all. *Jāti* is the same as *prakāra*; it is a kind of *viśeṣaṇa* or adjective. *Nyāya* logic has recognised that without the cognition of the *viśeṣaṇa* there cannot be the cognition of *viśeṣya* (*viśiṣṭa jñānam prati viśeṣaṇa-jñānam āvaśyakam*). For the cognition of *jāti*, class or universal which cannot be given by experience a special *faculty* has been recognised by the Nyāya logicians. This is what is known as *sāmānya-lakṣaṇā-pratyāsatti* (the perceptive *faculty* by which the knowledge of *jāti* or *sāmānya* is obtained). If the problem is to cognise a particular object (e.g., *dhūma*) then it cannot be done purely by *sāmānya-lakṣaṇā-pratyāsatti*. It will have to be obtained by *indriya sannikarṣa* or physical contact or by *yogaja-lakṣaṇā-pratyāsatti* which nevertheless may include *SLP*. In fact, *YLP* is *SLP* operating in the sphere of empirical particulars. *YLP* then can be regarded as a complex, 'process' of which *SLP* will be a distinguishable but inseparable aspect. Since the knowledge of the classes which are not empirical objects, cannot be obtained by any other *faculty*, the relation between them also cannot be obtained by any other *faculty*. They are obtained by *SLP* alone. The relations between two classes cannot be particular. Thus, a proposition like 'the pot is included in *pṛthvī*' or 'the pot is included in substance or existence' can be obtained by *sāmānya-lakṣaṇā-pratyāsatti*. Since

20. Though the Nyāya logic started an empirical discipline it had to introduce several non-empirical and *a priori* notions. I believe *sāmānya-lakṣaṇā-pratyāsatti* is one such notion. The earlier treatment of *jāti* knowledge is different from the later treatment. Earlier logicians thought that knowledge of *jāti* or class is got through *saṁyukta samavāya*. Though this notion was never discarded by the Nyāya logicians, introduction of the notion of *sāmānya-lakṣaṇā-pratyāsatti* was definitely a step forward from the empirical sphere to the non-empirical sphere.

such a proposition states the *vyāpti* between two non-particular, non-empirical notions, there is no necessity to substantiate the relation by giving an instance. For instance or *dṛṣṭānta* is a particular case to be obtained by sense-contact and so is strictly irrelevant in determining the relation between two classes. But when we arrived at a *vyāpti* like whenever there is smoke there is fire, we are not only concerned with a relation between two pure classes or concepts like *fireness* and *smokeness* but we are also concerned with particular fires and particular smokes. Here the *dṛṣṭānta* becomes necessary and the *pratyāsatti* that is operative is *YLP* (although this, in my opinion may include *SLP*).

When a proposition states a connotative relation between classes, it is not possible to deduce any particular proposition (which is its subaltern in the traditional logic) from it, for the relation between a class and its sub-class is entirely different from the relation between a class and its members. This latter relation gives us an idea of a class which is quantitative or denotative. Such a notion of class is a sum-total of all particulars under it. The logicians, both Eastern and Western, had an uneasy time with the notion of class. They pulled it either towards denotation or towards connotation. It should, however, be clear that if a class notion is understood in a connotative sense, merely giving a characteristic, then given a class we can never arrive at truths about particulars. Such a class notion is non-empirical; we arrive at truths about such classes not by observation and generalisation, but by intuitive induction. The Nyāya logic has such a notion of class, though from time to time it has also mixed up the other notion with it — the other notion where class is a sum-total of all individuals under it and is to be understood in a denotative way. This other notion of class is connected with *YLP*. When we take into consideration this other notion of class we can derive particular truths from universal truths. But there is always an air of indefiniteness about such universal propositions which are empirical and based on the observation of particulars. The notion of *vyāpti*, in the Nyāya logic, has at its back, the class membership notion, and so the *vyāptigraha* corresponds to the problematic induction of European logic. The pure *sāmānyā-lakṣaṇā-pratyāsatti* should give us the notion of pure class and a relation between two or more pure classes. It is important to note that the Nyāya logic has distinguished two kinds of relations, one existing between classes and the other existing between a class and its members. When a proposition is based on this second relation, it must make sure that the class is non-empty and this is safeguarded by instance or *dṛṣṭānta* in the *vyāpti* sentence.

As has been observed above, all *vyāptis* are not determined by pure relations between two classes. The proposition, 'wherever there is smoke there is fire' does not give us a relation between the class smoke and the class fire. In fact, there is no *vyāpti* between the class of smoke and the class of fire. They do not have a common substratum. The class of fire (or fireness) exists in fire and the class of smoke exists in smoke. Therefore, even if smoke and fire have a common substratum[21] and even if there is concomitance between the two, there cannot be a *vyāpti* between smokeness and fireness. Symbolising the class of fire by f, fire by F, the common substratum of fire and smoke by M, the class of smoke by s and smoke by S, we get the following two pairs:

(1) $(f \in F) \in M$

(2) $(s \in S) \in M$

(I am using the notation $\in$ to denote 'exists in a substratum'.) From these two instances it does not follow that f and s are directly related.

The *vyāpti*, wherever there is smoke there is fire, implies a more complicated relation than is found in the *vyāpti* between two classes. On the one hand, it relates two particulars, a particular smoke and a particular fire; on the other hand, it relates the two particulars (the particular smoke and the particular fire) to their class notions. This class-membership relation generates the idea of totality of smoke and totality of fire (*sakala-dhūmatva* and *sakala-vahnitva*). When there is a class-membership relation, the class is understood in terms of extension. In such an example, since the class is also understood in terms of extension it cannot be a pure

21. It acts as a container and so has a class-membership relation with the entities like smoke and fire, etc.

case of *sāmānya-lakṣaṇā-pratyāsatti*. It is rather a combination of ordinary perception and *sāmānya-lakṣaṇā-pratyāsatti*, a sort of a situation that we find in problematic induction. And it is this which is given the name *YLP*. Thus, in the case of *vyāpti* between smoke and fire, the particulars and the relation between particulars are obtained by ordinary perception, the class notion is obtained through *sāmānya-lakṣaṇā* and on the basis of the relation between particulars a relation is 'discovered' between the classes understood in terms of extension. Since the relation between two particulars is a case of matter of fact and since there is *a priori* necessity involved in such a connection, the relation that we find in experience should always be kept in mind and never overlooked. In order to specify that there is a relation between two particulars that a *vyāpti* proposition is always accompanied by an instance or a particular case. This particular case is the basis for regarding the class in extension. It is because the class in such *vyāpti*s is related to a particular that a particular conclusion can be obtained from a universal premiss. But it is this relation which makes the *vyāpti* probable and devoid of absolute certainty.

Sometimes even when the *vyāpti* is based on the relation of two particulars or denotes a class-membership relation it does not substantiate the *vyāpti* by giving an instance, thus, showing that the two elements are really co-existent. This is, for example, the case in 'wherever there is *gandhavatva* there is *itarabhedatva*'. It is impossible to show any instance of it, because on Nyāya theory *gandhavatva* and *itarabhedatva* exist only in *pr̥thvī*. In such a case the *vyatireka vyāpti*, the contrapositive of the original proposition is made the basis of argument. For if the original proposition is based on the class-membership relation then there should be a possibility of giving an instance after the contrapositive of the original is resorted to. Thus, in the case of the proposition,

yatra yatra gandhavatvam tatra itarabhedatvam

it is not possible to give an instance (for the case does not exist anywhere but in *pr̥thvī*) but as soon as its contrapositive is taken into account as in,

yatra yatra itarabhedābhāvaḥ tatra gandhavatvābhāvaḥ,

or

yat yat itarabhedābhāvavān tat tat gandhavatvābhāvavān,

an instance, e.g.., *yathā jalam*, can be given. As has been observed earlier it is not possible to give an instance in the case of propositions based on relations between classes (understood in a connotative way). Such propositions do not have existential import and they are signified in modern logic by the universal quantifiers. A proposition like, 'all honest men are virtuous' would be one such case. It is just a relation between two characteristics, 'honesty and virtue' and it is strictly irrelevant whether there is any honest man. 'All honest men' is not an enumeration of every particular honest man. Pure *sāmānya-lakṣaṇā-pratyāsatti* gives us such propositions.

However, problematic induction has a step which can be described as inductive leap. This step does require an uncommon imagination and perhaps because of this the term *sāmānya-lakṣaṇā-pratyāsatti* was also used by logicians to describe what may be called the problematic induction. Viśvanātha says that by *sāmānya-lakṣaṇā-pratyāsatti* the knowledge of the *prakāra* is obtained in the presence of a *viśeṣya* or substantive. It may, therefore, be obtained that *sāmānya-lakṣaṇā-pratyāsatti* cannot give us the knowledge of pure class, since knowledge of the class arises only in the presence of particulars.[22] It may, however, be pointed out that though the knowledge of universals arises in the presence of particulars, it need not necessarily be derived from particulars. The concepts arrived at in the presence of particulars may not refer to any particulars. For example, the notion of *nara-siṁha*[23] may be obtained by *SLP*, though it may not have any particular corresponding to it. The notions of *akhaṇḍopādhi* and *upādhi* should also answer to the objection.[24]

---

22. That is, it is not pure *SLP*. It is *SLP* mixed with ordinary perception or *YLP*.
23. Half-man and half-lion.
24. It may not be forgotten, however, that in the history of Indian logic the notion of *SLP* has been many times used very ambiguously and confusedly. And in actual use *SLP* and *YLP* may have been indiscriminately used.

The distinction that the logicians have made between *sāmānya-lakṣaṇā* and *yogaja-lakṣaṇā-pratyāsatti*[25] is very significant. The latter *faculty* claims to give us the knowledge of all the particulars, past, present and future along with the knowledge of class. It is a denotative faculty as against *sāmānya-lakṣaṇā-pratyāsatti* which is connotative. Some Nyāya logicians think that the *yogaja-lakṣaṇā-pratyāsatti* gives us such knowledge even in the absence of particular object or even when the particular object is destroyed or even when it has not come into existence. But this would make it mystical and take it out of the proper sphere of logic.

Jñāna-Lakṣaṇā-Pratyāsatti

Jñāna-lakṣaṇā-pratyāsatti like several other techniques of the Nyāya logic helps the inductive procedure. It approximately corresponds to the notion of analogy in modern inductive logic. Unfortunately it has been interpreted otherwise by most writers of Indian logic. It gives knowledge of particular as a *particular*. In *sāmānya-lakṣaṇā-pratyāsatti* the substratum (which is particular) and its class (*prakāra*) are separated and knowledge of the class of the particular is produced. In *jñāna-lakṣaṇā-pratyāsatti*, on the other hand, this separation is not yet effected. Thus, it is knowledge of the complex consisting of *viśeṣya* and *prakāra*. It is on account of *jñāna-lakṣaṇā-pratyāsatti* that we get knowledge of 'fragrance' in sandalwood. When a sandalwood (and not its fragrance) is presented to us still its fragrance is 'experienced'. Here knowledge process takes the following form. For Nyāya logicians, no object is perceived without its *prakāra* or universal characteristic. Thus, an object, say, a sandalwood will have to be analysed into two parts, (1) the

25. It is pointed out that, when we have a perception through *sāmānya-lakṣaṇā-pratyāsatti*, the sum-total of causes of the perception of that feature (*prakāra*) by the corresponding organ, in some object possessing that feature of *prakāra* are necessarily present — p. 102, *B.P.T. Mādhavānanda*. Without this one would not have the notion that the universal is related to particular. One does not have the knowledge of *all* particulars, since knowledge of a particular requires that it is connected with his sense-organs Re. S.M. on B.P. 64. The only exception to this is the perception by *yogaja-lakṣaṇā-pratyāsatti*.

viśeṣya or the substratum, and (2) the characteristic of being a sandalwood. Its second characteristic, viz., fragrance is also associated with its first characteristic. Thus, the sandalwood having fragrance has the following form:

$$A \text{ which has } p, \text{ has } q.$$

On the second occasion when the sandalwood is observed its form would be

$$A_1 \text{ has } p.$$

On the basis of the previous knowledge it is suggested that A_1 also has q. In Nyāya terminology it means q is the operation or *vyāpāra* of the knowledge of A having p.[26] *Jñāna-lakṣaṇā-pratyāsatti* is many times explained as the psychological faculty of preperception. Feeling cold is sensed by touch and not by eye. But we very often say ice looks cold. This is what is called preperception. However, it can be seen, without difficulty, that the logical procedure that is involved even in such a case is that of analogy alone.

Upamāna

Jñāna-lakṣaṇā-pratyāsatti should, however, be distinguished from *upamāna* which is usually translated as analogy. *Upamāna* is certainly an important means of knowledge which also is based on similarity and is useful for inductive procedure. But it is concerned with the relation between the name and its bearer and should not be confused with logical analogy.[27] In contrast with logical analogy, *upamāna* may be translated as philosophic or semantic analogy or class-apperception. In *upamāna* the process begins with verbal information and ends with the recognition of an object of perception which was not perceived before. This, however, is not only the case in *upamāna*, but also in all perceptions. There is only a difference of a degree between the *upamāna* knowledge and knowledge based on perception. In *upamāna* there is transition from one class of knowledge to another class of knowledge, e.g., from the class of cow

---

26. See B.P. 65a.
27. *Upamāna* of the *Pūrva Mīmāṁsakas* is like analogy.

there is a transition of the class of *gavaya* or *gayal*s, whereas in the perceptive knowledge, i.e., in apperception there is a transition from knowledge of one particular to that of another particular. But the logical form of process its essentially the same. *Upamāna* is, thus, the knowledge by comparative description. Let us explain the matter more closely.

Apperception — *A* perceives a cow. On another occasion when he perceives another object (another cow) he is struck by the similarity and recognises it as a cow (that is a particular belonging to the class of cow).

Upamāna — *A* perceives a cow. *B* tells *A* (and *A* knows) that there is an animal similar to cow, which has some properties similar to those of cow. Later *A* sees an animal. He observes a similarity between that animal and cow. (But the similarity is, indeed, not so great as to call it a cow). From the similarity *A* interprets the newly perceived animal as *gavaya* (which is similar to cow).

In ostensive definition the object is shown and a person is taught to call that object by a particular name. In *upamāna* the process is reversed. A person is taught the name first, and from the description of the object, he relates the name to the object. Thus, the knowledge of *upamāna* is ultimately based on *saṁjñā-saṁjñī*[28] relation. This is also the case in apperception.

The logical structure of *upamāna* is the following:

Quality q is similar to p

p belongs to the object A

$\therefore q$ also probably belongs to A_1 (a class of object similar to A). Here one goes from the quality to a substance, and from the name to the bearer. On the other hand, in *jñāna-lakṣaṇā pratyāsatti* one goes from the object to its properties. Thus, one is the process of perception similar to cognition and recognition, the other is the process of knowledge similar to inference. Both of them are useful for induction. By both one gets knowledge which is probable. Both help the inductive process and lead halfway to universal connections.

---

28. *Saṁjñā* — name; *Saṁjñī* — bearer of the name.

But of themselves they are not capable of giving a universal connection or *vyāpti.*

Elements in Causal Process

Ārambhavāda — The Nyāya theory of causation is based on the postulate that the whole is different from the sum of its parts. If the whole is broken the parts exist still. A mirror once broken cannot be conceived as one piece (whole) though parts of the mirror, to use ordinary language, still exist. When the whole exists its parts have a different significance. When the whole is destroyed its parts have a different significance. The Nyāya philosopher, therefore, thinks that when something comes into existence as a whole it is already non-existent as separate parts though the whole may still have parts. The effect has a new beginning. It comes into existence only when the cause 'dies'. On account of this peculiar doctrine, the Nyāya theory is termed as *ārambhavāda*. It is opposed to Saṁkhya theory of causation which regards effect as latent in the cause, and is thereby known as *satkāryavāda*. It is also opposed to the Buddhist theory which holds that there is no common substratum or continuum between the cause and the effect. Everything is a flux; there is nothing common between the first moment and the second. The effect is definitely different from the cause and has a new beginning for there is a definite discontinuity between the two moments. The Nyāya theory of causation is a compromise between the two opposed schools to Saṁkhya and Buddhism. With Buddhism it accepts that the effect is not present in the cause, and hence, both the philosophies fall under the category of *asatkāryavāda*. But unlike Buddhism, Nyāya believes in the common continuum between the cause and the effect. It believes in the *sānvayatā* or continuity and disapproves of the Buddhist *niranvaya*. Though it does not believe that the effect is present in the cause it believes that cause and effect are relative terms and become meaningful only in a common substratum. So though the effect is not present in the cause and comes into existence only when the cause becomes non-existent, it is present in the substratum in which the cause is (or was) present. These philosophic aspects of Nyāya theory seem to have been first worked out by Udyotakara, when perhaps he had to face Buddhism on the one hand and Sāṁkhya on the one other. Even the name *ārambavāda* seems to be due to him. There are other philosophic theories of causation too. But all these theories have only a metaphysical importance. Logically these theories are relatively insignificant. I have simply stated the Nyāya theory, because logical doctrines are worked out on the basis of this theory.

Cause — Cause has been defined as "the invariable immediate antecedent of what is not a superfluity"[29] The clause "What is not a superfluity" is very important. For what is already the cause of something else cannot be the cause of that which is under consideration. The effect has been defined as the *pratiyogī* of its previous non-existence. The definition appears to be circular. But it conveys the idea of an effect. The word *ananyathā-siddha* in the definition of cause is very important. For everything that immediately precedes the effect is not necessarily the cause.

According to Nyāya logic there are three kinds of causes. They are known a *samavāyī* or the material cause. *Asamavāyī* or the non-material cause and the *nimitta* or instrumental cause. The material cause of anything is the substance or *dravya*, the *asamavāyī* cause is either a quality or an action. The causes other than these are instrumental causes. If we take an example of a piece of cloth (regarded as an effect) the material out of which it is made, viz., the thread is its material cause. The material cause continues to exist in the effect. But the effect, cloth, is different from thread. When the thread exists as thread, the cloth is non-existent and when cloth comes into existence the thread, as thread, becomes non-existent; for the effect is the newly-born something. However, in order to turn the thread into cloth, a certain arrangement of threads or *tantu-saṁyoga* is required. This is what is termed as *asamavāyī* cause. The concept of *asamavāyī* cause is a very crucial concept. When something is destroyed, it is the effect of *asamavāyī* cause which is undone. A piece of cloth is destroyed only when the arrangement of threads is destroyed. The thread need not be destroyed at all. Nyāya metaphysics believes in permanent atoms which cannot be destroyed. So even in the final analysis the material is never destroyed. It is only the form that is destroyed.

---

29. B.P.T. Mādhavānand, p. 23.

According to the Nyāya Logic the *asamavāyī* cause is of two types. Annambhaṭṭa gives the definition of *asamavāyī* cause as follows — *kāryeṇa kāraṇena vā saha ekasmin arthe samavetatve sati yat kāraṇam tat asamavāyī kāraṇam, yathā tantu saṁyogaḥ paṭasya, tantu-rūpam paṭa-rūpasya.* The *asamavāyī* cause is the one which is inseparably united in the same object either with the effect or with the cause, as the conjunction of threads is of the cloth or the colour of threads is of the colour of the cloth."[30] The conjunction of the threads exists by *samavāya* or inherence in the thread which is the material cause of the cloth and so inheres in the cloth; it is one kind of *asamavāyī* cause. The colour (of the cloth) exists in the cloth which is the cause of the colour of the cloth. This is the second kind of *asamavāyī* cause.

Everything else (other than these two causes) which is necessary for the production of the effect but which can be separated from the effect comes under instrumental or efficient cause. The *nimitta* causes are again of two kinds, the common and the special. God, His desire, Space, Time, *adṛṣṭa* and prior non-existence of the effect are common causes for all effects. According to the school of Navya-Nyāya contactual non-existence or *saṁsargābhāva* of preventives or *pratibandhaka* is also a common instrumental cause.[31]

Of the different instrumental causes, *karaṇa* is the most important. The old school defines the notion as *vyāpāravat asādhāraṇam kāraṇam*. The new logicians define it as *phalāyoga-vyavacchinam kāraṇam*, that is the cause that immediately precedes the effect. The new logicians do not accept the other definition; for it applies to the agent or *kartā* who is not a *karaṇa* but only an instrumental cause.[32] The notion of *vyāpāra* is defined, as, *tat-janye-sati-tat-janya-janakatvam*, being the product of the cause it produces that which is produced by the cause. The wheel of the potter is said to be one of the causes of the pot. But the wheel cannot produce a pot unless it is in action. The action is the *vyāpāra*. According to the Navya-Naiyāyikas the notion of *vyāpāra* is

30. T.S. Athley, p. 206.

31. p. XXI, *Maṇikaṇa*, Dr. S. Sarma.

32. *Ibid.*, p. 92.

covered by *kāraṇa* itself.[33]

In addition to these causes, Indian logic also recognises auxiliary causes.

As we have seen the Nyāya logic gives three kinds of causes. If we add *prayojana* or final cause (which has also been recognised) the list would resemble the one given by Aristotle. The three causes, *samavāyī*, *nimitta* and the *prayojana*, exactly resemble the causes material, efficient and final, given by Aristotle. The *asamavāyī* cause of the Indian logic, however, is different from the formal cause attributed to Aristotle. It appears to me that the formal cause of Aristotle has not been properly interpreted by his commentators. They identify it with the form as thought of by Plato. Aristotle, however, distinguishes form from concept and uses two different words in Greek.[34] The commentators, however, translate it by only one word 'the form'. As a matter of fact on account of translating the word by 'form' (in a Platonic sense) the commentators have created a difficulty for themselves in distinguishing the formal cause from the cause. I think it would be better to regard the formal cause as the cause which gives 'form' to the existing material. It will be useful to add that Indian logic too diṣtinguishes a form (*ākr̥ti*) from concept (*jāti*). In fact, from the way Aristotle talks of form, the form resembles *ākr̥ti* and not *jāti*. This makes me think that the formal cause of Aristotle's concept is the same as the *asamavāyī* cause of Indian logicians.

It is interesting to point out that there is a recognition of inductive procedure, though very elementary and crude, in the *Nyāya-Sūtra* itself. Indian logic has grown out of the art of controversy or *vāda*. And the chief purpose of *vāda* is to establish a thesis or *siddhānta*. It should, therefore, be natural to have elements of induction present and discussed in the earliest treatise on Indian logic. Akṣapāda recognises *saṁśaya*, *prayojana*, *dr̥ṣṭānta* and *siddhānta* as elements in this procedure. He distinguishes four cases of *siddhānta*, (*a*) *sarvatantra siddhānta*, (*b*) *pratitantra siddhānta*,

33. The readers may refer to Section XXXVII of Sri Athaley's book for more detailed information.

34. Aristotle's work (Loeb Library).

(*c*) *adhikaraṇa siddhānta*, and (*d*) *abhyupagama siddhānta*. Of these (*a*) is the confirmed hypothesis and (*d*) is the hypothesis or the tentative presupposition.

Indian logic also gives a rule for accepting a hypothesis as correct out of a rival hypotheses. This is stated as *lāghava* or the law of parsimony or logical economy. It states that out of two or more hypotheses which explain certain evidence with equal plausibility, the one that is less complicated should be accepted, the only exception being *phalamukha-gaurava*. This is stated by the rule, *phalamukha-gauravasya-adoṣatvāt* (i.e., where the certainty of the hypothesis is otherwise determined by its workability).

Before I close this section it is necessary to point out that according to Indian logic we get universal propositions in five different ways, (1) by perception through *sāmānya-lakṣaṇā-pratyāsatti*, (2) by perception through *yogaja-lakṣaṇā-pratyāsatti*, (3) by perception through *sahacāragraha* and *vyabhicārāgraha*, by forming *abhyupagama siddhānta* or hypothesis, (4) by *śābda* knowledge, and (5) by inference. For *nigamana* is also a universal proposition, though not in the form of a *vyāpti*. The usual form of *nigamana* is $(x)\ (Fx)$ whereas the usual form of *vyāpti* is $(x)\ (Fx \supset Gx)$. But from two *vyāpti* propositions a third *vyāpti* proposition can be derived, e.g., from

1. *yatra ghaṭatvam tatra pṛthvitvam*

   and

2. *yatra pṛthitvam tatra dravyatvam*

   a third proposition

3. *yatra ghaṭatvam tatra dravyatvam*, can be derived. This proposition in its turn can be used as *vyāpti* proposition.

20

The Origin of Indian Idealism

COMRADE Sardesai in his monograph on Indian Philosophy, *The Ideological Conflict*, assumes that Advaita Vedānta is an idealistic system, and that the neglect of the materialist systems like Lokāyata and Saṁkhya, is responsible for the formation of a certain attitude of Indian people towards society. This is also the view of Late Debi Prasada Chattopadhyaya, the author of Lokāyata. All this can be challenged. It can, for example, be said that Advaita Vedānta does not propound Idealism. Nevertheless the problem remains as to how Indian mind thinks in terms of propositions which are idealistic in nature. It will, therefore, be important to find out the primary sources which may be significant from the point of view of the formation of Indian type of Idealism. The problem becomes more important because if Idealism is the fabrication of the common man and not the expert the remedy to alter the situation, would be altogether different.

First, let us see the premises of Idealism. I think, the first such premise is that the concrete reality that we perceive, that is, see, touch, hear, etc., does not exist. What exists is our idea. It is possible to argue in favour of such a proposition. For we do think that there is some kind of relation between being and knowing. But as soon as one thinks of a relation between being and knowing one also distinguishes *being* from *knowing*, knowing being mental and dependent on the knower. That which is dependent on the knower and is in the mind or is supplied by mind is naturally regarded as of the nature of idea. The link between the world and knowledge is, given up and knowledge is now supposed to depend, not on the thing, but on the knower. External concrete reality, thus, withers away. At some stage, however, we also believe that knowledge is not private, we communicate thoughts to others and, therefore, we begin to think that the thoughts themselves have the power to exist by themselves. Our concrete reality merely becomes an approximation of these universals or forms which are abstractions of our own making. This leads to yet another variety of Idealism, popularly known in Philosophy as Platonism.

How do all such philosophies arise? First, man and his surroundings form a very queer whole. He is born, he grows, he is continuously able to move from one place to another and he dies. All his actions are determined by space and time, and also limited by space and time. Two men, *A* and *B*, for example, form a contract. They may abide by it. But this contract is never permanent. *A* and *B* would not die at the same time except in an extraordinary condition and so *A* might not be able to fulfil his promise, duties or obligations towards *B*. The same could be the case with *B*. So although on account of the existing human order continuity of man's actions might be noticed over generations, *vis-a-vis* some individuals there is always an uncertainty which takes the form of 'unreality'; for reality and existence are grouped together. It is taken for granted that if a certain man does not exist he is unreal. This gives rise to two different propositions. First is the idea that the individual who is no more here, in this world 'must' live somewhere and, therefore, that 'somewhere' also must be more permanent than the present world. The world that is here and now and the individual in this world must, therefore, be unreal. Man also experiences dreams and he is able to distinguish between dream experience and his experience when he is not dreaming and which he regards as veridical. He naturally associates dreams with unreality which is determined on the basis of duration of time. That which lasts for a longer time is regarded as real and that which lasts for a shorter time is regarded as unreal. This in turn gives rise to degrees of reality. One begins to talk of less real and more real. Again man tries, as a part of his activity, to construct over the things given in nature. These constructions are always of the nature of forms given to things by man. The spatial forms, quite a large number of them, are reducible to their original nature because of a certain reversibility in space. The given forms are supposed to be effects and the matter on which the construction is made is called its cause. Man may make a brick out of the earth and this brick may be reduced to earth again. We may make ornaments out of gold and they may be reduced to gold again. This kind of reversibility makes one think that the material cause is everlasting and existential, and the forms it assumes are evanescent, and so are unreal. On account of the fact that every surrounding of man, including he himself, has this nature of growth and decay and on account of the belief that there is conservation of material cause one begins to think that the forms (and essences) are less real than the matter. It is forgotten that no form (or essence) in practice can be completely separated from matter (or existence). The result is that either the form the matter assumes is regarded as unreal or it is assumed that the form exists independently in an independent world and so is regarded as merely ideal.

To my mind it appears that the dichotomy which exists in the world with regard to matter and form or dream and the awakened state or the nature and construction over it gives rise to a certain deviation; one is regarded as real and the other is regarded as unreal. In the case of matter and form, matter continues to exist even though the form disappears, if they are spatial in nature. But man applies the logic of space to time and, therefore, that which is impermanent is also regarded as permanent in some other world, in some other space. If life is impermanent here, it must be perfect somewhere else. If life is imperfect here it must be perfect somewhere else. This gives rise to the second world consisting of heavens and the more perfect being (God). They come into existence on account of our application of *logic of space to* time. This concept of the other world and God and not necessarily idealistic. In Europe they have perhaps not played a supporting role to Idealism. But in Indian thought it appears that the dichotomy of an impermanent man *versus* a permanent soul and valueless world against the valuable heaven have played a major role in bringing forth the idea that the world is unreal. To me it appears that this dualism or dichotomy is not the creation of philosophers. It has naturally arisen in the world of ordinary man. In fact, the philosophers of the school of Lokāyata, Sāṁkhya, Bauddha, Jain and Advaita have continuously tried to correct the vision against the common sense prejudice, although all these systems have again and again fallen a prey to the original belief itself. Perhaps the only system which bases itself on these beliefs is the system of Pūrva Mīmāṁsā.

Let us try to understand as to what part does a belief in the supernatural, play in creating a hyphothesis that may be regarded as Idealism. It seems to be natural to think of a world is better than ours and it also seems natural to think of an individual who is superior to us. These two concepts give rise to the concepts of heavens and God. But once the superior world and superior individual is 'created' it is also natural to aspire for the superior world. Such an aspiration becomes our goal and simultaneously we also begin to think that we are being controlled by a superior world and superior individual. How are we to realise the intended goal? This again is treated on the basis of the casual functions with which we are ordinarily acquainted. Any attainment or realisation is now measured on the scale of such casual law which may act not only in regard to events in the present birth but is, on our belief, applied to 'events' beyond birth and death by creating a series of *birth and death*. Some kind of causation, joins this world with the other world and the other world, and the relation of this life with the other life may be invented. This invention is regarded as plausible on account of the control that the superior agent or God may exercise on us. Such causation takes the form of *karma* and *apūrva*. The longing for the other world makes the present world valueless and the concept of valuelessness gets identified with illusoriness or unreality of this world. We have, therefore, to discard everything in this world for attaining something superior in the other world. Although Judaism, Christianity and Islam have not developed a rebirth theory, the theory of reward for our actions and immortality of our souls and the control by God are present in all these faiths. To my mind it appears that it is this belief in a dichotomy between this world and the other world and preference for the other world which make a common man in India think that the world is illusory. The preferable is identified as real and the heaven or paradise was preferred to this world and since this could not be attained during the life time, life after death was recognised as real. A link between life and life after death was, thus, established through *apūrva* and *karma*.

Perhaps the efforts of philosophers of every variety except Pūrva Mīmāṁsā was to fight against this common belief. The dichotomy of the superior and inferior world was given up, as soon as the concept of *mokṣa* was introduced and it was thought that the concept of *karma* emerged through ignorance and, therefore, can be destroyed by knowledge. It really means the recognition of the fact that the categories which emerge for understanding this world cannot employed beyond this world resulting in the postulation of the other world.*

The question that is of primary importance is whether the thought has moulded the pattern of beliefs in the common man or the beliefs have moulded the pattern of our thought. My answer to this question is that although philosophers have tried to mould the pattern of beliefs they have not succeeded. May be the beliefs have consistently mitigated the normative thought which has again and again succumbed to the beliefs or even primitive beliefs. In my opinion these primitive beliefs are three, existence of an immortal soul (conceived as some kind of an animate 'thing'), reincarnation or rebirth of this soul which takes the form of a man or a woman (or even an animal) and the *karma* through which this transformation takes place. In addition to this primitive belief there is a belief in deities of supernatural powers. Sometimes a hierarchy of these supernatural powers is recognised and one of them is called God. But many a time the monarchy or oligarchy of spirit is not present and what we have is a pluralism in the spiritual kingdom. Perhaps the recognition of spiritual kingdom was also a part of European and middle-eastern belief systems, but rebirth does not seem to be present in their belief system. Reincarnation or rebirth seems to be the core of Indo-Hellenistic thinking. Even God is subjected to it. God's reincarnation required a cause, a kind of *karma* which was provided by bad deeds of demons when the Mother Earth taking the form of a cow went to God and requested him to take birth to destroyed the evil-minded demons. One cannot positively say as to why these two different basic patterns of beliefs were nurtured by the Europeans and Indo-Hellenic people. But the fact remains that

---

* It is possible to think that everywhere in the world idealism might not have sprung in the same way.

although the Europeans, the Semetics and the ancient Egyptians believed in the immortality of souls they never thought of the rebirth in the way the Indo-Helenic thought of Indians, for example, thought that the soul was immortal, and that his taking rebirth resembled to changing of clothes. The 'clothes' get soiled on account of the *karma*. Egyptian mummies were preserved because it was thought that sometimes that the souls might re-enter them and amongst the Christians, Jews or Muslim dead bodies are kept in the tombs in the hope that they may dwell there till day of resurrection. But among these people there is no belief that the souls of the dead re-enter other bodies. What must be the reason for such a difference? Perhaps India became an abode of several primitive tribes and a system of social beliefs was invented through the common beliefs of these tribes, although these tribes were not entirely absorbed in one homogeneous whole. I am aware that what I am saying cannot be the reason for accepting the rebirth theory and, therefore, one has to believe that the concept of rebirth was primitive among these tribes. Once, however, the immortality of soul and re-birth are accepted, a social order which would maintain inequality in the name of justice and would (at the same time) keep open the possibility of transformation in the social hierarchy would emerge. *Punarapi jananam, punarapi maraṇam, punarapi jananī jaṭhare śayanam* seems to be the answer to the possible inequality amongst men. Thus, *karma* theory in the name of justice defends inequality and allows the society to maintain its hierarchical pattern.

The philosophers of India tried to make a revolt against this position. Their arguments are of two kinds: (1) the question of immortality of souls does not arise because to be a soul requires self-consciousness, but beyond a certain point this self-consciousness evaporates and what you call soul or ego withers away in the cosmos or Brahmā. (2) Re-birth is merely lay-man's belief which has its source in ignorance and *karma theory* is merely an invention — a pseudo-intellectual tool to aid the soul. But since it is created on account of ignorance, with the dawn of knowledge the *karma* (and with it the concepts of re-birth also) vanishes. The question of taking birth in the social hierarchy or enjoying the fruits of heaven and coming back to the earth after the *puṇya* is exhausted simply does not arise. The concept of *mokṣa*, *nirvāṇa*, *kaivalya*, *apavarga*, etc., are recognition of the fact that it is only through ignorance that man creates *karma* theory and the other world or other stronger powers and gets himself involved in these beliefs. But in doing this the philosophers fell into the other trap. They created a dichotomy, if not of this world and the other world, of the real and the appearance. As soon as *Brahman* was regarded as real not only the concept of *karma*, rebirth and the other world became relatively unreal but also the individual and society became relatively unreal. There is indeed a difference between the world that is given to us and the world that man creates. One exists all the time. The other is evanescent as it continuously changes forms. That which is evanescent and impermanent was regarded as illusory. All the human powers and evolution became unmeaningful and the concept of action was rejected for inaction. Not only was the theological causation rejected, but in the ultimate analysis even social causation was rejected. For ultimately there may be many a manifestation of *Brahman*. The manifestation would be like the ripples of water and would be of no consequence to the Ultimate. Common Indian thus had no choice between the devil and the deep sea. Either he was a target of the *karma* theory or he lost his individuality into *Brahman*. The philosophy behind Indian thinking seems to be a tragedy, not of idealism as it is commonly understood but a tragedy of Buridan's ass who could not make a choice between the two alternatives and who had no capacity to think of the third alternative.

21

Four Phases of Hinduism

IF someone takes me unawares and asks me what my religion is I might reply Hinduism, but if I begin to think about my answer, I shall be puzzled. I shall not be able to decide either about the defining characteristics of Hinduism or about those characteristics which make me a Hindu. The reason for this is that Hinduism is not a religion in the sense Christianity, Islam or Judaism is a religion. Perhaps to Christians and Muslims a society without religion was unthinkable and whatever they observed in the Hindu way of life they regarded as the religion of the Hindus. The word Hindu is an adaptation of the word 'Sindhu (Indus)' and signified the country around Indus and also the people living in that country. The invaders used the word rather in a derogatory sense. I am not sure whether the word 'Hindu' is found in any of the scriptures of classical literature of the Hindus. It is not a Sanskrit word and I am doubtful whether the word 'Hindu' was actually used before the thirteenth or fourteenth century AD. However, we the people of India who are neither Christians nor Muslims, Jews or Parasis, accepted the name 'Hindu' and started to think that Hinduism is our 'religion'. Since followers of faiths like Jainism also identified themselves with the Hindus, the word Hindu denoted a joint family of different faiths, different people.

The Sociology and Ritual Phase

Although Hindus claim that Hinduism is very ancient, in its present traditional form it is one of the youngest religions in the world. It is evolved out of the heterogeneous ways of life of hundreds of tribes and communities that lived in India for ages. The present form of Hinduism is a multi-centred decentralised structure-formation of the ways of life of all these people. Of course, the central norms of this Hinduism is represented by the beliefs and thought of the Indo-Aryan group because of the dominating role of these people in the making of Indian History. But the influence of non-Indo-Aryan communities should not be minimised. Thus, though the peripheral beliefs will have no place in the religious books of the Hindus some of these beliefs will certainly be a part of Hindu practices. I shall refer to only one of these now — the institution of sacrifice or *yajña*. It is mentioned in the Vedic Scriptures and today it has taken the form of worship and prayer, partly through Buddhist influence and partly on account of the syncretism of different aboriginal cults in India. This institution of sacrifice is not to be confused with practices like *bali*, for although the central nucleus of both is similar, the history of the institute of *yajña* was progressive in character and at least partly sublimated. For example, at least at one stage of history it was associated with the phenomena of lighting fire and cooking. It indicates the discovery of fire and its preservation. The institution of sacrifice represents, very complex character and includes in it, sacrificing oneself for the sake of the clan. From human sacrifice to animal sacrifice was another stage in social evolution and represented the concept of ceremonial cooking and feasting. In the course of time however, Hinduism accepted the norm of non-violence largely due to the criticism from the Buddhists, Jains and the Cārvākas. The Cārvākas argued that if you are sacrificing the animal with the altruistic motive that it should go to heaven, why don't you sacrifice your own father, for, you certainly want your father to attain heaven, which is the goal of life. On account of such criticism the institution of sacrifice lost its original form and just became a religious symbol with a metaphorical sense superimposed on it. The institution of *bali* which was practised by the aborigines is in a sense similar to the institution of *yajña* and is sometimes associated with Hinduism because when one talks of Hinduism, one talks of all the beliefs of the heterogeneous people who got wholly or partly assimilated with Hinduism through the so-called caste system. But the logic behind *bali* would be based on a series of beliefs, such as the belief that there is a deity of a disease, which wants to eat men, and that if some other life (a goat, or a hen) is offered to the deity, the life of the diseased may be saved. Sometimes the motive may be enmity. The *bali* may be offered to pleased the deity which when satisfied, may kill the enemy. All these are indeed superstitions. But there is nothing Hindu about them. It is, of course, true that norms or Hinduism do not exist in their pure form in actual practice, they are partly vulgarised and partly mixed up with the religious superstitions of other people already living in India.

In fact, whenever I think of Hinduism and Hindu society in its present form the model of Australia stands before me. If history repeats itself I think whatever must have happened in India is happening in Australia today. Imagine that in spite of the superiority of Western civilization you have still retained place names such as *yanchep* and *kalamunda* and Wooloomooloo alongside Perth and Melbourne and Sydney. There are some full-blood and some half-blood aborigines. And though some of them have embraced Christianity, they have not given up their old religion, their old beliefs. Then there are atheists among Christians. But they go to Church for performing their marriages. If this continues Australian Christianity will be altogether different from other types of Christianity. But this means that Christianity is being trasformed into a cultural religion although Christians may not consciously admit it. When a religion becomes a cultural religion the walls which are built around it on account of dogmas and faith break. This is exactly what has happened in India.

I shall, however, confine myself to the religious norms of the Hindus, and they are of two different kinds. Firstly, the system of general beliefs and secondly the criticism of these beliefs. There may of course be a criticism of the criticism itself and in general the criss-crossing of this kind becomes apparent in the Hindus religious system.

The system of general-belief-norms which has arisen in the course of Indo-Aryan history is preserved in the Vedas, the scripture of the Hindus and is usually connected with what is known in Hindu thought as *karma-kāṇḍa*, or the chapter of rituals and actions.

The ends for which a Hindu is supposed to strive can be

classified under two heads:

The individual ends and the social ends.

The social end is of course the order and well-being of the society. This is expressed in the Vedic *mantra*: as in English

> Let us live together, let us eat together, let us show our valour together, let us learn from the illustrious and let us not hate anyone. O God, let there be peace, (peace, peace).

Although the social ideal is of living together, the society was conceived on the model of an individual and the sections of the society were compared to different organs like Head and Shoulders and hands and feet. In the beginning the profession of the members of the Society was not determined by birth and people could choose any profession they liked. But gradually, the profession of the people became a matter of inheritance. In the course of time this was further vulgarised into what is known today as the caste system. It must be added that the concept of justice of these people was very different from the concept of justice that we have today. Their concept of equality and justice varied from class to class. Perhaps in the beginning there was no feeling of superiority or inferiority attached to the different functions associated with different *varna*s, though the last section of the society was not treated very fairly by our present standards. Very soon this led to some kind of primitive apartheid.

The social end of the Indo-Aryans meant nothing but keeping the society going by performing the different functions in the society. What was supposed to be the individual end was the means to this social end and the individuals were trained to this end. Since the society was divided according to four different functions and four different aptitudes or abilities the individual training and individual ends also varied accordingly. Thus, the training of the man who wanted to become brāhmaṇa or a priest would be very much different from that of the man who wanted to become a vaiśya or a businessman. In the course of time, however, the *varṇa*s or professions began to be determined by birth and the training for each became stereotyped. All this sounds very secular; but what made the whole thing religious was some kind of religious halo which was associated with the individual training. There is, however, no ordaining of the priest class as is done amongst the Roman Catholics.

I shall now return to the individual ends which were divided into two broad classes, one, that which was relevant for a 'good' life in this world, and two, that which represented withdrawal from this world. At some stage it was thought necessary to withdraw from this world. Thus, the individual ends orbited round the concepts of life and death. Needless to say, the concept of death brought with it the concept of the other world, immortality of the soul and *karma* or the law of actions which governs the future actions. The individual ends are termed *dharma*, *artha* and *kāma* (or duty, prosperity and the objects of desires). The inclusion of *mokṣa* (emancipation) amongst individual end was a later development. Earlier, *kāma* itself signified both the desire for worldly prosperity and the desire for the other-worldly happiness which was in a way, the withdrawal from this worldliness. *Dharma* usually signified the means to other ends, and signified what man ought to do, whether it was a duty to himself or in interpersonal relations. On account of the religious halo attached to it, *dharma* also signified the other-worldly aspect and the notion of heaven was introduced. Heaven was, however, associated with pleasures in terms of this-worldly-pleasures (including the sexual desires) signified by *kāma*. Perhaps in the beginning *dharma*, *artha* and *kāma* signified one whole, which was predominantly dominated by this-worldliness and played a prominent role in the life of a married man. Very soon however, the *artha* and *kāma* aspects of human life were incorporated in *dharma* itself and *dharma* signified the only end of human beings, and was manifested in family life, the importance of which is pivotal to Hinduism. Thus, preservation of fire which is necessary for keeping the house-going becomes a duty of the couple. Procreation which is also compared to the preservation of fire is another duty.

In order to enter the family life a proper early training or education was required, and this included an emphasis on self-discipline.

Similarly, to a Hindu the withdrawal from this world was also an end. So, after living a happy married life in the society the man and his wife could withdraw at their own pleasure and this was known as *vānaprastha* (literally going to the forest).

A religion is usually associated with a mythology, rituals and a concept of God. Hinduism has retained several anthropological elements of the tribal religions existing in India and has, thus, created a rich mythology, a system of rituals and many Gods. Sometimes we lightly say that there are as many as 330,000,000 Gods. A large part of Hindu mythology and rituals however, was only a passing phase of the Hindu history. In Hinduism if there is a place for many Gods, it is for two reasons. In the first place Hinduism had to accommodate the gods of other tribes. Thus, for example, *liṅga* (phallus) worship was admitted to the Hindu fold and *liṅga* was identified with some of the Indo-Aryan Gods. But, secondly, amongst the Indo-Aryans themselves there was a tendency to recognise a deity for every action. To a stranger what appears to be a polytheistic attitude must be due to this phenomenon. However, underneath the tendency of polytheism there is a strong undercurrent of monotheism in Hindu religion and in the Hindu mind. The concept of Unity is indeed very very strong amongst the Hindus. Of course, one could argue that the Upaniṣads point to monistic and pantheistic tendencies and not to a monotheistic one. There is, however, enough evidence to show that the Hindus did believe in one God. For example, in the daily ritual of brāhmaṇas it is very clearly stated that as the water fallen from the skies goes to one ocean, similarly, the worship to all 'Godheads' goes to one God.

In the *Yoga Sūtras*, Īśvara or the god is regarded as one and is all mighty, all knowing, and omnipresent. Even in Hindu mythology which talks of many Devas or Gods, the belief in one Creator God is persistent. However, unlike Judaism, there is absence of any promise in Hinduism. It is true that many of the words of Lord Kṛṣṇa are interpreted as promises. But a proposition of the form, 'I confirm. . . ' is not equivalent to the proposition of the form 'I promise. . . . '

However, the beliefs in the immortality of the soul, and the Law of *karma* seem to be more integral to Hindu religion than the belief in God. In fact, *karma* should be supposed to persist only as something dependent on the soul. This can be deduced from the later thought where the *karma* and the soul form what is known as *liṅga śarīra* or a microscopic body. However, as soon as it is said that the soul is free and still subjected to the law of *karma*, a certain inconsistency would arise. This inconsistency can be resolved either by giving an absolute status to *karma* and by denying the soul or by making at absolute and independent of *karma* and denying any status to *karma* in the final analysis. The first alternative was chosen by the Buddhist and the second by the Hindu thinkers. Let me, however, not go into the intricacies of Hindu metaphysics. That the *karma* was supposed to belong to the individual and the future course of the individual, i.e., his sins and merits were determined by the *karma*, really meant that the individual was free to choose his own actions, he was responsible for them. It is a pity that time has changed the meaning of *karma* theory to its opposite and made it synonymous with Fatalism.

From what I have said the following tenets of Hinduism would emerge:

(1) Belief in one God. This was somehow compatible with beliefs in many supernatural powers personified as deities. The deities could be invoked and in a sense 'controlled' by prayer to occupy an object of worship, which a non-Indian may call a totem. Earlier there was no idol-worship in Hinduism.

(2) The concepts of sacrifice, prayer, worship and rituals. The first of these gradually disappeared.

(3) Absence of any promise by God.

(4) A belief in moral order, freedom of Man to choose and the concept of responsibility; the belief in social justice although it would be different from our concept of social justice.

(5) Immortality of soul and the concept of rebirth.

(6) A rich mythology.

(7) Social well-being as a social end, and social divisions into sub-sections or *varṇa*s according to individual skill and aptitude. This is what is known as *varṇāśrama-vyavasthā*.

The caste according to birth emerged out of it.

(8) *Dharma*, *artha* and *kāma* (duty prosperity and the objects of desires) as individual ends.

(9) Acceptance of the authority of the Vedas.

(10) No ordaining of priests.

(11) The notion of *svarga* or Heaven, associated with great happiness — though only of the worldly kind.

(12) The concept of merit and sin which would grow or diminish according to the *karma* performed. (Perhaps in Heaven it would only diminish).

The kind of system of religious beliefs I have explained goes by the name of Manu and is based on the concept of positive desires and attachments. Lord Kṛṣṇa, who is regarded as an incarnation of God, says in *Bhagavad Gītā*. "Those who drink the *soma* juice, who are well-versed in the three Vedas, and who are rid of sins, having (worshipped) me through sacrifices seek for a place in the heaven. Having, thus, enjoyed the vast heavenly world, they come back again to this world of mortals. This is the kind of *dharma* of the three Vedas and is followed by those who have attachments (literally who desires 'desires'). The makers of Hindu thought, including Lord Kṛṣṇa, however, criticised this outlook and took Hinduism to altogether a different level. I shall turn to this aspect of Hinduism now.

The Conceptual Phase

I have till now pointed out the growth of Hinduism in its historical setting. Some norms of religion did grow in this process of development. But several others were still to emerge. We have seen that the element of withdrawal in the form of *vānaprastha* did exist in Hinduism. But so long as attainment of heaven was the ideal, man was bound by desires, attachments and *karma* and was supposed to be entangled in the cycles of births and deaths. There was, thus, a rethinking whether heaven was the real goal and whether attachment in any form, even the attachment to merit or *puṇya* would make a man free. Since in this life a man cannot be thought some activity (*karma*) — voluntary or involuntary, the doctrine of *karma* became the focus of rethinking and questions like what is the nature of this *karma* and how to get rid of it, what is the nature of God, and what is the nature of reality began to be hotly discussed. We have seen that the dissatisfaction with the traditional Vedic religion based on rituals is seen even in *Bhagavad Gītā*. This dissatisfaction is apparent even in *Bhagavad Gītā*. This dissatisfaction is apparent even in the Upaniṣads which are supposed to be the parts of the Vedas. Hinduism was also being pounded to pieces at the hands of critics like Cārvākas and the Buddhists. A critical Hinduism emerged out of such criticisms and is known amongst the Hindus as *jñāna-kāṇḍa* or the chapter of knowledge as against *karma-kāṇḍa* or the chapter of rituals and actions which we have discussed earlier. The attainment of *svarga* or Heaven was discredited. The sensual pleasures whether on this earth or in heaven were regarded as of the same order. *The concept of mokṣa or Complete emancipation* was universally accepted as the goal, which superseded all other social goals like *dharma*, *artha* and *kāma*. Correspondingly at the social level also the institution of *saṁnyāsa* or renunciation or complete withdrawal came into being. To become a *saṁnyāsin* or a recluse, it was not actually necessary for a man to go through the stages of *brahmacarya*, *grahastha* and *vānaprastha*, although one could successively go through all these. The institution of *saṁnyāsa* was a negation of the institution of family. But both of them could exist side by side. Through the elimination of the Heaven as the goal and the acceptance of *mokṣa* and *saṁnyāsa*, the concept of *karma* also got a jolt and was completely modified. Only on the basis that *karma* was a part and parcel of an individual was the cycle of births and deaths justified. If a man was freed from *karma* then the very cause of rebirth was taken away. *Mokṣa* was regarded as freedom from births and deaths. Thus, if man was freed from *karma* he would be free and thus *attain mokṣa*. This led to the philosophic enquiry about the soul or the *ātman* which was regarded as identical with the *cosmic principle* or *Brahman*. *Karma* was also the product of attachment. If you are not attached to anything you cannot be supposed to have *done* that thing, although something may *happen* to you. You are *responsible* only for *doing something* not for *something that happens* to you. Action done through the spirit of detachment would not produce any real *karma*. It is in this spirit that Lord Kṛṣṇa says in *Gītā* that 'a man has authority over his actions (i.e., the choice of action) but has no control over the effects. Thus, *karma* is, in fact, not integral to the man or *ātman*. *Karma* is like a gear-box unless the *ātman* is put in the gear of *karma*, *karma*- *ātman*-complex would not act. It follows that man or *ātman* is essentially free. It is only through ignorance that he thinks he is bound. There is nothing new to be achieved or attained. *Mokṣa* or emancipation, therefore, only means the *cognition or the recognition* that man is free. The problem has yet another dimension. The moral problem of good or evil too is connected with human expectations and the meaning or value that we attach to happenings. One may suffer from moral indignation if one sees a bad man prospering and a good man suffering. But the fact is that goodness or truth does not seem to triumph although it is again and again asserted that it does. The philosophers of Hinduism solved this dilemma by affirming that the meaningfulness or the value loadedness of certain situations exists only in the anthropocentric world. Looked at from cosmic point of view events are only value-neutral happenings. Thus, *karma* loses all its meaning. Nothing is either good or bad, there is no sin nor merit. All these are fancies of the human brain. The very basis of the cause-effect series of *karma* is taken away. The cycle of births and deaths which as a matter of fact, never cristed, was only imagined purely on account of ignorance and is destroyed through the attainment of knowledge. Essential recognition that the concept of responsibility and *karma* are anthoropocentric concepts, that from cosmic point of view there is neither the cycle of births and deaths nor heaven or sin or merit had its effect even on the concept of God as creator. The never dying and ever existing soul could not be regarded as different from God. A non-difference, unity or identity between the two, the soul and God, was asserted in one of the very famous sentences in *Chāndogya Upaniṣad* — *tat tvam asi*, That thou art. God himself, however, was bereft of *karma* which was regarded as *māyā* or phenomenal nature of God. And this new outlook on religion was regarded as *paramārtha*, the highest purpose, as against *puruṣārtha* — the human goal. This dialectial process in Hinduism completely negated the old form of Hindu religion. It was recognised that when a man attaining knowledge in its true sense, there is no more any religion for him. All religions are nothing but based on superstitious ignorance or *ajñāna*. Hinduism in its true sense, therefore, is not a religion but a critique of religion, all religions. It is in this spirit that Puṣpadanta in what appears to be a prayer to Lord Śiva asks: What is *thy desire*? What is *thy* body? What is thy purpose? On what substratum dost thou (the creator) create this Universe? And what are the means or instruments for this creation?—Any thinking about these problems is beyond the comprehension of human beings. Any speculation based on bad logic will only increase the ignorance.

The Phase of Devotion

The spirit behind early Hinduism and critical Hinduism appeared to be lost in the course of time. Some of the Hindu religious institutions continued without life or spirit like the Egyptian mummies. The philosophy of Hinduism merely remained in the books. Through the influence of Mahāyāna Buddhism new *purāṇika* gods emerged and idol-worship became a part and parcel of Hinduism. New rituals were practised. *Karma* theory was identified with fatalism and Hinduism degenerated into superstition and tradition. It is this form of Hinduism which is known to Christian missionaries and foreign observers when, for example, they write:

"When we think of Indian religions, perhaps we think of a turbaned man lying on a bed or nails, or perhaps squatting cross-legged, wearing only a loincloth, as he meditates. Such images are so strange and so remote from our own experience that some of us may not try to understand why he does these things, but may regard him as an oddity, a mystery, perhaps even a joke."* It is hardly necessary to say that such a caricature of Hindu religion will not cut any ice. For even Hindus would not regard anyone religious or as spreading the gospel of Hinduism merely on the basis of dress or (extrovert) social behaviour.

However, behind this apparently degenerated form of Hinduism a new and simple form of Hinduism was already emerging. It was the religion advocated by the Hindu saints and was not for the select

*History of India, Habbett.

few but was for the masses. It consisted in complete surrender to God through prayer and worship. The distinction of castes was resented (though caste could not be eradicated) and the sophisticated forms of religious practices were looked down upon. The name of God became the sole symbol for prayer and worship. All the old forms of the Hindu religion institution and practices were synthesised with this new form and the greatness of God was contrasted against the helplessness of man. This new attitude kept Hinduism alive against the Muslim and the Christian onslaught and Hinduism continued to prosper both by anticipating and absorbing the Christian and Muslim teachings. Once again the Hindu way of life manifested its power to assimilate and absorb others' ideas and to have respect and tolerance for others' way of life.

This third way of Hinduism is connected with the *bhakti* movement. Of course, it is doubtful whether the name *bhakti* is given to this phase by the leaders of the movement themselves or it is given by outsiders. The second phase of Hinduism was a reaction against the *karma* concept and the philosophers aimed at pointing out that we regard as action was not, in fact, an action. We are neither the agents nor the controllers of those actions. What we call actions are merely happenings — a matter of course, so the concepts of merit or sin or rebirth or immortality of soul are to be completely ignored as they are creations of our own imagination and ignorance. But such a thought is likely to remove the distinction between a conscious and unconscious being. Although man obeys all the laws of Physics which are cosmocentric laws he also creates his own laws over and above the laws of Physics. It is a case of fait accompli that man is in the midst of society and unless the physical laws and happenings remove him from the universe, he and the society along with his relations to environment and society would continue. The relationships between two non-sentient things are just static. But the relationships between two sentient and self-conscious beings are not static. Some dynamism is operative between sentient beings. This is what is called communication and it is at the basis of all human and social constructions. The communication between I and others or I and you may take two forms. It may take the form of a relation of equality between two equal individuals or it may take the form of helplessness and frustration and, therefore, of complete surrender. Since this surrender is also connected with communication the surrender to whom would be a question. And it is here that the concept of a personal sentient God arises. This God is merely a symbol for communication. It is a variable for communicating our teachings to others and ultimately it takes an abstract form, when we begin to talk of society or humanity. This communication is not based on reason. The tools of communication here are compassion and sympathy. It is finally a kind of humanism. God does not mean God, it means the other human beings, something fine in other human beings, something personified. What we call *bhakti* seems to be the description of such communication. It is recognition of the fact that there are other individuals like you and the communication between other individuals and you, is not only possible but is factual. This communication immediately takes you to live in this world, to enjoy this world, not to withdraw from this world, although you are constructing this 'living' on the withdrawal concept. Naturally, you start with equality amongst yourselves and you only obey God or His substitute, perhaps a personified principle of communication. The old social order based on inequality is discarded. For, we now recognise 'the others' and we also recognise the miseries of others. It is once again, going together but now it is a different 'going'. Narsī Mehtā defines a man of God as one who understands the miseries of others. His God, as also the God of any of the sects which have flourished during this phase, locates him in the society and recommends compassion for others. The way of life which saints preached, perhaps has its origin in the concept of the earlier Buddhist and Jain *saṁghas*, where there is no hierarchy. It is worth noting that this phase of Hinduism based on *bhakti* gave rise to saints of all castes. Even untouchability was rejected by the Saints. A saint like Narsī Mehtā seems to be conscious of the fact that the scheduled caste people were being continuously persecuted. He wanted to re-admit them to society and to do this, he gave them the name Harijan. It was, in a way, an attempt to get rid of alienation which arises in human society.

It is usually forgotten that on account of alienation that man develops himself, discovers himself, and also loses his way. Although, the dichotomies like justice-injustice, equality-inequality, exploitation-non-exploitation, are present in the human world, to choose one of the alternatives and construct the society also seems to be the engineering of awareness. In my view, when Advaita philosophy talks of *ātman* it is talking about this awareness. The traditional Advaita philosophy forgets this and so arrives at the conclusion that the world is *māyā*. But such a conclusion is not necessary. If we may emphasise on the essential unity, of the human and the non-human world and if we realise that out of the alternatives created in the human world, man can also choose, man has freedom to choose, whatever he wants to choose, it can supply a good scaffold in social reconstruction. Although, such a thing has not been worked out there should be no difficulty in working it out.

The Political Phase

As India came in contact with the West, Hinduism underwent yet another restructuring. Raja Rammohun Roy (Brahmo Samāj) and Svāmī Vivekānanda, Jyotibā Phūle, Rānāde (Prārthanā Samāj) were the architects of this orientation. But, finally, the phase resulted in the political form of Hinduism.

1857 is a landmark in the history of India. Both the Hindus and the Muslims revolted against the British and although finally this revolt was unsuccessful it gave rise to one national consciousness. Although the revolutionaries, the hard nationalists and the moderates had their independent points of view, they were never divided on the basis of religion. At the same time it must be said that almost everyone in India whether Hindu, Muslim or Christian was very religious in the individual life. The British took advantage of this and followed the policy of divide and rule by encouraging one community and not giving similar facilities to others. Sometimes they even patronised followers of all religions. They hoped that if all of them grow strong in their religious convictions and blind beliefs they would finally split India. The British, thus, helped both Sir Sayed Ahamad, the moderate brāhmaṇas and the promoters of non-brāhmaṇa parties like the Justice-Party of Madras.

In this process the Hindu consciousness also grew and finally it started showing itself politically in the speeches of Barrister Savarkar, Pt. Madan Mohan Malviya, Dr. Munje and Dr. Hedgewar, the founder of R.S.S and several others. For Hedgewar and his followers organising a para-military organisation was the basic need for protecting the Hindus. Dr. Munje very honestly pleaded that the Hindus must adopt non-vegetarian diet in order to build their muscles and Barrister Savarkar said that there was nothing wrong in eating beef, that our Vedic forefathers did so; you cannot have self-realisation if you are weak *nayam ātmaḥ barhīnen labhyaḥ*. He had before himself the ideal of the Sikh Gurus. He and his brother Shri Babarao Savarkar wrote lives of all the ten Gurus and we, in our younger days had occasion to read them. Savarkar did not believe in the caste system for he wanted the unity of all Hindus and for the same reason made a campaign against untouchability in Hinduism. The problem of untouchability for him was different from the problem before Mahatma Gandhi or Dr. B.R. Ambedkar. He wanted a united Hindu clan, a clan which had Hindu origin and which accepted India as their mother-land. Savarkar said, those who regarded their holy-land was outside India, were not Hindus. The other religious and philosophical conditions of Hinduism did not matter to him. His was an attempt to create a hard-core Hinduism, just in the manner of the tenth Guru of the Sikhs, Guru Govind Singh. For Savarkar and for these hard-core Hindu leaders Sikhs belonged to Hindu community and Sikhism was a paradigm. But this rigidity in Hinduism did not bear dividends. Excepting a microscopic tradition Hindu community did not go either with the R.S.S. or Hindu Mahasbha or Jansangh. Of course, the rigidity of Hindus helped the two-nation theory and brought about the division of India, into India and Pakistan. It points out that when religions become rigid and political they lead to splinter groups within each religion. Events in the context of Sikh politics will bear testimony to this. The rigidity and the growing political ambition not only made Sikhism a separate religion but also made for Sikhs, a demand for a separate Sikh nation possible. It may be pointed out that in all its first three phases, Hinduism was not rigid. It absorbed and even swallowed other religions and kept Hinduism alive. The rigidity of Hinduism is likely to split it into several fragments. This is desirable neither from the religious point of view nor from the political.

I have discussed in this chapter, though briefly, the four phases of Hinduism. I call them, *karma-kāṇḍa*, *jñāna-kāṇḍa*, *bhakti-kāṇḍa* and the *artha-kāṇḍa*. One interesting thing, however, I find in this development. In the first phase Hinduism began as a geographical-cum-demographic notion. In the fourth phase also it has returned to this geographical-cum-demographic notion. But strangely when I look at Hinduism in its deeper perspective I find that Hinduism, in none of its phases, was really a religion. The second phase was just philosophy. And though *bhakti-kāṇḍa* may be thought to be a religion, except prayer to God, almost everything in this phase is really social and humanitarian. The most important thing is that even in this phase, there was no allegiance to any particular script nor was their any ordaining. In fact, people worshipped not only Hindu Gods, but also the Muslim Pīrs and Christian saints. Thus, to call Hinduism a religion is simply dogmatic or even fanatic.

22

Dialectics: Buddhist and Marxist

According to Buddhism everything is changing and impermanent and at the same time everything is continuous.

In Buddhist literature like *Dhammapada*, *Mahāparinirvāṇa Sūtra* and in Buddhaghoṣa there are references to impermanence. In the first parable of *Dhammapada* (Chinese version) Lord Buddha seems to have said, 'Whatever exists is without endurance'. . . 'The life of man is but as the earthen vesels made in a potter's mills.' And in yet another parable attributed to Buddha he says. "As the waters of river even hasten in and flow away, and once gone, never return, such is the life of man. That which is gone knows not any return." The same notion is again repeated in Buddhaghoṣa: "Just as a chariot wheel in rolling rolls merely at one point of the tyre and in resting rests only at one point, even so the life of living being endures only for the brief period of our thought and as soon as the thought has ceased, the being too, is said to have ceased. Thus, the being of a past moment has lived but does not live nor will it live; the being of a future moment will live but has not lived nor does it live; the being of the present moment does live but has not lived and will not live."[1] This main philosophy of Buddhism continues in later Buddhism also. Nāgārjuna, Diñnāga. Dharmakīrti and Ratnakīrti amongst others reiterate impermancence of everything in this world: *yat sat tat kṣaṇikam*.

According to Buddhism this impermanence, however, is of two

1. Warren's *Buddhism in Translation*, p. 150, as quoted by Yamakami Sogen's *Systems of Buddhistic Thought*, p .11.

kinds (*i*) impermanence of the life period and (*ii*) momentary impermanence. Even in the *mudrās* attributed to Buddha there is reference to momentariness. *Sarvaṃ kṣaṇikam.* Discreteness (*niranvayatā*) follows from it. The first is what is experienced (refer to the first parable), the second is what is presupposed by the first (the parable of the river). Impermanence of life period gives us immediate experience of duration and gives justification of the proposition that 'Everything is continuous'. When we are explaining experience from anthropocentric point of view, we need tools like causation, class and inference. This is clear from the Buddhist use of the concepts of *tad-utpatti* and *kārya-anumāna.* But when one tries to understand the nature of reality without subjecting it to human understanding and human categories, one may rather have to point out the limitations of concepts like causation, class and inference. I feel that Lord Buddha and following him his adherents like Diññāga, Dharmakīrti and Nāgārjuna are trying to point out such limitations of the human concepts when they talk of *pratītya-samutpāda* or *apoha.* In what follows I shall try to explain concepts like *pratītya-samutpāda* and show how these concepts point to the limitation of the tools of human thought like causality and class and indicate what may be regarded as the laws of dialectic.

My first contention is that as *pratītya-samutpāda* is the key concept[2] which is used for explaining that everything is of the nature of micro change, it does not give us any law of causation as thought by Mrs. Rhys Davids or following her most of the recent writers on Buddhism. Professor Hiriyanna, for example, while talking of *pratītya-samutpāda* regards it as the law of causation, although he qualifices it as the law of contingent causation. He writes: 'it was the knowledge of these factors, with the law of contingent casusation implicit in it, that flashed across Siddhārtha's mind at last and made him the Buddha.[3] If *pratītya-samutpāda* is interpreted as the law of causation the main thesis of Buddhism

---

2. *Yaḥ pratīya-samutpādaṃ paśyati sa dharmaṃ paśyati.*
   Quoted by Candrakīrti in his *Mādhyamaka-vṛtti*, Darbharnga edition p. 2
3. M. Hiriyanna, *Outlines of Indian Philosophy*, p. 144.

that everything is momentary, non-continuous and impermanent will suffer. In such a case the whole universe will be determined, events will be related to events and the unity of the self will not be liquidated. Moreover, to assert the law of causality would not be asserting anything new or novel. For, ordinarily, people have been accepting that things in the universe are determined causally.

It is true that the phrase *pratītya-samutpāda* is ambiguous and is variously interpreted in the Buddhist literature. Candrakīrti in the *Mādhyamikavṛtti,* his commentary on the *Mādhyamika-śāstra*, considers many such definitions although he rejects most of them. These definitions, however, presuppose the momentary character of occurrences or they lead us to think that causation does not have any status in its own right but is a kind of construct. It will be interesting to consider a few of these definitions. *Samutpāda* in ordinary language means 'coming into existence', and so on his first interpretation, points to cause-effect series.[4] But *pratītya* here means 'having known'.[5] Thus, on this interpretation *pratītya-samutpāda* is confined to the region of epistemology and is given phenomenal status only. This meaning may easily suggest that causation belongs to *sāmānya-lakṣaṇa*. On the second interpretation. *ityaḥ* is taken to mean momentary or fleeting existents.[6] *Prati* means occurring again and again.[7] *Pratītya-samutpāda* should, thus, mean coming into existence of momentary existence. Candrakīrti is inclined to reject this interpretation on the ground that literally *prati* means repetition of the same thing and the Buddhist philosophers want to reject this thesis. I venture to say that if *prati* is taken to mean similar, this definition of *pratītya-samutpāda* would fit in the Buddhist thesis. On the third interpretation, it means that causation is a construction after observing the particular cognitions or *pratyaya*s.[8] By this he excluded

4. *Samutpūrvaḥ padiḥ prādur-bhāvārtha hi samutpāda śabdaḥ prādurbhave vartate.*
5. *Pratīya śbdo'tra lyabantaḥ prāptāvapekṣāyāṃ vartate.*
6. *Itir gatin gamanaṃ vināśaḥ; itau sādhana ityāḥ.*
7. *Pratikirtyarthaḥ.*
8. *Tāṃstān pratyayān pratītya-samutpādaḥ.*

the ontic nature of causation or causality. On a still other interpretion it means 'that being present this becomes', an interpretation accepted by Professor Hiriyanna."[9] Candrakīrti makes it clear that it is not the case of the previous occurrences creating or causing the subsequent.[10] These co-occurrences do not have strength to occur on their own. They are not independent.[11] They are born not on their own, nor are they related to the previous occurrences by causal relation.[12] Thus, I think it is not necessary to understand *Pratītya-samutpāda* as the law of causation in any sense of the term.

Let me try to understand the problem before Buddhism. Like the philosophers of Sāṁkhya,Lord Buddha was also touched by suffering in this world and wanted to find a way out of it. He was not interested in any theoretical discussion of the problem, but was concerned with the removal of suffering. His doctrine of four noble truths is the proposed solution of this suffering. This concept of suffering occurs if we regard self as the unity of apperception. As Hiriyanna put it. "With the negation of self, selfish impulses necessarily disppear"[13] and misery being one of the selfish impulses, it can be immediately eradicated as soon as we know that there is no self. As the belief in self-identity arises out of ignorance, when this ignorance is removed the suffering naturally ends. The main problem of Buddhism, therefore, is to remove one continuous unity of self whether it is in *ātmavāda* or the theory of persistent self, or the identity of a thing in the multitude or *saṁghāta* of sense, or identity or one *sāmānya* or universal amongst particulars. Buddha and following him all Buddhists came to the conclusion that identity is due to intelligence-construction of *sāmānya-lakṣaṇa* and everything is in fact discrete (*niranvaya*) and impermanent. As a matter of fact what exists is nothing but discrete occurrents like

9. *Asmin sati idaṃ bhavati tasya utpādāt idam utpādyate.*
10. *Tena idānīm prāpya sambhavaḥ pratītya-samutpāda ity evam vyutpāditena pratītya-samutpāda-śabden nirviśeṣa-sambhavi-padārtha-parāmarś nigamitah.*
11. *Svabhāvena anutpannatvāt.*
12. *Utpādasya ca vivartatvāt.*
13. *Ibid.*, p. 147.

moments, and any kind of continuity that takes place is due to our own tendercy to organise the discrete moments or occurrents into one unity.[14] We do have a tendency to unify the discrete moments into a kind of flow or *santāna*. It is true that we do formulate concepts like causation, inference and class. But whether it is of macro level or micro level there is only contingency. Looked at from cosmic point of view there is no ontic reality corresponding to any of these unifications. They are all *vikalpas*.[15] From the cosmic or ontic point of view everything is of the nature of moments or momentary only. There may be time continuum or series, but our understanding of it would be of the nature of discrete moments or *kṣaṇas*. Lord Buddha could formulate such a thesis only by denying causation altogether and not by affirming it. His thesis is to assert discrete moments and their necessary series and deny the unity amongst them, the unity amongst them being a human construct; for he wanted to get rid of suffering which is concomitant with the unity. In fact, what dawned on him was the momentariness and disunity and not the unity, discretness and not the continuity, of what we experience as phenomenon. So what is usually interpreted as the formulation of the Buddhist law of causation, *pratītya-samutpāda,* known as the 'law of dependent origination', is in fact anything but the law of causation though today it goes in the name of the law of causation. Again, I think in is the application of the law of *pratītya-samutpāda* at macro level which gives us in the Buddhist theory of meaning the concept of *apoha* by which unity in respect of particulars is denied. Buddha does not seem to have formulated his second concept though it logically arises out of the fundamental concept of *pratītya-samutpāda*. It is, therefore, natural that logicians in the Buddhist tradition formulated this concept while dealing with the macro experience. The notion of *apoha* will incidentally take us to the discussion of the theory of classes and *vyāpti*, the notions of *tādātmya*, *tad-utpatti* and *svabhāva* and of *svatva*,

---

14. *Vartamāna-vyavidhim patita hi jaterastita — Apoha-siddhi Sa eva teṣāṃ sāmānya-samānādhāragocaraiḥ. Jñānabhudhanamuthyato vyavahāraḥ pratanyate,* etc., *P.V. Sva. pariccheda*, p. 51.

    Anyat sāmānyalakṣaṇam. Nyāyabindu. Ch. 1.

15. *Śabdajñānānupāti vastuśūnyo vikalpaḥ Yo Sū.*

although the discussion of all these concepts cannot be attempted within the scope of this paper.

The concept of *pratītya-samutpāda* is translated by Mrs. Rhys Davids in her book, *Buddhism,* as 'that being present this becomes'. I think Mrs. Rhys Davids translated this under the influence of some theory of causation. As Hiriyanna states it in his book,[16] "the Sanskrit expression means literally, 'arising in correlation with'.[17] There is no element of causal necessity involved in the theory of *pratītya-samutpāda.* Ordinarily, when we say that something *A* is the cause of something *B* we somehow think that *A* has the power to or ablitiy to create *B*; *A* can give birth to *B*, i.e., given *A, B* will necessarily follow. In other words we mean that if there is an event then that event must have come into existence on account of a certain cause. It will be pertinent here to refer to the distinction made by Hume between *sequence* and *consequence.* Hume said that we can never know *A* as the cause of *B*. We only know that *A* is followed by *B*. The relation of consequence, therefore, is denied by Hume. In matters of fact we can never establish a necessity between preceding and proceeding events. We are always governed by some contingency. Kant attempted to answer Hume by saying that though it is difficult, as Hume pointed out to prove the universality and necessity of causation, we can nevertheless show that at least in some matters of fact the element of necessity can be traced. In his second analogy (*Critique of Pure Reason*) Kant makes a distinction between subjective sequence and objective sequencce. If we look at a house we may decide to look at it in a way we like. The first view can be of the top, then of the middle, then of the bottom or we can go from right to left or from left to right and so on. It means that there is no objective order in our perception. The order of such perception is arbitrary and can be reversed. But if we perceive a boat going down the stream it is not possible for us to imagine at our will that the boat is sometimes going up the stream and sometimes down the stream. It is not that we perceive the boat and its movements: the boat and its movements rather show themselves and in such a case the order of each succeeding perception is not

16. *Ibid.*, p. 143.
17. *Ibid.*

determined by us but is determined by the objective situation. That is, when there is an objective succession like the above there is some kind of necessity involved. Objective sequence is very different from subjective sequence. I think Kant is right in distinguishing between objective sequence and subjective sequence and in further stating that there is an element of necessity involved in such objective sequence or process. Hume's argument against causation was based on the fact that there is no necessity involved in matters of fact. Kant says that since we have shown an instance of necessity in matters of fact we need not say on Hume's ground that there is no causation.

I need not go into the merits of Kant's argument. I only want to point out that when we talk of causation we talk of two different series and of necessity governing both these series. The first such series is the series of moments and the second series is the series of events or occurrents. When we talk of objective sequence we talk of a necessary series of moments. It is possible to conceive that a series of moments has of necessity a particular order and all the same the series of events or occurrents contingent. The law of causation cannot he proved unless the necessity element is accepted both in the moment series and in the event or occurrent series. *Pratītya-samutpāda*, according to me, accepts the first part of these two elements viz., the necessity of the moment series. The series of objective sequence too is governed by necessity although it is quite different from the necessity governing consequence. The necessity of moment series gives us only the ground for causation. If necessity in this series is denied the question of causation would not arise. But even if necessity in this series is confirmed, it does not mean that the law of causation would hold good. The relation between the moment series and the event or occurrent series is something like the relation that we find in the antecedent and consequent of a case of material implication. Buddha accepted the necessary order in objective sequence only so far as the discrete moments were concerned. What he really meant was that there was something like the law of objective sequence, that time was not reversible. If this law was misunderstood for the law of causation, it would create all the muddle in Buddha's thesis. In fact, Buddha's idea to deny the self and thereby to deny the misery or suffering cannot be achieved unless the two prongs of the law, one of moments and the other of events, or occurrents are separated. Buddha did not deny the *santāna*, i.e., flow. There is always an order in a flow; it is always in one direction: it is not reversible and this is signified by his *pratītya-samutpāda*. There is *utpāda, samutpāda* — an order, and it follows one particular direction. That is if there is a second moment, it cannot come into existence unless there was the first moment. If it is 2 o'clock now, 2 o'clock could not come into existence unless there was 1.59 and unless 1.59 carried out. We could, however, not say that 1.59 is the cause of 2, even though 2 necessarily followed 1.59.

Once you regard that unity or identity is the human construct, things, minds, soul, or universals fall to ground. Things are substituted by *saṁghāta, ātman* is simply negated, and universals are discarded. For they had occurred on account of the arrest of flow or *santāna*, on account of the imposition of some kind of unity in succeeding multitudes of states. So whereas we may go on using these concepts in ordinary language these concepts will really have the status of words in philosophical explanations and nothing else.[18] This is what the Buddhists mean when they say that class, universal or inference, etc., belong to *vikalpa* or *sāmānya lakṣana*. The concepts do not have any ontological existence; they belong to the sphere of language and social reality.

But perhaps the non-Buddhists (and may be even some of the Buddhists) have not grasped the distinction between *svalakṣaṇa* and *sāmānya-lakṣaṇa*, the distinction which the Buddhist philosophers aim at. Many a time both these are treated alike (e.g., in the *Kusumāñjali*). In ordinary language, i.e., cause-effect language, for example, we speak of a seed as the cause and a sprout as the effect. As a part of explanation in Buddhist style it will now be claimed that a seed is to be replaced by seed continuum and the sprout by sprout continuum. The seed at time t_1, t_2, t_3, etc., is not the same seed. One seed is replaced by another seed though the perceiver is never conscious of the change. And when the seed

18. *Tulya bhede yayā jātiḥ pratyāsatyā prasarpati*
Kvacinnānāca tenasu samyaejñāna-ṇibandhanam — P.V, III.181.

changes into a sprout there is another kind of change. So in order to distinguish a seed at time t_1 as the 'cause' of seed at time t_2 from the seed as the 'cause of sprout the concept of *kurvatrūpa* is supplied by some of the Buddhist writers. The fact is that the cause-effect series in which seed and sprout are elements is a different kind of cause-effect series from the *seed-seed* cause-effect series. In fact, the *seed-seed* cause-effect series becomes a cause-effect series only on account of our putting that which is a cause into the cause-effect mould. In fact, in the world to which cause-effect language belongs we do not speak of *one* seed replacing or causing another seed. What I mean to say is that the cause-effect language belongs to the sphere of *sāmānya-lakṣaṇa*, i.e., to the ontic-epistemic sphere where we treat the entities perceived as having some kind of duration or permanence and not to the ontic sphere. In the world of moments *qua* moments the cause-effect language is ineffective. But once we start with the theory of momentariness (*kṣaṇabhaṅga-vāda*) and also allow the cause-effect language to co-exist then we are led to the conclusion that seed at time t_1 is the cause of seed at time t_2 and so on. In fact, even the word 'seed' is inappropriate to the language of *kṣaṇabhaṅga-vāda*. What really undergoes a change is not the seed (but some ontological nucleus); seed is a name given to it by man and, hence, belongs to the sphere of *sāmānya-lakṣaṇa* or *vikalpa*. To ignore this will lead to category mistake. In fact, the movement of time series itself is not due to causation but is due to *dialectic* that is due to the notion of time itself. The proper understanding would be important for the understanding of history. Let us try to understand *pratītya-samutpāda* in this context. Thus, it will have to be understood in relation to two propositions (*i*) that everything is impermanent (*sarvam anityam*) and (*ii*) that everything is continuous (*sarvaṃ santānam*). Time has both these dimensions. Are these two statements inconsistent? Evidently, Buddha and his followers did not want to make any contradiction while asserting these propositions. We do experience that things change and still we identify them, we regard them as having the same identity. We have in our language such words as events, process, sequence, series, history. All these words indicate certain moments in time, also certain replacement in time, also a certain length in time. Since all these are words they belong to the world of language, knowledge or epistemology. All such words have certain length dimension which is indicated by the word 'time'. We need not try to analyse the nature of time here, either it is ontic or epistemological. But even if it is epistemological, it will be of a different order, different from other objects of knowledge since it is presupposed by such words or concepts as sequence, change, moments, etc.

What are moments and time length? Either the moments themselves have the length and so have a continuum or they are made of some kind of 'geometrical' points of a geometrical line. One can say, there are infinite points in a line, but even with infinite points we cannot construct a line. In the same way if we talk of moments by adding a number of them together we should not be able to make a temporal length. We will have to presuppose time and in this time alone we would be able to demarcate, a portion certain cross-sections which we could believe as moments. The moments would be a mathematical concept; what we experience would be merely the events. The events would succeed one another or we would grasp the events succeeding one another and so in the epistemic series we would go from finite events to their infinite extent, i.e., from impermanent things to the time continuum. The grasping of this time-continuum will be gradual. Nevertheless, a time-continuum would be in the background. It will be like a thread of a garland and the flowers of the garland will be events.

What is the nature of this process or series or a continuum? Like a cinematographic film the events will pass us and gradually will be stored in the past, i.e., will be no more. The future will be unfolded to us, i.e., will become present and the present will become the past. At each point we would be confronted with the present and both the future and the past would be ideationally conceived so that the continuum that is temporal would never be experienced at a glance. *Sarvaṁ anityam,* therefore, is a generalisation of experience. *Sarvaṃ santānam* is generalisation of ideation. What is the relation between the two? Buddha tried to explain this postulating what he called *pratītya-samutpāda.* Of necessity one event is followed by another. What is the relationship between one event and another and also between one moment and another? Of course, events occupy moments and as moments or as points in the series they are indeed different from one another. The question of how long an event remains the same and when it becomes different should confronts us now. But if these events are discrete each event would be so different from the other that when one event is replaced by another one could say that the first event had ceased to exist giving rise to another, i.e., each consequent or subsequent event would negate the first and if we stick ourselves to such events or moments the question whether the each succeeding moment is compatible with the earlier moments would not arise. And while grasping the series or continuum we would rather try to construct the series or continuum by adding discrete, unrelated events or moments. In formal language if there is a series of *a,b,c,d,e,* we could not say that *a* is replaced by 'not-*a*' and 'not-*a*' by 'not-not-*a*'. In logic this 'not-*a*' is the contradiction of '*a*' and the 'not-not-*a*' is the contradiction of 'not-*a*'. But in logic even if we use the word contradiction in time series and in the world of things this will be a mere negation and not a logical contradiction. In logic 'not-not-*a*' is equivalent to '*a*' but this does not happen in time-series. For in time-series there are not really 'not-*a*' and 'not-not-*a*', there are only *a*, *b* and *c*. And *a*, *b*, and *c* should form a continuum *c* although it is also only a part of the continuum). It is only for the sake of our convenient understanding that we are dividing a time continuum into moments and events continuum into events.If we regard the 'moments' or 'events' as discrete then they would be characterised by incompatibility. If we do not regard them as discrete and rather regard them as a part of a continuum then compatibility would be the characrteristic. There is a difference between difference that is compatible and difference that is incompatible, *a* is different from *b* and *b is* different form *c*, all *a,b,c*, etc, are different from one another and still they are compatible, *a*, not-*a*, etc., are different from each other but they are non-compatible. Such non-compatible difference can be thought of in formal logic but cannot be thought of in experience or in a dialectic of experience.

Another important thing which follows from the concept of continuum and compatible difference within it is that a continuum or series is governed by necessity. Each succeeding event necessarily comes after the pervious events. But since it is one series, one continuity, and it is broken into parts for our convenience and since the parts could be broken into parts for our convenience and since the parts could be broken into shorter or longer duration, we could not strictly talk of earlier events as the cause of subsequent events. The law of causation is either irrelevant or will be merely of the nature of 'because' and not of 'cause'.

If all that I have said is correct it will have, as said earlier, some important implications in respect of understanding of history. For we will have to reframe the laws of historical understanding. They will be somewhat different from those given to us by Marx in his dialectics, or at least they will be different from the laws understood by the followers of Marx. First, incompatibility concept will have to be explained in terms of compatibility concept. That is, we will have to recognize that that which is compatible in time when stretched for a sufficiently longer time will appear as incompatible. This will also explain the law of change of quantity into quality. Finally, the basic principle in history and time will be compatibility although in our understanding and interpretation we will also make use of the concept of incompatibility. Similarly, basically the two events will be different but nor contradictory. Both these would follow if we take the two propositions *sarvam santānaṃ* and *sarvam anityam* together. The concept of difference will also be of two kinds, that which belongs to the reality as such which is of the ontic world and that which belongs to the world of understanding. We will have to explain our world of understanding on the basis of *anyonyā bhāva* and it will take the form of *A* is different from *B*. The length of *A* and *B* will be determined again by our attitude and understanding.

All that Buddha does through the concept of *pratītya-samutpāda* is the analysis of time and motion.

Karl Marx following Hegel has given us these laws of dialectics.They are: (1) unity of opposites, (2) change of quantity into quality, and (3) negation of negation. To me the first two laws are important. Marx applied these laws to events unlike Hegel who applied them to ideas. Marx's laws, therefore, become temporal laws. He posited them as follows:

> First there is a thesis (he does not say of how long a duration), it is followed by its opposite, the antithesis (again no body knows of how long a duration) and finally a part of the thesis and a part of the antithesis are synthesised

> in a synthesis, i.e., a part of the thesis and antithesis accepted and a part of the thesis and antithesis is rejected. The synthesis in its own turn becomes a new thesis and is again followed by its opposite.

Marx also thought that we are moving upward or spirally although it is not immediately realised. But the events in history (and our understanding) accumulate in such a way that there is, so to say, an explosion. In a series of events one now looks so different, qualitatively different, from the other earlier events, that we are, so to say, lifted up by a jack. This, of course, happens because the events 1, 2, 3 may appear to be similar and compatible but the event 4 succeeding 3 may appear as unrelated and incompatible with event 1or 2. If we take cotton fibres of particular length we can make a thread out of it but the fibres have only a finite length and the 1st fibre may not be continued in the 5th, 2nd in the 6th and so on. So, finally a difference may come in such way that the succeeding events may be totally different from the earlier events. Cotton fibres have limited length and events are of finite duration. But events presuppose time and although we may be able to divide time into moments we do not say that time is made up of finite moments.

Marx, when he talks of reality, distinguishes social reality from the other given reality. Our social reality is largely a construction of man although it may be a construction on the given reality. In this social reality it is possible that the different creations of man may either be compatible or incompatible. If they are incompatible, it means that the first creation is rejected and the subsequent accepted. Evidently, the social reality is different from nature and yet it is a part of the nature. It is, so to say, a part of the epistemological world. The laws of social reality, in a way, will be the laws of human understanding and a change of quantity into quality will be a part of human understanding. Not that there would not be a counterpart of this in the given reality, but our saying that it has become qualitatively different will be a part of our understanding, a part of our language. When we grasp events in a series we may feel that at sometime they become qualitatively different. But this qualitative difference is connected with our awareness. While giving the explanation of dialectic it is conveniently forgotten that Marx also talked of social reality. Being of the world and understanding of the world are so thickly related and thinly demarcated that understanding cannot be completely eliminated from either, with the result that epistemological phenomenon is misunderstood as physical or ontological phenomenon. In the natural reality everything is compatible. Events are compatible because they co-exist. Incompatibility is the concept of human world. When difference-gap becomes more and more it tends to become incompatibility. When difference becomes exhaustive then the exhaustive differences together become contradiction. This can never be experienced or grouped at experiential level although it can be thought of at ideational level.

The point that I want to make is that the so-salled incompatibility is not incompatible with the compatibility inconsistent with the so-called qualitative difference. The paradox of compatibility-incompatibility in regard to time and events must have come Buddha's way also. This is how he talks of momentary impermanance along with impermanence of life period; he also talks of continuum *santānam* with *anityam* that which is momentary.

23

Indian Philosophy

Retrospect and Prospect

By Indian philosophy we usually understand the classical philosophy of Indian origin excluding Muslim, Christian, Jewish or Parsi thought. This is not to say that thinkers in this region did not write on Islam and Christianity, etc., or criticised Hindu philosophy from a third person's point of view. But their thought was kept away during contemporary times from the 'Hindus' and the mutual respect for each other's thinking necessary for communication was conspicuous by its absence. In the early past the case was different. When Varāhamihira wrote on astronomy, he began by giving salutations to the Yavanācāryas. These philosophers of astronomy and mathematics were perhaps Greeks settled in Greece, Palestine, Egypt and Crete. In the memoirs of Megasthenes, which have come down to us through McCrindle we find a reference to Dandamis who was a philosopher and whose philosophy was similar to that of the Vedānta of the Advaita type. Similarly, in a letter which Spinoza wrote to one of his students who took a leading part in Spinoza's excommunication from his religious community, Spinoza refers to Indian or Hindu philosophy and suggests that Europeans should leave their prejudices and narrow outlook and read the Hindu philosophy. Like mathematics perhaps the Upaniṣadic philosophy was also carried abroad to Europe through Morocco and Spain by Moors in the middle ages. The Buddhist philosophy was certainly spread outside India to Sri Lanka, Thailand, Kampuchia, Vietnam, Malaysia, Mongolia, Manchuria, Tibet, China and Japan. Perhaps, the historian-philosopher, Al-Biruni, of the court of Mohammed of

Gazni was also a learned scholar of Indian lore. Similarly, some Jaina thought also might have been carried outside India through the Jain traders.

But in the middle ages the broad-mindedness necessary for carrying a dialogue with others perhaps came to an end and Indians developed a closed social and cultural outlook which prohibited Indians from crossing seas or learn foreign languages. This culminated in the attitude that Hindus should not even read other philosophies of Indian origin. Some religious sects even tried to observe secrecy for preserving their religious thoughts and practices. The Mahānubhāva sect is one such example. The Mahānubhāva kept their literature away from those who were not Mahānubhāvas and developed a secret script for preserving it. The traditional Hindu philosophers, like those belonging to Nyāya, even said that we must not accept anything outside our own realm of thinking, even if it is good, useful and rational, just as we do not accept good milk if it is offered to us in a dog's skull. Thus, Indian philosophy tended to become sectarian.

This, of course, does not mean that there was no attempt at dialogue in one way of thinking or another. Perhaps, it might have been carried through criticism, even amounting to *chala* and *vitaṇḍa*. The criticism offered by Rāmānuja and Madhva against Śaṅkara can be cited as instances of such arguments. There are also a few instances of give and take amongst several philosophers of different schools. Such instances have, in fact, enriched the Indian theories of philosophy in one way or the other. Thus, both the process of segregation and syncretism occurred in India, and, in fact, philosophers of Vedānta rather adhered to the method of *samanvaya*, integrating different philosophical thoughts in their own system. In course of time, the synthesis in philosophical thought was also carried on in a different way. For example, Nyāya was valued more for its methodology and logic than for its philosophy proper. The Nyāya philosophers themselves assumed or accepted the Vaiśeṣika metaphysics. But the other systems of thought like Pūrva Mīmāṁsā and Uttara Mīmāṁsā accepted the style of Navya-Nyāya. Thus, some later works of Pūrva Mīmāṁsā and Vedānta like *Khaṇḍanakhaṇḍakhādya* and the *Advaita-siddhiḥ* were written in Navya-Nyāya style. Similarly, the basic rituals of Pūrva Mīmāṁsā were adhered to by people belonging to other sects or those following other philosophies. It must be pointed out at this stage that the basis of classification of philosophy in India was quite different from the one which we are accustomed to in the present age. Pure metaphysics, or pure formal logic, or pure ethics, was not the thing they aimed at. And since classification is not something natural and is dependent on some principle that one adopts, one need not necessarily follow the Western pattern. In fact, if one has to understand the Indian way of thinking, one must follow their own patterns rather than subjugating the Indian thoughts to the Western style.

In this kind of Indian way of thinking, they put emphasis on knowledge (*jñāna*) more than anything else. Of course, the concept of *jñāna* was broader than that of knowledge, that we, at present use as its equivalent.

The Indian philosophy was, so to say, an answer to our desire to know (*jijñāsā*). Thus, conceptual analysis of philosophy of language was not regarded as an independent discipline. But this does not mean that they did not pay any heed to, for example, the analysis of concepts. It would also not be correct to say that they did not take into consideration the analysis of language in their *bhāṣyas*. All Indian philosophers in general and Kāśmīra Śaiva philosophers in particular, talked of four kinds of language, although what they said is not clear to me and to most of the philosophers of the present-day who do philosophy through the current idiom. The *Parātriṁśikā* a work in Kāśmīra Śaivism is a thesis on *parā* language, though there may be some difficulty in understanding it today; and people may think that it is mystical. Similar would be the case with the *Spandakārikā*. The philosophy of Tantra has also to be given a second look. Perhaps, none of them need to be regarded as mystical as it is thought today; it could merely be some kind of philosophy of will or *icchā*. Of the four kinds of languages, *parā*, *paśyantī*, *madhyamā* and *vaikharī*. *Vaikharī* is a language in which we speak and write. It is ordinary language; and the philosophy of this language is also developed in philosophical grammar, particularly, of Patañjali and Bhartṛhari. Later, some of these ideas were employed, exploited and criticised by the Nyāya and Mīmāṁsā. The concepts in ordinary language, e.g., *śabda* and *artha*, were used in a slightly different sense in their philosophical treatises on art and poetry, e.g., in the sense in which medium is the language of art. An attempt to exemplify basic elements in arts like music and dance is seen in the concepts of *tāla* and *laya* and also *spanda*. There could be something common between such art languages and ordinary language also. Some kind of universal language could be at the back of all languages and could be inbuilt in the human species. Perhaps, when they talked of *parā* they had such a universal language in their mind. But it has to be accepted that the philosophy of Indian origin did not put emphasis on the philosophy of ordinary language only.

On the other hand, to the Western mind Indian philosophy appeared more religious, for at a certain stage it did look dogmatic. I do not know if it was religious in the strict sense. For the philosophical questions Indians asked, rather had a style of science. They usually did not ask the question — "Who created the world?" Rather they asked the question — "What is the world made of? What are the constituents of the world?" Of course, this does not mean that the question of the genesis of the world was completely ignored by them. In the Purāṇas, for example, they do ask the question regarding the genesis of the world, and also answer that the creator was sleeping in the ocean of milk on the snake-bed. The snake was named Śeṣa. From the navel of this Creator, grew a stem of lotus and in the lotus flower sat Brahmā who designed the present universe. A reference to such genesis of the universe, one can find even in the *Śāṅkarabhāṣya*. But the story of the genesis of the universe does not form the main core of Indian philosophical argument. All this shows that the ancient or medieval Indians did not emphasise on all those problems which a philosopher of the present generation includes in philosophy. It should not, however, suggest that the Indians did not pay any heed to these problems. Even today, a physicist does not bother himself with the problems of archaeology or linguistics, ethics, sociology and history. So, it is not proper to criticise the ancient Indian thinkers for not tackling the problems in which the philosophers of the present generation are interested.

After the British occupation of India, the ancient philosophical thought had to face another kind of problem. After the introduction of Macaulay's system of education, a large number of those who were devoting themselves to Indian philosophy, art, poetry, medicine, etc., gave up their old practice and tried to learn the thought which the British in particular had introduced in India. These people simply forgot the traditional thought and accepted the Western philosophy as was introduced in Indian educational system. Plato, Aristotle, the British empiricists in general, and Kant, Hegel, Berkeley, Mill, William James, Herbert Spencer and others in particular, were vigorously studied by the Indians. While the Indians were doing this, the Europeans, from William Jones onwards, tried to translate some Sanskrit classics in English; and this practice was followed by Jacobi, Max Müller, Keith, Stcherbatsky, and others. A series of Indian texts under the title *Sacred Books of the East* edited by Max Müller is an instance.

Ganganath Jha of Allahabad University also made a similar attempt. There were still *paṇḍit*s who were doing their Vyākaraṇa, Nyāya, Vedānta, etc. But now a new class of scholars who studied Sanskrit language in universities was regarded as experts in Vyākaraṇa, Mīmāṁsā and Vedānta. The Western scholars were great researchers in their own way, but they were also muddling through so far as the understanding of Indian lore was concerned. Thus, two camps emerged. In one camp were Sanskrit *paṇḍit*s — Eastern and Western — who had little training in either Indian or Western way of philosophising, but were scholars of Sanskrit and other allied languages. These came to be known as 'Orientalists'. In the other camp were philosophers who studied Western philosophy, but had nothing to do with Eastern thought. A bridge between these two worlds — the worlds of Orientalists and philosophers of the Western brand — was not built for a long time.

There was, however, a third group influenced by the Western ideas and was eager to find out what was living and what was dead in the Indian thought. This group could be regarded as the Renaissance group. The torch-bearers of this group in Bengal were Raja Rammohun Roy, Ishvarchandra Vidyasagar, Keshub Chandra Sen, and Devendranath Tagore. In Maharashtra, Jyotiba Phule, Rajaramshatri Bhagwat, Justice Mahadeo Govind Ranade, and Shri Neelakhantha Shastri Gorhe (who later became Rev. Gorhe) belonged to this group. In fact, people like Svāmī Vivekānanda should also be included in this group only. Shri Agarkar and Krishnaji Keshava Damle *alias* Keshava-suta also belonged to this group. In fact, the communist thinkers like Dange, D. D. Kosambi and Debi Prasad Chattopadhyaya also should be classified under this group. All these reformers were, in a way, pioneers of the enlightenment movement in India. They were, I think, influenced by two factors in particular. One was the spirit of Renaissance followed by the Industrial Revolution and the progress of science in the Western world. The other was the realisation of some lacuna in the Indian way of thinking, for the Indians in general believed that the world was illusory without understanding the philosophical significance behind it. Mr. Gorhe Shastri who was a believer in God thought, and in my opinion thought correctly, that the Advaita system was not theistic, that it was atheistic. He, therefore, preferred to embrace Christianity and became a Christian priest. The case of Prārthanā Samāj in Maharashtra and of Brahmo Samāj in Bengal has also to be studied in the proper perspective. We are confused by the term 'Brahmo' which, in fact, is the same as the word 'Brahma'. *Brahman* was thought to be attributeless and formless. The Brahmos thought that neither the Hindu rituals nor their concrete forms of God give us His real nature, that the potentiality or strength of any religion or philosophy does not lie in its ritualism or in its idol-worship. We must realise that the essence of the universe cannot be described in any such terms. Similarly, to think of re-incarnation of God, or re-birth, or the hierarchy of castes could also be unjustified. Raja Rammohun Roy who had studied the *Koran* and also the *Bible* came to this conclusion, and to distinguish his thinking from the traditional Indian thinking, he established Brahmo Samāj. This was, in a way, going back to Upaniṣads. In it was embodied the real spirit of 'Hinduism' and, in fact, should be called neo-Hinduism. They had also introduced prayer in this Samāj. Perhaps this was due to the influence of the *Bhakti* movement of Caitanya, Kabīr and others. But it could have also been due to the influence of Islam and Christianity. Almost similar was the case in Maharashtra with Prārthanā Samāj. Although both these Samājas divided the so-called Hindu society into orthodox and unorthodox groups, I should say that they emerged through the reflective thinking on Indian philosophy itself. The Ārya Samāj of Svāmī Dayānanda was also established in this age. Just as Brahmo Samāj took to the Upaniṣadic thinking. Svāmī Dayānanda Sarasvatī also tried to reform 'Hinduism' and thought that almost everything after the Vedic *Saṁhitā* period was an aberration and so we should go back to the Vedas proper.

On the background of such trends one should try to understand Svāmī Vivekānanda's contribution. He found that it was not proper to go out of the mainstream and, therefore, he called his philosophy Hindu philosophy. But, as a matter of fact, his philosophical preachings were not generally different from those of Brahmo Samāj. He did not believe in casteism. For him the worldly prosperity of India was as important as the spiritual prosperity. That is why he found his God in the poor, in the common man. He did not believe in idol-worship, though he did not discard it either. For him, *Brahman* was the sole reality. Thus, his way of thinking was not different from that of the Brahmos. We must remember that his early background was that of an atheist, a non-believer, and the Brahmo teachings suited him well. It should not be ignored that for a few years he was very close to Shri Keshub Chandra Sen who was the Brahmo Samāj leader then. So, although in the strict sense of the term he was talking of Hindu philosophy, his philosophy could be described as neo-Brahmo. By accepting the word 'Hindu' he managed to remain in the mainstream and he could, at the same time, absorb the principles of the Brahmo Samāj.

However, the development of the so-called Renaissance in India led to a sharp division between philosophers on the one hand and the protagonists of religious thought on the other. The religious thought had two prongs: one was concerning the mixture of metaphysical, mystical, ritualistic, traditional thought and the other was concerning the interpretations the Orientalists gave of the religio-metaphysical thought. Thus, philosophy was confined to European philosophy only, and Indian philosophy became the sole property of the Indian religious authority, Sanskrit *paṇḍit*s and Western Orientalists. This is not to say that Sāṁkhya, Nyāya-Vaiśeṣika, Navya-Nyāya, Mīmāṁsā and Vedānta were not studied in India. But those who studied them usually did not have any contact with Western philosophers and Western Orientalists studied

Indian philosophy in their own way and foisted their own opinions of Indian philosophical thought.

Some Indian and European teachers did take to philosophical study of Indian origin. But this was only by way of hobby and not by way of training the students. However, as the Western Orientalists studied Indian thought, they found some similarities between the European idealist thought and the Indian thought. Spinoza, Kant and Hegel, Berkeley, Hume and Bradley, were the important names in Western philosophy and the scholars realised that there was a great similarity between their thinking and thinking of Indian philosophers of the Upaniṣads and some of the systems like Vedānta. Some of the Western scholars like Max Müller, Jacobi and others showed their great appreciation for the thought of Indian philosophers. And Indian also had religiously accepted some of the Indian thinkers like Śaṅkara, Rāmānuja and Madhva. They did regard that these philosophers were great thinkers. But in order for accepting their greatness, a testimonial from Western scholars became necessary. The argument for the greatness of Indian thinkers was of the type that Śaṅkarācārya was a great philosopher because his philosophy was like that of Spinoza, or of the Kant, or of Hegel or of Bradley and that Western scholars accepted him as a great philosopher. One can easily see that this is a fallacious argument. Some re-thinking on Indian philosophy was also done in Indian universities and outside by people like K.C. Bhattacharyya and Lokamanya Tilak; but Indian philosophy was not studied seriously till recently.

Vidyabhushan's work on Indian logic, Athalye's work on the *Tarka Saṁgraha* and Kuppuswami Sastri's work on Indian Nyāya, were some serious attempts in trying to bridge the gap between philosophies of Western origin and Eastern origin. But the credit of bridging this gap should really go to Professors Dasgupta and Radhakrishnan. Dasgupta's work opened before the world scholars a treasure of Indian philosophy and Radhakrishnan who was trained in the contemporary philosophical idiom made people aware of the richness of thought in ancient and medieval Indian tradition. Indian philosophy was introduced in Indian universities and colleges only after the works of Radhakrishnan and Dasgupta were published, that is, in the third decade of this century. Today, Indian Philosophy is being taught in colleges and universities of India. But inclusion of Indian philosophy in the University curriculum is rather recent. The scholars of Indian philosophy like Radhakrishnan who introduced Indian philosophy to the whole world had not studied either Indian philosophy or Sanskrit during their college days. Ganganath Jha had translated a number of Indian philosophical classics into English. Later Pt. Gaurinath Shastri, Satkari Mookerji and a few others also wrote on Indian philosophy, Jacobi, Max Müller, A.B. Keith and a number of Western Orientalists also had written on Indian philosophy. But then Indian philosophy was not baptised as philosophy and even when it was introduced in Indian universities, the compartments of Indian philosophy and Western philosophy were separately maintained. Radhakrishnan's work made Western students of philosophy take to Indian philosophy seriously and even Indian scholars like R.D. Ranade, T.R.V. Murti, Rashvihari Das, Shaileshwar Sen, Kalipada Tarkacharya, Satkari Mookherji, G. R. Malkani, T. M. P. Mahadevan, Gopinath Bhattacharyya and several other followed suit. Stcherbatsky and Randle had already done some work on Buddhist and Nyāya logic. Now, Father Bochenski J.F. Staal, Schayer, Kunst, and Potter were also enthused to study Indian philosophy and logic.

Of course, philosophy and religion were mixed in Europe also, for a long time. But in Europe and particularly in the Anglo-Saxon world, the separation of philosophy from theology and religion took place for quite sometime. In India they still continue to be interdependent. Another thing that happened to philosophy of Indian origin was that at the time it was introduced to Indian scholars and introduced in Indian university curriculum, Western philosophy was under the spell of idealism. The well-known names in the field of philosophy at that time were Spinoza, Kant and Hegel, Bradley, Green and Taylor. All of them were idealists. Not that there were not other philosophers like Mill and Sidgwick, Herbert Spencer, William James, and so on. But the older generation did not pay heed to their thought; and in the next generation when they were studied, they were studied more or less for pointing out the contrast between them and the idealists.

According to the Indian traditions, there were only *ṣaḍ-darśanas*, and since *darśana* was translated as system, it was thought that there were six systems of philosophy and that Indian philosophy had to be studied as systems. This was also perhaps on account of the influence of Hegel. D.M. Dutta did not use the word 'system' for naming the varieties of Indian philosophy, but for him there were six ways of knowing. So, when people started learning Indian philosophy, they started exploring the consistency of each system. On the basis of consistency the whole thought of the system was to be either accepted or rejected. Again, of these six systems Advaita Vedānta became the subject of theoretical study and it was regarded as spiritual. It was monistic and it talked of *ātman*, which was regard as equivalent to self or soul. Again, it maintained that there was identity between *ātman* and *Brahman* and so not only the internal reality but also the external cosmic reality was regarded as spiritual or of the nature of spirit. Again, in attempting a synthesis of all systems, it accepted, for example, the methodology of the Nyāya system and the ritualism of Pūrva Mīmāṁsā, the practice of the Yoga system; and the Vaiśeṣika system was regarded as significant perhaps in *vyāvahārikī sattā*. The other kinds of philosophy like those of Buddha, Cārvāka and Jains, were called unorthodox and were used more or less like *pūrva-pakṣa* and it was thought that Vedānta solved all problems raised by unorthodox and other orthodox systems. Although people studied Vyākaraṇa, they never paid heed to the fact that Vyākaraṇa was of significance in philosophical discipline. Similar was the case with Cārvāka's theory. People brushed it aside on the ground that is was materialism. Ryle once said that in the twentieth century for the first time after Plato and Aristotle, philosophy became self-conscious, and asked the question, 'What is philosophy itself'? Our philosophers should have asked the question, what philosophy was before thinking about the philosophy of Cārvāka. They should not have simply assumed that the philosophy of Cārvāka was materialistic. In fact, when I started pondering about Cārvāka's philosophy, I found that there were many things common between Cārvāka and the philosophy of what is usually termed 'spiritualism'. He, for example, did not deny consciousness as a constituent of an organism called man, or for that matter any living being. He, of course, did not accept the duality of body and soul. Like Descartes, to use a modern phrase, he did not accept the ghost in the machine. If a living body is not to be separated from the soul (only because body and soul could be distinguished), how can Cārvāka be called a *jaḍavādī* or a materialist? In fact, his *śarīrātmavāda* should give us a position of monism similar to that of Advaita Vedānta. "What is the difference between the two philosophies" I thought, and came to the conclusion that the only difference between the two is that, whereas Advaita would say that, in the time series $A_1 \ldots A_n$, consciousness would exist from A_1 to A_n, — that is, it would occupy the whole of the time series, Cārvāka, like Loyd Morgan or Karl Marx, would say that it came into existence at some point of time and vanished at some other point of time. To me, it appeared, that such a theory could not be classified under materialism. Other aspects of Cārvāka's philosophy also could be looked at in a different perspective. There were reasons, I thought, to believe that Cārvāka was a robust common sense philosopher and perhaps it was equally necessary to re-examine the interpretations of Cārvāka's philosophy given by the rigid Indian traditionalists. In such a case, I thought that much of the Indian thought would be looked at in a new perspective. For this, two things were necessary. One should read the original text and not depend on translation or the commentaries alone. For, commentaries would also reflect the impressions of the commentator rather than the thought of the author. Similarly, one should not look to Indian *darśana*s necessarily as coherent philosophical systems, but rather try to select the useful rejecting the useless and make use of the flashes of the Indian thinkers. Of course, these two presuppositions of mine had one more presupposition, namely that our forefathers were honest people and were really enthused with the idea of finding out the essential, were eager to know the Reality and understand the nature of value. I thought that Indian philosophy should be studied in this new light.

We must also remember that philosophy in general and Indian philosophy in particular have now to face two more problems. First, both for theoretical and practical reasons the students are now more attracted to sciences. For practical considerations like employment opportunities, study of philosophy is now being discouraged. After we got our Independence, the Industrialisation process in the country was on the rise and it discouraged students to take to philosophy. It is only recently that people have started thinking that some kind of liberal education and philosophy are needed even in an Industrial civilisation, for they help build human relations and solve human problems. Thus, ethics and psychology, in particular, were introduced even in several engineering colleges. But while this was being done, psychology and later, logic broke their relation with philosophy. This was a major setback to philosophy in general and Indian philosophy in particular. How to get over this shock is a major problem before the contemporary Indian philosophers of the country. But there is yet another problem which philosophers in India have to face. I wonder whether it is inbuilt in philosophy itself or in the character of Indian philosophers, for although some new inspiring philosophy comes to the forefront from time to time, in a short time it becomes stagnated, stereotyped and traditional. Indian philosophy has to be rescued from such traditionalism.

I look at this problem from two points of view — organisational and theoretical. In order to tackle the organisational side, I started, for example, three philosophical journals, in English, Hindi and Marāṭhī for creating a forum for those who wanted to study and write. I think this should be done all over India. But the main problem is rather theoretical, I thought and do think that Indian philosophy is just philosophy. There is nothing special about it; and so we should enter into a dialogue between Indian philosophers and the philosophers of the Western mode and a synthesis should be arrived at. This could be done at two levels. First, by arranging a dialogue between the *paṇḍit*s and the Western scholars. What is living in Indian philosophy should be accepted and what it dead should be given up. But while doing this, we must also examine the interpretations given by commentators; and as far as possible we should understand the original text directly rather than depend on the commentaries. With this end in view, I arranged some seminars with the title of 'sequence seminars'. I am happy that ICPR is carrying on the work now under the leadership of Daya Krishna.

I also thought that our University syllabus should be so arranged that the problems that Indian philosophy raises should not be studied in isolation. They should rather be studied along with the Western problems. Where the problems are not similar, there also the study of Indian philosophy may throw some different light and perhaps enrich the theory. I made an attempt in this direction also; but, perhaps, the whole thing now is again reversed. Indian philosophy is again thought of as belonging to some different caste.

What will be the prospects of Indian philosophy? I do not try to answer this question systematically. I want the scholars to think over it, but I believe that philosophy in India will not die, whether it is included in the university curriculum or not and whether there are students to take to philosophy or not. Philosophy in India was not built in Indian universities, Sri Aurobindo, Tilak, Gandhi, Vivekānanda or Krishnamurthy developed their thought without paying any heed to what happened in the universities.

If we think of doing Indian philosophy today, we will have to tackle two kinds of problems. This is always the case when we try to integrate the history of philosophy with current philosophy or philosophising. This has happened with Greek and Medieval philosophy in Europe. The works of ancient writers of philosophy along with their own contribution or thought will have to be kept alive. But this thought has also to be integrated into the contemporary thinking considering all its pros and cons. All philosophy students cannot become, and are not expected to become, scholars of philosophical classics. But the mainstream of the classical thought should be open to contemporary scholars. It is necessary that they should breathe the air of these classics. So classical Indian philosophy would have to be studied at two levels. At one level, it would have to be studied through Sanskrit, Vedic language and also Prakrit, Ardhamāgadhī, Pāli, etc., and, it would also have to be studied through the idiom that would be current at that time. As suggested earlier, it would have, for example, to be studied through Navya-Nyāya language. These scholars would also have to take into account the Indian philosophy written in Chinese, Japanese, Tibetan, Simhalese and would have to give proper critical account of the modern Europe scholars like Max Müller, Jacobi, Stcherbatsky and others. But to use the ancient Indian philosophy, integrating it with modern thought, is a different question altogether. It is like a confluence of two rivers. Once the confluence takes place, it would be no more Indian or Western. It would be philosophy, and philosophy alone. To achieve this is certainly difficult, but an attempt will have to be made in this direction.

Index